Economics of Good and Evil

Economics of Good and Evil

The Quest for Economic Meaning from
Gilgamesh to Wall Street

Tomas Sedlacek

OXFORD
UNIVERSITY PRESS

OXFORD
UNIVERSITY PRESS

Oxford University Press, Inc., publishes works that further
Oxford University's objective of excellence
in research, scholarship, and education.

Oxford   New York
Auckland   Cape Town   Dar es Salaam   Hong Kong   Karachi
Kuala Lumpur   Madrid   Melbourne   Mexico City   Nairobi
New Delhi   Shanghai   Taipei   Toronto

With offices in
Argentina   Austria   Brazil   Chile   Czech Republic   France   Greece
Guatemala   Hungary   Italy   Japan   Poland   Portugal   Singapore
South Korea   Switzerland   Thailand   Turkey   Ukraine   Vietnam

Published by Oxford University Press, Inc.
198 Madison Avenue, New York, New York 10016
www.oup.com

First issued as an Oxford University Press paperback, 2013.

Oxford is a registered trademark of Oxford University Press

Library of Congress Cataloging-in-Publication Data

Sedlacek, Tomas, 1977–
   [Ekonomie dobra a zla. English]
   Economics of good and evil : the quest for economic meaning from
Gilgamesh to Wall Street / Tomas Sedlacek.
      p. cm.
   Includes bibliographical references and index.
   ISBN 978-0-19-976720-5 (cloth : alk. paper), ISBN 978-0-19-932218-3 (paperback).
1. Economics—Philosophy. 2. Economics—Moral and ethical aspects.
3. Good and evil. 4. Civilization—History. 5. Literature and morals. I. Title.

   HB72.S36513   2011
   174—dc22   2010030271

Editor of the Czech original: Jiří Nádoba, Co-editors: Martin Pospíšil,
Lukáš Tóth
Translation: Douglas Arellanes
Illustrations (inside): Milan Starý

First published in Czech as *Ekonomie dobra a zla*, 2009, by 65. Pole Publishing,
Konevova 121, Praha 3, Czech Republic.

9 8 7 6 5 4 3 2 1

Printed in the United States of America on acid-free paper

This book was translated into English with the kind support of ČSOB a.s.,
a member of KBC Group.

To my young son Chris, who I feel understands more than I ever will, as perhaps I also did long ago. Anyway, may you one day write a better book.

Know then thyself, presume not God to scan
The proper study of mankind is man.
Placed on this isthmus of a middle state,
A being darkly wise, and rudely great:
With too much knowledge for the sceptic side,
With too much weakness for the stoic's pride,
He hangs between; in doubt to act, or rest;
In doubt to deem himself a God, or beast;
In doubt his mind and body to prefer;
Born but to die, and reas'ning but to err;
Alike in ignorance, his reason such,
Whether he thinks too little, or too much;
Chaos of thought and passion, all confus'd;
Still by himself, abus'd or disabus'd;
Created half to rise and half to fall;
Great lord of all things, yet a prey to all,
Sole judge of truth, in endless error hurl'd;
The glory, jest and riddle of the world.

Alexander Pope, *The Riddle of the World*

Contents

12 The History of Animal Spirits: The Dream Never Sleeps 275

13 Metamathematics 285

14 Masters of Truth: Science, Myths, and Faith 299

Conclusion 319

Foreword

Václav Havel

I had the opportunity to read Tomas Sedlacek's book before it was published in the Czech Republic in 2009 under the same title, and it was obvious that it was an unconventional view on a scientific discipline that—as the general belief has it—is exceptionally dull. Of course I was taken with the book, and I was curious about the kind of interest it would provoke in other readers. To the surprise of both the author and publisher, it immediately drew so much attention in the Czech Republic that it became a bestseller within a few weeks, and both experts and the general public were talking about it. By coincidence, Tomas Sedlacek was at that time also a member of the Czech government's National Economic Council, which, in its behavior as well as its views on long-term goals, stood in sharp contrast to the quarrelsome political environment, which usually doesn't think further than the next election.

Instead of self-confident and self-centered answers, the author humbly asks fundamental questions: What is economics? What is its meaning? Where does this new religion, as it is sometimes called, come from? What are its possibilities and its limitations and borders, if there are any? Why are we so dependent on permanent growing of growth and growth of growing of growth? Where did the idea of progress come from, and where is it leading us? Why are so many economic debates accompanied by obsession and fanaticism? All of this must occur to a thoughtful person, but only rarely do the answers come from economists themselves.

The majority of our political parties act with a narrow materialistic focus when, in their programs, they present the economy and finance first; only then, somewhere at the end, do we find culture as something pasted on or as a libation for a couple of madmen. Whether they are on the right or left, most of them—consciously or unconsciously—accept and spread the Marxist thesis of the economic base and the spiritual superstructure.

It may all be related to how economics as a scientific discipline frequently tends to be mistaken for mere accounting. But what good is accounting when much of what jointly shapes our lives is difficult to calculate or is completely incalculable? I wonder what such an economist-accountant would do if given the task to optimize the work of a symphony orchestra. Most likely he would eliminate all the pauses from Beethoven concerts. After all, they're good for nothing. They just hold things up, and orchestra members cannot be paid for not playing.

The author's questioning breaks down stereotypes. He tries to break free of narrow specialization and cross the boundaries between scientific disciplines. Expeditions beyond economics' borders and its connection to history, philosophy, psychology, and ancient myths are not only refreshing, but necessary for understanding the world of the twenty-first century. At the same time, this is a readable book that is also accessible to laymen, in which economics becomes a path to adventure. We do not always find an exact answer to the permanent search for its end, only more reasons for even deeper considerations of the world and man's role in it.

In my presidential office, Tomas Sedlacek belonged to the generation of young colleagues who promised a new view on the problems of the contemporary world, one unburdened by four decades of the totalitarian Communist regime. I have the feeling that my expectations were fulfilled, and I believe you, too, will appreciate his book.

Acknowledgments

In the Czech edition of this book, I wrote a very brief thank-you. That was not a good idea, so I will be more verbose this time. This book took many years to be born, innumerable conversations, hundreds of lectures, and countless books read over many a long night.

I owe this book to my two great teachers, Professor Milan Sojka (who led me in this work) and H. E. Milan "Mike" Miskovsky (who inspired me on the whole topic, many years ago). This book is dedicated to their memory. Neither is with us anymore.

I owe thanks to my great teacher, Professor Lubomír Mlčoch, whom I had the honor to work as a teaching assistant in his Business Ethics classes. I give my great thanks to Professor Karel Kouba, Professor Michal Mejstřík, and Professor Milan Žák for their leadership. I thank my 2010 class of Philosophy of Economics for their comments and thoughts.

I would like to thank Professor Catherine Langlois and Stanley Nollen from Georgetown University for teaching me how to write, and also Professor Howard Husock from Harvard University. I would like to express my great gratitude to Yale University for offering me a very gracious fellowship, during which I wrote a substantial part of the book. Thank you, Yale World Fellows, and all at Betts House.

Great thanks to the outstanding Jerry Root, for welcoming us to stay in his basement for a month to work on the book in perfect quiet, and for the pipe and smokes; David Sween, for making it all happen; and James Halteman, for all the books. Thank you to Dušan Drabina, for support in the hardest times.

There are many philosophers, economists, and thinkers to whom I feel honored to express thanks: Professor Jan Švejnar, Professor Tomáš Halík, Professor Jan Sokol, Professor Erazim Kohák, Professor Milan Machovec, Professor Zdeněk Neubauer, David Bartoň, Mirek Zámečník, and my younger brother, the great thinker Lukáš. You have my thanks and admiration. I can never express enough thanks to the rest of my family, especially my father and mother.

Now, the biggest thanks for the most specific help with this book goes to the team who cooperated on the Czech and English versions. Tomáš Brandejs, for ideas, faith, and courage; Jiří Nádoba, for editing and management; Betka Sočůvková, for patience and endurance; Milan Starý, for drawings, creativity, and kindness; Doug Arellanes, for thorough translation; and Jeffrey Osterroth, for detailed English proofreading.

Now, there are two great minds who helped me to write and edit parts of the book: Martin Pospíšil and Lukáš Tóth, my two intellectual fellows. I cannot thank them enough for their brilliant thoughts, keen debates, and research, as well as their hard work on specific chapters, which they co-authored. I would also like to thank my colleagues at ČSOB, a.s. for a creative work environment and support.

My wife, Markéta, has stood with me in times when no other imaginable person would. Thank you also for your smiles and thoughts (she is a sociologist, so you can imagine our dinner discussions). This book really belongs to her.

But the biggest thanks go to the one whose name I actually don't even know . . .

Economics of Good and Evil

Introduction

The Story of Economics: From Poetry to Science

Reality is spun from stories, not from material.
Zdeněk Neubauer

There is no idea, however ancient and absurd, that is not capable of
improving our knowledge . . .

Anything goes . . .
Paul Feyerabend

Man has always striven to understand the world around him. To this end he was helped by stories that made sense of his reality. From today's standpoint, such stories often seem quaint—much as ours will appear to the generations that follow. However, the secret power of these stories is profound.

One such story is the story of economics, which began a long time ago. Xenophon wrote around 400 BC that "even if a man happens to have no wealth, there is such a thing as a science of economics."[1] Once upon a time, economics was the science of managing a household,[2] later a subset of religious, theological, ethical, and philosophical disciplines. But, little by little, it seems to have become something quite different. We may sometimes feel that economics has gradually lost all of its shades and hues to a technocratic world where black and white rule. But the story of economics is far more colorful.

Economics, as we know it today, is a cultural phenomenon, a product of our civilization. It is not, however, a *product* in the sense that we have intentionally *produced* or invented it, like a jet engine or a watch. The difference lies in the fact that we understand a jet engine or a watch—we know where they came from. We can (almost) deconstruct them into their individual parts and put them back together. We know how they start and how they stop.[3] This is not the case with economics. So much

---

[1] Xenophon, *Oeconomicus*, 2.12. Economics here means household management.
[2] From the Greek *oikonomia*; *oikos*—household, house, family, *nomos*—law.
[3] However, we still don't really know what *matter as such* is made of. We understand watches, so to speak, from a certain level up. Nor do we know what the real essence of *time* is. So we understand the *mechanics of a watch*, the parts that we have, ourselves, constructed.

originated unconsciously, spontaneously, uncontrolled, unplanned, not under the conductor's baton. Before it was emancipated as a field, economics lived happily within subsets of philosophy—ethics, for example—miles away from today's concept of economics as a mathematical-allocative science that views "soft sciences" with a scorn born from positivistic arrogance. But our thousand-year "education" is built on a deeper, broader, and oftentimes more solid base. It is worth knowing about.

MYTHS, STORIES, AND PROUD SCIENCE

It would be foolish to assume that economic inquiry began with the scientific age. At first, myths and religions explained the world to people, who ask basically similar questions as we do today; today, science plays that role. Thus, to see this link, we must dive into far more ancient myths and philosophy. That is the reason for this book: to look for economic thought in ancient myths and, vice versa, to look for myths in today's economics.

Modern economics is considered to have begun in 1776 with the publication of Adam Smith's *Wealth of Nations*. Our postmodern age (which seems to be significantly humbler than its predecessor, the modern scientific age)[4] is more likely to look further back and is aware of the power of history (path dependency), mythology, religion, and fables. "The separation between the history of a science, its philosophy, and the science itself dissolves into thin air, and so does the separation between science and non-science; differences between the scientific and unscientific are vanishing."[5] Therefore, we shall set out as early as the written legacy of our civilization allows. We shall search for the first traces of economic inquiry in the epic of the Sumerian king Gilgamesh and explore how Jewish, Christian, classical, and medieval minds considered economic issues. Additionally, we shall carefully investigate the theories of those who laid the foundations for contemporary economics.

The study of the history of a certain field is not, as is commonly held, a useless display of its blind alleys or a collection of the field's trials and errors (until *we* got it right), but history is the fullest possible scope of study of a menu that the given field can offer. Outside of our history, we have nothing more. History of thought helps us to get rid of the intellectual brainwashing of the age, to see through the intellectual fashion of the day, and to take a couple of steps back.

Studying old stories is not only for the benefit of historians, or for understanding the way our ancestors thought. These stories have their own power, even after new stories appear and replace or contradict them.

---

[4] We use the term "science" loosely here. A more detailed discussion of the "scientific" and the "unscientific" will take place in the second part of this book.
[5] Feyerabend, *Against Method*, 33–34.

An example could be drawn from the most famous dispute in history: the dispute between the story of geocentrism and the story of heliocentrism. As everyone knows, in the battle between helio- and geocentrism, the heliocentric story won, though even today we geocentrically say that the Sun *rises* and *sets*. But the Sun does not rise or set: if anything is rising, it's our Earth (around the Sun), not the Sun (around the Earth). The Sun does not revolve around the Earth; the Earth revolves around the Sun—so we are told.

Furthermore, those ancient stories, images, and archetypes that we will examine in the first part of the book are with us to this day and have cocreated our approach to the world, as well as how we perceive ourselves. Or, as C. G. Jung puts it, "The true history of the mind is not preserved in learned volumes but in the living mental organism of everyone."[6]

THE DESIRE TO PERSUADE

Economists should believe in the power of stories; Adam Smith believed. As he puts it in *The Theory of Moral Sentiments*, "the desire of being believed, or the desire of persuading, of leading and directing other people, seems to be one of the strongest of all our natural desires."[7] Note that this sentence comes from the alleged father of self-interest being the *strongest of all our natural desires*. Two other great economists, Robert J. Shiller and George A. Akerlof, recently wrote: "The human mind is built to think in terms of narratives . . . in turn, much of human motivation comes from living through a story of our lives, a story that we tell to ourselves and that creates a framework of our motivation. Life could be just 'one damn thing after another' if it weren't for such stories. The same is true for confidence in a nation, a company, or an institution. Great leaders are foremost creators of stories."[8]

The original quote comes from "Life isn't one damn thing after another. It's the same damn thing again and again." This is well put, and myths (our grand stories, narratives) are "revelations, here and now, of what is always and forever."[9] Or, in other words, myths are what "never happened, but always are."[10] However, our modern economic theories based on rigorous modeling are nothing more than these metanarratives retold in different (mathematical?) language. So it is necessary to learn this story from the

---

[6] Jung, *Psychology and Religion*, 41.
[7] Smith, *The Theory of Moral Sentiments*, 7.4.25.
[8] Akerlof, Shiller, *Animal Spirits*, 51 in the chapter "Stories."
[9] Campbell, *Myths to Live By*, 97.
[10] Sallust, *On the Gods and the World*, Part IV: *That the species of myth are five, with examples of each.*

beginning—in a broad sense, *for one will never be a good economist, who is only an economist.*[11]

And since economics wants imperially to understand everything, we must venture out of our field to truly try to *understand everything*. And if it is at least partially true that "salvation was now to be a matter of ending material scarcity, leading humankind into a new era of economic abundance, [and that] it followed logically that the new chief priesthood should consist of economists,"[12] then we must be aware of this crucial role and take a broader social responsibility.

THE ECONOMICS OF GOOD AND EVIL

All of economics is, in the end, economics of good and evil. It is the telling of stories by people of people to people. Even the most sophisticated mathematical model is, de facto, a story, a parable, our effort to (rationally) grasp the world around us. I will try to show that to this day that story, told through economic mechanisms, is essentially about a "good life," a story we have borne from the ancient Greek and Hebrew traditions. I will try to show that mathematics, models, equations, and statistics are just the tip of the iceberg of economics; that the biggest part of the iceberg of economic knowledge consists of everything else; and that disputes in economics are rather a battle of stories and various metanarratives than anything else. People today, as they have always, want to know from economists principally what is good and what is bad.

We economists are trained to avoid normative judgments and opinions as to what is good and bad. Yet, contrary to what our textbooks say, economics is predominantly a normative field. Economics not only describes the world but is frequently about how the world should be (it should be effective, we have an ideal of perfect competition, an ideal of high-GDP growth in low inflation, the effort to achieve high competitiveness…). To this end, we create models, modern parables, but these unrealistic models (often intentionally) have little to do with the *real world*. A daily example: If an economist on television answers a seemingly harmless question about the level of inflation, in one blow a second question will be presented (which an economist will frequently add himself without being asked) as to whether the level of inflation is *good* or *bad*, and whether inflation *should be* higher or lower. Even with such a technical question, analysts immediately speak of *good* and *bad* and offer *normative* judgments: It *should* be lower (or higher).

---

[11] The author's liberal paraphrase of John Stuart Mill's quote: "A person is not likely to be a good political economist, who is nothing else." From John Stuart Mill's *Essays on Ethics, Religion and Society*. Vol. 10 of *Collected Works of John Stuart Mill*, 306.

[12] Nelson, *Economics as Religion*, 38.

Despite this, economics tries, as if in a panic, to avoid terms such as "good" and "evil." It cannot. For "if economics were truly a value-neutral undertaking, one would expect that members of the economics profession would have developed a full body of economic thought."[13] This, as we have seen, has not happened. In my view, it is a good thing, but we must admit that economics is, at the end of the day, more of a normative science. According to Milton Friedman (*Essays in Positive Economics*), economics *should be* a positive science that is value-neutral and describes the world as it is and not how it should be. But the comment itself that "economics *should be* a positive science" is a *normative statement*. It does not describe the world as it is but as it should be. In real life, economics is not a positive science. If it were, we would not have to *try for it to be*. "Of course most men of science, and many philosophers, use the positivistic doctrine to avoid the necessity of considering perplexing fundamental questions—in short, to avoid metaphysics."[14] By the way, being value-free is a value in itself, a *great value* to economists anyway. It is a paradox that a field that primarily studies values wants to be value-free. One more paradox is this: A field that *believes* in the *invisible hand of the market* wants to be without mysteries.

So in this book I ask the following questions: Is there an economics of good and evil? Does it pay to be good, or does good exist outside the calculus of economics? Is selfishness innate to mankind? Can it be justified if it results in the common good? If economics is not to become simply a mechanical-allocational, econometric model without any deeper meaning (or application), it is worth asking such questions.

By the way, there is no need to fear words such as "good" or "evil." Using them does not mean we are moralizing. Everyone has some internalized *ethics* according to which we act. In the same way, we each have a certain faith (atheism is a faith like any other). It is like that with economics, too, as John Maynard Keynes puts it: "Practical men, who believe themselves to be quite exempt from any intellectual influence, are usually the slaves of some defunct economist. . . . Sooner or later, it is ideas, not vested interests, which are dangerous for good or evil."[15]

WHAT THIS BOOK IS ABOUT: META-ECONOMICS

This book is composed of two parts: In the first part we look for economics in myths, religion, theology, philosophy, and science. In the second part, we look for myths, religion, theology, philosophy, and science in economics.

---

[13] Nelson, *Economics as Religion*, 132.
[14] Whitehead, *Adventures of Ideas*, 130.
[15] Keynes, *The General Theory of Employment, Interest, and Money: Collected Writings of John Maynard Keynes*, 383.

We will search our entire history for answers, from the beginnings of our culture to our current postmodern age. Our goal is not to examine every moment that helped change later generations' (and our current) economic perception of the world; it is to look at the stops in the development, either at certain historical epochs (the age of Gilgamesh and the eras of the Hebrews, and Christians, etc.) or at significant personalities that influenced the development of man's economic understanding (Descartes, Mandeville, Smith, Hume, Mill, et al.). Our goal is to tell the story of economics.

In other words, we seek to chart the development of the *economic ethos*. We ask questions that come before any economic thinking can begin— both philosophically and, to a degree, historically. The area here lies at the very borders of economics—and often beyond. We may refer to this as *protoeconomics* (to borrow a term from protosociology) or, perhaps more fittingly, *meta-economics* (to borrow a term from metaphysics).[16] In this sense, "the study of economics is too narrow and too fragmentary to lead to valid insight, unless complemented and completed by a study of meta-economics."[17] The more important elements of a culture or field of inquiry such as economics are found in *fundamental assumptions* that adherents of all the various systems within the epoch unconsciously presuppose. Such assumptions appear so obvious that people do not know what they are assuming, because no other way of putting things has ever occurred to them, as the philosopher Alfred Whitehead notes in *Adventures of Ideas*.

What exactly are we doing? And why? Can we do (ethically) all that we can do (technically)?[18] And what is the point of economics? What is all the effort for? And what do we really believe and where do our (often unknown) beliefs come from? If science is "a system of beliefs to which we are committed," what beliefs are they?[19] As economics has become a key field of explaining and changing the world today, these are all questions that need to be asked.

In a somewhat postmodern fashion, we will try to have a philosophical, historical, anthropological, cultural, and psychological approach to meta-economics. This book aims to capture how the perception of man's economic dimension developed and to reflect on it. Almost all of the key concepts by which economics operates, both consciously and unconsciously, have a long history, and their roots extend predominantly outside the range of economics, and often completely beyond that of science.

---

[16] The term "metaeconomics" was first used by Karl Menger in 1936 in his paper *Law of Diminishing Returns. A Study in Meta-economics.* "When he coined the term 'metaeconomics' he did not think of a sort of reintegration of ethics in economics; he was thinking of modelling economics and ethics as well into a coherent logical pattern, without any connections between them." (Becchio, *Unexplored Dimensions*, 30).

[17] Schumacher, *Small Is Beautiful*, 36.

[18] To paraphrase a key question that the Czech theologician Tomáš Halik asks, see *Stromu zbývá naděje* [*There is hope*].

[19] Polanyi, *Personal Knowledge*, 171.

Let us now attempt to examine the beginnings of economic belief, the genesis of these ideas and their influence on economics.

TO ALL THE COLORS OF ECONOMICS

I argue that mainstream economists have forsaken too many colors of economics and have been overobsessed with the black-and-white cult of homo economicus, which ignores issues of good and evil. We have created a self-inflicted blindness, a blindness to the most important driving forces of human actions.

I argue that there is at least as much wisdom to be learned from our own philosophers, myths, religions, and poets as from exact and strict mathematical models of economic behavior. I argue that economics should seek, discover, and talk about its own values, although we have been taught that economics is a value-free science. I argue that none of this is true and that there is more religion, myth, and archetype in economics than there is mathematics. I argue that in economics nowadays there is too much emphasis on the method rather than on the substance. I argue and try to show that it is crucial for economists, and a wider audience as well, to learn from a wide group of sources, such as the Epic of Gilgamesh, the Old Testament, Jesus, or Descartes. The traces of our way of thinking are more readily understood when we look at their historical beginnings, when the thoughts were, so to speak, more naked—there we can see the origins and sources of such ideas easier. Only thus can we identify our principal (economic) beliefs—in the complicated web of today's society, in which they are still very strong but go unnoticed.

I argue that to be a good economist, one has to either be a good mathematician or a good philosopher or both. I argue that we have overemphasized the mathematical and neglected our humanity. This has led to the evolution of lopsided, artificial models that are often of little use when it comes to understanding reality.

I argue that the study of meta-economics is important. We should go beyond economics and study what beliefs are "behind the scenes," ideas that have often become the dominant yet unspoken assumptions in our theories. Economics is surprisingly full of tautologies that economists are predominantly unaware of. I argue that the nonhistorical perspective, which has become dominant in economics, is wrong. I argue that it is more important in understanding human behavior to study the historical evolution of ideas that shape us.

This book is a contribution to the long-lasting clash between normative and positive economics. I argue that the role normative myths and parables had in ancient times is now played by scientific models. This is fine, but we should openly admit it.

I argue that economic questions were with mankind long before Adam Smith. I argue that the search for values in economics did not start with

Adam Smith but culminated with him. The modern mainstream, which claims to descend from classical Smith-economics, has neglected ethics. The issue of good and evil was dominant in classical debates, yet today it is almost heretical to even talk about it. I further argue that the popular reading of Adam Smith is a misunderstanding. I argue that his contribution to economics is much broader than just the concept of the invisible hand of the market and the birth of the egoistic, self-centered homo economicus, although Smith never used that term. I argue that his most influential contribution to economics was ethical. His other thoughts had been clearly expressed long before him, whether on specialization, or on the principle of the invisible hand of the market. I try to show that the principle of the invisible hand of the market is much more ancient and developed long before Adam Smith. Traces of it appear even in the Epic of Gilgamesh, Hebrew thought, and in Christianity, and it is expressly stated by Aristophanes and Thomas Aquinas.

I argue that now is a good time to rethink our economic approach, because now, in the time of the debt-crisis, is a time when people care and are willing to listen. I argue that we have not really learned our economic lessons from the simplest Sunday school stories, such as the story of Joseph and the Pharaoh, although we have sophisticated mathematical models at hand. I argue that we should reconsider our growth-only thinking. I argue that economics can be a beautiful science that can appeal to a wide audience.

In a way, this is a study of the evolution of both homo economicus and, more importantly, the history of the animal spirits within him. This book tries to study the evolution of the rational as well as the emotional and irrational side of human beings.

THE BORDERS OF CURIOSITY, AND A DISCLAIMER

Since economics has dared to imperialistically apply its system of thought to provinces traditionally belonging to religious studies, sociology, and political science, why not swim against the current and look at economics from the viewpoint of religious studies, sociology, and political science? As long as modern economics dares to explain the operation of churches or conduct economic analyses of family ties (often resulting in new and interesting insights), why not examine theoretical economics as we would systems of religions or of personal relationships? In other words, why not attempt an anthropological view of economics?

To look at economics in such a way, we must first distance ourselves from it. We must venture to the very borders of economics—or, even better, beyond them. Following Ludwig Wittgenstein's metaphor of the eye observing its surroundings but never itself to examine an object (Wittgenstein, *Tractatus Logico-Philosophicus*, section 5.6), it is always necessary to step outside of it, and if that is not possible, at the very least, to use a mirror. In this book we will employ anthropological, mythical, religious, philosophical, sociological, and psychological mirrors—anything that provides us with a reflection.

Here, at least two apologies must be offered. First, if we look at our own reflection in anything and everything around us, we often get a fractured and disparate picture. This book does not wish to offer an intricately woven system (for the simple reason that no such system exists). Importantly, we will only deal with the legacy of our *Western* culture and civilization and will not study here other legacies (such as Confucian, Islamic, Buddhist, Hunduist, and many others, although we would certainly find a great deal of stimulating ideas if we did). Furthermore, we will not, for example, tackle the entirety of Sumerian literature. We will discuss Hebrew and Christian thought that concerns economics, but we will not study the whole of ancient and medieval theologies. Our goal will be to pick out the key influences and revolutionary concepts that created today's economic modus vivendi. The justification for such a broad and somewhat disjointed approach is the idea Paul Feyerabend explained long ago, that "anything goes."[20] We can never predict from which well science will draw inspiration for its further development.

The next apology concerns the possible simplification or distortion of those fields that the author finds important despite being located entirely within another realm. Today, science enjoys hiding behind an ivory wall built here from mathematics, there from Latin or Greek, from history, from axioms, and other sacred rituals, so scientists can enjoy undeserved sanctuary from critics from other fields and the public. But science must be open; otherwise, as Feyerabend aptly noted, it becomes an elitist religion for the initiates, radiating its totalitarian beams back at the public. In the words of the Czech-born, American economist Jaroslav Vanek, "unfortunately or fortunately, one's curiosity is not limited to one's professional field."[21] If this book inspires new insights in fusion of economics with these other areas, then it has fulfilled its raison d'être.

This is not a book on the thorough history of economic thought. The author aims instead to supplement certain chapters on the history of economic thought with a broader perspective and analysis of the influences that often escape the notice of economists and the wider public.

Perhaps it should be said that this text contains quite a number of quotations. This provides the closest approximation to the valuable ideas of distant ages in the words of the original authors. If we only paraphrased the ancient words, their authenticity and the spirit of the age would simply evaporate—a terrible loss. The footnotes provide the opportunity for deeper study of the problems given.

---

[20] Feyerabend, *Against Method*, 33: "There is no idea, however ancient and absurd, that is not capable of improving our knowledge."
[21] Vanek, *The Participatory Economy*, 7.

CONTENTS: SEVEN EPOCHS, SEVEN TOPICS

The book is divided into two parts. The first follows a line through history, which in seven stops focuses specifically on seven topics, which will then be summarized in the second part. The second part is therefore thematic; it harvests historical topics and integrates them. In this sense, the book is a bit like a matrix; you can follow it historically, or thematically, or both. The seven topics are as follows:

The Need for Greed: The History of Consumption and Labor

Here we start with the most ancient myths, in which labor figures as the original human calling, labor for pleasure, and later (through insatiability) as a curse. God or the gods either curse labor (Genesis, Greek myths) or curse too much labor (Gilgamesh). We will analyze the birth of desire and lust, or demand. We will then examine asceticism in various concepts. Later, Augustinian contempt for this world dominates; Aquinas turns the pendulum, and the material world gets attention and care. Until then, care for the soul dominated and the desires and needs of the body and the world were marginalized. Later, the pendulum would again swing the opposite way, in the direction of individualistic-utilitarian consumption. Nevertheless, from his beginnings, man has been marked as a naturally unnatural creature, who for unique reasons surrounds himself with external possessions. Insatiability, both material and spiritual, are basic human metacharacteristics, which appear as early as the oldest myths and stories.

Progress (Naturalness and Civilization)

Today we are intoxicated by the idea of progress, but in the very beginning, the idea of progress was nonexistent.[22] Time was cyclical, and humanity was expected to make no historical motion. Then the Hebrews, with linear time, and later the Christians gave us the ideal (or amplified the Hebrew ideal) we now embrace. Then the classical economists secularized progress. How did we come to today's progression of progress, and growth for growth's sake?

The Economy of Good and Evil

We will examine a key issue: Does good pay (economically)? We will start first with the Epic of Gilgamesh, where the morality of good and evil, it would appear, were not connected; on the other hand, later, in

---

[22] Sociologists still have the ideal of classical (rustic) society. Psychologists have the ideal of the harmony of the civilized and animal parts of our personality. They also have their ideal in the past and are often skeptical of development-progress. Among these fields, economists are probably the only social scientists who have their ideal in *the future*.

Hebrew thought, ethics ruled as an explanatory factor in history. The ancient Stoics did not permit the calculation of the yield of good, and the Hedonists, on the other hand, believed that anything that paid in its results was good as a rule. Christian thinking broke a clear causality between good and evil through divine mercy and shifted reward for good or evil to the afterlife. This theme culminates with Mandeville and Adam Smith, in the now-famous dispute on private vices that produce public benefit. Later, John Stuart Mill and Jeremy Bentham built their utilitarianism on a similar Hedonistic principle. The entire history of ethics has been ruled by an effort to create a formula for the ethical rules of behavior. In the final chapter we will show the tautology of Max Utility, and we will discuss the concept of Max Good.

The History of the Invisible Hand of the Market and Homo Economicus

How ancient is the idea of the invisible hand of the market? How long before Adam Smith was this concept with us? I will try to show that foreshadowing of the invisible hand of the market is almost everywhere. The idea that we can manage to utilize our natural egoism, and that this evil is good for something, is an ancient philosophical and mythical concept. We will also look into the development of the ethos of homo economicus, the birth of "economic man."

The History of Animal Spirits: Dreams Never Sleep

Here we will examine the other side of human beings—the unpredictable, often *arational* and archetypal. Our animal spirits (something of a counterpart to rationality) are influenced by the archetype of the hero and our concept of what is good.

Metamathematics

From where did economics get the concept of numbers as the very foundation of the world? Here we want to show how and why economics has become a mechanistically allocative field. Why do we believe that mathematics is the best way to describe the world (even the world of social interactions)? Is mathematics at the core of economics, or is it just the icing of the cake, the tip of the iceberg of our field's inquiry?

Masters of the Truth

What do economists believe? What is the religion of economists? And what is the character of truth? The effort to rid science of myth has been with us from the time of Plato. Is economics a normative field or positive science? Originally, truth was a domain of poems and stories, but today we perceive truth as something much more scientific, mathematical. Where does one go (to shop) for the truth? And who "has the truth" in our epoch?

PRACTICAL ISSUES AND DEFINITIONS

When we mention *economics* in this book, we mean the mainstream perception of it, perhaps as best represented by Paul Samuelson. By the term *homo economicus*, we mean the primary concept of economic anthropology. It comes from the concept of a rational individual, who, led by narrowly egotistical motives, sets out to maximize his benefit. We will avoid the question of whether economics is or is not, properly stated, a science. So although we may occasionally refer to it as a social science, we often only mean *the field* of economics. We understand "economics" to mean a broader field than just the production, distribution, and consumption of goods and services. We consider economics to be the study of human relations that are sometimes expressible in numbers, a study that deals with tradables, but one that also deals with nontradables (friendship, freedom, efficiency, growth).

I have been blessed with three experiences in life. I worked for many years in academia, studying, researching, and teaching theoretical economics (dealing with meta-economic dilemmas). I also served for many years as an economic advisor on economic policy—working as an advisor to our former Czech president, Václav Havel, to our minister of finance, and, eventually, to our prime minister (on the practical application of economic policy). It is also my duty and (often) pleasure to be a regular columnist at our leading economic daily, writing about the practical, as well as philosophical, aspects of economics for a wide audience (simplifying things, trying to create a fusion of different fields of inquiry). This experience has taught me the limits and advantages of each side of economics. This triple schizophrenia (What is the meaning of economics? How can we use it practically? and How can it be connected with other fields in an understandable way?) has always been with me. For good or for bad, this book, which I offer here, is the result.

Part I

ANCIENT ECONOMICS AND BEYOND

1

The Epic of Gilgamesh

On Effectiveness, Immortality, and the Economics of Friendship

Gilgamesh, wherefore do you wander? The eternal life you are seeking you shall not find. . . . Always be happy, night and day. Night and day play and dance.
The Epic of Gilgamesh

The Epic of Gilgamesh dates from more than four thousand years ago[1] and is the oldest work of literature available to humankind. The first written records come from Mesopotamia, as do the oldest human relics. This is true not only of our civilization but of humankind in general.[2] The epic served as an inspiration for many stories that followed, which dominate mythology to this day in more or less altered form, whether it is about the motif of the flood or the quest for immortality. Even in this oldest work known to men, however, questions we today consider to be economic play an important role—and if we want to set out on a trail of economic questioning, we can go no deeper into history than this. This is the bedrock.

Only a fraction of the material relics survive from the period before the epic, and only fragments remain of written records relating mainly to

---

[1] The oldest Sumerian version of the epic dates from the third Uru dynasty, from the period between 2150 and 2000 BC. The newer Akkadian version dates from the turn of the second millennium BC. The standard Akkadian version, on which this translation is based, dates from between 1300 and 1000 BC and was found in a library in Nineveh. For the rest of its chapters, the Epic of Gilgamesh is thought of as its "standard" eleven-tablet Akkadian version, which does not contain Gilgamesh's descent into the underworld, later combined with a twelfth clay tablet, and at the same time includes the meeting with Utanapishtim on the eleventh tablet and the conversation with Ishtar on the sixth tablet. Unless otherwise noted, we will use the Andrew R. George translation from 1999. The story plays out on the territory of what is today Iraq.

[2] The oldest writings come from the Sumerians; writings from other cultures (such as the Indian and Chinese) are from newer dates. The Indian *Vedas* come from the period around 1500 BC, as does the Egyptian *Book of the Dead*. The older parts of the Old Testament were written between the ninth and sixth centuries BC. The *Iliad* and the *Odyssey* come from the eighth century, and Plato and Aristotle's writings from the fourth century. The Chinese classics (such as Confucius) date from the third century BC.

economics, diplomacy, war, magic, and religion.[3] As the economic historian
Niall Ferguson (somewhat cynically) notes, these are "reminders that when
human beings first began to produce written records of their activities
they did so not to write history, poetry, or philosophy, but to do business."[4]
But the Epic of Gilgamesh bears witness to the opposite—despite the fact
that the first written clay *fragments* (such as notes and bookkeeping) of
our ancestors may have been about *business and war*, the first written
story is mainly about great friendship and adventure. Surprisingly, there is
no mention of either money or war; for example, not once does anyone in
the whole epic sell or purchase something.[5] No nation conquers another,
and we do not encounter a mention even of the threat of violence. It is a
story of nature and civilization, of heroism, defiance, and the battle against
the gods, and evil; an epic about wisdom, immortality, and also futility.

Despite being a text of such great importance, it seems to have completely escaped the attention of economists. There is no economic literature
on the Epic of Gilgamesh. At the same time, this is where we encounter
our civilization's very first economic contemplation; the beginnings of
well-known concepts such as the market and its invisible hand, the problem of utilizing natural wealth and efforts at maximizing effectiveness.
A dilemma appears on the role of feelings, the term "progress," and the
natural state, or the topic of the comprehensive division of labor connected with the creation of the first cities. This is the first feeble attempt
to understand the epic from an economic standpoint.[6]

First, though, let's briefly summarize the story line of the Epic of
Gilgamesh (we will develop it in greater detail shortly). Gilgamesh, the
ruler of the city of Uruk, is a superhuman semigod: "two thirds of him god
and one third human."[7] The epic begins with a description of a perfect,
impressive, and immortal wall around the city that Gilgamesh is building.
As punishment for the merciless treatment of his workers and subjects,
the gods call on the savage Enkidu to stop Gilgamesh. But the two become
friends, an invincible pair, and together they carry out heroic acts. Later,
Enkidu dies, and Gilgamesh sets out in search of immortality. He overcomes

---

[3] Kratochvíl, *Mýtus, filozofie a věda* [Myth, Philosphy, and Science], 11.

[4] Ferguson, *The Ascent of Money*, 27.

[5] Just as in (our own) modern epic (myth, story, fairy tale)—in the *Lord of the Rings* trilogy
by J. R. R. Tolkien—money plays no role. The "transaction" takes place in the form of a gift,
battle, fraud, trick, or theft. See Bassham and Bronson, *The Lord of the Rings and Philosophy*,
65–104.

[6] No search is ever totally complete, but despite some relatively comprehensive searching in the conventional EconLit archives (which is the most widespread and certainly
most respected database of economic literature of our time), the author did not manage
to find any book, or even a chapter of a book or academic article, that examined the Epic
of Gilgamesh from an economic point of view. We are therefore aware that this attempt to
analyze one of the oldest writings from a heretofore unexamined angle is predestined to all
the failures, simplifications, contradictions, and inaccuracies of a first excavation.

[7] The Epic of Gilgamesh, Tablet I (48), 2.

numerous obstacles and pitfalls, but immortality eludes him, if only by a hair's breadth. The end of the story returns to where the epic began—to the song in praise of Uruk's wall.

UNPRODUCTIVE LOVE

Gilgamesh's effort to build a wall like no other is the central plot of the entire story. Gilgamesh tries to increase his subjects' performance and effectiveness at all costs, even preventing them from having contact with their wives and children. So the people complain to the gods:

> The young men of Uruk he harries without warrant,
> Gilgamesh lets no son go free to his father (. . .)
> Gilgamesh lets no girl go free to her bridegroom.
> The warrior's daughter, the young man's bride.[8]

This has a direct relation to the emergence of the city as a place that manages the countryside around it. "The village neighbors would now be kept at a distance: no longer familiars and equals, they were reduced to subjects, whose lives were supervised and directed by military and civil officers, governors, viziers, tax-gatherers, soldiers, directly accountable to the king."[9]

A principle so distant and yet so close. Even today we live in Gilgamesh's vision that human relations—and therefore humanity itself—are a disturbance to work and efficiency; that people would perform better if they did not "waste" their time and energy on *non*productive things. Even today, we often consider the domain of *humanity* (human relations, love, friendship, beauty, art, etc.) to be *un*productive; maybe only with the exception of *re*production, the only one which is literally(!) productive, reproductive.

This effort to maximize effectiveness at any cost, this strengthening of the economic at the expense of the human, reduces humans across the breadth of their humanity to being mere production units. The beautiful, originally Czech word "robot"[10] perfectly expresses this: The word is based on the old Czech and Slavic word "robota," which means "work." A person reduced to being only a worker is a robot. How well the epic would have served Karl Marx, who could have easily used it as a prehistoric example of the exploitation and alienation of the individual from his family and himself![11]

---

[8] The Epic of Gilgamesh, Tablet I (67–68 . . . 77–78), 3.

[9] Mumford, *The City in History*, 41.

[10] The term "robot" was first used in 1920 by the Czech author Karel Čapek in his science-fiction drama *R.U.R.* [Rossum's Universal Robots] about an uprising of artificial beings built for the purpose of taking over human labor. Čapek originally wanted to call them *labori* (laborers), but his brother Josef (an outstanding artist) thought up the more suitable "robot."

[11] Marx expresses this reduction of man even more emphatically: "[the workman] becomes an appendage of the machine . . ." Rich, *Business and Economic Ethics*, 51 (originally published

Governing people reduced to human-robots has been the dream of tyrants from time immemorial. Every despotic ruler sees competition to effectiveness in family relations and friendships. The effort to reduce a person to a unit of production and consumption is also evident in social utopia or more accurately dystopias. For the economy as such needs nothing more than a human-robot, as has been beautifully—albeit painfully—shown in the model of homo economicus, which is a mere production and consumption unit.[12] Here are some examples of this kind of utopia or dystopia: In his vision of an ideal state, Plato does not allow guardian families to raise their children; instead they hand them over to a specialized institution immediately after birth.[13] This is similar to the dystopias in Aldous Huxley's *Brave New World* and George Orwell's *1984*. In both novels, human relations and feelings (or any expressions of personality) are forbidden and strictly punished. Love is "unnecessary" and unproductive, as is friendship; both can be destructive to a totalitarian system (as can be seen well in the novel *1984*). Friendship is unnecessary because individuals and society can live without it.[14] As C. S. Lewis puts it, "Friendship is unnecessary, like philosophy, like art. . . . It has no survival value; rather it is one of those things that give value to survival."[15]

---

in German: Rich, *Wirtschaftsethik*). We notice that today in economic models, we perceive a person through their work (L) or as human capital (H). In companies, human resource departments (HR) arise on a common basis, as if a person truly was a resource, the same as a natural resource or financial resource (capital).

[12] Homo economicus, or "economic human," is the concept that humans act rationally and are self-interested actors who make judgments so as to reach their own subjective ends. The term was originally used by the critiques of the economist John Stuart Mill as a simplification of broad human behavior. For he argued that political economy "does not treat the whole of man's nature as modified by the social state, nor of the whole conduct of man in society. It is concerned with him solely as a being who desires to possess wealth, and who is capable of judging the comparative efficacy of means for obtaining that end." Mill, *Essays on Some Unsettled Questions of Political Economy*, 1874, essay 5, paragraphs 38 and 48 (Mill, *Essays on Some Unsettled Questions of Political Economy*, 1844, 137). The model of homo economicus is a very controversial simplification of human behavior and was criticized by many, including economists.

[13] "[A]s children are born, they'll be taken over by officials appointed for that purpose . . . children of inferior parents, or any child of the others that is born defective, they'll hide in a secret and unknown place, as is appropriate" (Plato, *Republic*, 460b). Children were not to know who their real parents are and they should be bred deliberately to produce the best offspring ("best men must have sex with the best women," see Plato, *Republic*, 459d), as if they were a pack of hunting dogs (459a–d). Only when they are no longer (re)productive, when "women and men have passed the age of having children, we'll leave them free to have sex with whomever they wish" (461b).

[14] See Lewis, C. S., *The Four Loves*, 60. The economist Deirdre McCloskey frequently quotes C.S. Lewis in her book *The Bourgeois Virtues*.

[15] It must be noted that in the most modern stories and myths, in films such as *The Matrix*, *The Island*, *Equilibrium*, *Gattaca*, and so forth, people are robotized (frequently more or less unconsciously), enslaved to a certain production function, and emotions are strictly forbidden, which is probably best expressed in Kurt Wimmer's film *Equilibrium*.

To a large degree, today's mainstream economics is somewhat close to such a concept. Models of neoclassical economics perceive labor as an input to a production function. But such an economy does not know how to build humanity (so human!) into its framework—but human-robots would fit it just fine. As Joseph Stiglitz says,

> One of the great "tricks" (some say "insights") of neoclassical economics is to treat labour like any other factor of production. Output is written as a function of inputs—steel, machines, and labour. The mathematics treats labour like any other commodity, lulling one into thinking of labour like an ordinary commodity, such as steel or plastic. But labour is unlike any other commodity. The work environment is of no concern for steel; we do not care about steel's well-being.[16]

LET'S CHOP DOWN THE CEDARS

But there exists something that is frequently confused with friendship, something society and the economy greatly need: Even the earliest cultures were aware of the value of cooperation on the working level—today we call this collegiality, fellowship, or, if you want to use a desecrated term, comradeship. These "lesser relationships" are useful and necessary for society and for companies because work can be done much faster and more effectively if people get along with each other on a human level and are mutually amenable. Teamwork is a promise of improved performance, and specialized companies are hired to do *team-building*.[17]

But true friendship, which becomes one of the central themes of the Epic of Gilgamesh, comes from completely different material than teamwork. Friendship, as C. S. Lewis accurately describes it, is completely uneconomical, unbiological, unnecessary for civilization, and an unneeded relationship (as opposed to erotic relationships or maternal love, which are necessary from a purely reproductive standpoint).[18] But it is in friendship where—often by-the-way, as a side product, an externality—ideas and deeds are frequently performed or created that together can altogether change the face of society.[19] Friendship can go against an ingrained system in places where an individual does not have the courage to do so himself or herself.

---

[16] Stiglitz, *Globalization and Its Discontents*, 10.

[17] For our purposes, we can understand cordial relations among colleagues in the workplace as "lesser friendships." Just as society needs "lesser love," or at least some sort of weak feeling of mutual sympathy among strangers, a company functions better if internal battles are not constantly going on and colleagues are "lesser friends." We will return to the problem of sympathy, belonging, and therefore to a sort of "lesser love" in the chapter on Adam Smith.

[18] On the topic of love and economics, see McCloskey, *The Bourgeois Virtues*, 91–147.

[19] See Lewis, *The Four Loves*, 64.

In the beginning, Gilgamesh considers friendship unnecessary and unproductive until he himself experiences it with Enkidu and discovers that it brings unexpected things. Here we have a beautiful example of the power of friendship, one that knows how to transform (or break down) a system and change a person. Enkidu, sent to Gilgamesh as a punishment from the gods, in the end becomes his faithful friend, and together they set out against the gods. Gilgamesh would never have gathered the courage to do something like that on his own—nor would Enkidu. Their friendship helps them to hold their own in situations where either of them would not have succeeded alone. Mythic drama frequently contains a strong friendship bond—as religious scholars describe it, friends "are afraid and stimulate each other before the battle, seek solace in their dreams and are transfixed before the irreversibility of death."[20]

Bound by the ties of friendship and shared intent, Gilgamesh forgets about the building of his protective wall (in doing so abandoning what used to be his greatest goal) and instead heads *away* from the city, beyond the safety of its walls, his civilization, his known ground (which he himself built). Into the wilds of the forest he goes and there he wants to correct the order of the world—to kill Humbaba, the personification of evil.

> In the Forest of Cedar, where Humbaba dwells,
> Let us frighten him in his lair!(. . .)
> Let us slay him so that his power is no more!(. . .)
> Let me start out, I will cut down the cedar,
> I will establish for ever a name eternal![21]

Let's pause for a moment at the cutting of the cedars. Wood was a prized commodity in ancient Mesopotamia. Going out for this wood was very dangerous, and only the most courageous could do it. The danger of these expeditions is symbolized in the epic by the presence of Humbaba in the forest. "Humbaba was the guardian of the Cedar Forest, placed there by Enlil to deter would-be intruders seeking the valuable Timber."[22] In the epic, Gilgamesh's courage is emphasized by his intention to cut down the cedar forest itself (and thus gain the great wealth, which is the hero's right).

In addition, cedars were considered a holy tree, and cedar forests were the sanctuary of the god Shamash. Due to their friendship, Gilgamesh and Enkidu then intend to stand up to the gods themselves and turn a holy tree into mere (construction) material they can handle almost freely, thereby making it a part of the city-construct, part of the building material of civilization, thus "enslaving" that which originally was part of wild nature. This is a beautiful proto-example of the shifting of the borders between the sacred and profane (secular)—and to a certain extent also an

---

[20] Balabán and Tydlitátová, *Gilgameš* [Gilgamesh], 72.
[21] The Epic of Gilgamesh, Tablet II (Y100–102, Y98, Y186–187), 18–20.
[22] George, *The Babylonian Gilgamesh Epic*, 144.

early illustration of the idea that *nature is there to provide* cities and people with raw material and production resources.[23] "The felling of cedars was usually considered a 'cultural success' because Uruk did not have wood for construction. Gilgamesh is considered to have procured this valuable material for his city in this way. This act can also be a portent of our 'cultural successes,' which turn living beings, not only trees, into raw materials, supplies, goods (. . .) The transformation of a cosmic tree into construction material is an example given to us by Gilgamesh and one which we have feverishly pursued."[24]

Here we witness an important historical change: people feel more natural in an unnatural surrounding: the city. Among the Mesopotamians, it was the city that was the habitat of people; for Hebrews (as we will see later) it was still nature, as they originally were more of a nomadic tribe. It started with Babylonians—rural nature becomes just a supplier of raw materials, resources (and humans the source of human resources). Nature is not the garden in which humans were created and placed, which they should care for and which they should reside in, but becomes a mere reservoir for natural (re)sources.

The part of the epic mentioning Gilgamesh and Enkidu's expedition to Humbaba also conceals another reason why Gilgamesh is celebrated—he is ascribed in legends with the discovery of several desert oases that eased

---

[23] In Gilgamesh's time, it was necessary to approach nature with an honor pertaining to nonhuman things, consequently toward something a human did not create and was unable to control. There was even a completely "sacred" untouchability (which Gilgamesh incidentally breaches) related to certain parts of nature. Today such inviolability is becoming rarer with every passing day, but despite this we can still find modern "holy places" where the effective invisible hand of the market is not allowed entry. Such an example is the paradox of New York's Central Park. This park is surrounded by *sky-high* effectiveness—a big city where every square meter is utilized to the greatest possible degree in both height and depth. Perhaps it is appropriate to recall here that Babylon's holy towers, the ziggurats, were supposed to "reach unto heaven." Their role, of course, was the domestication of mountains, which from time immemorial were inhabited by (uncontrollable and innumerous) gods. The things we domesticate or produce ourselves are things we have control over; we can control them and we "see" into them. The ziggurat was consequently a likely result of an effort to relocate a natural mountain into the city, to build it with human hands and urbanize it (as was done with the feral Enkidu). ". . . the cave gave early man his first conception of architectural space (. . .) despite their differences, the pyramid, the ziggurat, the Mithraic grotto, the Christian crypt all have their prototypes in the mountain cave." (Mumford, *The City in History*, 17). But back to New York, the city of cities: As far as the price of land goes, Central Park is one of the most expensive places in the world; it is probably the most expensive nature in the world. This "holy" place takes up 3.5 square kilometers, which without regulation and under the action of genuine market forces would have long ago been swallowed up by city buildings. Of course, proposals to use at least part of its vast property for new construction would never succeed with either city leaders or local inhabitants, and so the city and its sky-high effectiveness are effectively banned from Central Park. And one last note: In a longer time frame, the "protected" nature in Central Park is not an anomaly; quite the opposite: the city all around it is. Nature is not the intruder into the city, even if it appears that way today. The city is an intruder into nature.
[24] Heffernanová, *Gilgameš* [Gilgamesh], 8.

traveling for traders in ancient Mesopotamia. "The discovery of various wells or oases that opened a passage across the desert from the middle Euphrates to Lebanon must have revolutionalized long-distance travel in upper Mesopotamia. If Gilgamesh was traditionally the first to make this journey on his expedition to the Cedar Forest, it would be logical for him to be given credit for the discovery of the techniques of survival that made desert travel possible."[25] Gilgamesh becomes a hero not only due to his strength, but also due to discoveries and deeds whose importance were in large part economic—direct gaining of construction materials in the case of felling the cedar forest, stopping Enkidu from devastating Uruk's economy, and discovering new desert routes during his expeditions.

BETWEEN ANIMAL AND ROBOT: HUMAN

The subjugation of wild nature was a bold act that Gilgamesh dared to try because of his friendship with Enkidu. But in the end, this revolt against the gods paradoxically served the gods' original plan: Through his friendship with the feral Enkidu, Gilgamesh renounces the construction of the wall. At the same time, inadvertently and through his own experience, he confirms his theory—that human relations *truly* stand in the way of the construction of his famed wall. He then leaves it unfinished and, with his friend, heads out *beyond* it. No longer does he seek immortality in the construction of his wall but in heroic acts with his friend for life.

The friendship changes both friends. Gilgamesh changes from a cold and hated tyrant, who reduces men to robots, into a person with feelings. He leaves his sober pride behind the walls of Uruk and indulges in adventures in the wild with his *animal spirits*.[26] Despite J. M. Keynes's thinking of this term as a spontaneous impulse to action, he did not necessarily have our animality in mind; but perhaps we could in this context consider

---

[25] George, *The Babylonian Gilgamesh Epic*, 98.

[26] *Animal spirits* is a term that the economist J. M. Keynes coined and introduced to economics. With it he means our souls, or what "animates" us, or consequently our spontaneous urge, which gives meaning and energy to our acts:

"... our positive activities depend on spontaneous optimism rather than on a mathematical expectation, whether moral or hedonistic or economic. Most, probably, of our decisions to do something positive, the full consequences of which will be drawn out over many days to come, can only be taken as a result of animal spirits—of a spontaneous urge to action rather than inaction, and not as the outcome of a weighted average of quantitative benefits multiplied by quantitative probabilities. Enterprise only pretends to itself to be mainly actuated by the statements in its own prospectus, however candid and sincere. Only a little more than an expedition to the South Pole, is it, based on an exact calculation of benefits to come. Thus if the animal spirits are dimmed and the spontaneous optimism falters, leaving us to depend on nothing but a mathematical expectation, enterprise will fade and die." Keynes, *General Theory*, 161–162.

For more on the topic of animal spirits, see Akerlof and Shiller, *Animal Spirits*.

for a moment the animal parts of our (would-be rational-economic) personae. The *animal* essence of his friend, Enkidu, is transferred onto Gilgamesh (they head out from the city into nature, giving in to the call of uncertain adventure).

And Enkidu's transformation? If Gilgamesh was a symbol for nearly godlike perfection, civilization, and a staid city tyrant who would rather see machines instead of his subjects, Enkidu originally represented something on the complete opposite pole. He is the personification of animality, unpredictability, indomitability, and wildness. His animalistic nature is also brought to mind physically: "All his body is matted with hair (. . .) the hair of his head grows thickly as barley."[27] In Enkidu's case, friendship with Gilgamesh symbolizes the culmination of the process of becoming a human. Both heroes change—each from opposite poles—into humans.

In this context, a psychological dimension to the story may be useful: "Enkidu (. . .) is Gilgamesh's alter ego, the dark, animal side of his soul, the complement to his restless heart. When Gilgamesh found Enkidu, he changed from a hated tyrant into the protector of his city. (. . .) Both titans are humanized by the experience of their friendship, and the half-god and half-animal become beings similar to us."[28] There seem to be two propensities in us, one economic, rational, seeking to be in control, maximizing, efficiency seeking, and so forth, and the other wild, animal-like, unpredictable, and brute. To be human seems to be *somewhere in between*, or *both* of these two. We shall come back to this topic in the second part of the book.

DRINK THE BEER, AS IS THE CUSTOM OF THE LAND

Now how did Enkidu become a part of the civilization, a human? At the beginning of Enkidu's transformation from an animal into a civilized person, Gilgamesh sets a trap for him. The harlot Shamhat is told to "do for the man the work of a woman"[29] and when Enkidu gets up after six days and seven nights of sex, nothing is as it was before.

> When with her delights he was fully sated,
> he turned his gaze to his herd.
> The gazelles saw Enkidu, they started to run,
> the beasts of the field shield away from his presence.
> Enkidu has defiled his body so pure,[30]

---

[27] The Epic of Gilgamesh, Tablet I (105 . . . 107), 5.

[28] Balabán and Tydlitátová, *Gilgameš* [Gilgamesh], 72.

[29] The Epic of Gilgamesh, Tablet I (185), 7.

[30] This certainly sounds paradoxical to us: How can sex be something in the epic that *civilizes and humanizes* Enkidu? Don't we frequently consider the sexual instinct as being something animal? It is perceived in the epic as the opposite, in large part because of the fertility cult, but also because the experience of sex was existentially considered at the time to be

his legs stood still, though his herd was in motion.
Enkidu was weakened, could not run as before,[31]
but now he had reason, and wide understanding.[32]

Enkidu eventually loses his animal nature because "his herd will spurn him, though he grew up amongst it."[33] He is brought to the city, dressed, given bread and beer:

Eat the bread, Enkidu, essential to life,
drink the ale, the lot of the land.[34]

With this, what happened is that he had "turned into a man."[35] Enkidu joined a (specialized) society that offered him something that nature in its uncultivated state was never capable of. He moved away from nature—he moved *behind* the city walls. Thus he became a human person. But this change is irrevocable. Enkidu cannot return to his previous life because "the beasts of the field shield away from his presence."[36] Nature will not allow a person back who has left her womb. "Nature, from where (a person) long ago came, remains outside, beyond the city walls. It will be foreign and rather unfriendly."[37]

At this moment of rebirth from an animal to a human state, the world's oldest preserved epic implicitly hints at something highly important. Here we see what early cultures considered the beginning of civilization. Here is depicted the difference between people and animals or, better, savages. Here the epic quietly describes birth, the awakening of a conscious,

---

something that elevates and emancipates man from the animal state. Sex was deified to a certain extent, as is shown by the role of the temple priestesses who devoted themselves to sex. The approach to sex is what truly distinguishes man from an absolute majority of creatures—only a handful of species in nature do *it* for pleasure: ". . . sex is flagrantly separated from reproduction in a few species, including bonobos (pygmy chimpanzees) and dolphins." (Diamond, *Why Is Sex Fun?* 3). The fact that eros paradoxically figures in our conscience something animal has also been noted by the economist Deirdre McCloskey, who criticizes that concept. See McCloskey, *The Bourgeois Virtues*, 92.

[31] There is a close relationship between the loss of naturalness and the development of humanity and the soul in the Epic of Gilgamesh; in economics this is marked by the term "trade-off," or the principle of quid pro quo—that nothing comes for free and everything has its price. In Enkidu's case, this meant that he could not be both a natural and civilized creature at the same time; the ascension of Enkidu's new personality suppresses his old naturalness.

[32] The Epic of Gilgamesh, Tablet I (195–202), 8.

[33] The Epic of Gilgamesh, Tablet I (145), 6. Nature becomes not only unfriendly to a civilized person, but even haunted and demonic. Animals such as mice, bats, or spiders do not attack people, but despite this they provoke irrational fear. Nature does not threaten us; nature haunts us. A dark forest, a swamp, a foggy valley—all of these provoke fear in a civilized person. The embodiment of these fears are creatures from fairy tales, who frequently symbolize a nature that is haunted (witches, vampires, werewolves, etc.).

[34] The Epic of Gilgamesh, Tablet II (P96–97), 14.

[35] The Epic of Gilgamesh, Tablet I (P109), 14.

[36] The Epic of Gilgamesh, Tablet I (198), 8.

[37] Sokol, *Město a jeho hradby* [The City and Its Walls], 288.

civilized human. We are witnesses to the emancipation of humanity from animals, similar to how a sculpture is brought forth from stone. From a state of individual satisfaction of his needs in a primary unmediated use of nature without any efforts to transform it, Enkidu moves to the city, the prototype of civilization and life in an *artificial* environment *outside* nature. "He will continue to live in a city, in a world created by people; he will live there richly, safely, and comfortably and will live on bread and beer, strange fare, which has been laboriosly prepared by human hands."[38]

The entire history of culture is dominated by an effort to become as independent as possible from the whims of nature.[39] The more developed a civilization is, the more an individual is protected from nature and natural influences and knows how to create around him a *constant* or controllable environment to his liking. Our menu is no longer dependent on harvests, the presence of wild game, or the seasons. We have managed to maintain a constant temperature inside our dwellings, regardless of whether there is piercing cold or burning summer.

We can also follow the first attempts at a desired *constantization* of the living environment in the Epic of Gilgamesh—and best in the example of the construction of a wall around Uruk, which will allow it to become a cradle of civilization.[40] This constantization also pertains to human activity, human labor. Humans do better at one thing they specialize in, and if they can depend on the work of others for the rest of their needs, society grows rich. It has been a long time since every individual has had to make their own clothes and shoes; to hunt, plant, or prepare their own food; to find a source of drinking water and build a dwelling.[41] These roles have been taken over by the institution of market specialization (which understandably functioned a long time before Adam Smith described it as one of the main sources of the wealth of nations[42]). Each therefore specializes

---

[38] Sokol, *Město a jeho hradby* [The City and Its Walls], 289.

[39] Nowadays we usually perceive unspoiled nature as an ideal of beauty and purity, but most Western-type people would not survive for long in nature's untouched locations. It is not a world of people.

[40] "In the prologue the poet claims the wall as Gilgamesh's handiwork, while at the same time relating that its foundations were laid by the Seven Sages, primeval beings who brought to man the arts of civilization. This view reflects an old tradition in which Uruk was considered (rightfully) the cradle of early civilization." George, *The Babylonian Gilgamesh Epic*, 91.

[41] At the same time, it is good to be aware of how great a change humanity has gone through in the past few generations. Our great-grandparents or great-great-grandparents commonly managed these "natural" skills and theoretically managed to secure themselves. But today most people have a hard time imagining that they would be capable or willing to kill a chicken, pig, or cow, despite being happy to consume meat on a daily basis.

[42] The concept of "doing one thing" has led to the extreme of factory production, where a person carries out almost-roboticized labor. It was in one such factory (a pin manufacturer) that even Adam Smith, who is considered the doyen of the idea of economic specialization, came to realize the magic of the division of labor. If every family had to produce its own pins

in what they know to be most valuable to society, and the remaining vast majority of their needs are left to others.

The epic captures one of the greatest leaps in the development of the division of labor. Uruk itself is one of the oldest cities of all, and in the epic it reflects a historic step forward in specialization—in the direction of a new social *city* arrangement. Because of the city wall, people in the city can devote themselves to things other than worrying about their own safety, and they can continue to specialize more deeply. The permanence of a city surrounded by a wall brings is also noticeable. Human life in the city gains a new dimension and suddenly it seems more natural to take up issues going beyond the life span of an individual. "The city wall symbolizes as well as founds the permanence of the city as an institution which will remain forever and give its inhabitants the certainty of unlimited safety, allowing them to start investing with an outlook reaching far beyond the borders of individual life. The prosperity and riches of Uruk are supported by the certainty of its walls. Provincials can honestly be amazed, and possibly envy them."[43]

From an economic standpoint, the creation of a fortified city brings important changes; aside from a deeper specialization for its inhabitants there is also "the possibility of crafts and trade, where one can become rich with the wave of a hand—and of course also become poor. The possibility of a livelihood for those who had no land, for younger sons, outcasts, speculators and adventurers from anywhere—from the entire world."[44]

But everything has its price, and no lunch is free—not even the course of prosperity, which specialization has laid out for us. The price we pay for independence from the whims of nature is dependence on our societies and civilizations. The more sophisticated a given society is *as a whole*, the less its members are able to survive on their own *as individuals*, without society. The more specialized a society is, the greater the number of those on whom we are dependent.[45] And so much so that it is existential.

Enkidu managed to survive in nature *independently* and without any kind of help, freely. Because Enkidu

> knows not a people, nor even a country (. . .)
> with the gazelles he grazes on grasses,
> joining the throng with the game at the water-hole,
> his heart delighting with the beasts in the water.[46]

---

at home, they would frequently not be able to, but thanks to specialized factory production they can simply buy them, and at a completely negligible price.

[43] Sokol, *Město a jeho hradby* [The City and Its Walls], 289.

[44] Ibid., 290.

[45] The societal importance of another object of economists' interests, *the market*, is thus increased. It becomes a *communications medium* for individuals dependent on a great number of other members of society; because of their numbers a lot of them would not be able to communicate or especially trade separately.

[46] The Epic of Gilgamesh, Tablet I (108 . . . 110–112), 5.

Enkidu is like an animal; he has no nation of his own and is a member of no land. Through his own acts he himself proves to take care of all his needs; he is without civilization, *non*civilized. Again we see the principle of quid pro quo: Enkidu is self-sufficient (just as many animals are), and in return (or precisely because of this), his needs are minimal. Animal needs are negligible compared to humans'. On the other hand, people are not able to satisfy their needs even with the riches and technology of the twenty-first century. It can be said that Enkidu was therefore happy in his natural state, because all of his needs were satiated. On the other hand, with people, it appears that the more a person has, the more developed and richer, the greater the number of his needs (including the unsaturated ones). If a consumer buys something, theoretically it should rid him of one of his needs—and the aggregate of things they *need* should be decreased by one item. In reality, though, the aggregate of "I want to have" expands together with the growing aggregate of "I have." Here it is appropriate to quote the economist George Stigler, who was aware of this human unsaturatedness. "The chief thing which the common-sense individual wants is not satisfactions for the wants he had, but more, and better wants."[47]

A change in the external environment (a transition from nature to the city) in the Epic of Gilgamesh very closely relates to an internal change—the change of a savage into a civilized person. The wall around the city of Uruk is, among other things, a symbol of an internal distancing from nature, a symbol of revolts against submission to laws that do not come under the control of man and that man can at most discover and use to his benefit.

"The practical purpose of the wall in the outside world had its parallel in the interior of a person: The forming ego-consciousness also serves as a sort of protective wall which separates it from other psyches. Defensiveness is an important characteristic trait of the ego. And Gilgamesh also ushers in man's isolation from the natural environment, both external and internal."[48] On the other hand, this isolation enables new, heretofore unrecognized forms of human development in relationship to the entire city society. "The expansion of human energies, the enlargement of the human ego (. . .) and differentiation at many points in the structure of the city were all aspects of a single transformation: The rise of civilization."[49]

NATURAL NATURE

When we talk about the city and nature, it is possible to take our thoughts in one more direction, one that will prove to be very useful, especially in comparison with later Hebrew and Christian thought. We consider the symbolism of nature as a natural state into which we are born and the city

---

[47] Stigler, "Frank Hyneman Knight," 58.
[48] Heffernanová, *Gilgameš* [Gilgamesh], 4.
[49] Mumford, *The City in History*, 44.

as a symbol of the exact opposite—development, civilization, the alteration of nature, and progress.

An unspoken message blows through the entire epic: Civilization and progress play out in the city, which is the true "natural" dwelling of the people. It seems from this perspective that it is not natural for us to be in the natural state of being. In the end, the city is the home not only of people but of gods as well:

> Said Uta-napishti to him, to Gilgamesh:
> (. . .)The town of Shuruppak, a city well known to you,
> which stands on the banks of the river Euphrates:
> the city was old—the gods once were in it—
> when the great gods decided to send down the Deluge.[50]

It is animals that live in nature, and the savage Enkidu rages there. Nature is where one goes to hunt, collect crops, or gather the harvest. It is perceived as the saturator of our needs and nothing more. One goes back to the city to sleep and be "human." On the contrary, evil resides in nature. Humbaba lives in the cedar forest, which also happens to be the reason to completely eradicate it. The wild Enkidu lives in nature; he looks like a human, but in his naturalness he is an animal—he does not live in the city, is uncontrollable,[51] and does damage. It is necessary to separate the city, as a symbol of people, civilization, nonnature, from its surroundings with a strong wall. Enkidu becomes a human by moving to the city.

The natural state of things, as at birth, is accordingly imperfect in the epic, evil. Our *nature* has to be transformed, civilized, cultured, fought against. Symbolically, then, we can view the entire issue from the standpoint of the epic in the following way: Our nature is insufficient, bad, evil, and good (humane) occurs only after emancipation from nature (from naturalness), through culturing and education. Humanity is considered as being in civilization.

For fuller contrast, let us compare the duality of the city and nature with a later Hebrew thought. In the Old Testament, this relationship is perceived completely differently. Man (humanity) is created in nature, in a garden. Man was supposed to care for the Garden of Eden and live in harmony with nature and the animals. Soon after creation, man walks naked and is not ashamed, de facto the same as the animals. What is characteristic is that man dresses (the natural state of creation itself is not enough for him), and he (literally and figuratively) covers[52] himself—in

---

[50] The Epic of Gilgamesh, Tablet XI (9 . . . 11–13), 88.

[51] The only way for Gilgamesh to be successful was the trick with the harlot. Gilgamesh never managed to subjugate Enkidu through force alone.

[52] The Czech philosopher and biologist Zdeněk Neubauer noted that the same is true for science: "It appears that science's naturalness, like every naturalness, likes to be hidden hermetically. (Incidentally, 'hermetic' also indicates secret, hidden . . .)." See Neubauer, O čem je věda? [What Science Is About?], 59, the chapter "Science as a Religion of Modern History." Neubauer further writes: "Science—considering its spirituality—is understandably ashamed

shame after the fall.[53] Dressing, which stems from shame at his natural state, for his state at birth, for his nakedness, distinguishes people from animals and from their natural, at-birth state. When the prophets of the Old Testament later speak of a return to paradise, they are at the same time portraying it as harmony with nature:

> The wolf will live with the lamb, the leopard will lie down with the goat. The calf and the lion and the yearling together; and a little child will lead them. The cow will feed with the bear, their young will lie down together, and the lion will eat straw like the ox. The infant will play near the hole of the cobra, and the young child put his hand into the viper's nest.[54]

AND SINFUL CIVILIZATION?

On the other hand, resistance to city civilization, to the sedentary way of life, can be found between the lines of many Old Testament stories. It is the "evil" farmer Cain (farming requiring a sedentary, city lifestyle) who kills the shepherd Abel (hunters and shepherds tended to be nomadic and did not found cities; their way of life on the contrary required constant motion from one hunting ground or pasture to the next). A similar dimension is in the background of the story of the staidly living Jacob, who *fools, tricks*[55] his brother Esau,[56] depriving him of his father's blessing in his own favor.

---

of this 'secret body'." Neubauer, *O čem je věda? (De possest: O duchovním bytí Božím)* [What Science Is About? (De possest: Of Spiritual Being of God)], 58.

[53] "He answered, 'I heard you in the garden, and I was afraid because I was naked; so I hid.' And he said, 'Who told you that you were naked? Have you eaten from the tree that I commanded you not to eat from?'" Genesis 3:10–11. What was hidden was our genitals, man's central point, as is shown by Leonardo Da Vinci's famous drawing, the Vitruvian Man.

[54] Isaiah 11:6–8. Unless noted otherwise, we use the New International Version of the Holy Bible (Grandville, MI: Zondervan, 2001).

[55] Trickery and swindling play an important role in ancient myth in general—the so-called Trickster is one of the fundamental archetypes of heroes. This understanding was emphasized by the American anthropologist Paul Radin in his most-read book, *The Trickster*, where he describes the basic archetype of heroes. The trick is a symbol of mankind's original emancipation and the beginning of the struggle against something stronger than man himself, against gods or nature, for example. It is the original revolt against the rule of law and givenness, the original refusal of passivity and the beginning of a struggle with a stronger (or abstract) principle. Even Gilgamesh had to use trickery against the feral Enkidu. The patriarch Abraham lies, passes off his wife as his sister and, in an effort to avoid unpleasantries, lets things go so far that he even sells her to the Pharaoh's harem. Jacob is a "trickster" for a substantial part of his life, which to a certain extent is contained in his name: In Hebrew, Jacob means "to hold by the heel," which in English is similar to "pulling one's leg." It is necessary to point out that in early cultures, trickery did not have the pejorative connotation it has today. Trick was simply a way of fighting, especially against stronger enemies. Even Odysseus is known by the epithet Odysseus the Cunning. To this day, tricksters often appear in such things as fairy tales as positive heroes. These tricksters frequently handle tasks that knights and princes are incapable of, and precisely for this reason he frequently gains the princess's hand and the royal crown.

[56] In the book *Tajemství dvou partnerů* [The Secret of Two Partners] by Heffernanová, the author sees in this story a struggle between the natural subconscious (the hairy hunter Esau)

The city was frequently (at least in older Jewish writings) a symbol of sin, degeneration, and decadence—nonhumanity. The Hebrews were originally a nomadic nation, one that avoided cities. It is no accident that the first important city[57] mentioned in the Bible is proud Babylon,[58] which God later turns to dust. When the pasture gets too small for Abraham and Lot, Lot chooses the city as his future (Sodom and Gomorrah), and Abraham goes further into the desert to lead a nomadic life. It is not necessary to recall the degeneration of these two cities—everyone knows.

The Old Testament uses poetry that elevates nature. We find nothing of the sort in the Epic of Gilgamesh. The Old Testament Song of Solomon describes the lovers' state with natural symbolism. It is no accident that all of the lovers' positive moments play out in nature, outside the city, in a vineyard, in a garden. But unpleasant events take place in the city: A guard beats and humiliates his lover; the lovers cannot find each other in the city. But in nature, in the vineyard, in the garden (reminding us of the original Garden of creation) it is safe and the lovers are together again, uninterrupted, as they wish.

In short, nature and naturalness had a rather positive value for the Hebrews, while city civilization was negative. God's original "altar" traveled, and when established was "only" placed in a tent (hence the term "the Lord's *Tabernacle*"). It is as if civilization could only spoil mankind—the closer it holds to nature, the more human it is. Here humans' natural state, their naturalness, needs no civilization to be good or human. As opposed to the Epic of Gilgamesh, it appears that for the Hebrews, evil is rather found *inside* the city walls and in civilization.

This view of naturalness and civilization had and continues to have a complicated development in the history of Jewish culture and our own. The Hebrews later also chose a king (despite the unanimous opposition of God's prophets) and settled in cities, where they eventually founded the Lord's Tabernacle and built a temple for Him. The city of Jerusalem later gained an illustrious position in all of religion. The city (the home of the Temple) holds an important position in Hebrew thought as well. Later development is even more inclined toward the city model, which is already evident in early Christianity. It is enough, for example, to read the Book of Revelation to see how the vision of paradise developed from the deep

---

and settled consciousness (Jacob, a "dweller in tents" and a master of language and the deceit language enables). With his hairiness, Esau also noticeably recalls the appearance of the animal, feral Enkidu. In this symbolism, both are classified as being in the world of nature.

[57] The very first city named in the Bible was the city founded by the heroic hunter Nimrod. "The first centers of his kingdom were Babylon, Erek, Akkad, and Calnech, in Shinar. From that land he went to Assyria, where he built Nineveh . . ." Genesis 10:10–11. Babylon is likely meant as the city where the tower/ziggurat of Babel was built, Erek most probably means Uruk, which in the twenty-seventh century BC was ruled by the mythical Gilgamesh. Other cities also have ties to our story: The Akkadian version is today considered the standard version of the Epic of Gilgamesh, and a copy of it was found in the library of the city of Nineveh.

[58] Genesis 11:9.

Old Testament period, when paradise was a garden. John describes his vision of heaven as *a city*—paradise is in New Jerusalem, a city where the dimensions of the walls(!) are described in detail, as are the golden streets and gates of pearl. While the tree of life is located here, with a river flowing from it, there is no other mention of nature in the last book of the Bible.

But even this tableau perfectly describes the transformation of man's perception and his naturalness that was playing out at the time. That is to say that by this time Christianity (as well as the influence of the Greeks) does not consider human naturalness to be an unambiguous good, and it does not have such an idyllic relationship to nature as the Old Testament prophets.

How does this affect economics? More than we would want to surmise. If we were to look at human *naturalness* as a good, then collective social actions need a much weaker ruling hand. If people themselves have a natural tendency (propensity) toward good, this role does not have to be supplied by the state, ruler, or, if you wish, Leviathan.[59] But on the contrary, if we accept Hobbes's vision of human nature as a state of constant latent violence and wars of everyone against everything, *homo homini lupus*, where man is dog eat dog (animal!) to his fellow man, then it is necessary to civilize man (and turn wolves into people) with a ruler's strong hand. If a tendency toward good is not naturally endowed in people, it must be imputed from above through violence or at least the threat of violence. For in a "natural state" there is "no culture of the earth . . . no knowledge of the face of the earth," and life is "solitary, poor, nasty, brutish, and short."[60] On the contrary, economic policy can be much freer if the ruler believes in human nature, which has in itself a tendency toward good and that this good only needs to be cared for, guided in coordination, and supported.

From the standpoint of the development of economic thought, it is interesting to note additional differences between the Old Testament and the Epic of Gilgamesh, even in seemingly similar stories. The epic, for example, mentions a great flood several times, which is strikingly similar to the biblical flood.

> For six days and seven nights,
> there blew the wind, the downpour,
> the gale, the Deluge, it flattened the land.
> But the seventh day when it came,
> The gale relented, the Deluge ended.
> The ocean grew calm, that had thrashed like a woman in labour,
> The tempest grew still, the Deluge ended.

---

[59] In the Bible, Leviathan is described as a great and ferocious monster (see the Book of Job 3:8, and Job 41:1–7). Thomas Hobbes uses this name in the metaphorical sense as a marking for the state or ruler, without whom society in Hobbes's conception would fall into chaos and disorder.

[60] Hobbes, *Leviathan*, 100 (the name of this chapter thirteen is "Of the Natural Condition of Mankind as Concerning Their Felicity and Misery").

I looked at the weather, it was quiet and still,
But all people had turned to clay.
The flood plain was flat like the roof of a house.[61]

In the Epic of Gilgamesh, the flood occurred long before the main
story itself. Only Utanapishti survived—because he built a ship that saved
everything living.

All the silver I owned I loaded aboard,
all the gold I owned I loaded aboard,
all the living creatures I had I loaded aboard,
I sent on board all my kith and kin,
The beasts of the field, the creatures of the wild,
and members of every skill and craft.[62]

Unlike Noah, Utanapishti loads silver and gold first, things that are not
mentioned in the biblical story at all. If in Gilgamesh the city acts as a
place of protection against the "evil beyond the walls," its primary and
positive relationship to wealth is logical. It is in cities that riches are concentrated. In the end, even Gilgamesh gained part of his fame by killing
Humbaba—an act in which he came into riches in the form of wood from
the felled cedars.

HARNESSING WILD EVIL AND THE INVISIBLE HAND
OF THE MARKET

Let us return for the last time to the humanization of the wild Enkidu,
which is a process we can perceive with a bit of imagination as the first
seed of the principle of the market's invisible hand, and therefore the
parallels with one of the central schematics of economic thinking.

Enkidu used to be an invincible terror to all hunters. He destroyed
their plans and stood in the way of hunting and cultivating nature. In the
words of one of the affected hunters:

I am afraid and I dare not approach him.
He fills the pits that I myself dig,
he pulls up the snares that I lay.
He sets free from my grasp all the beasts of the field,
he stops me doing the work of the wild.[63]

Nevertheless, after his humanization and civilization, a turnaround
occurs:

When at night the shepherds lay sleeping,
he struck down wolves, he chased off lions.

---

[61] The Epic of Gilgamesh, Tablet XI (128–136), 93.
[62] The Epic of Gilgamesh, Tablet XI (82–87), 91.
[63] The Epic of Gilgamesh, Tablet I (129–134), 6.

Sleeping lay the senior shepherds,
Their shepherd boy Enkidu, a man wide awake.[64]

By culturing and "domesticating" Enkidu, humanity tamed the uncontrollable wild and chaotic evil that had previously vehemently caused damage and did everything to work against the good of the city. Enkidu devastated the doings (the external, outside-the-walls) of the city. But he was later harnessed and fights at the side of civilization *against* nature, naturalness, the natural state of things. This moment has an interpretation that could be very important for economists. Enkidu caused damage and it was impossible to fight against him. But with the help of a trap, trick, this evil was transformed into something that greatly benefited civilization.

We understandably mean the image of the bad human inborn natural traits (for example, egoism, placing one's interests before those of one's neighbors). Enkidu cannot be defeated, but it is possible to use him in the service of good. A similar motif appears a thousand years after the reversal, which is well known even to noneconomists as the central idea of economics: the invisible hand of the market. Sometimes it is better to "harness the devil to the plow" than to fight with him. Instead of summoning up enormous energy in the fight against evil, it is better to use its own energy to reach a goal we desire; setting up a mill on the turbulent river instead of futile efforts to remove the current. This is also how Saint Prokop approached it in one of the oldest Czech legends.[65] When he was clearing a forest(!) and tilled the land gained in this way (how nature was civilized at the time), the legend tells that neighboring people caught sight of a plow with a devil harnessed to it.[66] Prokop, it seems, knew how to handle something dangerous, something that people fear. He understood well that it is wiser and more advantageous to appropriately make use of natural chaotic forces than to futilely try to suppress, exclude, and destroy them. He knew to a certain extent the "curse" of evil, which the devil Mephistopheles gives away in Goethe's play *Faust*:

Part of that force which would
Do evil evermore, and yet creates the good.[67]

In his book *The Spirit of Democratic Capitalism*, the economist Michael Novak deals with the problem of transforming evil into a creative force.[68] He argues that only democratic capitalism, as opposed to all alternative—frequently utopian—systems, understood how deeply evil nature is rooted in the human soul, and realized that it is beyond any system to uproot this

---

[64] The Epic of Gilgamesh, Tablet II (59–62), 14.
[65] See also Neubauer, *Přímluvce postmoderny* [Advocate of Postmodernity], 37–36, 53–55.
[66] Jan Heller examines this reference in his book *Jak orat s čertem* [How to Plow With the Devil], 153–156.
[67] Goethe, *Faust*, part one, scene 3. English translation: Goethe, *Goethe's Faust*, 159.
[68] A similar defense of capitalism is offered by such people as Deirdre McCloskey in her book *The Bourgeois Virtues*.

deeply embedded "sin." The system of democratic capitalism can "bring down the power of sin—i.e., to retransform its energy into creative force (and in doing so the best way to get revenge on Satan)."[69]

A similar story (reforming something animally wild and uncultivated in civilizational achievement) is used by Thomas Aquinas in his teachings. Several centuries later, this idea is fully emancipated in the hands of Bernard Mandeville and his *Fable of the Bees: or, Private Vices, Publick Benefits*. The economic and political aspects of this idea are—often incorrectly—ascribed to Adam Smith. The idea that later made him famous speaks of the societal good that comes from the butcher's egoism, yearning for earnings, and his own profit.[70] Of course, Smith takes a much more sophisticated and critical stand than is generally taught and believed today. We will also get to this later.

At this place, please allow a minor observation. Only the saint in the story of Prokop had the transformative power to harness evil and recast it, to force it to serve the general welfare.[71] In this day and age that quality is ascribed to the invisible hand of the market. In the story of Gilgamesh, the harlot was able to recast wild evil into something useful.[72] It appears that the invisible hand of the market is endowed with the historical heritage of moving in the dimensions of these two extremes—the saint and the harlot.

IN SEARCH OF THE BLISS POINT[73]

With his divine origin, Gilgamesh was predestined to something great. His efforts at finding immortality serve as a red thread through the

---

[69] Novak, *Duch demokratického kapitalismu* [The Spirit of Democratic Capitalism], 77–78 (quoted and translated from Czech version of the book).

[70] Smith, *An Inquiry into the Nature and Causes of the Wealth of Nations*, 266.

[71] As the Czech economist Lubomír Mlčoch frequently and accurately notes, in order for a person to harness evils, one would have to be at least a saint.

[72] In Babylonian culture, priestesses were at the same time temple "prostitutes" as part of the fertility cult. "Shamhat's position in Uruk is not revealed in the epic, for it is not material to the story, but one should note that, as the cult center of Ishtar, goddess of sexual love, Uruk was a city well known for the number and beauty of its prostitutes. Many of these women were cultic prostitutes employed in the temple of Ninsun and Ishtar" (George, *The Babylonian Gilgamesh Epic*, 148). "The harlot Gilgamesh sent is rather a priestess or a courtesan, and not a mere prostitute. (. . .) Aside from the pleasure of lovemaking, she had to know how to offer the savage human wisdom and convince him of the advantages of civilized life." (Balabán and Tydlitátová, *Gilgameš* [Gilgamesh], 139).

[73] A term used frequently by economists. The bliss point is a sort of consumer nirvana, a point at which utility is not only optimized within the given situation, but also approaches the ideal state. It takes no limits (such as budgets) into account. In economics, the term "bliss point" (or "saturation point") is used as an ideal, desirable level of consumption in which the given individual is completely blissful and it is impossible to improve his or her well-being in any way with further consumption. In economics, the function of utility is frequently drawn as a hill, and the bliss point is its peak.

entire epic.[74] This ancient goal par excellence, which only heroes previously dared attempt,[75] takes several different forms in the epic.

First, Gilgamesh tries to secure his immortal name in a relatively uninteresting way—building a wall around the city of Uruk. In the second stage, after finding his friend Enkidu, Gilgamesh abandons the wall and sets out beyond the city to maximalize heroism. "In his (. . .) search of immortal life, Gilgamesh went through the most extraordinary hardships and performed superhuman feats."[76] Here the individual does not try anymore to maximize his goods or profits, but what is important is writing his name in human memory in the form of heroic acts or deeds. The utility consumption function replaces the dimension of the maximization of adventure and renown. Such a concept of immortality is very closely tied to the creation of letters (the story must be recorded for the next generation), and Gilgamesh was the very first to attempt such immortality in the form of a written record of "immortal" fame—anyway the first to succeed. "His famous name introduces a new concept of immortality, one connected with letters and the cult of the word: A name and especially a written name survives the body."[77]

We also get, of course, to classical economic maximization of profit later in the epic. Gilgamesh's journey in the end is not as successful as the hero imagined. His lifelong friend Enkidu dies before him, and for the first time he hears the sentence that for the rest of the epic will serve as an echo of the futility of his deeds: "O Gilgamesh, where are you wandering? The life you seek you never will find."[78] After this disappointment, he comes to the edge of the sea, where the innkeeper Siduri lives. As tonic for his sorrow, she offers him the *garden of bliss*, a sort of hedonistic fortress of carpe diem, where a person comes to terms with his mortality and at least in the course of the end of his life maximizes earthly pleasures, or earthly utility.

Gilgamesh, wherefore do you wander?
The eternal life you are seeking you shall not find.

---

[74] Immortality, in any form, had a fundamental meaning for Babylonians—paradise did not await after death, and death was perceived as a transition into something between an unpleasant and repulsive state.

[75] The desire for immortality, as with many other primeval desires, remains to this day, but it has taken on a much more folk form: The cult of an eternally beautiful and young body created the imperative for efforts toward as healthy and long a life as possible, which overlooks its quality. It is not possible to achieve this long life through heroic acts, a rich or moral life, but, for example, through eating food that fulfills certain (constantly changing) criteria and avoiding other consumer habits. Even this modern movement takes the form of a "return to nature," at least as far as the content of their menus are concerned. At the same time, an effort toward the most exotic origin of herbs and mixtures, which are the content of these miracle youth elixirs, is laughably the same as in all ancient eras.

[76] Heidel, *Gilgamesh Epic and Old Testament Parallels*, 11.

[77] Heffernanová, *Gilgameš* [Gilgamesh: A Tragic Model of Western Civilization], 8.

[78] The Epic of Gilgamesh, Tablet IX (Si i 7–8), 71.

When the gods created mankind,
They established death for mankind,
And withheld eternal life for themselves.
As for you, Gilgamesh, let your stomach be full,
Always be happy, night and day.
Make every day a delight,
Night and day play and dance.
Your clothes should be clean,
Your head should be washed,
You should bathe in water,
Look proudly on the little holding your hand,
Let your mate be always blissful in your loins,
This, then, is the work of mankind.[79]

How does Gilgamesh respond to this offer, to this modern consumer-pleasure maxim? Surprisingly, he refuses her ("Gilgamesh said to her, to the tavern keeper: What are you saying, tavern keeper?"[80]) and sees in her only delays, obstacles in his path in search of Utanapishti, the only person to survive the great flood and in whom Gilgamesh sees the promise of finding the cure for mortality. The hero refuses hedonism in the sense of maximizing terrestrial pleasure and throws himself into things that will exceed his life. In the blink of an eye, the epic turns on its head the entire utility maximization role that mainstream economics has tirelessly tried to sew on people as a part of their nature.[81]

After finding Utanapishti, Gilgamesh gets from the seafloor his coveted plant, one that should give him youth forever. But he immediately falls asleep and loses the plant: "Exhausted by his great deeds, Gilgamesh cannot resist the most gentle and most unspectacular thing: He gives in to sleep, the brother of death, the creeping exhaustion which accompanies life as tiredness and aging."[82]

Of the plant's fragrance a snake caught scent,
came up in silence, and bore the plant off.
As it turned away it sloughed its skin.[83]

---

[79] The Epic of Gilgamesh, Tablet X (77–91), 75.
[80] The Epic of Gilgamesh, Tablet X (92–94), 75.
[81] It is only fair to acknowledge that this part of the epic underwent significant development over the centuries. In the ancient Babylonian version of the epic, the tenth tablet was the last, and the story ended with Gilgamesh heading out after his conversation with the innkeeper for another journey toward immortality, and accepting his role as a mortal of royal status. In the original version, then, Siduri had a similar influence on Gilgamesh as Shamhat did on Enkidu—she humanized him and returned him to the human collective, where he could continue to be beneficial. Only after the later addition of the eleventh tablet with the story of the meeting between Gilgamesh and Utanapishti did Siduri become a seductress offering pleasure, which Gilgamesh refuses.
[82] Patočka, Kacířské eseje o filosofii dějin [Heretical Essays in the Philosophy of History], 23.
[83] The Epic of Gilgamesh, Tablet XI (305–308), 99.

And in the eleventh and final tablet, Gilgamesh again loses what he sought. Like Sisyphus, he misses his goal just before the climax and does not find his notional bliss point. But in the end, Gilgamesh nevertheless becomes immortal—to this day his name is not forgotten. And regardless of whether chance played any kind of major role in this historical development of events, we today remember Gilgamesh for *his story* of heroic friendship with Enkidu, not for his wall, which no longer reaches monumental heights.

CONCLUSION: THE BEDROCK OF ECONOMIC QUESTIONING

In this first chapter we have attempted the first economic contemplation of our civilization's oldest text. I allowed myself to do so in the hope that through this ancient epic we would discover something about ourselves, about the society that has developed over five thousand years into an incredibly complicated organism and entanglement. Orienting oneself in today's society is now naturally much more complicated. It is simpler to observe the main features of our civilization at a time when the picture was more readable—at a time when our civilization was just being born and was still "half-naked." In other words, we have tried to dig down to the bedrock of our written civilization; under this, nothing else exists.

Was the study of the epic useful? Has it shown something about itself in an economic sense? And is there something from it that is valid today? Have we found in Gilgamesh certain archetypes that are in us to this day?

I have tried to show that the mystical relationship to the world also has its "truths." Today we take these truths reservedly and tolerantly put them inside quotation marks, but we must be aware that the next generations will just as unhumbly put today's truths into quotation marks as well. In ancient times people answered questions with stories, tales. In the end, the Greek word "myth" means "story." "A myth is every story that anticipates some kind of 'why.'"[84] We will soon return in this book to the question of to what extent mythical storytelling differs from the mathematical or the scientific.

The very existence of questions similar to today's economic ones can be considered as the first observation. The first written considerations of the people of that time were not so different from those today. In other words: The epic is understandable for us, and we can identify with it. Sometimes too much—for example, as far as efforts to turn people into robots go. The thought that the human in us is only a drag on work (on the wall)[85] is still with us. Economics frequently uses this and tries to

---

[84] Kratochvíl, *Mýtus, filosofie, věda I a II* [Myth, Philosophy, and Science], 17.
[85] Which we recognize from the Pink Floyd song "Another Brick in the Wall." As can be seen, the theme of the wall survives to this day. Isn't it significant that the fall of communism has been reduced to the symbolism of the fall of the Berlin Wall?

neglect everything human. The thought that humanity comes at the expense of efficiency is just as old as humanity itself—as we have shown, subjects without emotion are the ideal of many tyrants.

We have also been witnesses to the very beginnings of man's culturing—a great drama based on a liberation and then a distancing from the natural state. Gilgamesh had a wall built that divided the city from wild nature and created a space for the first human culture. Nevertheless, "not even far-reaching works of civilization could satisfy human desire."[86] Let us take this as a memento in the direction of our restlessness, our inherited dissatisfaction and the volatility connected to it. Considering that they have lasted five thousand years and to this day we find ourselves in harmony with a certain feeling of futility, perhaps these characteristics are inherent in man. Maybe we feel it even stronger and more burning than Gilgamesh or the author of the epic himself.

The epic later crashes this idea through the friendship of Gilgamesh and Enkidu. Friendship—the biologically least essential love, which at first sight appears to be unnecessary from a societal standpoint as well. For effective economic production, for the welfare of the society, it's enough to become a member of a team without major emotional engagement. Of course, to change the system, to break down that which is standing and go on an expedition against the gods (to awaken, from naïveté to awakening) requires friendship. For small acts (hunting together, work in a factory), small love is enough: Camaraderie. For great acts, however, great love is necessary, real love: Friendship. Friendship that eludes the economic understanding of quid pro quo. Friendship gives. One friend gives (fully) for the other. That is friendship for life and death, never for profit and personal gain. Friendship shows us new, unsuspected adventures, gives us the opportunity to leave the wall and to become neither its builder nor its part—to not be another brick in the wall.

In another sense, the relationship between Gilgamesh and Enkidu can be compared to the civilized and animal essence of man (Enkidu later dies, but in a certain sense he lives on in Gilgamesh). We shortly paused on Keynes's notion of "animal spirits," which lead uneconomically and frequently irrationally to adventures: The builder Gilgamesh—he who separates humanity from its primitive animal state and brings about the civilized (one wants to say "sterile") culture, the one hidden behind the walls and a careful ruler—becomes friends with the wild Enkidu and heads out to subjugate heretofore untouched nature.

At the same time, with the phenomenon of the creation of the city, we have seen how specialization and the accumulation of wealth was born, how holy nature was transformed into a secular supplier of resources, and also how humans' individualistic ego was emancipated. This moment, of course, paradoxically relates to an increase in the individual's dependence

---

[86] Kratochvíl, *Mýtus, filosofie, věda I a II* [Myth, Philosophy, and Science], 12.

on other members of society, even if a civilized person feels more independent. The less a civilized, city person is dependent on nature, the more he or she is dependent on the rest of society. Like Enkidu, we have exchanged nature for society; harmony with (incalculable) nature for harmony with (incalculable) man.

We have compared this view with the view of the Hebrews, to whom we will devote ourselves in greater detail in the next chapter. The Hebrews came to cities much later, and an essential part of the Old Testament describes a people who lived in greater harmony with nature. Which, then, is more natural? Is man a naturally (full) man in his natural state, or does he become so in the framework of a (city) civilization? Is human nature good or evil? To this day these questions are key for economic policy: If we believe that man is evil in his nature, therefore that a person himself is dog eat dog (animal), then the hard hand of a ruler is called for. If we believe that people in and of themselves, in their nature, gravitate toward good, then it is possible to loosen up the reins and live in a society that is more laissez-faire.

Finally we have shown that the principle that a thousand years later materialized as the economic idea of the "invisible hand of the market" had its predecessors as early as Gilgamesh, in the form of harnessing wild evil, which in the end served to benefit humanity. We can find a whole range of predecessors of the invisible hand of the market in our ties. Finally, at the end of the chapter, a sort of pre-Greek hedonism got its word, in the form of the offer by the innkeeper Siduri. Gilgamesh rejects this offer, only for this thinking to be fully embraced by the economic ethos some 4,500 years later at the hands of utilitarians.

The end of the epic finishes at a dismal cyclical note, where nothing has changed, no progress was made, and—after a small adventure—everything returns to its original setting; the epic is cyclical and ends where it started, with the building of the wall. History heads nowhere, and everything cyclically repeats itself with minor variations, as we see in nature (the repeating of the seasons, cycles of the moon, etc.). In addition, nature, which has surrounded people, is the embodiment of unpredictable deities who have the same weaknesses and vagaries as people (according to the epic, the flood was called for by the gods because people were making too much noise, which bothered the deities). Because nature is not undeified, it is beyond consideration to explore it, let alone intervene in it (unless a person was a two-thirds god like Gilgamesh). It is not safe to investigate the preserves of capricious and moody gods.

For a concept of historical progress, for the undeification of heroes, rulers, and nature, mankind had to wait for the Hebrews. The entire history of Judaism is the history of waiting for the Messiah, who is to come in historical time, or rather at its end.

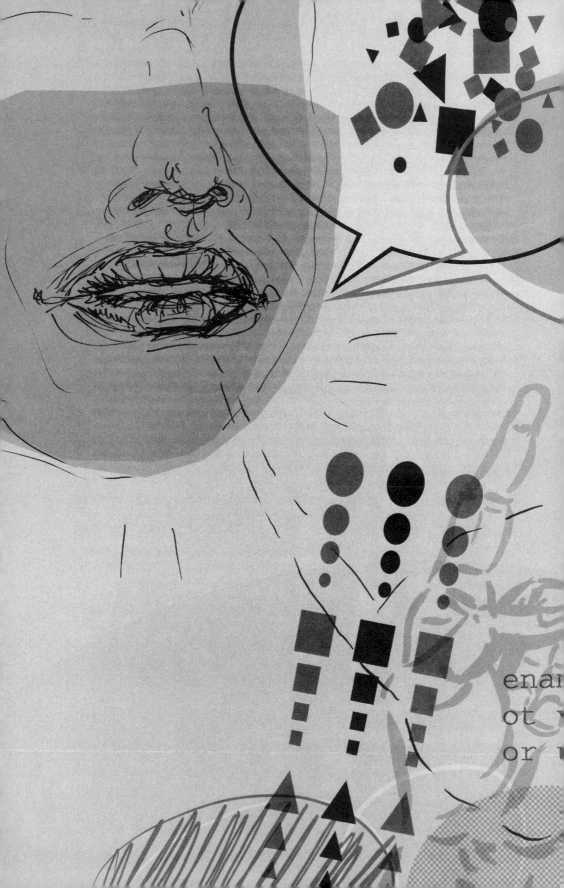

2

The Old Testament

Earthliness and Goodness

Let me avow it right away: I think that the Jewish religion has the same
leading ideas as Capitalism.
I see the same spirit in the one as in the other.
Werner Sombart

Although the Jews of the Old Testament[1] played a key role in forming
today's Euro-American culture and economic systems, not much space
has been devoted to them in either the leading textbooks of economic
ideas or other economic texts.[2] Max Weber believed that we owe the

---

[1] Following Bimson, (*The Compact Handbook of Old Testament Life*, 7–8, it may be useful
to mention the correct use of names for the people to whom the "promised" land was
given by God. If we follow biblical precedent, it is certainly correct to call them "Hebrews"
from Abraham onward (see Genesis 14:13). "Israel" was the new name given by God to
Jacob, Abraham's grandson (Genesis 32:28, 43:6, etc.), and so the descendants of Jacob are
"Israelites." In Exodus 3:18 and 5:1–3 "Hebrews" and "Israel" appear to be used as synony-
mous terms. "Israel" also has a secondary and more specific meaning in the Old Testament,
since it can signify the northern tribes as distinct from Judah, especially after the division of
the kingdom. Although the terms "Hebrew" and "Israelite" continued in use into the New
Testament period (e.g., Romans 9:4; 2 Corinthians 11:22; Philippians 3:5), by then the term
"Jew" was more commonly used. This originally referred to a member of the southern tribe
of Judah (which is its use in Jeremiah 32:12; 34:9), but after the Babylonian Exile it came
to replace "Israelite" as the most widely used term for one of God's covenant people. This
was because, by that time, virtually all Israelites were in fact members of the tribe of Judah,
as the northern tribes ("Israel" in the narrow sense) had lost their identity after the fall of
Samaria in 722 BC "Jew" and "Jewish" should not be used in the generally accepted sense
when speaking of the period before the Exile. For the purpose of our text, however, we will
treat "Israelites," "Hebrews," and "Jews" as synonyms.

[2] To the author's knowledge, the issue of economic thinking in Judaism has probably been
considered the most by Max Weber (*Ancient Judaism, Economy and Society, Sociology of
Religion*) and later, to a lesser extent, by Werner Sombart (*The Jews and Modern Capitalism*)
and Karl Marx (*On the Jewish Question*), but none of them (possibly with the exception of
certain parts of Max Weber's texts) set as their goal to analyze the economic aspects of the
fundamental texts of the ancient Jewish faith. Economic journals (the *Journal of Business
Ethics, Business Ethics Quarterly*, and others) have published a number of articles on Jewish
business ethics, but none of the articles known to the author examine the economic aspects
of the historical and philosophical foundations of Judaism as a whole. Regarding textbooks
on economic thought: As one example of many we may present the book by MacIntyre,

birth of capitalism to Protestant ethics;[3] Michael Novak, on the other hand, emphasizes the influence of Catholic morals and perception of humans;[4] nevertheless, according to Sombart,[5] it is the Jewish faith that is behind the birth of capitalism.

However, all of the leading lights in this discussion admit the important role Jewish culture has played. In no way may we doubt the important contribution of Jewish thought and its role in the development of modern capitalist economics.[6] For this reason, there is no way the Old Testament could be absent from our exploration of prescientific economic viewpoints—not only because Christianity is built on it, which later had an important influence on the formation of capitalism and economic teachings, but also for its distinctive contribution to a change in the perception of economic anthropology and ethos.

In many areas, Jewish economic habits anticipate the development of modern economics. As early as the "dark" ages, the Jews commonly used economic tools that were in many ways ahead of their time and that later became key elements of the modern economy:

> They practiced money lending, traded in many assets (. . .) and especially were engaged in the trading of shares on capital markets, worked in currency exchange and frequently figured as mediators in financial transactions (. . .), they functioned as bankers and participated in emissions of all possible forms. As regards modern capitalism (as opposed to the ancient and medieval periods) . . . there are activities in it which are, in certain forms, inherently (and completely necessarily) present—both from an economic and legal standpoint.[7]

Even those who attack Jewish traditions usually speak about these aspects. As Niall Ferguson notes, "Marx himself wrote a review article 'On the Jewish Question,' which identified the capitalist, regardless of his religion, as 'the real Jew.'"[8] Even according to Heinrich Class, one of the

---

A Short History of Ethics. In the chapter "The History of Moral Philosophy from Homer to the 20th Century," there is not a single mention of Hebrew teachings. A similar approach prevails in other textbooks as well. An exception among textbooks of the history of economic thought which consider the issues more deeply are somewhat older and little-used today, such as Haney, *History of Economic Thought*, and to a certain extent Roll, *A History of Economic Thought*, or Spiegel, *The Growth of Economic Thought*. The contributions of the Hebrews to the intellectual life of Western civilization are discussed by such scholars as Thorstein Veblen in his article "The Intellectual Pre-Eminence of Jews in Modern Europe" (see Veblen, *Essays in Our Changing Order*).

[3] Weber, *Protestant Ethic and the Spirit of Capitalism.*

[4] Novak, *The Catholic Ethic and the Spirit of Capitalism.*

[5] Sombart, *The Jews and Modern Capitalism.*

[6] This is one of the points that Max Weber is trying to make; he devoted a whole book to this topic; see Weber, *Ancient Judaism.*

[7] Weber, *Wirtschaft und Gesellschaft*, 369–370.

[8] See Ferguson, *War of the World*, 32. For more on Marx's views on the influence of the Hebrews, see also Mini, *Philosophy and Economics*, 201.

prewar instigators of racist propaganda,[9] the Jews were "a people born to trade in money and goods."[10] How did this development come about? For a nation originally based on nomadism, where did this Jewish business ethos come from? And can the Hebrews truly be considered as the architects of the values that set the direction of our civilization's economic thought?

PROGRESS: A SECULARIZED RELIGION

One of the things the writers of the Old Testament gave to mankind is the idea and notion of progress. The Old Testament stories have their *development*; they change the *history* of the Jewish nation and tie in to each other. The Jewish understanding of time is linear—it has a beginning and an end. The Jews believe in historical progress, and that progress is *in this world*. This progress is to be climaxed by the arrival of the Messiah, who frequently in chiliastic notions will even take on a specific political role.[11] Hebrew religiosity is therefore strongly connected with this world, not with any abstract world, and those who take pleasure in worldly possessions are not a priori doing anything wrong.

> The observance of God's Commandments in Judaism leads not to some ethereal other world, but to an abundance of material goods (Genesis 49:25–26, Leviticus 26:3–13, Deuteronomy 28:1–13) (. . .) There are no accusing fingers pointed at those engaged in normal economic activities for the earning of material goods. There are no echoes of asceticism nor for the cleansing and spiritual effect of poverty. It is fitting therefore, that the founders of Judaism, the Patriarchs Abraham, Isaac and Jacob, were all wealthy men.[12]

Before this linear understanding of time, a cyclical-Sisyphean perception held rule. In the Epic of Gilgamesh, history does not go in any direction. Everything is a cyclical repetition with minor variations, as we see in nature (the repetition of seasons, life and death, the cycle of the weeks, months, etc.). And stories take place in a strange time-loop: Gilgamesh's story ends where it began. There is a consistency in this with Greek myths and fables: At the end of the story, no progress occurs, no essential historic change; the story is set in indefinite time, something of a temporal limbo. It could play out anywhere and any number of times, because nothing has changed since its completion and everything returns to its old routine.[13]

---

[9] Class, *Wenn ich der Kaiser wär* [If I Were the Emperor].

[10] See Ferguson, *War of the World*, 35.

[11] For this, see Yoder, *Politics of Jesus*, especially the chapter "The Kingdom Coming," which deals with the political expectations that the Jews had in connection with Messiah, specifically, in this case, with Jesus.

[12] Tamari, *The Challenge of Wealth*, 47–48.

[13] After Gilgamesh loses Enkidu and fails to find immortality, he returns to his city of Uruk in Sisyphean futility, to his unfinished city wall, as if nothing had happened: "For whom

The idea of progress,[14] which would later become the moving force for the creation of science and the hope of our civilization in general, only came about due to a linear understanding of history. If history has a beginning as well as an end, and they are not the same point, then exploration suddenly makes sense in areas where the fruits are borne only in the next generation. Progress gains new meaning.

Our civilization, therefore, is especially indebted to the Hebrews for the idea of progress. In the course of history, however, the idea of progress itself underwent major changes, and today we perceive it very differently. As opposed to the original spiritual conceptions, today we perceive progress almost exclusively in an economic or scientific-technological sense.[15] What's more, economic progress has almost become an assumption of modern functional societies. We expect growth. We take it automatically. Today, if nothing "new" happens, if GDP does not grow (we say it *stagnates*) for several quarters, we consider it an anomaly. But this wasn't always the case. As Keynes wrote almost a hundred years ago, strong growth and significant material progress have been with us only in the past three centuries:

> From the earliest times of which we have record back, say, to two thousand years before Christ down to the beginning of the eighteenth century, there was no very great change in the standard of life of the average man living in the civilised centres of the earth. Ups and downs certainly. Visitations of plague, famine, and war. Golden intervals. But no progressive, violent change. Some periods perhaps 50 per cent better than others—at the utmost 100 per cent better—in the four thousand years which ended (say) in AD 1700 (. . .) At some epoch before the dawn of history—perhaps even in one of the comfortable intervals before the last ice age—there must have been an era of progress and invention comparable to that in which we live to-day. But through the greater part of recorded history there was nothing of the kind.[16]

---

are my shoulders exhausted? For whom does the blood spill from my heart? Not an iota of good have I achieved for myself." (Epic of Gilgamesh, Tablet X, (III.15–16), 80). Gilgamesh is now the kind of hero as he was described at the beginning of the epic. From Utanapishti he brings news of events before the flood, but otherwise it is as if the entire epic could play out again. From a historical perspective it was "only" an adventure, a sort of historical outlier, nothing more. The phenomenon of adventure was dealt with interestingly by the sociologist Georg Simmel in his book *The Philosophy of Money*. It corresponds to the archetypal cyclical notion of time, which was dominant in early cultures.

[14] For more see Eliade: *The Myth of Eternal Return*, especially the chapter "Regeneration of Time."

[15] And we consider civilizations that are less technically or materially equipped as less developed societies that have yet to reach our phase. We perceive them as being "behind us," that they have "something to catch up to."

[16] Keynes, *Economic Possibilities for Our Grandchildren*, 360–361. It is not without interest to quote one more paragraph here:

"Almost everything which really matters and which the world possessed at the commencement of the modern age was already known to man at the dawn of history. Language, fire, the same domestic animals which we have today, wheat, barley, the vine and the olive,

After emancipating ourselves from a cyclical conception of time and after several centuries, humanity was not accustomed to a visible rise in the standard of living. We might supplement Keynes's quote by saying that the furnishings of a typical household barely changed over those four thousand years. In this respect, a person who fell asleep in the time long before Christ and woke up in the seventeenth century would not necessarily have noted any major changes in the day-to-day material equipment. Now, however, we live in a time where waking up a generation later would mean absolute disorientation in operating common household equipment. Only since the period of scientific-technological revolution (and at a time when economics was born as an independent field) is material progress automatically assumed.

Despite the fact that Keynes expressed hope for the economic satisfaction of our needs most explicitly, a strong faith in the beneficial effect of material progress is professed by a majority of the key figures of economic thought of our time. This is *why* we must constantly grow, because we (deep down and often implicitly) believe that we are headed toward an (economic) paradise on Earth. Because care for the soul has today been replaced by care for external things, as the Czech philosopher Jan Patočka writes, economists have become key figures of great importance in our time (*Kacířské eseje o filosofii dějin* [*Heretical Essays in the Philosophy of History*]). They are expected to perform interpretations of reality, give prophetic services (macroeconomic forecasts), reshape reality (mitigate the impacts of the crisis, speed up growth), and, in the long run, provide leadership on the way to the Promised Land—paradise on Earth. Paul Samuelson, Milton Friedman, Gary Becker, Frank Knight, and many others have become passionate evangelizers of economic progress, used not only within their own country but also toward other cultures, globally. We will return to this topic more thoroughly in the latter part of the book.

REALISM AND ANTIASCETICISM

Aside from ideas of progress, the Hebrews brought another very fundamental contribution to our culture: The desacralization of heroes, nature, and rulers. It could be said with some exaggeration that Jewish thought is the most grounded, most realistic school of thought of all those that have

---

the plough, the wheel, the oar, the sail, leather, linen and cloth, bricks and pots, gold and silver, copper, tin, and lead and iron was added to the list before 1000 BC—banking, statecraft, mathematics, astronomy, and religion. There is no record of when we first possessed these things" (360–361).

influenced our culture.[17] An abstract world of ideas was unknown to the Jews. To this day it is still forbidden to even *depict* God, people, and animals in symbols, paintings, statues, and drawings. They were not permitted to create representative symbols and symbolic representations (in a way, models) of reality:

> You saw no form of any kind the day the Lord spoke to you at Horeb out of the fire. Therefore watch yourselves very carefully, so that you do not become corrupt and make for yourselves an idol, an image of any shape, whether formed like a man or woman, or like any animal on earth or any bird that flies in the air, or like any creature that moves along the ground or any fish in the waters below. And when you look up to the sky and see the sun, the moon, and the stars—all the heavenly array—do not be enticed into bowing down to them and worshiping things the Lord your God has apportioned to all the nations under heaven.[18]

As opposed to Christianity, the concept of an extraterrestrial paradise or heaven was not developed much in Hebrew thought.[19] The paradise of the Israelites—Eden—was originally placed on Earth at a given place in Mesopotamia[20] and at a given time, one which has measured the exact genealogy from Adam and Eve. Jews to this day calculate the years from the creation of the world. The concept of heaven is not elaborated at all, and in any case it is not used in (theological) argumentation. Even Voltaire writes: "It certain fact is, that in his public laws he [Moses] never so much as once made mention of a life to come, limiting all punishments and all rewards to the present life."[21]

Directed and intentional asceticism was foreign to ancient Hebrew thought, as well disdain for anything material or physical, as would later happen under the influence of traditions built on the work of Socrates and Plato.[22] This Greek ascetic tradition makes its way into Christianity

---

[17] "In the Western world, a complete "division" of the body and soul occurred only with Greek thought. [The important anthropologist] Jaynes dates this event in the 6th century BC. The concept of the soul as something essential differs from the concept of the body especially as prepared by Plato and Aristotle, and Christianity later developed this further. Early Judaism did not differentiate so sharply between the body and the soul, but then later accepted the concept of the immortal soul." Heffernanová *Tajemství dvou partnerů* [The Secret of Two Partners], 61.

[18] Deuteronomy (The fifth book of Moses) 4:15–19. Visual depiction is forbidden; on the other hand, a strong emphasis is placed on interpretation, or oral presentation. Only a few verses earlier, the Lord urges: "Only be careful and watch yourselves closely so that you do not forget the things your eyes have seen or let them slip from your heart as long as you live. Teach them to your children and to their children after them." (Deuteronomy 4:9). In contrast to other nations, oral tradition plays a major role in Hebrew culture. In other nations, the maintenance of cultural heritage (history) through representations—whether through pictures or sculptures—dominated. Especially the Greek hero had to fulfill all the requirements for attractive depiction.

[19] For more see Weber, *Ancient Judaism*, 141.

[20] See Genesis 2:10–14.

[21] Voltaire, *The Philosophical Dictionary for the Pocket* [*Dictionnaire Philosophique*], 308.

[22] This work does not set as its goal to follow the later development of Judaism (especially the diaspora), where ascetic elements frequently appear. We will only concentrate on Old Testament economic anthropology.

later through the teachings of Paul of Tarsus and the neo-Platonist Augustine (354–430), who of course agreed with it only to a certain extent. (We will return to the Greek and medieval Christian scholars in relation to the topic of asceticism.)

Jewish groundedness (earthiness) was noted by Max Weber, who wrote that "Judaism is at least oriented to the world in the sense that it does not reject the world as such but it only rejects the prevailing social rank order in the world. . . . Judaism differs from Puritanism only in the relative (as always) absence of systematic asceticism. . . . The observance of the Jewish law has little to do with asceticism."[23] The Hebrews consider the world to be *real*—not just a shadow reflection of a *better* world somewhere in the cloud of ideas, something the usual interpretation of history ascribes to Plato. The soul does not struggle against the body and is not its prisoner, as Augustine would write later. On the contrary, the body and the material world—and therefore the economic world—is the creation of a good God. The land, the world, the body, and material reality are for Jews the paramount setting for divine history, the pinnacle of creation.

This idea is the *conditio sine qua non* of the development of economics, something of an utterly earthly making, and is thus warranted and justified, despite by itself not having a "spiritual dimension," but serving the fulfillment of completely earthly needs and desires.[24] Old Testament teachings rarely disdain wealth or sing the praises of poverty. It is in the New Testament that we find the austerity of radical contempt for riches— see for example the parable of Lazarus. But for Hebrews, when a person does well in the (economic) world, it is frequently understood as an expression of God's favor. The economizing sociologist Sombart handles it accurately:

> Look through Jewish literature, more especially through the Holy Writ and the Talmud, and you will find, it is true, a few passages wherein poverty is lauded as something higher and nobler than riches. But on the other hand you will come across hundreds of passages in which riches are called the blessing of the Lord, and only their misuse or their dangers warned against . . . in all of this nothing is said against riches; and never is it stated that they are abomination to the Lord.[25]

Together with the concept of earthiness, the Hebrews carried out other desacralizations. In the Old Testament teachings, heroes, rulers, and nature

---

[23] Weber, *Economy and Society*, 611.

[24] "So economic wants or desires are treated by Judaism in exactly the same way as all other basic human tendencies. They are not something which can or have to be destroyed, but rather tendencies that people can and must sanctify, and themselves be sanctified thereby. . . . Therefore, earning and keeping economic assets is considered by Judaism as legitimate, permissible and beneficial, yet restricted and sanctified by the observance of God's revealed Commandments." Tamari, *The Challenge of Wealth*, 47.

[25] Sombart, *The Jews and Modern Capitalism*, 216.

are all stripped of their deity. This all plays a major role for changes in economic considerations.

THE HERO AND HIS UNDEIFICATION: THE DREAM NEVER SLEEPS

The concept of the hero is more important than it might appear. It may be the remote origin of Keynes's *animal spirits*, or the desire to follow a kind of internal archetype that a given individual accepts as his own and that society values. Each of us probably has a sort of "hero within"—a kind of internal role-model, template, an example that we (knowingly or not) follow. It is very important what kind of archetype it is, because its role is dominantly irrational and changes depending on time and the given civilization. This *internal animator* of ours, our internal mover, this dream, never sleeps and it influences our behavior—including economic behavior—more than we want to realize.

First we perceive that the Old Testament has at its disposal a much more realistic archetype of hero than the surrounding civilizations. The Jewish "heroes," as opposed to those in the Epic of Gilgamesh for example, or in Greek fables and legends, are more real and realistically, three-dimensionally imaginable people. We already know the Sumerian idea of a hero, so let's pause for a moment for the second culture that had a strong influence on the Jews—the Egyptians. The Jews spent several centuries there at the beginning of their history, leaving (probably) sometime during the rule of the famous Ramses II.[26] From the writings preserved (if anyone founded the tradition of bureaucrats and registrars, it was the Egyptians), we can roughly create a picture of what such a hero should look like in the imaginings of the time. The mythology of the hero-king was strongly developed in that period, which Claire Lalouette summarizes into these basic characteristics: Beauty (a perfect face, on which it is "pleasant to look upon," but also "beauty," expressed in the Egyptian word *nefer*, not only means aesthetics, but contains moral qualities as well),[27] manliness and strength,[28] knowledge and intelligence,[29] wisdom and

---

[26] See Lalouette, *Ramessova říše* [L'empire des Ramsès], 194.

[27] Incidentally, it is interesting to note that to this day we connect morality with aesthetics. Evil characters are unpleasing to the eye, while the positive ones tend to be beautiful. Readers will certainly think of many examples they will not have to go far for. Demons and monsters from modern myths—books and films—are similar to death, corpses, and if they are beautiful, it is only deceptive (temporary) beauty and they use that beauty only as a (sexual) lure. There are truly few negative characters in our most modern mythology that are beautiful.

[28] Ramses II is "a hero with no equal, with strong shoulders and a brave heart."

[29] Ramses II "has a heart as clever as Thvot." It is not uninteresting to note that for Egyptians, intelligence was located in the heart; the heart was the location of thought. Today the heart is considered the location of emotion; what's more, it is frequently in conflict with reason,

understanding, vigilance and performance, fame and renown (fame which overcomes enemies because "a thousand men would not be able to stand firmly in his presence");[30] the hero is a good shepherd (who takes care of his subordinates), is a copper-clad rampart, the shield of the land, and the defender of heroes. It is also necessary to point out that the Egyptian ruler, just as the Sumerian, was partly a god, or the son of a god.[31]

We find no similar demigods in the Torah, no musclemen heroes who are gifted with superhuman physical abilities and predestined to great things. The only exception was the "muscleman" Samson (but even he had his superhuman strength subject to divine discretion). The Torah's *heroes* (if that term can be used at all) frequently make mistakes and their mistakes are carefully recorded in the Bible—maybe precisely so that none of them could be deified.[32] We do not have to go far for examples. Noah gets so drunk he becomes a disgrace; Lot lets his own daughters seduce him in a similar state of drunkenness. Abraham lies and (repeatedly) tries to sell his wife as a concubine. Jacob defrauds his father Isaac and steals his brother Esau's blessing of the firstborn. Moses murders an Egyptian. King David seduces the wife of his military commander and then has him killed. In his old age, King Solomon turns to pagan idols, and so on.[33]

Every society and era has its ideals, according to which we unconsciously behave; most are combined from things that have already been. Anthropology knows several archetypes of heroes. The Polish-born American anthropologist Paul Radin examined the myths of North American Indians and, for example, in his most influential book, *The Trickster*, he describes their four basic archetypes of heroes. The oldest was the so-called Trickster—a fraudster; then the culture bearer—Rabbit; the musclebound hero called Redhorn; and finally the most developed form of hero: the Twins. For example, Gilgamesh had the signs of all Radin's archetypes at his disposal; the twin who complements him

---

which on the contrary we note is located in the head. See Pascal, *Pensées*: "The heart has its reasons, which reason does not know" (part 277, Section IV, "Of the Means of Belief"). We could easily replace the word "reason" with the word "head."

[30] This moral weapon, as Lalouette calls it, has the same effect every time: The fall or at least the perfect paralysis of an enemy without a single blow. At this point it is appropriate to recall that during the fall of Jericho, the first city the Hebrews occupied, its walls (walls, not people) fall similarly, without a single blow. See Joshua 6.

[31] See Lalouette, *Ramessova říše* [L'empire des Ramsès], 277–283 from the chapter "Portrait of a Hero."

[32] In the vast majority of the Old Testament stories there are also efforts to precisely give the date (which are mostly derived from the year of rule of a given king or according to genealogy) and location of the event.

[33] This is especially true for important rulers of the Hebrew nation. However, even the prophets (for whom deification is not such a threat) frequently have their mistakes recorded. The prophet Jonas refuses to hear God and curses haughtily after God shows compassion on the city of Nineveh. Jeremiah yearns to die, and so forth. A shining exception is the prophet Daniel—he is one of the few characters for whom not a single character "flaw" is recorded.

is Enkidu.[34] To a certain extent it can be said that the Hebrews—and later Christianity—added another archetype, the archetype of the heroic Sufferer.[35] Job was one of these, or in large part Isaiah (in Christianity the ideal is understandably personified by Jesus Christ, who projects his strength through weakness, his victory through loss, and his magnificence through humiliation on the cross. His role, it would seem, was to show the way and to suffer representatively). As we have seen from the list above, the Hebrew heroes correspond most to the Tricksters, the Culture Bearers, and the Twins. The divine muscleman, that dominant symbol we think of when we say hero, is absent here.

This is very important for democratic capitalism, because the Jewish heroic archetype lays the groundwork much better for the development of the later phenomenon of the hero, which better suits life as we know it today. "The heroes laid down their arms and set about trading to become wealthy."[36] And, as is well known, muscles are not necessary for trade, nor is beauty or being a half-hero. For the heroes who moved our civilization to where it is today, the heroic archetypes of the cunning trickster, culture bearer, and sufferer are rather more appropriate.

NATURE IS NOT SACRED

Aside from the undeification of heroes, the Old Testament strongly emphasizes the undeification of nature.[37] Nature is God's creation, which speaks of divinity but is not the domain of moody gods such as those we saw in the Epic of Gilgamesh.[38] Undeification, however, does not mean a call to pillage or desecration; man was put here to take care of nature (see the story of the Garden of Eden or the symbolism of the naming of the animals). This protection and care of nature is also related to the idea of progress that we discussed at the beginning of the chapter. In the case of a linear perception of time, it is obviously an issue of legacy for generations to come. "Judaism views human economic development as positive, and nature is subservient to this. However (. . .), the growth will be of

---

[34] See Heffernanová, *Gilgameš* [Gilgamesh], 6.

[35] It appears that this is the archetype that F. Nietzsche attacks the most.

[36] Lalouette, Ramessova říše [*L'empire des Ramsès*], 118.

[37] In *Genesis*, the Sun and Moon—the traditional deities of early cultures—are not even named; they are only marked as the larger and smaller lights.

[38] As we may recall, in that epic, nature, which surrounded people, was the embodiment of capricious deities who had the same weaknesses and whims as people. For example, according to the epic, the deities brought on the great flood because the people were making too much noise, which bothered the gods. Nature was not undeified, and it was out of the question to examine it scientifically, let alone to interfere with it (unless that man was two-thirds god, as was Gilgamesh), because it is not safe to systematically, thoroughly (and scientifically) examine the forest of capricious and moody gods. And also there is no point—since there are no regularities which are reliable.

necessity limited. The needs of future generations will have to be considered; after all humankind are the guardians of God's world. Waste of natural resources, whether privately owned or nationally owned is forbidden."[39]

RULERS ARE MERE MEN

In a similar historical context, the Old Testament teachings carried out a similar desacralization of rulers, the so-called bearers of economic policy. God called on the Jews, through Moses, to rise up against the pharaoh—something unheard at the time. The ruler was equal to a god or, at worst, a god's son—ultimately in a similar sense as Gilgamesh, ruler of the Uruk, was two-thirds god. But in an Old Testament context, the pharaoh was a mere man (whom one *could* disagree with, and who could be resisted!).

Even the later Israelite kings were constantly reminded by the prophets that they were not omnipotent; they were not equal to God, but His subordinates. Ultimately the entire idea of a political ruler stood against the Lord's will, which is explicitly presented in the Torah. The Lord unequivocally preferred the judge as the highest form of rule—an institution that is capable of arbitrating, but will not explicitly rule in the modern sense of the term of executive power.[40] The rule of kings was almost literally stamped out of the land by the Jews, and it was to be regarded in this sense by later readers of Torah. This was not, therefore, about a divine institution; being king was a completely earthly affair. Since then humility has been in effect for rulers as one of the most essential virtues. King David, the most important of the Israelite kings, writes in Psalm 147, which is attributed to him, "The Lord sustains the humble but casts the wicked to the ground."[41] Politics lost its character of divine infallibility, and political issues were subject to questioning. Economic policy could become a subject of examination.

The entire institution of kingly reign is therefore in the Old Testament something that is not recommended, and is even warned against. Before the Israelites elected (drew lots for) their kings, "rule" in Israel was carried out by judges who had far less executive authority than kings had. In the following citation, the Hebrew Lord warns people through the prophet Samuel not to institute a king above them:

> He said: "This is what the king who will reign over you will do: He will take your sons and make them serve with his chariots and horses, and they will run in front of his chariots. Some he will assign to be commanders of

---

[39] Tamari, *The Challenge of Wealth*, 51.

[40] This has interesting implications as regards Tocqueville's division of legislative, judicial, and executive power. The Lord was supposed to be the lawmaker and the judges His assigned prophets.

[41] Psalms 147:6.

thousands and commanders of fifties, and others to plow his ground and reap his harvest, and still others to make weapons of war and equipment for his chariots. He will take your daughters to be perfumers and cooks and bakers. He will take the best of your fields and vineyards and olive groves and give them to his attendants. He will take a tenth of your grain and of your vintage and give it to his officials and attendants. Your menservants and maidservants and the best of your cattle and donkeys he will take for his own use. He will take a tenth of your flocks, and you yourselves will become his slaves. When that day comes, you will cry out for relief from the king you have chosen, and the Lord will not answer you in that day." But the people refused to listen to Samuel. "No!" they said. "We want a king over us."[42]

So, even without blessing, the institution of the ruler as a bearer of executive power was born in Israel. From the very beginning, when God distances Himself from the entire idea, there is an anticipation that there is nothing holy, let alone divine, in politics. Rulers make mistakes, and it is possible to subject them to tough criticism—which frequently occurs indiscriminately through the prophets in the Old Testament.

THE PRAISE OF ORDER AND WISDOM: MAN AS A PERFECTER OF CREATION

The created world has an *order* of sorts, an order recognizable by us as people, which for the methodology of science and economics is very important because *dis*order and chaos are difficult to examine scientifically.[43] Faith in some kind of rational and logical order in a system (society, the economy) is a silent assumption of any (economic) examination.

At the beginning of creation, it would appear, this was not the case—everything was, in the true meaning of the word, only *one* formless and colorless mass; nothing had a name or marking, and everything melted into one.[44] God first *creates* with the word and then on individual days He *divides* light *from* darkness, water *from* dry land, day *from* night, and so forth—and He gives *order* to things.[45] The world is created *orderly*—it is *wisely, reasonably* put together. The way of the world is put together at least partially[46] decipherably by any other wise and reasonable being who

---

[42] 1 Samuel 8:11–19.

[43] Modern science is, however, able to study certain chaos. For example, chaos theory studies the behavior of dynamical systems that are highly sensitive to initial conditions.

[44] This motif of Chaos appears in other ancient tales and mythologies as well.

[45] It is important to note that *naming* also relates to any kind of creation, separation. If a thing is not named, i.e., not separated from others, it is not itself—it is not delineated and therefore not defined.

[46] As yet, not even the queen of exact sciences, theoretical physics, has been able to fathom the foundations of "objective reality" itself. So to this day physicists do not know how to properly answer basic questions such as what is matter—and neither do we. The deep issues are still shrouded in mystery.

honors rational rules. The principles governing the world can be examined. The Book of Proverbs emphasizes specifically several times that it was *wisdom* that was present at the creation of the world. Wisdom personified calls out:

> The Lord brought me forth as the first of his works, before his deeds of old. I was appointed from eternity, from the beginning, before the world began. When there were no oceans, I was given birth, when there were no springs abounding with water, before the mountains were settled in place, before the hills, I was given birth, before he made the earth or its fields or any of the dust of the world. I was there when he set heavens in place, when he marked out the horizon on the face of the deep (. . .) Then I was the craftsman at his side.[47]

The citation above continues:

> I was filled with delight day after day, rejoicing always in his presence (. . .) and delighting in mankind. Now then, my sons, listen to me; blessed are those who keep my ways (. . .) Blessed is the man who listens to me, watching daily at my doors, waiting at my doorway. For whoever finds me finds life and receives favor from the Lord. But whoever fails to find me harms himself; all who hate me love death.[48]

God, and Wisdom with Him, therefore urge us toward learning the order of the world. The world is not entirely incomprehensible to us. And especially, examination is not *forbidden*. The fact that *order* can be grasped by human reason is another unspoken assumption that serves as a cornerstone of any scientific examination. There are more *urgings* to gain wisdom in the Old Testament. "Wisdom calls aloud in the street (. . .): 'How long will you simple ones love your simple ways?'"[49] Or several chapters later: "Wisdom is supreme; therefore get wisdom. Though it cost all you have, get understanding."[50]

Examining the world is therefore an absolutely legitimate activity, and one that is even requested by God—it is a kind of participation in the Creator's work.[51] Man is called on to understand himself and his surroundings and to use his knowledge for good. Nature exists for man, and the possibility opens up to explore and change it, something that man is called on, if not directly created, to do.

Hebrew culture laid the foundations for the scientific examination of the world. It is worth noticing that the rational examination of nature has its roots, surprisingly, in religion. While this world will always hold many

---

[47] Proverbs 8:22–30.
[48] Proverbs 8:30–36.
[49] Proverbs 1:20–22.
[50] Proverbs 4:7.
[51] The fact that this participation is God's wish is shown when God has Adam name all of creation. In older cultures, and to a certain extent today as well, the giving of names is a privileged activity. In the Jewish understanding, it reflects a certain dominion over the named.

mysteries that will never be solved by reason alone, we are set in a world that we can try to understand with a combination of intuition, reason, experience, and so forth.

MAN AS A FINISHER OF CREATION

The creation of the world, as it is explained in Jewish teachings, is described in the Book of Genesis. Here God (i) creates, (ii) separates, and (iii) names [my emphasis]:

> In the beginning God **created** the heavens and the earth (. . .) he **separated** the light from the darkness. God **called** the light "day," and the darkness he called "night." (. . .) God **made** the expanse and **separated** the water under the expanse from the water above it. And it was so. He **called** the expanse "sky."(. . .) God **called** the dry ground "land," and the gathered waters he called "seas."[52]

Without naming, reality does not exist; it is created together with language. Wittgenstein tightly names this in his *tractatus*—the limits of our language are the limits of our world.[53] Also, we cannot think of something that does not have a representative symbol in our mind (such as a name, sign, etc.). What we do not know how to consider we cannot rightfully name[54] and vice versa.

The Naming *itself* (the capital N is appropriate) traditionally belongs to the crowning act of the Creator and represents a kind of grand finale of creation, the last move of the brush to complete the picture—a signature of the master. A noteworthy moment occurs in Genesis: The last act, final stroke of the brush of creation, naming of the animals—this act is given to a human, it is not done by God, as one would expect. Man was given the task of completing the act of creation that the Lord began:

> [T]he Lord God had formed out of the ground all the beasts of the field and all the birds of the air. He brought them to the man to see what he would **name** them; and whatever the man **called** each living creature, that was its **name**. So the man gave **names** to all the livestock, the birds of the air and all the beasts of the field.[55]

A single paragraph speaks of the naming and designating four times. God hands over His creation to man in a somewhat incomplete state (one could almost say as a semifinished product) and leaves man to put on the finishing touches and thus to complete the creation. Naming is a symbolic expression. In Jewish culture (and also in our culture to this day), the right

---

[52] Genesis 1:1–10.
[53] Wittgenstein, *Tractatus Logico-Philosophicus*, 56.
[54] Ibid., 57.
[55] Genesis 2:19–20.

to *name* meant sovereign rights and belonged, for example, to explorers (new places), inventors (new principles), or parents (children)—that is, to those who were there at the genesis, at the origin. This right was *handed over* by God to mankind. The motif of putting on the *finishing touches* can also be seen in the notion of the garden, a place a person is supposed to cultivate, or to bring to perfection. Man was placed into a garden, not a jungle, forest or meadow. Gardens need constant care and cultivation; forests and meadows are fine even when left alone.[56]

How does this relate to economics? Reality itself, our "objective" world, is *cocreated*, man himself participates in the *creation*; creation, which is somewhat constantly being *re*-created.

Reality is not a given; it is not passive. Perceiving reality and "facts" requires man's active participation. It is man who must take the last step, an act (and we perceive the noteworthy proximity of *fact* and *act*) so that reality may continue to be created. A *real*-ization act on our part represents the creation of a construct, the imputation of sense and order (which is beautifully expressed by the biblical act of *naming*, or categorization, sorting, ordering). Our scientific models put the finishing touches on reality, because (1) they interpret, (2) they give phenomena a name, (3) they enable us to classify the world and phenomena according to logical forms, and (4) through these models we de facto perceive reality. Through this order (imputed by us), reality begins to truly appear; it loses sense without it. And as the leading Czech philosopher Neubauer puts it: "And that which makes no sense does not appear at all."[57]

Through his theories, man not only discovers the world but also *forms* it. Not only in the sense of remolding nature (increasing efficiency or fertility through plowing fields, breeding plants, building dikes), but also in a deeper ontological meaning. When man finds a new linguistic framework or analytical model, or stops using the old one, he molds or remolds reality. Models are only in our heads; they are not "in objective reality." In this sense, Newton *invented* (not merely discovered!) gravity.[58] He invented

---

[56] Genesis 2:15. A corrective for the interpretation of naming may be the fact that Adam also named woman—Eve. But this occurred after the Fall; before it Adam did not name Eve.

[57] Neubauer, *Respondeo dicendum*, 23.

[58] Neubauer, *O čem je věda* [What Science Is About], 173–174. Also see Pirsig, *Zen and the Art of Motorcycle Maintenance: An Inquiry into Values*, 32–37, from which I quote here:
"Do you believe in ghosts?"
"No," I say.
"Why not?"
"Because they are un-sci-en-ti-fic, they . . . do not exist except in people's minds."
(. . .)
"For example, it seems completely natural to presume that gravitation and the law of gravitation existed before Isaac Newton. It would sound nutty to think that until the seventeenth century there was no gravity . . . if you think about it long enough you will find yourself going round and round and round and round until you finally reach only one possible, rational, intelligent conclusion. The law of gravity and gravity itself did not exist before Isaac Newton. . . . law of gravity exists nowhere except in people's heads! It's a ghost! . . .

(fictitiously and completely abstractly!) a framework that was generally accepted and soon "made into" reality. Marx invented similarly; he created the notion of class exploitation. Through his idea, the perception of history and reality was changed for a large part of the world for nearly an entire century.

Now we are getting to a purely economic topic. Let's return to putting the finishing touches on reality in the simpler (nonmodel) sense of the term. John Locke deals with this in an interesting fashion, when he deals with the "value added" of human labor and care:

> For the provisions serving to the support of human life, produced by one acre of enclosed and cultivated land, are (to speak much within compass) ten times more than those which are yielded by an acre of land an equal richness lying waste in common. . . . I have here rated the improved land very low, in making its product but as ten to one, when it is much nearer an hundred to one.[59]

Michael Novak even speaks of raw creation,[60] or the creation of a kind of "natural state," which remains left alone and unrefined by man in "the sweat of his face." Man is established as the manager over the created world; he becomes responsible for leading creation to its full flourishing. As if through the raw (not completely ready) creation of the world, God connects man with the task of guarding and protecting the Garden of Eden, and thus man actually cocreates the cultural landscape. The Czech philosopher Zdeněk Neubauer also describes this: "Such is reality, and it is so deep that it willingly crystallizes into worlds. Therefore I profess that reality is a creation and not a place of occurrence for objectively given phenomena."[61]

Even in this viewpoint it is possible to see how Jewish thought is mystical—it admits the role of the incomprehensible. Therefore, through its groundedness, Jewish thought indulges mystery and defends itself against a mechanistic-causal explanation of the world: "The Jewish way of thinking, according to Veblen, emphasizes the spiritual, the miraculous, the intangible. On the other hand, pagans instead see the mechanical and scientific."[62] Many years later, Keynes enters into the history of economic thought from the same intellectual cadence; his greatest contribution to economics was precisely the resurrection of the *imperceptible*—for example in the form of *animal spirits* or *uncertainty*. The economist Piero Mini

---

Logic exists in the mind. Numbers exist only in the mind. I don't get upset when scientists say that ghosts exist in the mind. It's that only that gets me. Science is only in your mind too, it's just that that doesn't make it bad. Or ghosts either."

[59] Locke, *Two Treatises of Government*, book 2, chapter 5, §37, 304–305.
[60] Novak, *The Catholic Ethic and the Spirit of Capitalism*, 150–151.
[61] Neubauer, *Respondeo dicendum*, 28.
[62] Mini, *Philosophy and Economics*, 228; or see Veblen, *The Intellectual Preeminence of Jews in Modern Europe*.

even ascribes Keynes's doubting and rebellious approach to his almost Talmudic education.[63]

GOOD AND EVIL IN US: A MORAL EXPLANATION
OF WELL-BEING

We have seen that in the Epic of Gilgamesh, good and evil are not yet addressed systematically on a moral level. In the epic, there is a mention of evil, but it is presented as something that occurs exogenously, outside (the city), *beyond us*. The personification of evil, Humbaba, dwells *beyond* the city in the cedar forest; Enkidu was an evil who raged *beyond* the city—on the contrary, at the moment of his *urban*ification he becomes beneficial.

A reader of the epic cannot resist the feeling that evil correlates with nature and good with the city, civilization, progress. Incidentally, the Egyptians indulged in a similar deification of the city; for them cities represented divine entities. In Egyptian texts and poems, the city was identified with the gods who inhabited them.[64] But in the epic, good and evil are not envisaged morally—they are not the result of an *(a)moral* act. Evil was not associated with free moral action or individual will. This was not about moral-human evil, but rather a kind of *natural* evil. It is as if good and evil were not touched by morality at all. Evil simply occurred. Period.

Hebrew thought, on the other hand, deals intensively with *moral* good and evil. A moral dimension touches the core of its stories.[65] What's more, history seems to be based on morals; morals seem to be the key determining factors of history. For the Hebrews, history proceeds according to how morally its actors behave. Human sin has an influence on history, and that is why the authors of the Old Testament prepared a complicated moral code that was to guarantee a *better world*. Evil does not lie beyond the city, somewhere in nature, or in the forest, *beyond us*. In many stories, the exact opposite can be read—the natural represents good, and the artificial city civilization means evil.

Evil cannot, of course, be gotten rid of with a trek into the forest, as Gilgamesh and Enkidu resolve when they head out "to kill Humbaba and cut down the cedars." The Sumerians believed in dualism—good and evil deities exist, and the earth of people becomes their passive battlefield. The Jews believed the exact opposite. The world is created by a good God, and evil appears in it as a result of immoral human acts. Evil, therefore,

---

[63] Mini, *Philosophy and Economics*, 229.

[64] See Lalouette, *Ramessova říše* [L'empire des Ramsès], 336.

[65] As Sombart writes: "But like all other alien elements [i.e., stories they took from other nations] in Judaism, they, too, were given an ethical meaning, in accordance with the genius of the religion," *The Jews and Modern Capitalism*, 215.

is induced by man.[66] History unwinds according to the morality of human acts. As an example, let us take the expulsion from paradise: It occurred after Adam and Eve's disobedience.[67] The difference is illustrated in the story of the flood. The Old Testament presents human decadence and the multiplication of amoral evil as the reason for the flood:

> The Lord saw how great man's wickedness on the earth had become, and that every inclination of the thoughts of his heart was only evil all the time.[68]

As opposed to this, in the epic the flood happens because people behaved loudly and disturbed the gods. The epic therefore does not give any moral dimension to the flood, while Genesis on the other hand explains the flood through (a)morality. We find countless examples in the Old Testament where an (a)moral act preceded history. The obliteration of Sodom and Gomorrah came as a result of those cities' sins,[69] forty years in the desert before entering the Promised Land was the punishment for the uprising on Mount Sinai,[70] and so on. The entire history of the Jewish nation is interpreted and perceived in terms of morality. Morality has become, so to speak, a mover and shaker of Hebrew history.

MORAL BUSINESS CYCLE AND ECONOMIC PROPHECIES

In the story of the Jewish nation we also encounter the first notion of the economic cycle—the first ever recorded economic cycle in our written history. Here we also find the first attempt to *explain* the reasons for the cycle. There are many theories about economic cycles, and no regular agreement prevails among economists about what causes cycles even today. Some blame psychological factors, some discrepancy between savings and investment, and others are convinced of the monetary essence of the cycle, yet others see its causes in sunspots. The Hebrews came up with the idea that morals were behind good and bad years, behind the economic cycle. But we would be getting ahead of ourselves.

---

[66] It could even be said that it is induced by recognition. See Bonhoeffer's *Ethics*, where he argues that "the knowledge of good and evil is therefore a separation from God. Only against God can man know good and evil.... 'The man is become as one of us, to know good and evil' says God (Gen. 3:22) ... To know good and evil is to know oneself as the origin of good and evil, as the origin of an eternal choice and election ... this secret has been stolen from God ... Man's life is now disunion with God, with men, with things, and with himself," 21–24.

[67] Genesis 3. In both stories, the Epic of Gilgamesh and Genesis, it is a *snake* that deprives humanity of its immortality. It steals and eats Gilgamesh's flower—the elixir of youth; in the story of Eden, it talks Eve into eating the fruit of the Tree of Knowledge of Good and Evil.

[68] Genesis 6:5. The only exception was Noah: "The Lord then said to Noah, 'Go into the ark, you and your whole family, because I have found you righteous in this generation.'" Genesis 7:1.

[69] Genesis 18:20–21.

[70] "Not a man of this evil generation shall see the good land I swore to give your forefathers," Deuteronomy 1:35.

Pharaoh's Dream: Joseph and the First Business Cycle

To prevent this from being too simple, of course, the very first historic economic cycle is connected with a mystery. It is the Pharaoh's well-known dream of seven fat and seven lean cows, which he told to Joseph, the son of Jacob. Joseph interpreted the dream as a macroeconomic prediction of sorts: Seven years of abundance were to be followed by seven years of poverty, famine, and misery.

> Pharaoh had a dream: He was standing by the Nile, when out of the river there came up seven cows, sleek and fat, and they grazed among the reeds. After them, seven other cows, ugly and gaunt, came up out of the Nile and stood beside those on the riverbank. And the cows that were ugly and gaunt ate up the seven sleek, fat cows. Then Pharaoh woke up.[71]

Joseph later interprets the Pharaoh's dream:

> Seven years of great abundance are coming throughout the land of Egypt, but seven years of famine will follow them. Then all the abundance in Egypt will be forgotten, and the famine will ravage the land.[72]

Later Joseph offers the Pharaoh advice on how to de facto avoid the results of the prophecy—how to avert both famine and de facto seven years of abundance.

> And now let Pharaoh look for a discerning and wise man and put him in charge of the land of Egypt. Let Pharaoh appoint commissioners over the land to take a fifth of the harvest of Egypt during the seven years of abundance. They should collect all the food of these good years that are coming and store up the grain under the authority of Pharaoh, to be kept in the cities for food. This food should be held in reserve for the country, to be used during the seven years of famine that will come upon Egypt, so that the country may not be ruined by the famine.[73]

In this we certainly can handily recognize later Keynesian anticyclical fiscal policy. On the specific application of this rule for today's economic policy, see the second part of the book.

Self-Contradicting Prophecy

Here, let's make several observations on this: Through taxation[74] on the level of one-fifth of a crop[75] in good years to save the crop and then open granaries in bad years, the prophecy was de facto prevented

---

[71] Genesis 41:1–4.
[72] Genesis 41:29–30.
[73] Genesis 41:33–36.
[74] The very first mention of taxes in the book of Genesis.
[75] Interestingly, modern states tax their citizens with much higher overall tax rates, although they are not able to sustain cyclically balanced budgets. Some countries have not even achieved a budget surplus in decades.

(prosperous years were limited and hunger averted—through a predecessor of fiscal stabilization). This nicely points out that if the prophecy were "true," accurate, what was prophesied would often actually never happen. Therefore there is a paradox here: If we are able to anticipate problems and take appropriate measures, they do not have to occur at all.[76] The Old Testament prophesies therefore were not any deterministic look into the future, but warnings and strategic variations of the possible, which demanded some kind of reaction. If the reaction was adequate, what was prophesied would frequently not occur at all.[77] This principle of the "accursed prophet" or the "self-contradicting prophecy" can be also shown from the story of the prophet Jonah; he seemed to be aware of this (that prophecies, when adhered to, never actually materialize) and for this reason did not want to be a prophet: the city of Nineveh was never destroyed, although (or more accurately *precisely because*) he prophesied against it.[78]

If the threat is anticipated, it is possible to totally or at least partially avoid it. Neither Joseph nor the pharaoh had the power to avoid bounty or crop failure (in this the dream interpretation was true and the appearance of the future mystical), but they avoided the impacts and implications of the prophecy (in this the interpretation of the dream was "false")—famine did not ultimately occur in Egypt, and this was due to the application of reasonable and very intuitive economic policy.[79] In other words, no one knows the future—not even prophets—and this is simply because people react in a certain way to information about the future; that, in and of itself, changes the future and the validity of the prophecy. This principle stands directly against *the self-fulfilling prophecy*,[80] the well-known concept of social science. Certain prophecies become

---

[76] The important exception is when we are aware of forthcoming problems but nobody has the courage to solve them. Current economic policy in many countries serves as the best example of postponing necessary reforms beyond the horizon of short-term political cycles.

[77] Nassim Taleb discusses a similar principle in his book *The Black Swan*.

[78] "On the first day, Jonah started into the city. He proclaimed: 'Forty more days and Nineveh will be overturned.' The Ninevites believed God. They declared a fast, and all of them, from the greatest to the least, put on sackcloth. . . . When God saw what they did and how they turned from their evil ways, he had compassion and did not bring upon them the destruction he had threatened," Jonah 3:4–10. This "failed yet successful prophecy" greatly displeased Jonah and he became angry: "O LORD, is this not what I said when I was still at home? That is why I was so quick to flee to Tarshish. I knew that you are a gracious and compassionate God, slow to anger and abounding in love, a God who relents from sending calamity," Jonah 4:2.

[79] The Pharaoh is not presented as a god or son of a god, as his fellow citizens took him at the time, and the fact that he struggles with adversity technically and humanly suggests something interesting. The pharaoh uses no magic to ward off the crisis; readers are treated to the secrets of his kitchen, so to speak, and the "secret" of economic policy, which was a wise reaction to the given information.

[80] Despite the fact that we find examples of such prophecies in many places in history, the detailed problem of the self-fulfilling prophecy was first described by the sociologist Robert K. Merton in his book *Social Theory and Social Structure*.

self-fulfilling when expressed (and believed) while others become self-contradicting prophecies when pronounced (and believed).

Let us further note that the first "macroeconomic forecast" appears in a *dream*. A dream—that irrational, pictorial, and difficult to understand phenomenon which has long caused serious people to shake their heads and which has only recently been rehabilitated by psychology—becomes the bearer of the economic future.

It isn't clear why economists today are asked to predict the future. Of all the social sciences, or I'll even say all humanities, economics is the most focused on the future; other fields do not deal with it as much.[81] Perhaps this issue is related—one easily gets the feeling that for economists paradise is situated in the future, while paradise for sociologists, ecologists, or even for psychologists is in the nostalgic past (when man lived in harmony with his family, nature, or his psyche). Also, economics believes itself to be the most exact science among all the humanities; this may also be because it senses the future.

But back to Torah: Later in this story we will notice that there is no *reason* offered as to *why* the cycle occurs (that will come later). Fat years will simply come, and then lean years after them. For the Bible, which has some kind of (mainly moral) explanation for nearly everything, this is quite unique. Actually, in this regard it recalls the Epic of Gilgamesh: Evil (or good) simply occurs, and our acts have no general influence on it. The cycle is not explained in any way, and no answer at all is given to the question "*why?*"[82]

Moral Explanation of a Business Cycle

That is fundamentally different from later Hebrew interpretations, when the Jewish nation tries to offer *reasons* why the nation fared well or poorly. And those reasons are moral. If the nation or its representatives (most frequently kings and priests) behave according to God's commands, then Israel wins in battle,[83] enjoys the honor of surrounding nations,[84] and what is more important for us: prospers economically:

---

[81] Other political scientists do deal with the future, but the difference is that economists are much more convinced of their ability to precisely predict future developments. What's more, they are pressured to produce long-term predictions because a large number of decisions on all levels of the economy are accepted based on them. States, companies, and households are arranged according to them.

[82] In addition, this valuable secret is entrusted not to the Jews, but to the Pharaoh. And thanks to it, Egypt fundamentally strengthens his position, enslaves surrounding nations (the sons of Joseph are an example), and grows stronger both financially and in power because he sells grain in times of need or exchanges it for land.

[83] The myriad examples arise in the settlement of the Promised Land in the Book of Numbers (the fourth book of Moses) in chapter 31 and so on.

[84] Let the crowning example here be the times of the reigns of David and Solomon. See, for example, 2 Chronicles 9.

If you pay attention to these laws and are careful to follow them, then the Lord your God will keep his covenant of love with you, as he swore to your forefathers. He will love you and bless you and increase your numbers. He will bless the fruit of your womb, the crops of your land—your grain, new wine and oil—the calves of your herds and the lambs of your flocks (. . .) You will be blessed more than any other people; none of your men or women will be childless, nor any of your livestock without young. (. . .)[85]

Without being timid, we can say this is the first documented attempt to *explain* the economic cycle. The economic cycle, the explanation of which is to this day a mystery to economists, is explained *morally* in the Old Testament. At times when Israel maintained law and justice, when widows and orphans were not oppressed, and when the Lord's commandments were obeyed, the nation prospered. Economic and social crises occurred when the opposite was the case:

Do not take advantage of a widow or an orphan. If you do and they cry out to me, I will certainly hear their cry. My anger will be aroused, and I will kill you with the sword.[86]

The following passage could serve as another example:

In the twenty-third year of Joash son of Ahaziah king of Judah, Jehoahaz son of Jehu became king of Israel in Samaria, and he reigned seventeen years. He did evil in the eyes of the Lord by following the sins of Jeroboam son of Nebat, which he had caused Israel to commit, and he did not turn away from them. So the Lord's anger burned against Israel, and for a long time he kept them under the power of Hazael king of Aram.[87]

From today's perspective, we can state that the moral dimension entirely disappeared from economic thought for a long time, especially due to the implementation of Mandeville's concept of private vices that contrarily support the public welfare (I devote a separate chapter to Mandeville). Individual morals are irrelevant in such a system because something that would later be mystically called the *invisible hand of the market* also transforms private vices into public welfare.

Only in recent times have some currents of economics again become aware of the importance of morals and trust in the form of measuring the quality of institutions, the level of justice, business ethics, corruption, and so forth, and examining their influence on the economy, not to mention economic growth.

---

[85] Deuteronomy 7:12–16. Another example is Exodus 23:25: "Worship the Lord your God, and his blessing will be on your food and water."

[86] Exodus 22:22–24.

[87] 2 Kings 13:1–3: To be complete, the Israelite king Jereboah II was very successful economically, even though he was wicked . . . "he did evil in the eyes of the Lord." But the economic success is noted in the Bible with the words "The Lord had seen how bitterly everyone in Israel, whether slave or free, was suffering; (. . .) he saved them by the hand of Jeroboam, son of Jehoash." 2 Kings 14:26–27.

But how do we consolidate these two conflicting interpretations of the economic cycle: Can ethics be responsible for it or not? Can we influence reality around us through our acts? Does ethics have an influence on the future? With this, we come to one of the most important questions of ethics and economics.

THE ECONOMICS OF GOOD AND EVIL: DOES GOOD PAY OFF?

This is probably the most difficult moral problem we could ask. The fact that we are asking this question in the middle of a discourse on Hebrew thought indicates that there are probably more opinions on this than there are participants in the discourse. We are also suggesting that it is not within the scope of this book to answer that question; justice has been done to the question if it manages to sketch out the main contours of possible searches for answers.

It could follow from the text above that good deeds pay. For the Hebrews, morals meant the best investment one could make. Nothing could help an economy more than being very particular about justice. Adherence to rules and a moral life would pay off *very well for them materially*.[88] Let us not forget that the Hebrews had it more difficult to answer this question. In the Old Testament, there is little mention of heaven or hell—as if this concept did not exist for the Hebrew thought; it was not possible (somewhat noncommittally) to place payback for good or evil in the form of a just recompense that comes posthumously (as, in the end, Christianity does; see below). It speaks of *justice in the context of life here on Earth*. Moral accounting had to be carried out during life on earth; it could not be deferred into the preserve of life after death.

Sombart puts it this way:

> The oldest form of Judaism knows nothing of another world. So, weal and woe can come only in this world. If God desires to punish or to reward, He must do so during man's lifetime. The righteous therefore is prosperous here, and the wicked here suffer punishment. Obey my precepts, says the Lord, "so that thou mayest live long and prosper in the land which the Lord thy God hath given unto thee." Hence the bitter cry of Job, "Wherefore do the wicked live, become old, yea, wax mighty in power? . . . But my way He hath fenced up, that I cannot pass . . . He hath broken me down on every side . . . He hath also kindled His wrath against me" [Job xxi.7; xix.8, 10, 11].

---

[88] We will not deal with the reasons why the rules were not adhered to. There are many reasons (explored for instance by game theory), where it pays for a person on the individual level not to play by the rules, to be an unticketed passenger on others' trust and adherence to the rules. Of course this leads to a general decline in well-being on the social level. For more, see Sedláček, "Spontaneous Rule Creation."

"Why hath all this evil come upon me, seeing that I walked in His path continually?"[89]

As far as reward for good, we can find an interesting parallel in a different context, on the payment of tithes:

"You are under a curse—the whole nation of you—because you are robbing me. Bring the whole tithe into the storehouse, that there may be food in my house. Test me in this," says the Lord Almighty, "and see if I will not throw open the floodgates of heaven and pour out so much blessing that you will not have room enough for it. I will prevent pests from devouring your crops, and the vines in your fields will not cast their fruit," says the Lord Almighty. "Then all the nations will call you blessed, for yours will be a delightful land," says the Lord Almighty.[90]

Inquiring about the economics of good and evil, however, is not that easy. Where would Kant's "moral dimension of ethics" go if ethics paid? If we do good *for profit*, the question of ethics becomes a mere question of rationality. Immanuel Kant, the most important modern thinker in the area of ethics, answers on the contrary that if we carry out a "moral" act on the basis of economic calculus (therefore we carry out an hedonistic consideration; see below) in the expectation of later recompense, its morality is lost. Recompense, according to the strict Kant, annuls ethics.

The same issue figures in all its thorniness in the Torah. The issue of the "algorithm of recompense for sin,"[91] the search for the rules of God's justice on this earth, has become an important topic of the Hebrew thought. The pious Hasidim and their successors, the Pharisees, who are known mainly from the New Testament, considered their piety as being in their adherence to the given, and very strict, rules. As opposed to this, the prophetic schools emphasized that there was no algorithm between good and reward. We find a good example in one of the most beautiful—and at the same time most complicated—books of the Old Testament, the Book of Job. The role of devil's advocate is (conveniently) awarded to Satan (incidentally, the only place in the Old Testament where the devil figures explicitly[92]):

---

[89] Sombart, *The Jews and Modern Capitalism*, 214–215.

[90] Malachi 3:9–12. This direction can be read in many places in the Old Testament. As an example, let us consider: "for I, the Lord your God, am a jealous God, punishing the children for the sin of the fathers to the third and fourth generation of those who hate me, but showing love to a thousand [generations] of those who love me and keep my commandments," Exodus 20:5–6.

[91] As Jan Payne accurately names it in his book *Odkud zlo?* [Whence Evil?], 69. The following division of the Hasidic tradition and the prophetic school refers to Hengel, *Judentum und Helenismus*, 310–381, 394–453.

[92] If we omit the reference to the "snake" in the story of the Garden of Eden, where the snake placed in direct equivalence to Satan. Otherwise we find direct reference to Satan only once in the Old Testament, and very briefly (in the Book of Malachi). Compare this with the number of appearances this word makes in the New Testament. Robert Muchembled, in *A History of the Devil*, 1–2, even argues that despite the fact that "The [concept of] devil has been a part of the fabric of the European life since the Middle Ages, and has

Then the LORD said to Satan, "Have you considered my servant Job? There is no one on earth like him; he is blameless and upright, a man who fears God and shuns evil." "Does Job fear God for nothing?" Satan replied. "Have you not put a hedge around him and his household and everything he has? You have blessed the work of his hands, so that his flocks and herds are spread throughout the land. But stretch out your hand and strike everything he has, and he will surely curse you to your face."[93]

After Job's misfortunes (by the way, three of the four misfortunes relate to his possession, his assets), which are supposed to show (it almost sounds like a divine bet between God and devil) that Job does not do good *for profit*, his friends stop by to see him. Their debate (which is among the high points of Jewish poetry and philosophy) more or less turns around how Job's friends try to show that he *must* have sinned in some way and, in doing so, *deserved* God's punishment. They are absolutely unable to imagine a situation in which Job, as a righteous man, would *suffer without (moral) cause*. Nevertheless, Job insists that he deserves no punishment because he has committed no offense: "God has wronged me and drawn his net around me."[94]

At first sight, this idea collides with the aforementioned thesis of reward for the righteous. But Job remains righteous, even though it *does not pay* to do so:

Though he slay me, yet will I hope in him.[95]

And

till I die, I will not deny my integrity
I will maintain my righteousness and never let go of it;
my conscience will not reproach me as long as I live.[96]

Job does not live morally because it is advantageous. He remains righteous, even if his only reward is death. What economic advantage could he have from that?

Good Outgoing, Good Incoming

In life it often happens that the righteous suffer and the unrighteous live in prosperity. What ontological status, then, does good have? What logic?

---

accompanied all its major changes . . . He represents the dark side of our culture, the exact antithesis of the big ideas it has generated and exported all over the world." In this context, let us cite this book once again on the influence of the representation of the devil on history. When Muchembled describes the work of the well-known author Daniel Defoe, *The Political History of the Devil*, he concludes that "Like Locke and Hume, and before Kant, he [Daniel Defoe] is moving towards a definition of the devil as a motor of history," (166).
[93] Job 1:8–11.
[94] Job 19:6. For other lists and evidence of Job's righteousness, see Job 31:1–40.
[95] Job 13:15.
[96] Job 27:5–6.

Is there a correlation at all between the (outgoing) good or evil we do and the good or evil (just reward) that comes to us (incoming)? From what is presented above, it would appear that this relationship is created *randomly*. Why do good rather than evil (outgoing), if its consequent state (incoming) is random? Aside from the Book of Job, this characteristic is noted by the author of the biblical book of Ecclesiastes:

> There is something else meaningless that occurs on earth: righteous men who get what the wicked deserve, and wicked men who get what the righteous deserve. This too, I say, is meaningless.[97]

The Psalmist also perceives this similarly and in full scope and bitterness:

> But as for me, my feet had almost slipped; I had nearly lost my foothold. For I envied the arrogant when I saw the prosperity of the wicked. They have no struggles; their bodies are healthy and strong. They are free from the burdens common to man; they are not plagued by human ills.[98]

So why do good? After all, suffering is the fate of many biblical figures. The answer can only be: For good itself. Good has the power to be its own reward. In *this sense*, goodness gets its reward, which may or may not take on a material dimension. Nevertheless, in the proper sense of the term, morals cannot be considered in the economic dimension of productivity and calculus. The role of the Hebrews was to do good, whether it paid off or not. If good (outgoing) is rewarded by incoming goodness, it is a bonus,[99] not a *reason* to do outgoing good. Good and reward do not correlate to each other.

This reasoning takes on a dimension of its own in the Old Testament. Good (incoming) has already happened to us. We must do good (outgoing) *out of gratitude* for the good (incoming) shown to us in the past.[100]

One more comment about morals and asceticism. As we will see later, especially in connection with the teachings of the Stoics and Epicureans, the question of whether one can *enjoy* life on earth plays an important role in the economy of good and evil. Consequently, whether he or she has the right to expect the maximization of *utility*. Can we lay claim to

---

[97] Ecclesiastes 8:14.

[98] Psalms 73:2–5.

[99] At the end of the book, Job gets his property back ("the LORD made him prosperous again and gave him twice as much as he had before," Job 42:10), but going through this suffering (for the "reward") hardly would be called a good deal and mainly is *not* the point of the book. The reward was a bonus, not a calcul.

[100] As regards evil, Socrates offers an interesting view on the difference between evil (incoming) and evil (outgoing): In the *Phaedo*, the arrested Socrates chooses to commit suicide by drinking hemlock rather than run away. He would rather have evil done to himself than do something he himself considers wrong—escaping from prison and banishment. According to Socrates, evil (outgoing) is more serious than evil (incoming): "It is better to suffer wrong than to do wrong" (*Gorgias* 473a–475e).

material or emotive rewards for good that has been performed? Immanuel Kant was of the opinion that if good (outgoing) is reciprocated with good (incoming), then we have done nothing meritorious or moral, because the increase in our utility (whether precalculated or unexpected) negates the morality of our acts.

Now, the Hebrews offered an interesting compromise between the teachings of the Stoics and Epicureans. We will go into it in detail later, so only briefly here: The Stoics could not seek their enjoyment—or, by another name, utility. They could not in any way look back on it, and in no way could they count on it. They could only live according to rules (the greatest weakness of this school was to defend where exogenously the given rules came from and whether they are universal) and take a indifferent stand to the results of their actions.

The Epicureans acted with the goal of maximizing utility without regard for rules (rules developed *endogenously, from within the system,* computed from that which increased utility—this was one of the main trumps of the Epicurean school; they did not need exogenously given norms, and argued that they could "calculate" ethics (what to do) for every given situation from the situation itself).

The Old Testament offers an option somewhere in the middle:

Be happy, young man, while you are young, and let your heart give you joy in the days of your youth. Follow the ways of your heart and whatever your eyes see, but know that for all these things God will bring you to judgment.[101]

In other words, clear (exogenously given) rules exist that must be observed and cannot be contravened. But within these borders it is absolutely possible, and even recommended, to increase utility. In the language of the more modern economic mainstream, individuals are recommended to carry out the optimalization of utility limited by their *budgetary constraint.* It calls for bounded optimalization (with limits). A kind of symbiosis existed between the legitimate search for one's own utility (or *enjoyment* of life) and maintaining rules, which are not negotiable and which *are not* subject to optimalization. The religion of the Old Testament did not act as an ascetic religion forbidding earthly pleasures. On the contrary, the world was given to man so that he could draw enjoyment from it. However, the mining of enjoyment must not come at the expense of exogenously given rules. "Judaism comes therefore to train or educate the unbounded desire . . . for wealth, so that market activities and patterns of consumption operate within a God-given morality."[102]

---

[101] Ecclesiastes 11:9.
[102] Tamari, *The Challenge of Wealth*, 45.

Christianity later returned again to a more ascetic view[103] on the search for utility, or enjoying life. A good example could be, among the many possible, the parable of Lazarus:

> There was a rich man who was dressed in purple and fine linen and lived in luxury every day. At his gate was laid a beggar named Lazarus, covered with sores and longing to eat what fell from the rich man's table. Even the dogs came and licked his sores. The time came when the beggar died and the angels carried him to Abraham's side. The rich man also died and was buried. In hell, where he was in torment, he looked up and saw Abraham far away, with Lazarus by his side. So he called to him, "Father Abraham, have pity on me and send Lazarus to dip the tip of his finger in water and cool my tongue, because I am in agony in this fire." But Abraham replied, "Son, remember that in your lifetime you received your good things, while Lazarus received bad things, but now he is comforted here and you are in agony."[104]

In other words, what appears to be said here is: The rich man enjoyed himself on Earth, and as if that is *why* he must suffer after death, and on the other hand the poor man will be blessed in heaven, because he did not experience good on Earth. Ultimately, we cannot read anything into the morality of the rich man or of Lazarus (we can only extrapolate it from the story, but nevertheless, the story itself does not consider this dimension to be important). The only difference between them is that the rich man enjoys a high standard of enjoyment on Earth while Lazarus suffers.

We shall return to the relation between good outgoing and good incoming in a separate chapter in the latter part of the book, where various moral views are summarized on a symbolical Axis of Good and Evil.

To Love the Law

The Jews not only had to observe the law (perhaps the word covenant would be more appropriate), but they were to *love* it because it was good. Their relationship to the law was not supposed to be one of duty,[105] but one of gratitude, love. Hebrews were to do good (outgoing), because goodness (incoming) has *already been done* to them.

---

[103] Also under the influence of the cultural heritage of the Greeks as well as due to the religious stew of the Middle East in the first centuries of the growth of "mainstream" Christianity. If we were to understand such things as regular fasting as an ascetic element, then we find it in a very limited measure in the Old Testament, while it is abundant in the piety of Christians (and Jews) in the first centuries.

[104] Luke 16:19–25.

[105] The key element of Kantian ethics (ethics which to this day are a very influential school) is duty. "Kant stands at one of the great dividing points in the history of ethics. For perhaps the majority of later philosophical writers, including many who are self-consciously anti-Kantian, ethics is defined as a subject in Kantian terms. For many who have never heard of philosophy, let alone of Kant, morality is roughly what Kant said it was." MacIntyre, *A Short History of Ethics*, 122.

And now, O Israel, what does the Lord your God ask of you but to fear the Lord your God, to walk in all his ways, to love him, to serve the Lord your God with all your heart and with all your soul, and to observe the Lord's commands and decrees that I am giving you today for your own good? To the Lord your God belong the heavens, even the highest heavens, the earth and everything in it. Yet the Lord set his affection on your forefathers and loved them. . . . He defends the cause of the fatherless and the widow, and loves the alien, giving him food and clothing. . . . He is your God, who performed for you those great and awesome wonders you saw with your own eyes. Your forefathers who went down into Egypt were seventy in all, and now the Lord your God has made you as numerous as the stars in the sky.[106]

This is in stark contrast with today's legal system, where, naturally, no mention of love or gratefulness exists. But God expects a full internalization of the commandments and their fulfillment with love, not as much duty. By no means was this on the basis of the cost-benefit analyses so widespread in economics today, which determines when it pays to break the law and when not to (calculated on the basis of probability of being caught and the amount of punishment vis-à-vis the possible gain). Let us present just a few examples:

Fix these words of mine in your hearts and minds; tie them as symbols on your hands and bind them on your foreheads.[107]

Even the Psalmist speaks of loving the law rather than its slavish fulfillment: "Oh, how I love your law! I meditate on it all day long. (. . .) Because I love your commands more than gold, more than pure gold."[108] Or elsewhere: "Blessed is the man who does not walk in the counsel of the wicked . . . But his delight is in the law of the LORD, and on His law he meditates day and night."[109] This motif is repeated many times in the Old Testament, and the principle of doing good (outgoing) on the basis of a priori demonstrated good (incoming) was also taken over by the New Testament. Atonement itself is based on an a priori principle; all our acts are preceded by good. The well-known sociologist Werner Sombart also notes the love and esteem the Jews have for the Law:

As Josephus [meaning Flavius] so well put it: "Ask the first Jew you meet concerning his 'laws' and he will be able to tell you them better than his own name." The reason for this may be found in the systematic religious instruction given to every Jewish child, as well as in the fact that divine service partly consists of the reading and explanations of passages from Holy Writ. In the course of the year the Torah is read through from beginning to end. Moreover, it is one of the primary duties of the Jew to study

---

[106] Deuteronomy 10:12–22.
[107] Deuteronomy 11:18.
[108] Psalms 119:97,127.
[109] Psalms 1:1–2.

the Torah. "And you shall teach them diligently to your children, and shall talk of them when you sit in your house, and when you walk by the way, and when you lie down, and when you rise up." [Deuteronomy vi.5](. . .) The Talmud was the greatest wealth; it was the breath of their lives, their soul itself. [110]

The aforementioned citation beautifully shows what a central role laws and rules have in the Jewish religion. Their absolute understanding is of course typical only for rules and laws presented in the Torah—laws given by God.[111]

The following difference is also characteristic: The Egyptians had to love their rulers,[112] while the Hebrews were to love their Lord and His law.[113] Laws given by God are binding for Jews, and God is the absolute source of all values, and for this reason a way to overcome human laws must exist. Human laws, if they are in conflict with the responsibilities given by God, are subordinate to personal responsibility, and a Jew cannot simply join the majority, even if it is legally allowed. Ethics, the concept of good, is therefore always superior to all local laws, rules, and customs: "Do not follow the crowd in doing wrong. When you give testimony in a lawsuit, do not pervert justice by siding with the crowd."[114]

THE FREEDOM OF THE NOMAD AND THE SHACKLES OF THE CITY

Owing to the Hebrew's liberation from Egyptian slavery, *freedom* and *responsibility* become the key values of Jewish thought. The Hebrews, originally a nomadic tribe, preferred to be unrestrained and grew up in constant freedom of motion. They preferred this way of life to settled agricultural city life, which seemed to tie them down.[115] The Jews were shepherds—agricultural life would have required settling in one place.

The Hebrew ideal is represented by the paradise of the Garden of Eden, not a city.[116]The despised city civilization or the tendency to see in

---

[110] Sombart, *The Jews and Modern Capitalism*, 134, 136. In reality, it was an imprecise citation, not from Deuteronomy 6:5, but two verses onward, 6:7. As we can see, even Sombart suffered from imprecision.

[111] There are a total of 613 laws mentioned in the Torah, most of them in the Book of Leviticus.

[112] *See* Lalouette, *Ramessova říše* [L'empire des Ramsès], 284.

[113] As mentioned, a part of the word "economics" means *nomos*: law or the spirit of law. *Nomos* is the origin of the suffix -onomy, as in astronomy, economy, or taxonomy.

[114] Exodus 23:2.

[115] Sokol, *Člověk a svět očima Bible* [Man and the World in the Eyes of the Bible], 30. Sokol further argues that to a certain extent the founding fathers of American society were also originally nomads who had similar preferences for freedom as the Jews did.

[116] The transformation of natural *paradise* into the notion of a heavenly *city* only occurs later and is brought in at the end of the New Testament in the Book of Revelation, where life after

it a sinful and shackling way of life appears in glimpses and allusions in many places in the Old Testament. The construction of the fabled Tower of Babel is presented with the preamble: "Then they said, 'Come, let us build ourselves a city, with a tower that reaches to the heavens, so that we may make a name for ourselves and not be scattered over the face of the whole earth.'"[117] Abraham chooses pastures, while Lot bets on (alas the sinful) cities of Sodom and Gomorrah.[118] Numerous mentions even occur in the Song of Solomon, where the lovers look forward to their love in the gardens and vineyards outside the city, while the episodes that take place in the city give a despondent impression.

The nomadic Jewish ethos is frequently derived from Abraham, who left the Chaldean city of Ur on the basis of a command: "The LORD had said to Abram, 'Leave your country, your people and your father's household and go to the land I will show you.'"[119] The ability to be in motion and not be tied down with ownership is a highly valued attribute. This way of life had understandably immense economic impacts. First, such a society lived in much more connected relationships, where there was no doubt that everyone mutually depended on each other. Second, their frequent wanderings meant the inability to own more than they could carry; the gathering up of material assets did not have great weight—precisely because the physical weight (mass) of things was tied to one place.

In addition, they were aware of a thin two-way line between owner and owned. We own material assets, but—to a certain extent—they own us and tie us down. Once we become used to a certain material comfort, it is difficult to bid farewell to it, pick up, and live freely. We encounter the dilemma of comfort and freedom in the story in the Sinai Desert. After the Jews were led out from slavery in Egypt, they start to grumble against Moses:

> The rabble with them began to crave other food, and again the Israelites started wailing and said, "If only we had meat to eat! We remember the fish we ate in Egypt at no cost—also the cucumbers, melons, leeks, onions and garlic. But now we have lost our appetite; we never see anything but this manna!"[120]

One of Moses's greatest deeds was that he managed to explain to his nation once and for all that it is better to remain hungry and liberated than to be a slave with food "at no cost."[121] If the term "free lunch" comes to mind, we can be sure that a whole nation was deceived that they were

---

death is described in a heavenly Jerusalem, or therefore in a city. In Hebrew, "Jerusalem" literally means *city of peace*.

[117] Genesis 11:4.

[118] Genesis 13:10.

[119] Genesis 12:1.

[120] Numbers 11:4–6.

[121] Sokol, *Člověk a svět očima Bible* [Man and the World in the Eyes of the Bible], 33.

getting a "free lunch" and nobody realized that that "free lunch" cost them their freedom, and—to a large degree—their whole existence.

SOCIAL WELFARE: NOT TO ACT IN THE MANNER OF SODOM

A remarkable complex of socioeconomic regulations is developed in the Old Testament, one we hardly find in any other nation of the time. In Hebrew teachings, aside from individual utility, indications of the concept of maximalizing utility *societywide* appear for the first time as embodied in the Talmudic principle of *Kofin al midat S'dom*, which can be translated as "one is compelled not to act in the manner of Sodom" and to take care of the weaker members of society. Later in this chapter we will look at tithes, alms, years of pardons, and other responsibilities that were to create a more stable social environment and a kind of basic social safety net.

Sabbath: Year of Rest

One of these social measures is the institution of sabbath years. This system is discussed in detail especially in chapter 25 of the Book of Leviticus:

> When you enter the land I am going to give you, the land itself must observe a sabbath to the Lord. For six years sow your fields, and for six years prune your vineyards and gather their crops. But in the seventh year the land is to have a sabbath of rest, a sabbath to the Lord. Do not sow your fields or prune your vineyards. Do not reap what grows of itself or harvest the grapes of your untended vines. The land is to have a year of rest.[122]

Now every forty-nine years[123] there is a year of forgiveness, when land is returned to its original owners (according to original plans, as the land was divided among individual tribes that entered Canaan).[124] In a jubilee year, debts were to be forgiven,[125] and Israelites who fell into slavery due to their indebtedness were to be set free.[126]

---

[122] Leviticus 25:2–5. The crops of the sixth year were supposed to last for three additional years; see Leviticus 25:20.
[123] The symbolism of this number is based on the square of 7.
[124] Leviticus 25:8.
[125] "Consecrate the fiftieth year and proclaim liberty throughout the land to all its inhabitants. It shall be a jubilee for you; each one of you is to return to his family property and each to his own clan. The fiftieth year shall be a jubilee for you; do not sow and do not reap what grows of itself or harvest the untended vines. . . . In this Year of Jubilee everyone is to return to his own property. . . . You are to buy from your countryman on the basis of the number of years since the Jubilee. And he is to sell to you on the basis of the number of years left for harvesting crops. When the years are many, you are to increase the price, and when the years are few, you are to decrease the price, because what he is really selling you is the number of crops. Do not take advantage of each other, but fear your God. I am the LORD your God." Leviticus 25:10–17
[126] "If one of your countrymen becomes poor among you and sells himself to you, do not make him work as a slave. He is to be treated as a hired worker or a temporary resident

Such provisions can be seen as the antimonopoly and social measures of the time. The economic system even then had a clear tendency to converge toward asset concentration, and therefore power as well. It would appear that these provisions were supposed to prevent this process (without the need for a regulatory body). A period of fifty years roughly corresponded to the life span at the time, and at the same time evidently was supposed to act to remove the problem of generational indebtedness. The generation following the indebted or poor father got their land back and had a chance to start farming again. The sins of the fathers (bad management) did not fall as heavily on the heads of their sons and daughters. Successes were also not inherited linearly, as in a common economic system. The Sumerian Code of Hammurabi had something similar: regular forgiveness of debt, which was even prescribed once every three years.[127] This is interesting because it appears that the oldest society to (with light suspicion) allow interest had at the same time instruments of *forgiveness*, which annulled the power of debt (after some time).[128]

Land at the time could be "sold," and it was not sale, but rent. The price (rent) of real estate depended on how long there was until a forgiveness year. It was about the awareness that we may work the land, but in the last instance we are merely "aliens and strangers," who have the land only rented to us for a fixed time. All land and riches came from the Lord. "The earth is the Lord's, and everything in it, the world, and all who live in it."[129] Man is only a tenant on the land, and all ownership is only temporary. Rent had to be paid in the form of a tithe and in adherence to the laws given by the Lord. Forgiveness years are also a reminder that in reality, land does not belong to its human owners.

> In this Year of Jubilee everyone is to return to one's own property. If you sell land to one of your countrymen or buy any from him, do not take advantage of each other. You are to buy from your countryman on the basis of the number of years since the Jubilee. And he is to sell to you on the basis of the number of years left for harvesting crops. When the years are many, you are to increase the price, and when the years are few, you are to decrease the price, because what he is really selling you is the number of crops.[130]

A responsibility existed on all land sold, or people sold into slavery, that the new owner would sell off the land, or sell back the slave, as soon

---

among you; he is to work for you until the Year of Jubilee. Then he and his children are to be released, and he will go back to his own clan and to the property of his forefathers. Because the Israelites are my servants, whom I brought out of Egypt, they must not be sold as slaves. Do not rule over them ruthlessly, but fear your God." Leviticus 25:39–43.

[127] See Ferguson, *The Ascent of Money*, 30.

[128] A different problem was that these regulations were rarely adhered to in practice, as historic accounts indicate from both Mesopotamia and the time of the Old Testament.

[129] Psalm 24:1.

[130] Leviticus 25:13–16.

as they could work up enough to buy the lost ownership themselves or with the help of their relatives. If the slave was not able to do that, he had to wait—for in the jubilee year he would be released for free. "The land must not be sold permanently, because the land is mine and you are but aliens and my tenants."[131]

These provisions express a conviction that freedom and inheritance should not be permanently taken away from any Israelite. Last but not least, this system reminds us that no ownership lasts forever and that the fields we plow are not ours but the Lord's. The forgiveness years again emphasize that we are only wanderers here; nothing material from this world will save us, we take nothing with us and *everything* we have is a certain type of rental. We only pass through here; material things will stay here, even when we are gone.

Glean

Another social provision was the right to glean, which in Old Testament times ensured at least basic sustenance for the poorest. Anyone who owned a field had the responsibility not to harvest it to the last grain but to leave the remains in the field for the poor.

> When you reap the harvest of your land, do not reap to the very edges of your field or gather the gleanings of your harvest. Leave them for the poor and the alien. I am the Lord your God.[132]

Or elsewhere:

> When you are harvesting in your field and you overlook a sheaf, do not go back to get it. Leave it for the alien, the fatherless and the widow, so that the LORD your God may bless you in all the work of your hands.[133]

Tithes and Early Social Net

Every Israelite also had the responsibility of levying a tithe from their entire crop. They had to be aware from whom all ownership comes and, by doing so, express their thanks. If it was a crop, the first fruits of the harvest belonged to the Lord. They did not consider everything they produced to be exclusively their property, but they handed over every tenth sheaf to the Lord. This ten percent was handed over to the temple. And every third year they gave it to the Levite, the stranger, the fatherless, and the widow.[134] For centuries, religious institutions—even in the Christian era—have held the function of a social safety net.

---

[131] Leviticus 25:23.
[132] Leviticus 23:22.
[133] Deuteronomy 24:19.
[134] Deuteronomy 26:12–15.

Among the Israelites we can find not only the roots of the modern widespread redistribution of wealth for the benefit of the poorest but also the well-substantiated concept of economic regulation, which closely relates to social policy. In Judaism, charity is not perceived as a sign of goodness; it is more of a responsibility. Such a society then has the right to regulate its economy in such a way that the responsibility of charity is carried out to its satisfaction. "Since the community has an obligation to provide food, shelter, and basic economic goods for the needy, it has a moral right and duty to tax its members for this purpose. In line with this duty, it may have to regulate markets, prices and competition, to protect the interests of its weakest members."[135]

Alms and various other acts of charity expressed for the poor functioned as another factor strengthening the social network. Through His prophets, the Lord many times reminds us that He wants mercy, not sacrifice.[136] These were voluntary gifts in that the donor was in contact with the recipient and therefore knew who he was giving money to, who needed it, and how it was being used.

According to Moses's law, family members had to take care of individuals whose breadwinner had died (widows, orphans). The deceased's brother had to marry the widow. The first son born to him was considered the son of the deceased husband, and, when the son was grown, he had to take care of his mother. It is worth noting that widows inherited nothing from the deceased and sometimes had to return to their families after being widowed. In times of war, widows had the right to part of the spoils of war, and their money in times of threat was stored in the temple, where they were often employed as helpers to the Levites. The entire Old Testament and especially the Book of Deuteronomy remembers widows and orphans. They stand under special protection and those who are unkind to them face God's judgment:

> He raises the poor from the dust
> and lifts the needy from the ash heap;
> he seats them with princes
> and has them inherit a throne of honor.[137]

Or elsewhere:

> He who oppresses the poor shows contempt for their Maker,
> but whoever is kind to the needy honors God.[138]

---

[135] Tamari, *The Challenge of Wealth*, 52.

[136] "For I desire mercy, not sacrifice, and acknowledgment of God rather than burnt offerings." Hosea 6:6. See also Isaiah 1:11; this has a New Testament counterpart in Matthew 9:13: "But go and learn what this means: 'I desire mercy, not sacrifice.' For I have not come to call the righteous, but sinners." And also Matthew 12:7: "If you had known what these words mean, 'I desire mercy, not sacrifice,' you would not have condemned the innocent."

[137] 1 Samuel 2:8.

[138] Proverbs 14:31.

If a man shuts his ears to the cry of the poor, he too will cry out and not be answered.[139]

Do not mistreat an alien or oppress him, for you were aliens in Egypt.[140]

As one can see, aside from widows and orphans, the Old Testament also includes immigrants in its area of social protection.[141] The Israelites had to have the same rules apply for them as for themselves—they could not discriminate on the basis of their origin. "You are to have the same law for the alien and the native-born. I am the Lord your God."[142] Foreigners had the same right to glean as any Israelite. In relation to this, the Israelites are frequently reminded that they too were slaves in Egypt. They should remember their most miserable state and should behave kindly to their slaves, let alone to their guests: "Do not go over your vineyard a second time or pick up the grapes that have fallen. Leave them for the poor and the alien."[143]

All the rules described above show what a central role community and its cohesion play in Judaism. With a number of responsibilities, however, comes the difficulty of getting them into practice. Their fulfillment, then, in cases when it can be done, takes place gradually "in layers." Charitable activities are classified in the Talmud according to several target groups with various priorities, classified according to, it could be said, rules of subsidiarity.

> Judaism recognizes different levels of responsibility to those in need. Interpreting the biblical obligation to loan funds to the needy (Exodus 22:24), the Talmud concludes that one has a primary obligation to meet the legitimate financial needs of the members of one's own family. Only after satisfying family needs does one have an obligation to meet the needs of one's own city. Finally, after satisfying the needs of one's own city, only then does one have an obligation to meet the needs of other towns (Baba Mezia 71a).[144]

The most marked differences are in responsibilities to various socially distanced groups, as can be seen in the example of lending money with interest, where there is a dividing line between the (non)membership of the debtor to the Jewish community.

ABSTRACT MONEY, FORBIDDEN INTEREST, AND OUR DEBT AGE

If it appears to us that today's era is based on money and debt, and our time will be written into history as the "Debt age," then it will certainly be

---

[139] Proverbs 21:13.
[140] Exodus 22:21.
[141] Leviticus 25:47.
[142] Leviticus 24:22.
[143] Leviticus 19:10.
[144] Pava, *The Substance of Jewish Business Ethics*, 607.

interesting to follow how this development occurred. Money, debt, interest—these are all things we cannot imagine being without in modern society. Keynes even considers interest and the accumulation of capital as the trigger of modern progress.[145] But at the very beginning it was connected with ethical rules, faith, symbolism, and trust.

The first money came in the form of clay tablets from Mesopotamia, on which debts were written. These debts were transferable, so the debts became currency. In the end, "It is no coincidence that in English the root of 'credit' is 'credo,' the Latin for 'I believe.'"[146] These tablets have been preserved from more than five thousand years ago and are the oldest writings we have preserved. Coins appeared around 600 BC and were found at the Ephesian temple to the goddess Artemis. The coins did not differ much from today's; they had a symbol of a lion on them and the shape of the goddess Athena or an owl. China introduced coins in 221 BC.[147] To a certain extent it could be said that credit, or trust, was the first currency. It can materialize, it can be embodied in coins, but what is certain is that "money is not metal," even the rarest metal, "it is trust inscribed,"[148] and money actually has nothing in common with its material bearer (coin, note). "Money is a matter of belief, even faith."[149] This is nicely expressed by the Czech term for lender, věřitel, literally meaning believer. It is someone who believes the debtor. Money is a social abstractum. It is a social agreement, an unwritten contract.[150] Calling for the gold standard has similar significance as calling for the clay standard. The primeval nations were aware that the currency, the medium of circulation, has nothing in common with its bearer. Metals sometimes tend to be carriers of trust, but it could also be clay; clay, the most common "commodity" at our

---

[145] "The modern age opened, I think, with the accumulation of capital, which began in the sixteenth century. I believe for reasons with which I must not encumber the present argument that this was initially due to the rise of prices and the profits to which that led, which resulted from the treasure of gold and silver which Spain brought from the New World into the Old. From that time until today the power of accumulation by compound interest, which seems to have been sleeping for many generations, was reborn and renewed its strength. And the power of compound interest over two hundred years is such as to stagger the imagination." Keynes, *Economic Possibilities for Our Grandchildren*, 358.

[146] Ferguson, *The Ascent of Money*, 30.

[147] Ibid., 25, 28.

[148] Ibid., 30.

[149] Ibid., 29.

[150] At the same time money enables even great societies to become connected. Because of it we can trust a person whom we do not know but who honors the same (monetary) values. As Simmel points out in the chapter "Economic Activity Establishes Distances and Overcomes Them" (the heading pretty much explains it all), at the end it's money that bases more ties among people than have ever existed before (see Simmel, *Philosophy of Money*, 75–79). That money is in some way institutionalized trust is ensured by the various ornaments, signs, and symbols that dot banknotes and coins to this day. They are a kind of "holy" symbol of statehood, of our holy or important historical personalities. As if the given banknote or its user "swears" on its authority: With this I believe, I respect these, I will accept these.

feet ubiquitously. From the same clay, from the "dust of the earth" that Adam was created from, according to Genesis. The first man and the first money were both products of the earth.[151]

It is interesting that we find in Genesis the first mention of all of the first monetary transaction, in the story of Abraham, and it is accompanied with a unique puzzlement. The story is about the sale of a field that Abraham buys from the Hittites so that he can bury Sarah.[152] But the Hittites want to *give it* to him, not to sell it. Until then, all asset *transactions* documented in Genesis were nonmonetary, and ownership changed through gifts[153] or violence (Abraham gains substantial spoils of war from a king who attacked Sodom and Gomorrah).[154] In the first monetary transaction, Abraham insists that he wants to buy the field "for the full price as a burial site among you." He refuses an offer to receive the tomb for free, even doing so twice. It's almost surprising how this process is described in detail without them even haggling over the price. We will examine the symbolism of the gift in greater detail in the chapter on Christianity.

Inseparably, with the original credit (money) goes interest. For the Hebrews, the problem of interest was a social issue: "If you lend money to one of my people among you who is needy, do not be like a moneylender;

---

[151] See also Simmel, *Philosophy of Money.*

[152] Genesis 23:3–16:

"Then Abraham rose from beside his dead wife and spoke to the Hittites. He said, 'I am an alien and a stranger among you. Sell me some property for a burial site here so I can bury my dead.' The Hittites replied to Abraham, 'Sir, listen to us. You are a mighty prince among us. Bury your dead in the choicest of our tombs. None of us will refuse you his tomb for burying your dead.' Then Abraham rose and bowed down before the people of the land, the Hittites. He said to them, 'If you are willing to let me bury my dead, then listen to me and intercede with Ephron son of Zohar on my behalf so he will sell me the cave of Machpelah, which belongs to him and is at the end of his field. Ask him to sell it to me for the full price as a burial site among you.' Ephron the Hittite was sitting among his people and he replied to Abraham in the hearing of all the Hittites who had come to the gate of his city. 'No, my lord,' he said. 'Listen to me; I give you the field, and I give you the cave that is in it. I give it to you in the presence of my people. Bury your dead.' Again Abraham bowed down before the people of the land and he said to Ephron in their hearing, 'Listen to me, if you will. I will pay the price of the field. Accept it from me so I can bury my dead there.' Ephron answered Abraham, 'Listen to me, my lord; the land is worth four hundred shekels of silver, but what is that between me and you? Bury your dead.' Abraham agreed to Ephron's terms and weighed out for him the price he had named in the hearing of the Hittites: four hundred shekels of silver, according to the weight current among the merchants."

[153] Abraham receives a large gift from Abimelech, whom Abraham misled when he said that his wife, Sarah, was his sister: "Then Abimelech brought sheep and cattle and male and female slaves and gave them to Abraham, and he returned Sarah his wife to him. And Abimelech said, 'My land is before you; live wherever you like.' To Sarah he said, 'I am giving your brother a thousand shekels of silver. This is to cover the offense against you before all who are with you; you are completely vindicated.' Genesis 20:14–16.

[154] Genesis 14.

charge him no interest."[155] The discussion of whether collecting interest was a sin or not has lasted for millennia. In the Old Testament, there is an explicit ban on Jews collecting interest from their fellow Jews.

> Do not charge your brother interest, whether on money or food or anything else that may earn interest. You may charge a foreigner interest, but not a brother Israelite, so that the Lord your God may bless you in everything you put your hand to in the land you are entering to possess.[156]

Christians later placed this prohibition on themselves, and for a long time the collecting of interest was forbidden and publicly punished. Nevertheless, everyone had to borrow money at some point, and no one would lend without interest. And while paradoxically the Christians considered the Jews to be an unclean nation, Christian authorities allowed—or rather assigned—them to lend money with interest. This represented one of the few vocations they could pursue in medieval central Europe.

William Shakespeare leaves a famous picture of this in the play *The Merchant of Venice*, where one of the main antagonists, the Jew Shylock, wants a pound of the borrower's flesh as collateral in the event of nonpayment of a loan. In fourteenth-century Venice, Jews acted as lenders. As the economic historian Niall Ferguson notes, when Shylock says of Antonio that "Antonio is a good man," he does not have his moral quality ultimately in mind, but rather his ability to repay (despite this, residual risk is ensured—nonmonetarily—with a pound of his flesh). It was at this time when the Jews learned this trade better than anyone else. In the end, the term "bank" comes from the Italian *banci*, or the benches that Jewish lenders sat on.[157]

But the ancient Hebrews not only approached interest, but debt as a whole with caution. Aside from the previously mentioned forgiveness of debts, there were also clearly set rules setting how far one could go in setting guarantees and the nonpayment of debts. No one should become indebted to the extent that they could lose the source of their livelihood: "Do not take a pair of millstones—not even the upper one—as security for a debt, because that would be taking a man's livelihood as security."[158]

But back to the Old Testament ban on interest collection. At the time, the ban was intended as a social tool. At the time, when the poor borrowed out of necessity, they were social loans (unlike today when most of our loans are not out of necessity but out of abundance). When the poor borrowed in an emergency or need, the poor were not to be further burdened by additional interest.

---

[155] Exodus 22:25.
[156] Deuteronomy 23:19–20; also see Leviticus 25:36–37, Ezekiel 24.
[157] Ferguson, *The Ascent of Money*, 35.
[158] Deuteronomy 24:6.

If one of your countrymen becomes poor and is unable to support himself among you, help him as you would an alien or a temporary resident, so he can continue to live among you. Do not take interest of any kind from him, but fear your God, so that your countryman may continue to live among you. You must not lend him money at interest or sell him food at a profit.[159]

In the course of history, however, the role of loans changed, and the rich borrowed especially for investment purposes, just as it is in the case of Shylock and Antonio's guarantor (Antonio was a merchant whose riches were sailing somewhere out at sea). In such a case a ban on interest did not have great ethical significance. Thomas Aquinas, a medieval scholar (1225-1274), also considers similarly; in his time, the strict ban on lending with usurious interest was loosened, possibly due to him.

Today the position and significance of money and debt has gone so far and reached such a dominant position in society that operating with debts (fiscal policy) or interest or money supply (monetary policy) means that these can, to a certain extent, direct (or at least strongly influence) the whole economy and society. Money is playing not only its classical roles (as a means of exchange, a holder of value, etc.) but also a much greater, stronger role: It can stimulate, drive (or slow down) the whole economy. Money plays a national economic role. There is even one economic school that has money directly in its name: Monetarism. This school, as represented especially by Milton Friedman, teaches that the management of monetary supply is the primary means of influencing economic activity. This could only happen in a highly monetized society that has a reliance on debt and interest as one of its key characteristics.

Incidentally, banknotes and coins (or the symbolic bearers of value) do not belong to us.[160] It is the property of the national bank, and this is also why you cannot, for example, deface it (nor can you print it; here competition simply does not work).[161] What's more, you do not have the freedom not to receive money, to accept it, to respect it.

---

[159] Leviticus 25:35–37.

[160] "Because the majority of modern people must focus on the acquisition of money as their proximate goal for most of their lives, the notion arises that all happiness and all definitive satisfaction in life is firmly connected to the possession of a certain sum of money; ... But when this goal has been attained, then frequently deadly boredom and disappointment set in which are most conspicuous among business people who retreat into retired life after having saved up a certain sum. ... money reveals itself in its true character a mere means that becomes useless and unnecessary, as soon as life is concentrated on it alone it is only the bridge to definitive values, and one cannot live on a bridge." Simmel, *Simmel on Culture*, 250.

[161] Despite this, scholars such as F. A. Hayek, who will be mentioned later, wished for every institution to print its own money, and that these compete among themselves.

MONEY AS ENERGY: TIME TRAVEL AND GROSS DEBT PRODUCT (GDP)

Let us add here that condemning interest also had a strong ancient tradition, one which came from the pen of Aristotle. Aristotle condemned interest[162] not only from a moral standpoint, but also for metaphysical reasons. Thomas Aquinas shared the same fear of interest and he too argued that time does not belong to us, and that is why we must not require interest.

And it is the relationship between time and money that is very interesting. For money is something like energy that can travel through time. And it is a very useful energy, but at the same time very dangerous as well. Wherever you put this energy in a time-space continuum, wherever you plant it, something happens there. As a form of energy, money can travel in three dimensions, vertically (those who have capital lend to those who do not) and horizontally (speed and freedom in horizontal or geographic motion has become the by-product—or driving force?—of globalization). But money (as opposed to people) can also travel through time. This time-travel of money is possible precisely because of interest. Because money is an abstract construct, it is not bound by matter, space, or even time. All you need is a word, possibly written, or even a verbal promise, "Start it, I'll pay it," and you can start to build a skyscraper in Dubai. Understandably, banknotes and coins cannot travel through time. But they are only symbols, a materialization, an embodiment or incarnation of that energy. Due to this characteristic, we can energy-strip the future to the benefit of the present. Debt can transfer energy from the future to the present.[163] On the other hand, saving can accumulate energy from the past and send it to the present. Fiscal and monetary policy is no different than managing this energy.

If we shift to the present day, money's energy characteristic can be shown in such things as GDP statistics. Due to time indeterminacy, the debate on GDP growth frequently tends to be nonsensical. GDP growth

---

[162] "The most hated sort, and with the greatest reason, is usury, which makes a gain out of money itself. For money was intended to be used in exchange, but not to increase at interest . . . That is why of all modes of getting wealth this is the most unnatural." Aristotle, *Politics*, 1258a39–1258b7.

[163] With a certain amount of exaggeration, it could be said that money can do something similar to alcohol, which has a similar unique power. It cannot improve the overall mood or energy of the person in question, but it is as if it can transfer the energy from the following day. In other words, the "energy value" of the weekend is constant. It's just that a part of energy is shifted from the future (Saturday morning) to the present (Friday night). Just as with monetary debt, alcohol vacuums up energy from Saturday morning and shifts it, invests it into Friday night. And we suddenly have so much energy that we start to behave differently, not normally. We are more audacious, consume more . . . we simply have a really good time. Now money energy has a much longer reach than the weekend.

can simply be influenced with the help of debt (and either through fiscal policy in the form of deficits or budget surpluses)[164] or through the help of interest rates (monetary policy). So what sense do GDP growth statistics make in a situation with a several times larger deficit in its background? What sense does it make to measure riches if I have borrowed to acquire them?[165]

The Jews as well as Aristotle behaved very guardedly toward loans. The issue of interest/usury became one of the first economic debates. Without having an inkling of the future role of economic policy (fiscal and monetary), the ancient Hebrews may have unwittingly felt that they were discovering in interest a very powerful weapon, one that can be a good servant, but (literally) an enslaving master as well. Fiscal as well as monetary policy are powerful weapons, but they are deceitful.

It's something like a dam. When we build one, we are preventing periods of drought and flooding in the valley; we are limiting nature's whims and, to a large extent, avoiding its incalculable cycles. Using dams, we can regulate the flow of water to nearly a constant. With it we tame the river (and we can also gain energy from the dam), we acculture it—it will not be as wild, and it starts to behave as we imagine it. Respectively, it will certainly appear that way over time. But if we do not regulate the water wisely, it may happen that we would overfill the dam and it would break. For the cities lying in the valley, their end would be worse than if a dam were never there.

The management of money's energy through fiscal and monetary policy is similar. Manipulation of state budget surpluses or deficits and manipulation of the central interest rate are gifts of civilization that can serve and do great things. But if we start to use them unwisely, our end could be worse than if they were never there.

LABOR AND REST: THE SABBATH ECONOMY

As opposed to the negative connotation of work ascribed to labor (manual labor is suitable only for slaves)[166] by ancient Greeks, labor was not considered degrading in the Old Testament. On the contrary, the subjugation

---

[164] State budgets today are so large that the growth of the economy can be manipulated through their imbalance, either to activate it or slow it down.

[165] An example: If I borrow 10 percent of my income, only a true madman would argue that I am 10 percent richer, or to put it more accurately, more productive. I am not, not even by a cent. But optically my income really did grow, and I can (thanks to a loan!) spend 10 percent more.

[166] It is interesting to realize that if we understand manual labor as work for slaves, and slaves as machines, Plato wasn't so far from today's truth. Today all manual labor really is left to machines, and work needing creativity, reason, or free will decisions is reserved for people. That was Plato's notion of the function of a free person (nonslave)—intellectual activity.

of nature is even a mission from God that originally belonged to man's very first blessings.

> God blessed them and said to them, "Be fruitful and increase in number; fill the earth and subdue it. Rule over the fish of the sea and the birds of the air and over every living creature that moves on the ground."[167]

Only after man's fall does labor turn into a curse.[168] It could even be said that this is actually the only curse, the curse of the unpleasantness of labor, that the Lord places on Adam. Instead of taking care of the Garden of Eden, now "in the sweat of your face you shall eat bread."[169] A pleasant labor—people to this day tend gardens outside their homes as a hobby—suddenly becomes an unpleasant curse. If man lived in harmony with nature before, now, after the fall, he must fight; nature stands against him and he against it and the animals. From the Garden we have moved unto a (battle)field.

We can only speculate about the extent to which today, several thousand years after the writing of these lines in Genesis, we have managed to set ourselves free from this primary curse. It could be said that an essential number of people in the developed world now do not have to *eat bread in the sweat of our face*, but nevertheless it is still far from it to have pleasure from work similar to the pleasure we have in cultivating our gardens. Those who take their work in this way, it could be said, have managed to liberate themselves from this primary curse. Work was originally supposed to be something that we enjoy, that fulfills us, something that we consider pleasant, our calling.

Work is also not only a source of pleasure but a social standing; It is considered an honor. "Do you see a man skilled in his work? He will serve before kings."[170] None of the surrounding cultures appreciate work as much. The idea of the dignity of labor is unique in the Hebrew tradition.[171] And one of the most frequent blessings was: "God may bless you in all the work of your hands."[172]

Both Plato and Aristotle consider labor to be necessary for survival, but that only the lower classes should devote themselves to it so that the

---

[167] Genesis 1:28. Labor changes into something difficult after the curse in Genesis 3:17–19.

[168] Genesis 3:17–19: "To Adam he said, 'Because you listened to your wife and ate from the tree about which I commanded you, "You must not eat of it," cursed is the ground because of you; through painful toil you will eat of it all the days of your life. It will produce thorns and thistles for you, and you will eat the plants of the field. By the sweat of your brow you will eat your food until you return to the ground, since from it you were taken; for dust you are and to dust you will return.'"

[169] Genesis 3:19.

[170] Proverbs 22:29.

[171] Then in the course of history the price of labor was taken to extremes, as is the position of workers in communism, in which labor is not only highly prized but also becomes the only source of value.

[172] Deuteronomy 24:19.

elites would not have to be bothered with it and so that they could devote themselves to "purely spiritual matters—art, philosophy, and politics." Aristotle even considers labor to be "a corrupted waste of time which only burdens people's path to true honour."[173]

The Old Testament adopts a very different view on labor. It is celebrated in many passages:

> Lazy hands make a man poor, but diligent hands bring wealth.[174] (. . .) The sleep of a laborer is sweet, whether he eats little or much, but the abundance of a rich man permits him no sleep.[175] (. . .) The sluggard's craving will be the death of him, because his hands refuse to work.[176]

On the other hand, labor as a unit of production also had its limits. Despite this, labor was considered a natural human destiny. Hebrew thinking is characterized by a strict separation of the sacred from the profane. In life, there are simply areas that are holy, and in which it is not allowed to economize, rationalize, or maximize efficiency.[177] A good example is the commandment on the Sabbath. No one at all could work on this day, not even the ones who were subordinate to an observant Jew:

> Remember the Sabbath day by keeping it holy. Six days you shall labor and do all your work, but the seventh day is a Sabbath to the Lord your God. On it you shall not do any work, neither you, nor your son or daughter, nor your manservant or maidservant, nor your animals, nor the alien within your gates. For in six days the Lord made the heavens and the earth, the sea, and all that is in them, but he rested on the seventh day. Therefore the Lord blessed the Sabbath day and made it holy.[178]

Although from an economic viewpoint it was certainly possible to spend the seventh day much more productively, the message of the commandment on Saturday communicated that people were not primarily created for labor. Paradoxically, it is precisely this commandment out of all ten that is probably the most violated today. In this sense, the message of the Old Testament stands directly against Gilgamesh's reasoning, where he tries to make his subjects into *robot*-ers, who work constantly until rest is absolutely necessary. The Jewish Sabbath is not such a *necessary* rest, which is de facto just as necessary as the rest of a strained machine or an overheated saw. What are we? Machines? Must we, as the overworked saw after difficult work, *take a break* for a while so that we do not overheat, do not jam up? Do we rest only so that, after the break, we could say

---

[173] Hill, *Historical Context of the Work Ethic*, 1.
[174] Proverbs 10:4.
[175] Ecclesiastes 5:12.
[176] Proverbs 21:25.
[177] See also Eliade, *The Sacred and the Profane: The Nature of Religion* and *Cosmos and History: The Myth of the Eternal Return*.
[178] Exodus 20:8–11.

(to use the maxim from Orwell's *Animal Farm* horse called Boxer) "I will work harder!"? Is that the meaning of rest? To increase efficiency? To avoid workplace injuries?

Saturday was not established to increase efficiency. It was a real ontological break that followed the example of the Lord's seventh day of creation. Just as the Lord did not rest due to tiredness or to regenerate strength; but because He was done. He was done with His work, so that He could enjoy it, to cherish in His creation. The seventh day of creation is enjoyment. The Lord created the world in six days, and we have six days to perfect it. On Saturday, the world, as imperfect as it certainly is and with all its cracks, should *not* be perfected. Six-sevenths of time either be dissatisfied and reshape the world into your own image, man, but one-seventh you will rest and not change the creation. On the seventh day, enjoy creation and enjoy the work of your hands.

The observance of the Sabbath bears the message that the *purpose of creation was not just creating* but that it had an *end*, a *goal*. The process was just a process, not a purpose. The whole of Being was created so that we may find in it rest, accomplishment, joy. The meaning, the peak of something created, does not lie in the next creation but in the resting in the midst of all we have cocreated. Translated into economic language: The meaning of utility is not to increase it permanently but to rest among existing gains. Why do we learn how to constantly increase gains but not how to enjoy them, to realize them, to be aware of them?

This dimension has disappeared from today's economics. Economic effort has no goal at which it would be possible to rest. Today we only know growth for growth's sake, and if our company or country prospers, that does not mean a reason for rest but for more and higher performance.[179] If we believe in rest at all today, it is for different reasons. It is the rest of the exhausted machine, the rest of the weak, and the rest of those who can't handle the tempo. It's no wonder that the word "rest" is not used today (it has become almost pejorative); we say we *need a break*, or a *day off*. It is also interesting that we have days when we must not toil connected (at least lexically) with the word meaning *emptiness*: the English term "vacation" (or *emptying*), as with the French term, *les vacances*, or German *die Freizeit*, meaning *open time, free time*, but also *empty time*. As if these days were hollow, empty, well, days *off*.

When I met one of my current friends, I asked what he does, as is common in conversation. He answered me with a smile: "Nothing. I've got it all done." And he wasn't even a millionaire or a gentleman of means. I've been thinking about that ever since. Our hurrying, the economy of

---

[179] As the economist Jagdish Bhagwati accurately notes in his book *In Defense of Globalization*, 33, not long ago 2 percent GDP per year would have been considered decent growth. But now, if certain developing economies had not grown by at least 6 percent in recent years (before the crisis broke out), that would have been considered a failure.

our civilization, has no goal at which it may rest. When do we say "We're done"?

CONCLUSION: BETWEEN UTILITY AND PRINCIPLE

The influence of Jewish thought on the development of market democracy cannot be underestimated. The key heritage for us was the lack of ascetic perception of the world, respect to law and private property, but it also established the basis of our social net. The Hebrews never despised material wealth; on contrary, the Jewish faith puts great responsibility on property management. Also the idea of progress and the linear perception of time gives our (economic) life meaning—and we owe this to the Old Testament times. We have tried to show how the Torah desacralized three important areas in our lives: the earthly ruler, nature, and the concept of the hero. We have tried to show that the quest for a heaven on Earth (similar to the Jewish one) has, in its desacralized form, actually also been the same quest for many of the most distinguished economists in our history.

In this chapter we have also discussed good and evil and their relation to utility. What is the relationship between the good and evil that we do (outgoing) and the utility or disutility that we (expect to) get as a reward (incoming)? We have seen that there are two answers in Hebrew thought. Related to this, we have studied the first mention of a business cycle with the pharaoh's dream as well as seen a first attempt (that we may call Keynesian) to tackle this (natural) fluctuation. We have also seen that the Hebrews tried to explain the business cycle with morality and ethics. For the Hebrews, morality was the key driver of history.

We have devoted some time to study the principle of Sabbath rest—perhaps as a reminder that we are not here to work all the time and that there are holy places and times in life (Sabbath) where we are not allowed to maximize our productivity. In Hebrew thought, yes, we are finishers of the creation, keepers of the Garden, but as such, we are to work within limits. We have a role as finishers of creation—both specifically, but also in a more abstract ontological meaning. We have also talked about the stark difference between independent nomadic life and the civilized city. We have also spent a couple of pages looking at the history of abstract money that can travel in time as credit thanks to the instrument of charging interest. Consequently, we also looked at the history of debt and the risks that it carries with it.

A lot of Hebrew economic thought will be developed in the first chapters of the second part of this book. Here the key teaching will be integrated with other observations in the history of economic thought in an attempt to draw some conclusions.

In the next chapter, which is devoted to the ancient Greek economic ethos, we will examine two extreme approaches to laws and rules. While the Stoics considered laws to be absolutely valid, and utility had infinitesimal meaning in their philosophy, the Epicureans, at least in the usual historical explanation, placed utility and pleasure in first place—rules were to be made based on the principle of utility. It cannot be overlooked that the Hebrews managed to find something of a happy compromise between both of these principles. The Torah stands in first place and is undoubtable, but it nevertheless enables the growth of utility within limits that are set in advance—by the rules of the Torah.

3

Ancient Greece[1]

> *. . . the safest general characterization of the European philosophical*
> *tradition is that it consists of a series of footnotes to Plato.*
> Alfred Whitehead

European philosophy was born in the ancient Greek world; the foundations of Euro-Atlantic civilization, and economics as well, were inspired here in many ways. We will not be able to completely understand the development of the modern notion of economics without understanding the disputes between the Epicureans and the Stoics; it is here that the part of philosophy was born which later became an indivisible part of economics. It was the hedonism of the philosopher Epicurus that would later receive a more exact economization and more technical mathematization at the hands of J. Bentham and J. S. Mill. The foundations of rational idealization and the topic of scientific progress expressed in mathematics can be found in ancient Greece, especially in the teachings of Plato, and both helped to define the development of economics. "Plato's most important and enduring contribution to formal thought was the elevation of mathematics to a primary position in scientific inquiry. All sciences, including economics, which use mathematical analyses must comprehend the essence of Platonic idealism in order to properly evaluate the significance and limits of mathematics in their discipline."[2] But first we will look shortly at other early philosophers, and even before that at the prephilosophical, poetic ancient tradition.

FROM MYTH: THE TRUTH OF THE POETS

The poetic tradition, as culminated in Homer's *Iliad* and *Odyssey*, played a major role in the beginnings of Greek civilization. In his book *The Masters of Truth in Ancient Greece*, the Belgian historian Marcel Detienne highlights the fact that before the development of the Greek sophist and philosophical traditions, poetry played a much more important role than

---

[1] The co-author of this chapter is Lukáš Tóth, who also co-edited this book.
[2] Lowry, "Ancient and Medieval Economics," 19.

we can imagine today. This tradition, based on oral presentation and the development of complicated mnemonics, bore a completely different notion of truth and justice, and philosophy was rooted in it together with mythology and art. Only much later did the notion of *truth* "tear away" from the exclusive refuge of poets and become the domain of philosophers. So Plato does not consider poets to be "colleagues in another department, pursuing different aims, but as dangerous rivals," as Nussbaum writes.[3] The first philosophers tried to fight myths, get rid of narration, orient knowledge toward the unchanging—and take over the role of "masters of the truth" for themselves. The same thing would later be achieved by priests, theologists, and finally scientists, to whom questions on the content of truth are directed today.

What did such a "poetic" notion of truth look like in ancient Greece? This is what the poetic Muses say of themselves: "Field-dwelling shepherds, ignoble disgraces, mere bellies: we know how to say many false things similar to genuine ones, but we know, when we wish, how to proclaim true things."[4] Muses demand the right to proclaim truth (or deception). In addition, "epic and tragic poets were widely assumed to be the central ethical thinkers and teachers of Greece; nobody thought of their work as less serious, less aimed at truth, than the speculative prose treatises of historians and philosophers."[5] Truth and reality were hidden in speech, stories, and narration. Successful stories that arose from the hands of the poets were repeated, survived both their creators and their main heroes, and existed permanently in people's thoughts. Poetry is an image of reality; this is beautifully illustrated by the quote attributed to the poet Simonides: "Poetry is painting with the gift of speech."[6] But poets actually went even further, and with their speech they *shaped* and established reality and truth. Honor, adventure, great deeds, and the acclaim connected with them played an important role in the establishment of *the true, the real*. With praise from the lips of poets they achieved fame, and those who are famous will be remembered by people. They become more real, part of the story, and they start to be "realized," "made real" in the lives of other people. That which is stored in memory is real; that which is forgotten is as if it never existed.

Truth did not always have today's "scientific" form. Today's scientific truth is founded on the notion of exact and objective facts, but poetic truth stands on an interior (emotional) consonance with the story or poem. "It is not addressed first to the brain . . . [myth] talks directly to the feeling system."[7] If a poet writes "she was like a flower," from a scientific

---

[3] Nussbaum, *The Fragility of Goodness: Luck and Ethics in Greek Tragedy and Philosophy*, 12.
[4] Hesiod, *Theogony*, 25.
[5] Nussbaum, *The Fragility of Goodness: Luck and Ethics in Greek Tragedy and Philosophy*, 12.
[6] Detienne, *The Masters of Truth in Archaic Greece*, 128 in Czech translation, original citation comes from Psellos, M.: *Energeias Daimonon*, 821B, Migne, PG, CXXII.
[7] ". . . after which the brain might come along with its interesting comments," the quote continues. Campbell, *Myths to Live By*, 88. In later chapters we will try to show that even

point of view he is lying; every poet is a liar. The human female has almost nothing in common with a plant—and what little it does have in common is not worth mentioning. Despite this, the poet could be right and not the scientist. Ancient philosophy, just as science would later, tries to find constancy, constants, quantities, inalterabilities. Science seeks (creates?) order and neglects everything else as much as it can. In their own experiences, everyone knows that life is not like that, but what happens if the same is true for reality in general? In the end, poetry could be more sensitive to the truth than the philosophical method or, later, the scientific method. "Tragic poems, in virtue of their subject matter and their social function, are likely to confront and explore problems about human beings and luck that a philosophical text might be able to omit or avoid."[8]

Just as scientists do today, artists drew images of the world that were representative, and therefore symbolic, picturelike, and simplifying (but thus also misleading), just like scientific models, which often do not strive to be "realistic." Throughout its tradition, painting has been the art of illusion, the art of "pointing out," and so, from a different angle, "misleading." It is in art, as the author of *Dissoi logoi* says, where those who mislead "in such a way as to make most things similar to the real ones" are the best.[9]

But poets have their truth. The Greeks believed that the muses can reveal the hidden truth and see the future: "They breathed a divine voice into me, so that I might glorify what will be,"[10] Hesiod writes. At the same time, let us note that for Greeks the privileged time for truth revelation (*aletheia*) was mainly sleep: "She invented dreams which told the future freely, though, it would seem, confusedly."[11] We have already encountered something similar in the Hebrew thought, when Pharaoh sees the future in a dream and Joseph predicts the business cycle. But the dream, or an imitation of a dreamlike state, is also the beginning of the scientific method of René Descartes. He used the dream (detachment from senses) as a method of seeing pure truth. We will get to this in later chapters.

Speaking of Descartes, it seems that he was searching for a different sort of the truth. He was looking for the *stable truth*, truth that is free from doubts.[12] Furthermore, he even seems to be aware of that, as his major

---

today this internal "harmony with the story" (or model, with assumptions, conclusions, paradigms, etc.) also plays a major role in today's economics and in science in general.

[8] Nussbaum, *The Fragility of Goodness: Luck and Ethics in Greek Tragedy and Philosophy*, 13.

[9] Detienne, *The Masters of Truth in Archaic Greece*, 128, in Czech translation.

[10] Hesiod, *Theogony*, 28 and 38.

[11] Euripides, *The Iphigenia in Tauris*, 92. Or 1240: "[T]hen Earth produced the Dreams, nocturnal apparitions, and these to mortal multitudes divined things primeval, things of the time of telling, and what she would bring to pass." See 1261 nn and 1278. See also "All too prophetic, out of dreamland came/The vision, meting out our sire's estate!" Aeschylus, *The Seven against Thebes*, from *The Complete Greek Drama*, vol. 1, 109.

[12] "I ought to reject as absolutely false all opinions in regard to which I could suppose the least ground for doubt. . . . I considered that all objects that had ever entered into my mind when awake, had in them no more truth than the illusions of my dreams." Descartes, *Discourse on the Method*, part 4, 28.

book is called *Discourse on the Method of Rightly Conducting One's Reason and of Seeking the Truth in the Sciences*. Descartes was searching for truth in sciences *only*. He was searching for *doxa*. The truth of the poets seems to be *alethia*, a different sort of truth. That truth is, on the contrary, fleeting, irrational, and dreamlike.

Poet Economists

Hesiod, one of the greatest and at the same time last leaders of the Greek poetic tradition who lived around hundred years before the first famous philosopher Thales, can be considered to be the first economist ever.[13] He examined such things as the problem of scarcity of resources, and, stemming from that, the need for their effective allocation. His explanation of the existence of scarcity is thoroughly poetic. According to him, the gods sent shortage down on humanity as a punishment for Prometheus's acts:

> [T]he gods keep the means of life concealed from human beings. Otherwise you would easily be able to work in just one day so as to have enough for a whole year even without working, and quickly you would store the rudder above the smoke, and the work of the cattle and of the hard-working mules would be ended. But Zeus concealed it, angry in his heart because crooked-counselled Prometheus had deceived him.[14]

Hesiod's explanation is very interesting and we see something very fundamental in this "analysis" (we will get back to this later): the archetype of human labor.

According to Hesiod, labor is humans' fate, virtue, and the source of all good. Those who do not work deserve nothing but scorn. People and the gods alike hate the lazy, who are "like the stingless drones that waste the labour of the bees, eating it without working."[15] Aside from being the first attempt at an analysis of human labor, Hesiod's *Works and Days* is interesting for us as contemporary economists especially in its criticism of usury, which centuries later resonates in the works of Plato and Aristotle, as we will see later in this chapter.

First Philosophers

Economic topics did not play a main role in the teachings of the Greeks too often, either in poetry or philosophy. But Thales, who was considered

---

[13] "The honour of being the first Greek economic thinker goes to the poet Hesiod, a Boeotian who lived in the very early ancient Greece of the middle of the eighth century BC. . . . Of the 828 verses in the poem [*Works and Days*], the first 383 centred on the fundamental economic problem of scarce resources for the pursuit of numerous and abundant human ends and desires." Rothbard, *Economic Thought before Adam Smith: Austrian Perspectives on the History of Economic Thought*, 8.

[14] Hesiod, *Works and Days*, 42–49.

[15] Ibid., 305.

the first Greek philosopher ever, made his living as a trader. He is marked as the author of "evidence that he is able to win even in commercial competition, if he wants to show his [philosophical] superiority over it. He allegedly predicted a bad olive crop and used this to gain wealth, so as to show how easy and narrow-minded pursuit it was."[16] In ancient Greece, economic affairs are therefore, from the first philosopher, considered to be subordinate to all things spiritual. Economic considerations, as opposed to philosophical considerations, already have in their essence a quite limited subject of interest. Philosophical reflection in economic considerations is therefore justified and desired. This is what Thales tried to show in his "olive business." Philosophy is not empty speech but an endeavor with widespread practical impacts. Thales was involved in philosophy not because he could not make a living otherwise, but because in its essence it offered the widest horizons for consideration. For this reason philosophy was considered to be the queen of the "sciences" in ancient Greek philosophy. With a bit of exaggeration, we could argue the exact opposite of today's world. Philosophy to us often seems to be an unnecessary icing on the cake, a useless endeavor that never solves anything—so unlike economics!

Numerical Mystics

The key ideas of the original Ionian philosophic tradition have strongly inspired economic science. The Ionian tradition created the search for *one*(!) *original* principle of all things. For us, one of the most inspiring philosophers is Pythagoras, who beheld the essence of the world in the numerical proportions of its forms. He argued that "number is the essence of things."[17] "As such, it has magical force," for the speculations of the Pythagoreans about numbers "not only had an intellectual nature, but were also permeated by a mystical significance."[18] "Number is the essence of things—Everything is a number. When the question is asked whether such language is to be understood in literal or symbolic sense, here the highest authorities are at issue."[19] Aristoxen, Pythagoras's student noted that Pythagoras "diverted the study of numbers from mercantile practice, and compared everything to numbers."[20] Interestingly for us economists, "Aristoxen implies that it was this commercial insight which gave birth to the project of discovering the true 'measure' of everything . . . he claims

---

[16] Kratochvíl, *Filosofie mezi mýtem a vědou od Homéra po Descarta* [Philosophy between Myth and Science from Homer to Descartes], 53.

[17] See Aristotle, *Metaphysics*, 986a1–987b30: "Pythagoreans . . . supposed the element of numbers to be the elements of all things . . . they say that the things themselves are numbers."

[18] Bunt, Jones, and Bedient, *The Historical Roots of Elementary Mathematics*, 82.

[19] Mahan, *A Critical History of Philosophy*, Volume 1, 241.

[20] Aristoxen of Stobaia, 58 B 2. See Guthrie, *A History of Greek Philosophy*, Volume I, 177.

that the comparison of everything with numbers began from economic and commercial observations."[21] If this is true, then it wasn't mathematics that served as an inspiration for economists, but the other way around.

It is also interesting that the Pythagoreans, similar to the Hebrews and other nations, created numerical mysticism.[22] Incidentally, the leading logician and mathematician of the first half of the last century, Bertrand Russell, sees precisely the combination of mysticism and science (at which the Pythagoreans excelled)[23] as the key to achieving philosophical perfection. For Pythagoras, a number[24] was not just a mere quantity, the count of something; it is also a *quality*, which should become a means of describing the principle of a harmonized world, the *cosmos*.[25] And this teaching later, through Plato, entered the mainstream of European scientific consideration. "Plato was basically elaborating the ideas of the secret Pythagorean societies. They held that the world was a rational entity built by the 'great Geometer' from the basic unit; that is, the point or the 'one.'"[26] The Pythagoreans were the first to consider the possibilities of reducing the world to numerical form. We will see later just how much this would be an inspirational approach for twentieth-century economists.

As opposed to his contemporaries, Heraclitus envisaged reality as being nonstationary. Unmovability, unemotiveness, and staticness were at his time synonyms for perfection and divinity. The efforts of economists to involve a constantly changing reality with abstract, *unchanging* principles certainly go this far back. Heraclitus's world was, on the other hand, paradoxically held together by antithetical forces as in *the bow and lyre*.[27] Harmony is created from the antithetical and discordant, and it is realized as motion.

---

[21] Harris, *The Reign of the Whirlwind*, 80.

[22] Just for illustration, here are a couple of examples of what such mathematical mysticism looked like originally: Love and friendship, something of an expression of harmony, has the same number as an octave in music, or the number 8. The essence of health is the number 7. Justice is given a 4 because it relates to revenge, which should equate to crime; a wedding is defined according to the founders of mathematics with the number 3; space is 1. This mysticism later became the foundation of the old books of dreams. See Rádl, *Dějiny Filosofie: Starověk a středověk* [History of Philosophy: Ancient and Medieval], 89. See also Kirk, Raven, and Schofield, *The Presocratic Philosophers*, chapter 7.

[23] In his essay "Mysticism and Logic," Bertrand Russell shows how the ancient Greeks thought scientifically and combined scientific observation with their mystic conceptions. Russell, *Mysticism and Logic and Other Essays*, 20.

[24] Pythagoras was also the first to come up with the concept of *irrational numbers*. Isn't that an interesting name for this group of numbers? After all, we frequently consider numbers to be the most rational possible representation of anything. Can we consider ourselves as objective and rational beings in anything, if something as absolute as a number can seem irrational only because it in some way resists our everyday experience, only because it falls among the irrational numbers and cannot be used for such things as counting sheep?

[25] Pythagoras used the term *cosmos* as one of the first among philosophers. So he did with the term *philosophy*.

[26] Lowry, "Ancient and Medieval Economics," 19.

[27] Herakleitos, B51.

Now, Parmenides, a philosopher of the schools of Elea, could be a certain antithesis to Heraclitus. This priest of Apollo also considers the world that we perceive with our senses as constantly changing and flowing, but he marks it as *unreal*. What is *real*, according to him, comprises only processes of reason, abstract thoughts that are stable and unchanging. From this standpoint, truth lies in the area of ideas or theories. The imperfect empirical world (the world of phenomena), which suffers at the hands of constant changes, is not the arena of truth; the truth is in the abstract. The real empirical world is not *real*—for it to be real a mental model must be forged, and the changing world "put to death" in order to "stabilize" the idea.

Parmenides could therefore be considered a predecessor to the Socratic and Platonic philosophies of ideal forms, which among other things greatly influenced economics (as well as physics and other scientific disciplines) and laid the foundation for the creation of models as stable abstract constructions considered by many to be *more real than reality*. Modern science in effect constantly flows between the Parmenidean and Heraclitean notions of the world. On the one hand, it creates models as reconstructions of reality, or assumes that reality *can* be reconstructed, and thus implies its permanence in some sense at least. On the other hand, many scientists see rational models only as "untrue, unreal" crutches, which should help with predictions of the future in an ever-changing, dynamic reality.

XENOPHON: MODERN ECONOMICS FOUR HUNDRED YEARS BEFORE CHRIST

We can find the pinnacle of ancient political economics in the works of the economist Xenophon, who was also a philosopher, albeit an average one. In his texts, this Athenian described the economic phenomena that modern economists laboriously rediscovered only in the nineteenth century, more than two thousand years after his death, and despite the fact that "as late as the 18th century his 'Ways and Means' was studied for its practical analysis of economics and administrative problems."[28] In-depth and straightforward economic considerations have been with us from the beginnings of philosophy and Greek-European culture. Xenophon's economic analyses are no more superficial than Smith's.

Xenophon, Plato's contemporary, divided most of his ideas on economics into two books, *Oeconomicus* and *De vectigalibus* (*On Revenues*, which is sometimes called *Ways and Means*). The first of these deals with the principles of good household management, and the second advises Athens on how to increase revenues in the state's coffers and

---

[28] Lowry, *Archaeology of Economic Ideas*, 46.

be more prosperous. Without major exaggeration, it can be said that Xenophon wrote the very first stand-alone textbooks for micro- and macroeconomics. Incidentally, Aristotle also wrote a book called *Economics* (*Oeconomica*),[29] in which he reacts to Hesiod's *Works and Days*. Aristotle's book is more a tract on the management of housekeeping—the dominant part of the book deals with relations between husbands and wives, and especially the role of women. The book overall gives the impression that it was written for women, since a "good wife should be the mistress of her home"[30] because she is more likely to take care of the household's indoors, while the husband is, according to Aristotle, "less adapted for quiet pursuits but well constituted for outdoor activities."[31]

But back to Xenophon. In his book *On Revenues*, he exhorts Athenians to *maximize* the state's treasury and advises on how to achieve it. However, he does not advise nationalization or wartime maneuvers as the best path to achieving maximum tax revenues. He considered the expansion of Athens's trade activities as more appropriate, which at the time was truly a revolutionary idea, one that had to be rediscovered only much later. He calls for the stimulation of Athenian citizens' economic activity, and especially that of immigrants, for whom he proposes the foundation of a "board of Guardians of Aliens."[32] Together with the construction of homes for immigrants, such a board would increase not only their numbers but also their *goodwill*, and with that Athens's economic strength:

> [T]hat too would add to the loyalty of the aliens, and probably all without a city would covet the right of settling in Athens, and would increase our revenues. . . . If, moreover, we granted the resident aliens the right to serve in the cavalry and various other privileges which it is proper to grant them, I think that we should find their loyalty increase and at the same time should add to the strength and greatness of the state.[33]

Xenophon did not take wealth and prosperity in the context of a zerosum game,[34] as was common at the time, but in the relatively modern sense of common gains from trade. Increased trade activity by foreigners brings benefits to all of Athens; foreigners are not getting rich at our expense but are on the contrary enriching their environs. Therefore, he proposed approaching the stimulation of foreign trade and investment:

> It would also be an excellent plan to reserve front seats in the theatre for merchants and shipowners, and to offer them hospitality occasionally, when the high quality of their ships and merchandise entitles them to be considered benefactors of the state. With the prospect of these honours before

---

[29] Modern scholars sometimes ascribe this work to Theophrastus, a student of Aristotle.
[30] Aristotle, *Economics*, 1353b27.
[31] Ibid., 1344a3.
[32] Xenophon, *Ways and Means*, 2.7.
[33] Ibid., 2.4–7.
[34] Game where gain is possible only if someone else ends up worse off by the same amount.

them they would look on us as friends and hasten to visit us to win the honour as well as the profit.[35]

Xenophon reveals himself to be a highly talented and forward-thinking economist who takes into account human motivation and the businessman's desire for the feeling of being exceptional, which frequently plays a role in today's economies as well.

From the point of view of contemporary economics, Xenophon's theory of value is also very interesting; modern economists would label it the subjective theory of value. Its essence is probably best seen in the following excerpt from Xenophon's text of an imaginary conversation between Socrates and Critobulus:

> "We now see that to persons who don't understand its use, a flute is wealth if they sell it, but not wealth if they keep it instead of selling."
>
> "Yes, Socrates, and our argument runs consistently, since we have said that what is profitable is wealth. For a flute, if not put up for sale, is not wealth, because it is useless: if put up for sale it becomes wealth."
>
> "Yes," commented Socrates, "provided he knows how to sell; but again, in case he sells it for something he doesn't know how to use, even then the sale doesn't convert it into wealth, according to you."
>
> "You imply, Socrates, that even money isn't wealth to one who doesn't know how to use it."
>
> "And you, I think, agree with me to this extent, that wealth is that from which a man can derive profit. At any rate, if a man uses his money to buy a mistress who makes him worse off in body and soul and estate, how can his money be profitable to him then?"
>
> "By no means, unless we are ready to maintain that the weed called nightshade, which drives you mad if you eat it, is wealth."
>
> "Then money is to be kept at a distance, Critobulus, if one doesn't know how to use it, and not to be included in wealth."[36]

It can be seen in Critobulus's example with the flute that Xenophon was aware of the further essential distinction between *value in use* and *value in exchange*,[37] on which Aristotle, John Locke, and Adam Smith would later base their theories.

We will stay with Adam Smith for a moment. One of his greatest contributions to modern economics was the analysis of the division of labor and the increasing importance of specialization for the development and rationalization of production processes. Xenophon took note of the importance of the division of labor more than two thousand years before

---

[35] Xenophon, *Ways and Means*, 3.4.

[36] Xenophon, *Oeconomicus*, 1.11–14.

[37] Value in use indicates the utility of consuming a good. Value in exchange is based on the relative rarity of the given good. Water, for example, has a high value in use, because we cannot live without it. But its value in exchange (its market price, for example) is low, because there is a lot of water.

Adam Smith. He also put it in the context of the size of the community where this division takes place.

> In a small city the same man must make beds and chairs and ploughs and tables, and often build houses as well; and indeed he will be only too glad if he can find enough employers in all his trades to keep him. Now it is impossible that a single man working at a dozen crafts can do them all well; but in the great cities, owing to the wide demand for each particular thing, a single craft will suffice for a means of livelihood, and often enough even a single department of that; there are shoe-makers who will only make sandals for men and others only for women. Or one artisan will get his living merely by stitching shoes, another by cutting them out, a third by shaping the upper leathers, and a fourth will do nothing but fit the parts together. Necessarily the man who spends all his time and trouble on the smallest task will do that task the best.[38]

In many ways, Xenophon was ahead of his time and its greatest thinkers. As Todd Lowry writes, "Plato should have had no idea of that connection between the size of the market and the degree of division of labor which Adam Smith was to make famous. Plato's contemporary, Xenophon, however, who gives in his *Cyropaedia* a similar account of the division of labor, seems to have gone a little further in his appreciation of the nature of private exchange, for he distinguishes between the big cities in which division of labor is developed and the small cities in which it hardly exists."[39]

Limits of Future and Calculating

Xenophon, this brilliant economist, who among other things dealt with the issue of utility and the maximization of yield,[40] also clearly set limits for his analyses. He was very modest about the possibility of predicting economic success or failure at a time when agriculture played a much more essential role in the economy than it does today. According to this ancient economist, "in husbandry a man can rely very little on forecast. For hailstorms and frosts sometimes, and droughts and rains and blight ruin schemes well planned and well carried out."[41] At the same time he showed awareness that economic events must be placed in cultural contexts, and that as a subject of analysis they can never be entirely separated from the real world, which is governed not only by the laws of supply and demand.

---

[38] Xenophon, *The Education of Cyrus*, 7, C.2, 5.
[39] Lowry, *Archaeology of Economic Ideas*, 90.
[40] "keep down the cost of administration . . . and invest the balances over and above that amount . . . so that the investment will bring in the largest revenue." Xenophon, *Ways and Means*, 4.40.
[41] Xenophon, *Oeconomicus*, 5.18.

In *On Revenues* Xenophon closes with the words that in various forms we know from history as the *Conditio Jacobaea*,[42] a kind of opposite to today's economic mantra, *ceteris paribus* (all other things being equal): "[I]f you decide to go forward with the plan, I should advise you to send to Dodona and Delphi, and inquire of the gods whether such a design is fraught with wealth for the state both now and in days to come."[43] According to Xenophon, not even the best economic advice and analysis can contain all the relevant factors, whether they're called the *will of Heavens* or *animal spirits* or anything else.

Xenophon dealt with a very wide scope of economic considerations. His ideas include work with such phenomena as, for example, the relation between employment and price,[44] innovation,[45] and "state" infrastructure investment.[46] As we have seen above, he deals in detail with specialization, offers a lot of advice on both the micro and macro levels, examines the favorable effect of incentives for "foreign investors," and so on. To a certain extent, it could be said that his economic scope is wider and in many ways deeper than Adam Smith's considerations.

And lastly, one final thought to which we will return later: Xenophon's reflection on the satiability of real desires is interesting, but more so the

---

[42] From the New Testament, James 4:13–17. "Now listen, you who say, 'Today or tomorrow we will go to this or that city, spend a year there, carry on business and make money.' Why, you do not even know what will happen tomorrow. What is your life? You are a mist that appears for a little while and then vanishes. Instead, you ought to say, 'If it is the Lord's will, we will live and do this or that.' As it is, you boast and brag. All such boasting is evil. Anyone, then, who knows the good he ought to do and doesn't do it, sins." This means the effort to place all events in relation to the wider context of the world. Not to divide the future and the acts that lead to it from events in the cosmos.

[43] Xenophon, *Ways and Means*, 6.2.

[44] "An increase in the number of coppersmiths, for example, produces a fall in the price of copper work, and the coppersmiths retire from business. The same thing happens in the iron trade. Again, when corn and wine are abundant, the crops are cheap, and the profit derived from growing them disappears, so that many give up farming and set up as merchants or shopkeepers or moneylenders." Ibid., 4.6.

[45] "If (. . .) trade or commerce is advantageous to the common-wealth; if he were to be most honoured, who applied himself with the greatest diligence to trade, the number of merchants would be increased in proportion. And if it were publicly made known, that he who should discover a new method of increasing the public revenue, without detriment to individuals, should be well rewarded; neither would this kind of speculation be so much neglected." Xenophon, *Hiero*, 19.

[46] "I have now explained what regulations I think should be introduced into the state in order that every Athenian may receive sufficient maintenance at the public expense. Some may imagine that enough money would never be subscribed to provide the huge amount of capital necessary, according to their calculations, to finance all these schemes. But even so they need not despair. For it is not essential that the plan should be carried out in all its details . . . whatever the number of houses built, or of ships constructed, or of slaves purchased, they will immediately prove a paying concern. In fact in one respect it will be even more profitable to proceed gradually than to do everything at once . . . by proceeding as our means allow, we can repeat whatever is well conceived and avoid the repetition of mistakes." Xenophon, *Ways and Means*, 4.33–37.

insatiability of the abstract, monetary ones (as expressed in silver at the time): "Neither is silver like furniture, of which a man never buys more when once he has got enough for his house. No one ever yet possessed so much silver as to want no more; if a man finds himself with a huge amount of it, he takes as much pleasure in burying the surplus as in using it."[47]

PLATO: BEARER OF THE VECTOR

Socrates and Plato[48] are undoubtedly among the founders of our culture's philosophical tradition, and to a certain extent they demarcated and essentially formed the boundaries of the entire discipline for thousands of years to come (and it is still a question whether we will ever get beyond their framework). With Socrates, his student Plato, and Plato's student Aristotle, these three generations' ideas started questions and disputes that continue in our civilization to this day.

We are still not clear on whether or not to give preference to the rational or the empirical, whether the Platonic ideal exists, or whether all structures are a human creation, as Aristotle argued. It was the ancient Greek tradition that endowed us with the heritage of this eternal search; no such duality was created in the Hebrew or Sumerian traditions, for example. "Know thyself," the sentence which Alexander Pope ironizes in his own way, was carved into the Temple of Apollo at Delphi. And the same phrase returned to us in the popular film *The Matrix*: It hangs above the Oracle's door right in the first part, and it summarizes the message the Oracle has for the hero, Neo: "Know thyself. I can't tell you anything about you."

In a Cave of the Real

Plato plays a huge part in the way we think today, which questions we ask, and how we answer them. The second legacy, which is key for us, is the idea of abstraction from the world. In reference to Parmenides, Plato strengthens the rational tradition, founded on the idea that the world is best known through reason. In his best-known parable of the cave, he lays the foundation for a completely different perception of the world: This world is not the main world but a world of shadows, a secondary world. "It follows by unquestioned necessity that this world is an image of something."[49] Plato thus opens the door to a nearly mystical reticence

---

[47] Xenophon, *Ways and Means*, 4.7.
[48] We will no longer distinguish between these two thinkers. Socrates himself wrote nothing, and all we know of his ideas comes from Plato's version. It is therefore difficult to distinguish between Plato and Socrates, so philosophers frequently distance themselves from this. We will follow this custom as well. For more see Kahn, *Plato and the Socratic Dialogue*.
[49] Plato, *Timaeus*, 29b.

toward this world, to asceticism, and to the beginnings of faith in abstract rational theories. The truth is not clear, is not before our eyes but is instead *hidden*. And rationality is the path to this (unchanging) truth. The very first topic of the later ancient Greeks was getting rid of variability and irregularity. The goal was to cut through the confusing and variable empirical world toward unchanging and constant (therefore "real") rational truths.

But back to the parable of the cave. In it, Plato describes a prisoner who lives his entire life bound in a cave and who does not see real things but only their shadow reflections on the walls. He considers these to be real, studies them, and learnedly discusses their essence, even without having any idea of the existence of something else: "the prisoners would in every way believe that the truth is nothing other than the shadows of those artifacts."[50]

These "experts" are *guessers of shadows*. With this, Plato probably wanted to say that empirical phenomena only *appear* and do not capture the essence of things, *reality*, which can ultimately only be approached through abstract considerations and model rationalizations. For *enlightenment*, we must be freed of the bonds that connect us to this empirical world, step out from the cave,[51] and see things as they really are. A person who could would gain his vision after being blinded by the light when leaving the cave, and see *real* things, the *way* reality really is "he'd be pained and dazzled and unable to see the things whose shadows he'd seen before."[52] If he were to go back to the cave (which to me appears to be the main message of the parable) and tell the prisoners who were accustomed only to their shadows about real things, they would not believe him and would not accept him. This fate, for example, awaited Plato's great teacher Socrates.[53]

Invariability was the leading light for Plato. He tried to draw attention away from variable (and therefore ephemeral) things or phenomena. According to Plato, the tracks of truth (or if you prefer, the structure, the equation, or the matrix)[54] of this world lie somewhere deep within us, where they are written even before we are born. If we were to search for them, it would suffice to turn to our own interiors. Searching for truth in

---

[50] Plato, *The Republic*, 7, 515c.

[51] Or from television. In a certain sense, the televised version of reality is only a shadow of reality. A person who gets up from the television and starts to see things as they are is frequently disappointed, and after a long period of comfort "ruins his eyes."

[52] Plato, *The Republic*, 7, 515c.

[53] "[I]f he had to compete again with the perpetual prisoners in recognizing the shadows, wouldn't he invite ridicule? Wouldn't it be said of him that he'd returned from his upward journey with his eyesight ruined and that it isn't worthwhile even to try to travel upwards? And, as for anyone who tried to free them and lead them upward, if they could somehow get their hands on him, wouldn't they kill him?" Plato, *The Republic*, 7, 517a.

[54] The film *The Matrix* develops this idea in detail: We are slaves (used for generating energy) who see (colorful) shadows that are projected by someone.

the outside world is misleading and distracting, because it leads us to a path of following and examining shadows (the path Aristotle apparently took; see below). It is possible to take in real things—but not with our eyes or other senses, which can be fooled—but through *reason*.[55] Popper summarizes Plato's key teaching in the following manner: "He believed that to every kind of ordinary or decaying thing there corresponds also a perfect thing that does not decay. This belief in perfect and unchanging things, usually called the 'Theory of Forms or Ideas,' became the central doctrine of his philosophy."[56]

Thus the rationalist tradition was founded, which eventually gained an important standing in economics as well. It is precisely this logic, which tries *rationally* to uncover the principle of reality and forms model behavior. The tendency to fit the "real" world into mathematical models and exact, constant, valid-here-and-everywhere curves is noticeable in economics to this day.

But it is important to say here that Descartes, generally considered to be the founder of modern science, ties into Plato: He does not search for the truth in the outside world, but in interior meditation, looking inside oneself, freeing oneself from the fooling of the senses, memory, and other sensations or their records. Descartes found the truth by way of dreaming, freed from the (disappointing) senses, alone with his rationality. Descartes will play an important role in our story, and we will get to him later.

Myth as a Model, Model as a Myth

According to Plato, a hierarchy of being and a hierarchy of knowledge exist, knowledge of ideas rests at the top, while at the bottom lies knowledge of trickery, illusions, shadows dancing on cave walls. By the way, mathematical knowledge is not in the highest position; philosophical knowledge is. Mathematics can't describe the whole truth—even if we were to describe the entire world in precise mathematical equations, we would not have full knowledge. (More on this in the final chapters.) Incidentally, the ability to describe the functioning of things still does not mean that we understand the given relationship.

This is why Plato uses myths and considers them as a potential means of discovering the truth. The *fuzziness* (they are not exact) of myths is a *strength*, an *advantage*, not a disadvantage. As a form of expression, myth has a much larger "frame" or reach than the "exact scientific" or mathematical

---

[55] We are born into this world with imprinted ideas that we must discover, and which themselves are objective. In the dialogue *Protagoras*, Plato criticizes ungoverned subjectivism coined in the winged comment ascribed to the eponymous philosopher: "Man is the measure of all things." Plato, *Protagoras, 361c*. In Plato's world, we do not *learn* anything new; we only *discover* everything within ourselves we already knew.

[56] Popper, *The Open Society and Its Enemies*, volume 1, *The Spell of Plato*, 19.

approach. Myth reaches places where science and mathematics cannot, and it can contain the dynamics of a constantly changing world. What is interesting is that a modern person has the opposite tendency: to take his assistance from mathematics or other precise methods if he is heading out to the difficult places where senses cannot tread. The word *method* (*meta-hodos*) means "along the way," but also "beyond the way." Method should be a guiding light for a (frequently erstwhile) precise approach to avoid getting lost, or losing one's way in this mental exercise, which goes so far that the natural light of our intuition or of our sense experience is not enough.

Myth is of course an abstraction—a model, a parable, a story (even if a mathematical one). Perhaps these concepts can be joined together if we approach it differently and suggest that science creates myths around these facts, namely, its theories. We do not see facts physically; we see that which we interpret to be their expressions. In the end, we all see the sun "rise"—but why, how, and for what purpose is up for interpretation. Here is where the story, the narrative, comes in.

According to Plato, the secrets of the world can be understood only through the construction of a "higher order," which is something of a metanarrative, or a generally accepted myth, an archetype, a civilizational story or model, or, if you prefer, a matrix (the matrix), which lies above us (or in us?). Above the lower constructs stand philosophical truths—forms derived from the utmost ideas of Good. According to Plato, the functionality of mathematical definitions and derivations from them is guaranteed, because they exist *beyond us* and we gradually reveal it—we do not shape it. Models *reveal* the invisible laws of being.

It would appear that Aristotle's view of this principle of abstraction fundamentally differs: "Reflecting a fundamental disagreement with Plato, Aristotle argued that ideas do not exist independently, but that 'universals are reached from particulars.'"[57] Of course, one possible reading of Aristotle could be that the abstract construct does not stand *beyond* us, one we can not only come to understand (the notion that we approach it closer and closer as our knowledge grows), but we (co)create it.

The contemporary economist Deirdre McCloskey at the same time finds the intercept point of the foundations of mathematics and religion in Plato's good, in the faith in God as a principle of all things:

> The mathematicians Philip Davis and Reuben Hersh note that 'underlying both mathematics and religion there must be a foundation of faith which the individual must himself supply.' Mathematicians, they observe, are practising neo-Platonists and followers of Spinoza. Their worship of mathematics parallels the worship of God. Both God and the Pythagorean theorem, for example, are believed to exist independent of the physical world; and both give it meaning.[58]

---

[57] Nelson, *Reaching for Heaven on Earth*, 34–35, about Aristotle, *Nicomachean Ethics*, trans. T. Irwin (Indianapolis: Hackett Publishing, 1985), 166.
[58] McCloskey, *The Bourgeois Virtues*, 152, about Davis and Hersch: *Descartes' Dream*.

Religion in the Platonic world[59] is not mutually exclusive with mathematics and science; instead they complement each other—they mutually require each other. Standing behind both is faith in some principle that watches over all and without which one or the other does not make sense.[60] In the words of Michal Polanyi, the twentieth-century philosopher, even science is "a system of beliefs to which we are committed."[61] "Faith is not an attack on science or a turn to superstition";[62] on the contrary, faith stands at the foundations of all science and all knowledge, for example, the elementary faith that the world is knowable. Myth, a faith in something unproven which we even sometimes *know* is not real (assumptions in economics, for example), starts to play a role as a superstructure.

Here the question arises about how much of economics is mythmaking; respectively, how many myths does it need or draw from? Economics considers itself to be in the best position to interpret the social world of our time, but we are finding that it needs myth for this role. Economics uses myth in several regards or several ways. First, it draws from myth in its assumptions (the unconscious use of myth), and second it creates myths and stories. The model of homo economicus is such a myth-model. That a story is told by clouding it in mathematical fleece changes nothing about its mysticism. As an example, take the myths and stories about the complete rationality and assumptions like perfect information, or the invisible hand of the market, but also the story of human freedom and self-determination, or the myth of eternal progress or self-balancing markets. Nobody ever saw any of these, but they are stories, faiths, or myths that strongly resonate (not only) in economics. And our disputes, experiments, and statistics lead to the confirmation or overturning of these narratives.

There is nothing derogatory or shameful about myths. We cannot exist without faith in the unproven. But one must admit it and work with it as such. Only a myth can be set against another myth. Myth does not lead a fight with empiricism, with the real world (which revels in a large number of myths), but with other adepts at explanation, with other myths.

The Greeks did not take their myths "literally," they were acknowledged as myths. And as Sallust writes about myth, "Now these things never happened, but always are."[63] We know, as well as our ancestors knew, that we speak here of myths, fictions—not "realistic," literal *images*

---

[59] Deirdre McCloskey goes even further on the beautiful verbal similarity between "Good" and "God" with a reference to Plato's allegory of the sun illuminating our thoughts and bringing them closer to understanding Good. A convinced Christian would certainly prefer the rephrasing "Sun of Good" to "Son of God." See McCloskey, *The Bourgeois Virtues*, 365.
[60] Something similar is indicated in the catchphrase of mathematicians and physicists related to the statistical interpretation of coincidences: *God does not play dice.*
[61] Polanyi, *Personal Knowledge*, 171.
[62] McCloskey, *The Bourgeois Virtues*, 153.
[63] Sallust, *On the Gods and the World*, part 4.

or *representations*[64] of "objective" reality (even if one happens to believe that there is such a thing).

Now, this may seem a little strange to us, but we do exactly the same thing today. The question is placed before economists: Do we *truly* believe in our models? Do we believe that man is *truly* rational, narrowly egoistic, that markets regulate themselves and that the invisible hand of the market exists, or are these just myths? Both answers are possible, but then we must not get them confused. If we say, perhaps together with Milton Friedman,[65] that models and their assumptions are unrealistic[66]—for example, the assumption that man is rational—then we cannot say or create ontological-theological conclusions that man is *truly* rational in reality. If our models (whether in assumptions or conclusions) are admitted fictions (useful or not), then they do not imply *anything about man*.

On the other hand, if we think that our models are realistic, then we *believe in* our model-myths. And we are in the captivity of an undeclared myth even more than our archaic predecessors. The ancients took their myths with a grain of salt; they were useful fictions for them, abstractions, stories that never *actually happened*, but were useful for explaining things, for humans' orientation in the world and frequently also for practical activity.

Economists must decide; both are not possible.

Flee from the Body and Its Demand

Plato had no, or very little, regard for the body. Plato calls bodily pleasures "so-called pleasures"[67] and "it is the body and the care of it, to which we are enslaved."[68] The body is the seat of evil, and its pleasures deceptive: "As long as we have a body and our soul fused with such an evil, we shall never adequately attain what we desire."[69] As if all evil came from the body: "Only the body and its desires cause war."[70]

---

[64] But mark here that *everything* is a *representation* or an *image* of reality (not, so to speak, reality itself)—scientific "truths" and principles as well as mythological ones.

[65] "Truly important and significant hypotheses will be found to have "assumptions" that are wildly inaccurate descriptive representations of reality, and, in general, the more significant the theory, the more unrealistic the assumptions. . . . To be important, therefore, a hypothesis must be descriptively false in its assumptions; it takes account of, and accounts for, none of the many other attendant circumstances, since its very success shows them to be irrelevant for the phenomena to be explained." Friedman, *Essays in Positive Economics*, 14.

[66] The question is *what are our models?* Do they strive to *be true*, or are they just instrumental or (more or less useful)? But how can they be instrumental *or* useful, if they don't claim to be *in some way* true, valid?

[67] Plato, *Phaedo*, 64d.

[68] Ibid., 66d.

[69] Ibid., 66b.

[70] Ibid., 66c.

The body is an obstacle; if the soul "attempts to examine anything with the body, it is clearly deceived by it . . . soul reasons best when . . . it is most by itself, taking leave of the body as far as possible, having no contact or association with it [body] in its search for reality . . . Then he will do this most perfectly who approaches the object with thought alone."[71] The soul is better off without the body, the body is just a nuisance: "It seems likely that we shall, only when we are dead, attain that which we desire and of which we claim to be lovers, namely wisdom, as our argument shows, not while we live . . . . While we live, we shall be closest to knowledge if we refrain as much as possible from association with the body and do not join with it more than we must, if we are not infected with its nature but purify ourselves from it until the god himself frees us."[72]

It is precisely this conception of cutting off the demand side that early Christianity ties into, to a certain extent, especially the Apostle Paul and, later, Augustine. Augustine's conception of the body as a prison for the soul (see further) sounds in this context like an addition to the aforementioned Plato citation. "Physicality" and care for the material becomes the antithesis of the superior spiritual, the physical is disdained and suppressed, and material things are marginalized. The implications for economics offer themselves. Ascetic societies, which compared to our own hamper demand for possessions, can never develop into a high stage of specialization. Ascetic societies, whose individuals demand only the absolute minimum of possessions, can never be able to achieve high material prosperity (and would not have cared about it). In the end, not even economics, a field that takes interest and care especially of demand of the bodily pleasures (i.e., especially satisfaction of the unessential needs which are not necessary for life), would most certainly not develop into the forms we know today. For economists, the condemnation of physical pleasures—utility—has a clear meaning. The ideal is not found in consumption and producing assets, but in breaking free of both. In this, Plato is a staunch Stoic, as we will see later.

Since the time of Socrates, a broad discussion on this topic has been under way: "Callicles seems to attach a positive value to the very having of these appetitive needs: for Socrates's claim that those who need nothing are living well (are *eudaimón*) fills him with distaste. 'In that case,' he replies, 'stones and corpses would be living superlatively well.'"[73]

Ultimately, not even Socrates can manage to control his erotic needs, and even he is torn between his erotic and philosophical desires. The erotic love affair with Alcibiades was not actually in Socrates's control. Nevertheless, it was the tradition of the Stoics to avoid ties that were

---

[71] Plato, *Phaedo*, 65b–66a.
[72] Ibid., 66e–67a.
[73] Nussbaum, *The Fragility of Goodness: Luck and Ethics in Greek Tragedy and Philosophy*, 142.

random and uncountable, which tends to be the case with ties to the material world or relations overall.

And as far as the supply side goes, Plato took a very distant stand toward it as well. Manual labor, production, smelled of uncleanliness and was suitable only for the lowest class of people or, even better, slaves. The ideal was found in intellectual and spiritual contemplation—in self-knowledge, where the answers could be found, the key to truth, which means therefore also to a good, happy life.

Demand versus Supply: Freedom and Discrepancy

Today we believe that a person is freer the more property he has. The Stoics had it exactly the opposite: The *fewer* things one was dependent on, the freer he felt. Thus it is here from which calls for freedom from the wants (demands) of the flesh come. The best-known example of such liberation and getting rid of dependence on the world was Diogenes, who minimized his demand and threw away everything he did not need—including one of his last things, a jug, because water could be drunk with just one's hands. The program of the Stoics was therefore clear: Let's cut demand for possessions, and with this we will be able to decrease our supply side, or labor. He who gets by with few things is satisfied with few things. He who needs only a little does not have to toil as much. If a discrepancy exists between supply and demand (which is probably the default state of the human psyche), then for the Stoics the prescription for a happy life was to decrease demand, not to increase supply (or production), which the Hedonists saw as the prescription for a happy life.

Ideal Society: Politics and the Economy

Plato and Aristotle have in many ways defined the discussion space to this day. This is also true for questions of the functioning of society and on which foundations human coexistence stands. "Samuelson in *Economics* was implicitly addressing a question as old as the debates between Plato and Aristotle—when is self-interested behavior acceptable in society and when should individual behavior be directed to the realization of a broader good of society?"[74]

The area that is essential for our topic is Plato's economic-political teachings, even though there are disputes to this day about his interpretations, and Plato invited some criticism for them. For example, Karl Popper (but others as well[75]) charges Plato with becoming the inspiration, in

---

[74] Nelson, *Economics as Religion*, 105.

[75] Starting with Nietzsche, the criticism of totalitarianism strengthened, and after World War II it became almost a custom to see Plato as the great-grandfather of totalitarianism (see K. Popper Z. Baumann, J. Habermas, M. Foucault, etc.).

The Republic, for all utopian thinkers and even of communism.[76] "Both Plato and Marx offered a vision of 'apocalyptic revolution which will radically transfigure the whole social world.'"[77] Marx himself directly referred to Plato; in *Das Kapital* there are frequent references to him.[78]

For Aristotle, man was a social creature, "zoon politikon." But not for Plato. In Plato's conception, we are just (good) citizens of society because it pays for us to be, not out of our nature, as Aristotle was to later argue. "The second line of argument for a stable social structure is the rational self-interest of the individual members of the city. The Platonic argument is that individuals know that their best interests are served by rational decision-making. The conclusion is, for Plato, quite obvious. Any intelligent person will welcome the supervision and guidance of those more skilled and more intelligent."[79]

Plato divided society into three layers representing the various sets of human qualities—the class of rulers represents reason, the class of warriors embodies courage, and the class of craftsmen represents sensuality (which Plato considered the lowest). The ruling classes did not know private property, their own interests, or even their individuality. This stems from Plato's negative conception of private property—the higher classes should not entertain such (earthly) affairs at all; they should take care of the whole. The ruling elites take neither wives nor husbands. *Re*production is ensured almost clinically, and the raising of children was entrusted to special civic institutions. The elite class of rulers was to have applied itself to the purest possible philosophy, of course in a more radical way than where today's concept of the enlightened philosopher-ruler reaches. "*The Republic* also argues that the best life is a life 'ruled' by reason, in which reason evaluates, ranks and orders alternative pursuits."[80] Rulers were to have submitted to the impartial search for ideas and the "mystical vision of the absolute,"[81] not just issues of the state. In short, with regard to the desires and needs of the human body, Plato was "according them no positive value at all."[82] As in George Orwell's famous novel *1984,*

---

[76] Platonism's second life, including references to the thousands of possibilities of its "use" (even by J. V. Stalin), is provided by Novotný, F., *The Posthumous Life of Plato.*

[77] Nelson, *Economics as Religion,* 270, see also Popper, *The Open Society and Its Enemies,* 38, 164.

[78] Karl Marx in volume 1, chapter 12 of his *Capital* even complains, "Le platonisme oú va-t-il se nicher! [All the places Platonism made its nests!]." He refers to Plato as someone who "sees in the division of labour the basis for dividing society into statuses. A worker must adapt to his work, not the work to the worker." Plato then bears the epithet: "reactionary utopianism of consumer communism of the aristocratic classes."

[79] Lowry, "The Economic and Jurisprudential Ideas of the Ancient Greeks: Our Heritage from Hellenic Thought," 25.

[80] Nussbaum, *The Fragility of Goodness: Luck and Ethics in Greek Tragedy and Philosophy,* 138.

[81] Rádl, *Dějiny Filosofie: Starověk a středověk* [History of Philosophy: Ancient and Medieval], 185.

[82] Nussbaum, *The Fragility of Goodness: Luck and Ethics in Greek Tragedy and Philosophy,* 139.

things such as property or family or similar earthly hurryings were only appropriate for the proletarian class.

It appears that, according to Aristotle and contrary to Plato's view, it is unrealistic for ruler-philosophers not to desire property. "Aristotle found the proposals to abolish private property—such as Plato had made for his guardian class—failed to take account of the natural propensities of men."[83] A major difference between the outlooks of Aristotle and Plato on human nature can be found in this disagreement. For Plato, the corrupting tendency of property and its tendency to lead man away from what is truly important (getting to know the world of abstractions) plays a fundamental role. Aristotle instead points out the positive motivations that stem from desires for material security. "If the writings of Aristotle encouraged worldliness, optimism, practicality, common sense, empiricism, and utilitarian outlook, the writings of Plato proved more likely to lead to withdrawal, pessimism, radicalism, revelation, and an ascetic outlook."[84]

As a citizen of educated Athens, Plato is a great admirer of Sparta, a "totalitarian" military state. Physical labor, as merely procurement and satiation of needs, in his vision is left to the sphere of working people. This lowest societal class can own material assets, can indulge in family life and have their own children, while leaders and soldiers live communally and completely without private ownership.[85]

Plato sees the principle of decline in the rampancy of requests and treats them through a new establishment of hierarchy—the philosopher rules to the benefit of the whole, leads to the moderation of all walks of life, and himself owns nothing. The higher one stands, the less he owns in private ownership. Progress is found in *non*consumption, just as in *non*production. So Plato calls for or counts on the voluntary moderation of the ruling class and overcoming the tendency to gather up assets, which for many economists could represent a similarly tough problem as the later medieval appeals to asceticism (as presaged by Plato).

Progress

At the same time, Plato's vision of an ideal state casts light on his vision of social progress. According to Plato, it is not enough to be oriented toward social events and the direction of society as a whole only by generally accepted principles. Society needs regulatory ideas, goals that it may take guidance from. Of course, Plato's vision of a society in which children have as their parents all of the citizens as a collective and who are brought up by the state under the leadership of a philosopher without property is not a call for the immediate and brutal establishment of such order. It is

---

[83] Nelson, *Reaching for Heaven on Earth*, 36.
[84] Ibid., 61.
[85] Plato, *The Republic*, 5.

an ideal[86] that should pull society from its kinship nepotism and relation-ships twisted by blood ties and rather toward an order where everyone has the same opportunity to display their qualities without the burdens of familial background; on the basis of this they can be sorted through the most appropriate possible means to a place in society, and therefore most beneficial to themselves.[87]

Leaders in Plato's ideal society resist corrupting temptations that draw them away from their search for a higher good. This is not only about property but about sex as well. As Robert Nelson writes: "Sexual ties also, as both Plato and the Roman Catholic Church recognized, could create powerful feelings of individual possessiveness, perhaps deeper even than the ownership of private property. Plato's solution in *The Republic* was to remove the possessive element by abolishing marriage and other limits on free sexual expression, further establishing common ownership of children (the mother should not know the identity of her child). More pragmatically, the Roman Catholic Church took the opposite track, requiring its priests and nuns to be celibate, seeking to ensure that their highest loyalties were not to another person but to God and the Church."[88]

Man needs *more than learnedness* to lead the right life; he needs to be visionary to be able to move from his place. For this reason, society needs philosophers as leaders, people who can see ideals and mediate the sur-veyed "cosmic" order to others. Abstraction mediated by the governing elite leading the entire state should then be a benchmark for the orientation of everyone's everyday actions. The word "elite" itself has its origins in "eligo," meaning released. From here comes the elite as a group of released, selected for the service of the common good. The entire *Republic* is pulled by the harmonization of three levels: the cosmos, the community, and man. And harmonization takes place by the lower classes adapting to the upper classes. Without ideas and vision, no pragmatic decisions can take place. The vision of the whole, not just the general rules of the game, should govern our acts and become the motor of social progress.

It is worth noting that the social upbringing of children could have other important goals related to the idea of progress: the reduction of contingency. "Socrates argues that really decisive progress in human social

---

[86] In its literal meaning, "utopia" is made up of "ou" (not) and "topos" (place). It is therefore a vision that has no specific place for its existence, its fulfillment.

[87] "In his *Antigone*, Sophocles goes a step further. In it, he marks as the *worst* those who for whatever reason do not give the maximum for the community within the framework of their abilities; there is no place for any kind of individual comfort due to the inter-ests of the whole. The 'worst' (*kakitos*) person is the one who withholds his abilities from the city out of self-interest (Ant. 181). The 'bad' (*hoi kakoi*) are contrasted with 'whoever is well-minded to the city,' as if there were polar opposites (Ant. 108–109)." Nussbaum, *The Fragility of Goodness: Luck and Ethics in Greek Tragedy and Philosophy*, 55.

[88] Nelson, *Economics as Religion*, 271.

life will be made only when we have developed a new *techné*, one that assimilates practical deliberation to counting, weighing, and measuring."[89] From this angle, the whole history of men and our civilization is "a story of gradually increasing human control over contingency."[90] The reduction of contingency and the growing development of mathematics and measurement, according to Plato, led to man ridding himself of the rule of passion and gaining control over the fate of himself and his community as such. The probability that randomness would set progress back is therefore much lower.

As we will show in the practical example below (from Plato's dialogue *Timaeus*), Plato believed, as did the Hebrews, in a shining past and in decline as an expression of civilization's progress, as Popper summarizes nicely: "All social change is corruption or decay or degeneration. This fundamental historical law forms, in Plato's view, part of a cosmic law—of a law which holds for all created or generated things. All things in flux, all generated things, are destined to decay."[91] Nevertheless, "Plato believed that the law of historical destiny, the law of decay, can be broken by the moral will of man, supported by the power of human reason."[92] In this sense, he introduced a scientific program that was to reopen a blissful state for people. With this, Plato gave Europe a program for progress: science.

City, Civilization, and the Golden Age

The city, the community, is a symbol of progress in ancient Greece, even if in a somewhat different conception than we have witnessed in the case of the Sumerians or the Hebrews. Good and evil come from human beings; wildness can no longer be pointed to as the home of evil. And it would be this way for the rest of our civilization. At the same time, the ancient community undoubtedly tied their development to the order in the state. For Plato and Aristotle, the philosopher is important as part of the hoped-for harmony with the cosmos, because such harmonization could be found, and they could advise people and communities on how to assimilate to such an order. Even such a secular affair as the arrangement of the city-state was subordinate to the philosophy of seeing the cosmos.

What are interesting are also the parallels between the populace who live in cities and those in the country. Those who lived outside the city were uncivilized; they did not know how to either read or write. At the same time, this conception corresponds to how these "simple people"

---

[89] Nussbaum, *The Fragility of Goodness: Luck and Ethics in Greek Tragedy and Philosophy*, 89–90.

[90] Ibid., 91.

[91] Popper, *The Open Society and Its Enemies*, vol.1, *The Spell of Plato*, 17.

[92] Ibid., 18.

(the people who still knew somewhat how to live in uncivilized harmony) were outside the wrath of the gods: "Whenever the gods send floods of water upon the earth to purge it, the herdsmen and shepherds in the mountains preserve their lives, while those who live in the cities, in your region, are swept by the rivers into the sea. . . . It sweeps upon you like plague, and leaves only your illiterate and uncultured people behind. You became infants all over again," Timaeus says in Plato's eponymous dialogue.[93] Here as well we encounter the idea that civilization, culturing, the growing up of the human child, takes place in cities. Here we also find parallels with the "human child," who probably still does not have the conflict between good and evil internalized (accustomed), and as an animal (or a child) who "does what he wants," has no internal, only external (natural) limits. This seems to have been a time when man was in harmony with "the simple 'I want' of one's animal nature," as Joseph Campbell writes.[94] It seems to have been a time when one's "I want" was in perfect harmony with "I should," which later became disjointed.

Nevertheless, here as well there is an interesting overlap that we also see with other Greek classic works—the idea that the primordial race was better: "Second, you are unaware of the fact that the finest and best of all the races of humankind once lived in your region. This is the race from whom you yourself, your whole city . . . are sprung, thanks to survival of a small portion of their stock." This ancient race was superior, even though for "many generations the survivors passed on without leaving a written record."[95] These "ancient citizens" thus knew no *technai*, didn't even read or write, yet they lived in harmony[96] as if not yet "cursed" by the "gift" of Prometheus. The idea of progress was, in this case anyway, an idea of decay. Our predecessors were not savage apes but a superior race. Later on, people became more cultured, more "adult," and moved to the city, which is seemingly more shielded from the whims and changes of nature. But even there people are not shielded from the wrath of the gods; on the contrary, it is this city civilization that is often visited by floods[97] and other curses. It is the hills, the uncivilized parts of earth where people are safer, as can be seen in the story of Sodom and Gomorrah in the Bible.[98]

---

[93] Plato, *Timaeus*, 22e–23b.

[94] Campbell, *Myths to Live By*, 72.

[95] Plato, *Timaeus*, 23c.

[96] Elsewhere Plato writes: "And the people of old, superior to us and living in closer proximity to the gods." *Philebus*, 16d.

[97] "[Y]our people remember only one flood, though in fact there were many before." Plato, *Timaeus*, 23b.

[98] Genesis 19:16–17: "[T]he men grasped his hand and the hands of his wife and of his two daughters and led them safely out of the city . . . As soon as they had brought them out, one of them said, 'Flee for your lives! Don't look back, and don't stop anywhere in the plain! Flee to the mountains or you will be swept away!'" A similar topic can be seen in the warning of Jesus in Matthew 24:15–16: "So when you see standing in the holy place 'the abomination

The topic of "blissful ignorance" and the trade-off between harmony on the one hand and technical advances on the other appear quite frequently in Greek thought. People have been cast out, disconnected from their natural state, and now they work to earn their way back—to try to approach a more blissful state.

ARISTOTLE

We could present Aristotle as one of the first rigorous and systematic scholars—"Parmenides and Plato's Socrates compare themselves to initiates into a mystery religion. Aristotle's philosopher, by contrast, is what we might call a professional human being"[99]—and perhaps even the first rigorous scientist. His moral teachings are in this sense absolutely primal religious references or arguments (as opposed to Plato, in whose case we could be witnesses to a sort of transitional state between myth and analysis). The pre-Socratics used aesthetics and mnemonics (such as rhythm and rhyme) as bearers of truth. Plato sought the truth in dialogue and abstraction, and to a certain extent an emphasis on fantasy. The argumentation and style of Aristotle's writings are in no way different from today's narrative scientific discourses. It was Aristotle who was the first to begin acting like a scientist in today's meaning of the word.

His understanding of philosophy and science were, despite this, much wider than we understand it today. First, he did not strictly distinguish science from philosophy (as happened later), and second, he classified things as science that we probably would not so classify today. For Aristotle, "all science (*dianoia*) is either practical, poetical or theoretical."[100] He included poetry and practical fields into science. By practical science, he means ethics and politics; by poetical science, he means the study of poetry and the other fine arts; by theoretical science, he means physics, mathematics, and metaphysics. The majority of his scientific work was qualitative, not quantitative, and to him mathematics was very close to theoretical philosophy and metaphysics.

It was Aristotle who, figuratively speaking, brought earth to the center of attention. It was he who argued that "we need philosophy to show us the way back to the ordinary."[101] Instead of having his head in the world of ideas, he swam with the fish on the island of Lesbos, observing the behavior of octopii and animals in the forest. He argued that the form of an apple exists *in the apple*, not in the world of ideas. For this reason he examined apples and in general classified all creation into genii

---

that causes desolation,' spoken of through the prophet Daniel—let the reader understand—then let those who are in Judea flee to the mountains."

[99] Nussbaum, *The Fragility of Goodness: Luck and Ethics in Greek Tragedy and Philosophy*, 261.
[100] Aristotle, *Metaphysics*, 1025b25.
[101] Nussbaum, *The Fragility of Goodness: Luck and Ethics in Greek Tragedy and Philosophy*, 260.

and species. He was what we could call today an empiricist, while Plato would be classified today rather as the beginning of the rationalist tradition.

All of this was surprising for its time, "unnatural" to the point of being irritating, and occasionally met with resistance. "Aristotle's audience seems to have rebelled against his taste for the ordinary and the worldly, demanding instead the lofty and rarefied concerns."[102] And so earthly things as presented by Aristotle get attention, and the world of Platonic ideas is somewhat pushed to the shadowy background. Aristotle devoted his attention to precisely the things that for Plato—grandly stated—were *shadowplay*. This is how "strategy, economics, rhetoric" got the same attention as "even the most highly esteemed of capacities."[103]

If we were to summarize Aristotle's teachings in a few sentences, then aside from his groundedness, we would have to mention his sense for the *purpose* of things, *telos*. As opposed to Plato, he did not examine *invariability* as much but concentrated on the sense, the goal of movement, because "wish is for the end."[104] Similar to other ancient schools (moreover the same as with the Hebrews and Christians), he places a major role on morals (specifically on the ethics of virtue, which today is being rediscovered[105]), and the good life is unimaginable without the study of good and evil.

To present a practical example: Aristotle explains the falling of material things toward the ground as their nature. The stone comes from the earth and wants to return there; its meaning is to be on/in earth. This is similar to gas, fire, or the soul wanting to go upward. This explanation sufficed for a long time, until it was replaced by Newtonian gravitation.

The history of economic thought in many textbooks actually starts with Aristotle. It was he who defends private ownership, for example,[106] criticizes usury,[107] distinguishes between productive and unproductive economic activity,[108] categorizes the role of money,[109] notes the tragedy of

---

[102] Nussbaum, *The Fragility of Goodness: Luck and Ethics in Greek Tragedy and Philosophy*, 260.
[103] Aristotle, *Nicomachean Ethics*, 1094b3.
[104] Ibid., 1113a15.
[105] By "virtue ethics" we mean the ethics based on virtue (not on responsibility, benefit, utility, or the calculus of impact outcomes). For more see MacIntyre, *After Virtue*. MacIntyre was originally an Aristotelian who later became a Thomist, who in his own words was "a better Aristotelian than Aristotle himself." MacIntyre, *After Virtue*, x. Plato was the founder of virtue ethics, but Aristotle really established it. Virtue ethics was the dominant ethical school of our civilization until the Enlightenment, when it was partially replaced with utilitarianism or Kantian deontology (morals founded on responsibility, on good intentions, following rules).
[106] Aristotle, *Politics*, 2.5.
[107] Ibid., 1258b. 1.10.
[108] Ibid., 1.10. Aristotle distinguishes here between good *economics* practiced for the general benefit and bad *chremastics*, the unbridled accumulation of wealth for wealth itself.
[109] Ibid., 1.8–10.

the community's commons,[110] and deals with the issue of monopolies.[111] Nevertheless, here we want to focus on those of his observations that were key for the development of the economy but have not been much elaborated on by economists. For example, Aristotle deals in depth with utility and its role in life, deals with maximization functions, which economics to this day is obsessed with (the only difference being that today we consider them only in their mathematical form, which frequently conceals deeper philosophical discussion), and other key areas we would today call *meta*economics, or that which goes far beyond "household management" and asks about the meaning and purpose (*telos*) of these efforts.

Eudemonia: "Happiness Being a Sort of Science"

Aristotle asks about the things probably everyone is interested in: How to live a happy life? What does it mean for a person to live in such a way as to achieve the life we all desire? A question of happiness—*eudaimonia*—is far from theoretical: "the present inquiry does not aim at theoretical knowledge like the others (for we are inquiring not in order to know what excellence is, but in order to become good)."[112] His second book on ethics, *Eudemian Ethics*, starts in a similar way to *Nicomachean Ethics*: How to acquire a good life, for "happiness is at once the most beautiful and best of all things,"[113] as he states right in the first paragraph of the book. How much a blissful life is bound with good and how to achieve it ("happiness being a sort of science"[114]) is something we will present below.

First, it must be said that Aristotle sees private good only in the context of good for the society as a whole. He is famous for his statement that "man is by nature a political animal."[115] In addition, he did not attribute a mechanistic character to society, as was later taken up in economics, but rather an organic one: Without the rest, one part not only makes no sense at all, but mainly it cannot live.[116] At the same time, man does not associate into societies for his benefit, but because it is in his nature.[117]

Utility is nevertheless a complicated thing, and it is constantly transforming. The question is: What has an essential *influence on utility*? Aristotle does not see utility as something that exists for a moment and is then gone, but as a state that man can but does not have to be aware of. He also notes that there is something of a hierarchy of utility, as if to

---

[110] Aristotle, *Politics*, 2. 3, 1261b.

[111] Ibid., 1.11.

[112] Aristotle, *Nicomachean Ethics*, 1103b27–29.

[113] Aristotle, *Eudemian Ethics*, 1214a6–7.

[114] Ibid., 1214a18–19.

[115] Aristotle, *Politics*, 1.1253a2.

[116] For a different reading of social and economic processes in the *Nicomachean Ethics* and *Politics*, see Polanyi, "Aristotle Discovers the Economy."

[117] Aristotle, *Politics*, 2.1.1261a18, 3.1.1275b20.

say that we will not perceive utility from higher needs unless basic (natural) needs are fulfilled. He also notes that pleasures mutually crowd each other out: "activities are hindered by pleasures arising from other sources . . . the more pleasant activity drives out the other . . . e.g., in the theatre the people who eat sweets do so most when the actors are poor."[118]

MaxU versus MaxG

Whether or not man does everything because he is maximizing utility, pleasure, is to a large degree a nonsensical question for Aristotle. Pleasure, according to him, only "completes activity," which he repeats many times. "But whether we choose life for the sake of pleasure or pleasure for the sake of life is a question we may dismiss for the present. For they seem to be bound up together and not to admit of separation, since without activity pleasure does not arise, and every activity is completed by pleasure."[119] The term "pleasure," however, is not inseparably joined with the concept of perfection and good: The highest pleasure in the most perfect activity, pleasure is just a reward, a bonus—"Pleasure completes the activity."[120] Pleasure is not the purpose; goodness and perfection are. Pleasure therefore is something like the cherry on top of perfection and the activities pointing to it.[121] It is not the meaning of activity, but its accompanying expression. The purpose of activity (*telos*) is good.

In today's economics, we are somehow automatically used to the command MaxU, where man maximizes utility. There are tens of thousands of mathematical exercises that maximize utility functions, optimize utility and derivations seeking marginal utility, or balance marginal utility with marginal price, respectively profits with costs. In the vast majority of cases, however, we do not realize at all the astounding philosophical and ethical storm raging under those columns.

The concept of utility as good (and therefore also as a goal) was one of the main cores of the dispute between the Epicureans and the Stoics. Like Plato, Aristotle was closer to the Stoics. At the same time, Aristotle knew a sort of precursor of the maximization function. But instead of utility, he maximizes good, MaxG.

Right in the first sentence of *Politics*, he says:

[E]veryone always acts in order to obtain that which they think good.[122]

---

[118] Aristotle, *Nicomachean Ethics*, 1175b2–13.

[119] Ibid., 1175a19–22.

[120] Ibid., 1174b23.

[121] MacIntyre, one of the key modern Aristotelians, defines "eudemonia" as "the state of being well and doing well in being well, of a man's being well-favored himself and in relation to the divine." MacIntyre, *After Virtue*, 148.

[122] Aristotle, *Politics*, 1.1.1252a2–3.

This is similar to the first sentence of the *Nicomachean Ethics*:

> Every art and every inquiry, and similarly every action and choice, is thought
> to aim at some good; and for this reason the good has rightly been declared
> to be that at which all things aim.[123]

He goes into greater detail on the term "pleasure" in the tenth book of
Nicomachean Ethics. This book starts with the following sentence: "[W]e
ought perhaps next to discuss pleasure. For it is thought to be most intimately connected with our human nature . . . men choose what is pleasant
and avoid what is painful." Yes, this sounds like an introductory economics
textbook. But Aristotle continues: "For some say pleasure is the good,
while others, on the contrary, say it is thoroughly bad."[124]

When, for example, at the end of *Nicomachean Ethics* he has a dispute
with the hedonist Eudoxos, who "thought pleasure was the good because
he saw all things, both rational and irrational, aiming at it," he tells him:
"This argument seems to show it [pleasure] to be one of the goods, and no
more a good than any other."[125] Aristotle does not deny that pleasure is
part of good, but it is not in its identity, as the Hedonists argued.

To this day, economists still have to deal with a question similar to the
one Aristotle asked: "[B]oth the general run of men and people of superior
refinement say that it is happiness, and identify living well with and faring
well with being happy; but with regard to what happiness is they differ."[126]
To this day, you can drive economists mad with the same question: "If people
maximize their utility, what is the term 'utility' understood to mean?" That
is a more complicated question than it may appear, and we will discuss it
later, in the second part of the book. We will be very brief here.

Along with Aristotle we can argue that man in reality does not maximize his utility, but that he maximizes good. Man simply does what he
considers good. And doesn't everyone imagine something different under
the term "good"? Yes, and that is the point: The same is also true for *utility*.
If we take Aristotle's point of departure seriously, that "everyone does
everything for the sake of what they believe to be good,"[127] then it is possible that utility is only a subset of "that which we consider good." We get
no utility from certain things (or very halting and clumsily defensible), we
would be speaking more simply if we said that a given person did something because he considered it to be good, instead of saying "for maximizing his or her utility." It might be much more natural to say that Francis of
Assisi gave away all of his possessions because he considered it good, not

---

[123] Aristotle, *Nicomachean Ethics*, 1094a1–3 and on the household, as a sort of subset of
the city-state ". . . the end of medical art is health . . ., that of economics wealth." Aristotle,
Nicomachean Ethics, 1094a8–9.

[124] Ibid., 1172a19–29.

[125] Ibid., 1172b10–28.

[126] Ibid., 1095a14–23.

[127] Aristotle, *Politics*, 1.1.1252a1–7.

for utility; that Socrates decided not to renounce his teachings and run away but to drink poison, not because he expected utility after death, but because he considered it good. MaxG is therefore more defensible and, what's more, a more useful concept than MaxU.

Utility of Good and Evil

If we make this alteration, we can already see how tightly bound our perceptions are with the economics of good and evil. It is hard to imagine that a person would voluntarily and freely do something that he considers at a given moment to be completely evil. If a person steals, for example, they do not steal for stealing's sake (which they themselves would certainly consider to be evil) but, for example, to get richer, which they consider good. The goal is not to steal but to have more money. Ultimately we could hold a similar discussion with the assumption of MaxU.[128] Why does a person steal? Because it increases their utility? Never. They do not steal for the stealing itself but because it has utility from getting rich, for example. Or adrenaline or revenge. But whatever the reason why a person steals (or carries out other crimes), they do so for some good (therefore the goal of *telos*, which they see behind it).[129] MaxG can therefore explain the same things as MaxU, but in addition is able to explain the wider context of these actions. If we want to consider the theorem of MaxG as absurd (and to a certain extent it is, because it cannot be refuted, as we will see in the second part of the book), then the theorem of MaxU must also be absurd. Except that the absurdity of MaxG appears to be more visible. Maybe because of this, economics hides behind MaxU: so that the trick isn't so visible.

That we do not do things with the goal of momentary and unilateral MaxU, which Aristotle considers in the term "pleasure," will be shown in the following example: "And there are many things we should be keen about even if they brought no pleasure, e.g., seeing, remembering, knowing, possessing the excellences. If pleasures necessarily do accompany these, that makes no odds; we should choose these even if no pleasure resulted."[130] We want these things because they are good, and they are good because they are a natural part of humanness. So a human is more human if he sees, remembers, knows, and is virtuous.

---

[128] In this, Aristotle is closer to the Stoics: "[M]ost men, and men of the most vulgar type, seem (not without some reason) to identify the good, or happiness, with pleasure; which is the reason why they love the life of enjoyment." *Nicomachean Ethics*, 1095b15–17. "But people of superior refinement and of active disposition identify happiness with honour . . . but the good we divine to be something of one's own and not easily taken from one. Further, men seem to pursue honour in order that they may be assured of their merit." *Ibid.*, 1095b24–29.

[129] In this he is in agreement with Plato's teachings: "[T]he man who is truly good and wise, we think, bears all the chances of life becomingly and always makes the best of circumstances." Ibid., 1101a1–2.

[130] Ibid., 1174a4–9.

We have the feeling of bliss, pleasure, or happiness if we manage to achieve a good goal. It is hard for utility to be a goal in and of itself; the goal is goodness, and utility is its by-product, an externality. That which is good for a man is also the source of pleasure (for example, food); thus is our world built. We do not eat for pleasure only, but we have pleasure eating.

Aristotle would most likely protest against today's approach, where the *maximization* of utility is often automatically considered human nature. He considers what can simply be considered moderation to be the greatest virtue: "evil belongs to the class of unlimited"[131] and "good to that of the limited . . . for these reasons also, then, excess and defect are characteristic of vice and the mean of excellence."[132] This is therefore not about the maximization of utility, as the Epicureans argued, but about *temperance*. The goal is somewhere in between. Let's use an example: "With regard to giving and taking of money, the mean is liberality, the excess and the defect prodigality and meanness."[133] Or on a more general level: "So too it is, then, in the case of temperance . . . the man who indulges in every pleasure and abstains from none becomes self-indulgent, while the man who shuns every pleasure, as boors do, becomes in a way insensible; temperance and courage, then, are destroyed by excess and defect, and preserved by the mean."[134] "It is thus, then, that every art does its work well—by looking to the intermediate and judging its work by this standard."[135]

So, the key is not maximization at any cost but aiming for the center.

> For in everything it is no easy task to find the middle. e.g., To find the middle of a circle is not for every one but for him who knows; so too, any one can get angry—that is easy—or give or spend money; but to do this to the right person, to the right extent, at the right time, with the right aim, and in the right way, *that* is not for every one, nor is it easy; that is why goodness is both rare and laudable and noble.[136]

To this it could be added that such a point (the middle) is not easy to recognize. "Hence it is no easy task to be good. For in everything it is not easy task to find the middle";[137] a person must feel about for it. We do not recognize the bliss point easily.[138]

---

[131] Aristotle, *Nicomachean Ethics*, 1106b29–30.
[132] Ibid., 1106b31–34.
[133] Ibid., 1107b9–10.
[134] Ibid., 1104a19–27.
[135] Ibid., 1106b6–7.
[136] Ibid., 1109a25–29.
[137] Ibid., 1109a24.
[138] Searching for the mean is one of the greatest questions of Aristotelianism—it is not trial and error, empirical, but may be according to Plato *fronésis*—practical wisdom; see Gadamer, *The Idea of the Good in Platonic-Aristotelian Philosophy*.

THE STOICS VERSUS THE HEDONISTS

Surprisingly, it is Adam Smith, the founder of economics, who probably has the best description of the moral systems of ancient Greece in his book *The Theory of Moral Sentiments*. In the final, most interesting part of his monumental work,[139] we find an excellent study of the philosophical ideas of the ancient Greeks. Smith divides the moral teachings of the ancients into two different and de facto competing schools—the Stoics and the Hedonists. Their central dispute lies in the answer to the question of whether it pays to do good. Can it be calculated that good deeds bring us some kind of countervalue? That outgoing good correlates with incoming good?

The Stoics

The Stoics did not find any relationship between good and *pleasure* or *utility*,[140] and for this reason, any calculus was forbidden in advance. Certain good deeds tend to be paid back in pleasure (increased utility), others not at all, but the doer of the deed should remain perfectly blind to the results or impacts of his actions. The morality of the individual is judged on the basis of observance of the rules, regardless of the outcome of the given act.[141]

In other words, the morality of individual actions is judged only from the point of view of adherence to the rules, not the results or impacts of a given act. The result should simply be left to Fate.[142] If man behaves

---

[139] Smith, *The Theory of Moral Sentiments*, 395–430.

[140] Ibid., 415.

[141] "A wise man . . . [a]ssured of the wisdom which directs all events of human life, whatever lot befalls him, he accepts with joy, satisfied that, if he had known all the connections and dependencies of the different parts of the universe, it is the very lot which he himself would have wished for . . . If it is life, he is contented to live; and if it is death, as nature must have no further occasion for his presence here, he willingly goes where he is appointed. 'I accept,' said a cynical philosopher, whose doctrines were in this respect the same as those of the Stoics—'I accept with equal joy and satisfaction whatever fortune can befall me— riches or poverty, pleasure or pain, health or sickness, all is alike.'" Ibid., 405–406.

[142] "Human life the Stoics appear to have considered as a game of great skill; in which, how- ever, there was a mixture of chance . . . the whole pleasure of the game arises from playing well, from playing fairly, and playing skillfully. If, notwithstanding all his skill, however, the good player should, by the influence of chance, happen to lose, the loss ought to be a matter rather of merriment than of serious sorrow. He has made no false stroke; . . . he has enjoyed completely the whole pleasure of game. If, on the contrary, the bad player, notwithstanding all his blunders, should in the same manner happen to win, his success can give him but little satisfaction. He is mortified by the remembrance of all the faults which he commit- ted. Even during the play, he can enjoy no part of pleasure which it is capable of affording." Ibid., 409.

unethically, "his success can give him but little satisfaction."[143] According to the Stoics, the morality of a given act is not found in the repercussions of the act, whether it increases or decreases utility, but in the *correctness of the act itself*. For this reason, according to the Stoics, we must not analyze the costs or yields of the act.

Today Adam Smith is considered the founder of classical economics, for which the targeted maximization of utility is a central topic. Yet he considered himself a Stoic. He promotes this ancient philosophical direction[144] and admired how they managed to free themselves from thinking about utility.[145] (We will return to the paradox of how Smith's legacy is understood today.)

The Hedonists

The Hedonist (Epicurean) school, as represented especially by Epicurus, professed the exact opposite. According to them, neither good nor rules are exogenous, given from above. The goodness of an act lies in its *results* of the deed itself—in the utility it brings. In addition, its utility is judged from the personal point of view of the actor. The source of Epicurean ethics is egoism, the means to it calculation, prudence. Epicurus does not acknowledge any higher or altruistic principles. Only in case of friendship is he willing to make an exception. Utility thus became the main assumption for a good life and the guiding principle in deciding on every act. While the Stoics were not allowed to calculate the results of their actions (who is capable of overseeing the ends of our acts?), for the Hedonists (Epicureans) it was, on the contrary, the sine qua non of their morals.[146] "[B]odily pleasure and pain were the sole ultimate objects of natural

---

[143] Smith, *The Theory of Moral Sentiments*, 409.

[144] "The few fragments which have come down to us of what the ancient philosophers had written upon these subjects form, perhaps, one of the most instructive as well as one of the most interesting remains of antiquity. The spirit and manhood of their doctrines make a wonderful contrast with the desponding, plaintive, and whining tone of some modern systems." Smith, Ibid., 415.

[145] "'If I am going to sail,' says [Stoic] Epictetus, 'I choose the best ship and the best pilot, and I wait for the fairest weather that any circumstances and duty will allow. Prudence and propriety, the principles which the gods have given me for the direction of my conduct, require this of me, but they require no more; and if, notwithstanding, a storm arises, which neither the strength of the vessel nor the skill of the pilot are likely to withstand, I give myself no trouble about the consequence. All that I had to do is done already. The directors of my conduct never command me to be miserable, to be anxious, desponding, or afraid. Whether we are to be drowned, or to come to a harbour, is the business of Jupiter, not mine. I leave it entirely to his determination, nor ever break my rest with considering which way he is likely to decide it, but receive whatever comes with equal indifference and security.'" Ibid., 406.

[146] "Prudence, for example, though, according to this philosophy, [was] the source of all the virtues." Ibid., 434.

desire and aversion."[147] The Epicureans laid down an equals sign between good and utility—the morality of an act lies only and exclusively in how it decreased or increased personal benefit.[148]

It is important to emphasize that the Epicureans were completely consistent on this point and argued that "[a]ll the pleasures and pains of the mind were, according to Epicurus, ultimately derived from those of the body."[149] On the other hand, physical experiences were defined relatively widely and also included intellectual experiences. A Hedonist was supposed to use his reason to oversee his acts to their end in the long term. He does not accept or excuse short-run pleasures: "It is impossible to live a pleasant life without living wisely and well and justly, and it is impossible to live wisely and well and justly without living pleasantly."[150]

Egoism, forethought, calculus, and calculation made up the source of Epicurean ethics. Of course, according to the Hedonists, even these principles (the principles on which modern economics stands) have their exceptions. The principle of egoism, for example, is not valid in the case of friendship, where sympathy plays a role as the primary motive of our acts.

Economics of Good and Evil

If we wanted to express the aforementioned in the technical language of economics, then the Stoics demarcated the space for human behavior through certain "moral constraints" (just as today's economics works with budget constraints). For the Epicureans, of course, moral constraints completely disappear and morality is de facto implicitly incorporated in utility curves. Only external limits (budgets, for example) can limit the increases in utility. On the other hand, however, Hedonist teachings have a major advantage in that they do not have to take any exogenous (externally given) moral system or set of rules, which will always be the weak point of the Stoics or anyone else who is founded on rules or responsibility. The Hedonist principle creates its own rules.

Another difference between the Stoics and the Epicureans is in the relativization of good as such. As a moral quality in the teachings of the Hedonists, good loses its inherent sense and becomes a mere subset of utility. Virtuous acts can sometimes lead to greater utility and must be committed at that time. Good becomes something of a set of rules that can lead to increased utility, which stands completely in conflict with the teachings of the Stoics. While good for the Stoics was the reason for all of their acts, and pleasure stems from adhering to rules (including disregarding

---

[147] "That they were always the natural objects of those passions, he [Epikuros] thought required no proof." Smith, *The Theory of Moral Sentiments*, 431.
[148] Ibid., 431.
[149] Ibid., 432.
[150] Epicurus, *Principal Doctrines*, 1.

their results), the Hedonists completely turned this logic around: Good became the achievement of utility.

As has already been said, this philosophy of utilitarian economic teaching goes mainstream in the hands of J. S. Mill.[151] Adam Smith, on the other hand, ends his chapter on the Epicureans with the words: "This system is, no doubt, altogether inconsistent with that which I have been endeavouring to establish."[152] He refuses Hedonism as having too simplistic a view of the world. "By running up all the different virtues, too, to this one species of propriety, Epicurus indulged a propensity, which is natural to all men, but which philosophers in particular are apt to cultivate with a peculiar fondness, as the great means of displaying their ingenuity—the propensity to account for all appearances from as few principles as possible."[153]

One unintended irony is that it was this criticism from Adam Smith that predicted the future development of economic thought—to this day most economists consider the principle of self-love or egoism to be the only driving force of human behavior. An even greater irony is that Adam Smith is considered the father of this principle. Another methodological irony is that it is economics which tries to "account for all appearances from as few principles as possible."

The polar tension between the teachings of the Stoics and the Hedonists in the economics of good and evil is highlighted most clearly by Immanuel Kant, when these two schools again were set against each other as two of the fundamental prototypes of the morality of decision-making.[154] In his ethics, Kant joins the Stoics, whose teachings he revived and even made stricter. But this direction did not make it into economic thinking.

CONCLUSION

Greeks stood at the beginnings of our philosophy, and they significantly contributed to our way of living today. We started with the concept of truth of the poets, then talked about the birth of philosophy and of the numerical mystics. We went into some detail to see how interesting the economic thought of Xenophon is.

Plato was the bearer of the vector of our philosophy. He talked about the world of ideas and warned against the world of shadows, in which we now live. He has no respect for the desires of the body. Here we talked at some length about models and myths and about the idea of progress, about the Golden Age and the debate between a cultured and natural life. Aristotle could be considered the first scientist who, unlike Plato, devoted a lot of energy to this carnal world. We debated his thinking about a

---

[151] Mill, *Utilitarianism*.
[152] Smith, *The Theory of Moral Sentiments*, 436.
[153] Ibid., 438.
[154] See, for example, Kant, *Introduction to the Metaphysics of Morals*.

happy life and the question of whether it lies in the maximization of utility. We also introduced the key concept of Maximization of Goodness as a meaning and purpose in life.

Finally, we opened the debate between Hedonists and Stoics, something to which Adam Smith devoted a lot of ink. Economics as a science is a clear follower of the Hedonistic approach equating goodness with utility. Only the Hedonist program—maximize your supply of goods until it reaches your demand for goods, has not been fulfilled, although we have tried very hard for many generations, to the present day.

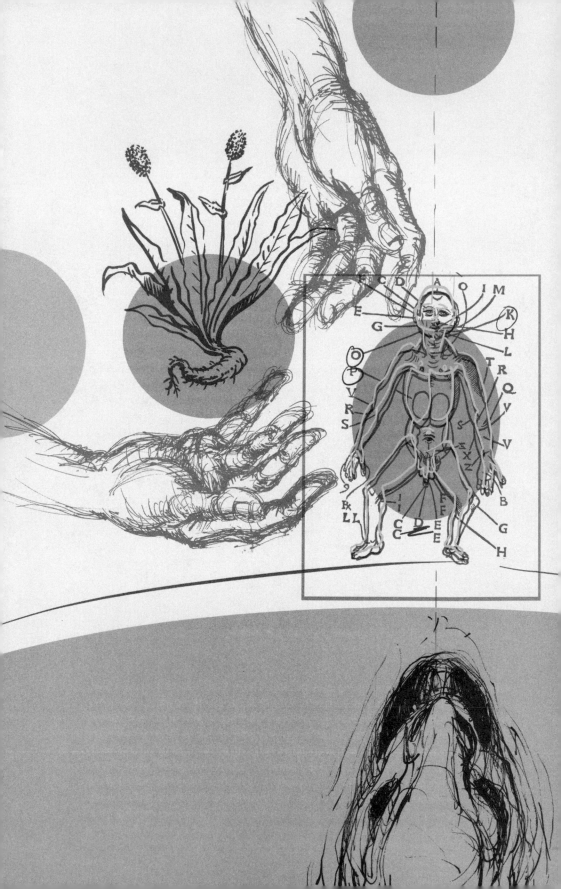

4

Christianity

Spirituality in the Material World

> *It is written, "Man does not live on bread alone."*
> The Bible, New Testament

Jesus's "Man does not live on bread alone"[1] is certainly true, just as it is true that people cannot live without bread. We were endowed with both body and soul, and we are both spiritual and material beings. In an extreme approach, both of these positions are inhuman; both are lethal in a certain sense. Without the material, we will die; without the spiritual, we stop being people. We must care for both, but at the same time it definitely does not have to be true that one comes at the expense of the other, as is frequently said. On the other hand, it would be a mistake to think that these two areas are independent of one another and do not influence each other. The very fact that we need external, material factors so that we can stay alive through *the sweat of our face*[2] is given as a reason to ease up on this rushing and think about economics.

In this chapter we will take a look at how Christianity searches for harmony between these two poles. How does Christianity view the hurrying we do on Earth? What does it think about consumption, material-physical requests, and asceticism? I will try to point out the economic ideas in Christianity, predecessors to the concept of the invisible hand of the market, the question of good and evil, and organizing people in society. Here we will also pause to consider how Christianity looks at the question of whether good or evil pays.

As the most widespread religion in Western civilization, Christianity has had a huge influence on the formation of the modern economy. This faith frequently had the decisive word, especially in normative questions (that which *should* be done). It would be hard to imagine our contemporary Western market democracy without it.

---

[1] Matthew 4:4.
[2] Genesis 3:19: "By the sweat of your brow you will eat your food."

Christianity is built on Judaism,[3] takes over numerous elements of Greek thought, and adds its own completely new dimension of salvation. In this form it is a faith that became a completely essential part of the development of Euro-Atlantic civilization in the last two millennia. But this isn't the single reason why Christianity should be studied. Some economists write[4] that economics is closer to Thomas Aquinas than to Isaac Newton precisely because its rhetoric and argumentation[5] all too often bring to mind theological disputations rather than the arguments among those who study physics. This is in stark contrast to what economics itself proclaims to be.

ECONOMIC PARABLES

The Bible and economics are much more closely tied than one would think. Of Jesus's thirty parables in the New Testament, nineteen (!) are set in an economic or social context: the parable of the lost coin;[6] of talents, where Jesus rebukes a servant who did not "put my money on deposit with the bankers;"[7] of the unjust steward;[8] of the workers in the vineyard;[9] of the two debtors;[10] of the rich fool;[11] and so forth.[12] Some authors have

---

[3] The era of Christianity was the first time that the fundamental ideas of the Jewish faith were so well received that they began to meaningfully influence the history of all of Western civilization.

[4] Nelson, *Economics as Religion*, 329.

[5] McCloskey, "Rhetoric of Economics."

[6] Luke 15:8–10: "Or suppose a woman has ten silver coins and loses one. Does she not light a lamp, sweep the house and search carefully until she finds it? And when she finds it, she calls her friends and neighbors together and says 'Rejoice with me; I have found my lost coin.' In the same way, I tell you, there is rejoicing in the presence of the angels of God over one sinner who repents."

[7] Matthew 25:27: "Well then, you should have put my money on deposit with the bankers, so that when I returned I would have received it back with interest."

[8] Luke 16:5–12: "So he called in each one of his master's debtors. He asked the first, 'How much do you owe my master?' 'Eight hundred gallons of olive oil,' he replied. The manager told him, 'Take your bill, sit down quickly, and make it four hundred.' Then he asked the second, 'And how much do you owe? A thousand bushels of wheat,' he replied. He told him, 'Take your bill and make it eight hundred.'... And if you have not been trustworthy with someone else's property, who will give you property of your own?" See also Luke 19:13–24.

[9] Matthew 20:8: "When evening came, the owner of the vineyard said to his foreman, 'Call the workers and pay them their wages, beginning with the last ones hired and going on to the first."

[10] Luke 7:41–43: "Two men owed money to a certain moneylender. One owed him five hundred denarii, and the other fifty. 42: Neither of them had the money to pay him back, so he canceled the debts of both. Now which of them will love him more? Simon replied, 'I suppose the one who had the bigger debt canceled.' 'You have judged correctly,' Jesus said."

[11] Luke 12:16–21. "But God said to him, 'You fool! This very night your life will be demanded from you. Then who will get what you have prepared for yourself?' This is how it will be with anyone who stores up things for himself but is not rich toward God."

[12] Let's name only a few: Parable of the Hidden Treasure (Matthew 13:44), the Parable of the Pearl (Matthew 13:45), the Parable of the Good Samaritan (Luke 10:25–37), the Parable

even counted that thousands of verses can be found on economic or social issues, of justice, wealth, or money, and that the second most frequent topics of both the Old and New Testaments are socio-economic (after idolatry[13]). As regards the New Testament, economic inquiries are discussed on average every sixteenth verse; in the Gospel of Luke, it is as often as every seventh.[14]

The Sermon on the Mount, Jesus's longest and probably most important speech, starts with the words: "His disciples came to him, and he began to teach them, saying: 'Blessed are the poor in spirit, for theirs is the kingdom of heaven.'"[15] Poverty, a dominant economic theme, is present (albeit in the context of the poverty of the soul) right at the beginning. Blessed also are those "who hunger and thirst for righteousness, for they will be filled." Without wanting to go into deeper theological exegesis, it is certain that Jesus is turning the maximization theorem inside out. Shortage and poverty (of both the belly and the soul) are considered a high value. The beginning of Jesus's model prayer, which has taken on the name of Pater Noster (Our Father), presents the plea "give us today our daily bread"[16] just after the desire for the coming of the kingdom of God. Incidentally, a key term of the New Testament, *gospel*, originally meant a *tip*, a small payment for the conveyance of good news (such as an unexpected victory). We will soon return to these economic themes when we discuss the topic of gifts.[17]

And finally one example of how important economic dealings are in the New Testament comes from the last book of the Bible, Revelation. During the end times, during the reign of the Antichrist, the ones not marked with the "mark or the name of the beast" will be punished by not being *able to buy and sell*.[18]

CANCEL OUR DEBTS

As we have seen, Christianity builds a large amount of its teaching on economic terminology and uses economic and social context. Probably the

---

of the Faithful Servant (Mark 13:33–37; Luke 12:35–48; Matthew 24:42–51), the Parable of the Prodigal Son (Luke 15:11–32). Harmony according to Cox, Easley, Robertson, and Broadus, *Harmony of the Gospels*, 348.

[13] This in and of itself can also be elegantly joined with the inordinate concentration on the material. "No one can serve two masters. Either he will hate the one and love the other, or he will be devoted to the one and despise the other. You cannot serve both God and Money." Matthew 6:24. Also in Luke 16:13.

[14] Willis, *God's Politics: Why the Right Gets It Wrong and the Left Doesn't Get It*, 212. See also Colins and Wright, *The Moral Measure of the Economy*.

[15] Matthew 5:2–3.

[16] Matthew 6:11.

[17] Liddel and Scott, *Greek-English Lexicon*: "reward of good tidings, given to the messenger."

[18] Revelation 13:17, "so that no one could buy or sell unless he had the mark, which is the name of the beast or the number of his name."

most important connections between Christianity and economics can be found in the continuation of Jesus's prayer:[19] "Forgive us our debts, as we also have forgiven our debtors."[20] For in New Testament Greek, *debt* means *sin.*[21] In this sense, these words—debt, debtor—speak to our time much more audibly than the distant terms *sin* and *those that sin against us.*

Jesus was speaking of something even deeper here. In those days, people whose debt increased so unbearably that they were not able to repay became "debt slaves."[22] There is very rich literature in the Old Testament about the whole concept of the release of debt slaves.[23] The New Testament takes this social institution to a higher and more fundamental level. Someone had to pay a ransom for people who fell into slavery. These people had to be bought out, ransomed, or, to use a more modern term, bailed out. Forgiveness (of debts, sins) is the key feature of Christianity, which makes it unique among the major religions. Jesus's role was to redeem men, purchase us at a price[24] buy us out of debt from the arms of sin, debt. "To give His life as a ransom for many."[25] "In him we have redemption through his blood, the forgiveness of sins, in accordance with the riches of God's grace,"[26] and further, "in whom we have redemption, the forgiveness of sins."[27] For the Jewish community of the time, which was used to the concept of the representational sacrifice of animals (such as the lamb at Passover), he provided a new covenant: "He did not enter by means of the blood of goats and calves; but he entered the Most Holy Place once for all by his own blood, having obtained eternal redemption....,

---

[19] See also Horsley, *Covenant Economics*, 81, 95.

[20] Matthew 6:12.

[21] In the Greek original the word "opheilēmata" is used, which means a debt, "opheilo." All English translations of the Bible (save for two) translate it as such. This prayer is also recorded in Luke 11:2–4. Here the Greek "amartias" is used, which at the same time means sin, from the early root "hamart," but it means "to miss the mark, do wrong, sin." These two words are frequently synonyms. (*Amartias* appears in the New Testament 181 times, *hamarant* 36 times, *opheilo* 36 times.)

[22] See Leviticus 25:39.

[23] Exodus 21:1–6; Leviticus 25:8–10, 41–42; Deuteronomy 15:1–6, 12–15. Cancellation of debts also appears in the Code of Hammurabi §117. See Horsley, *Covenant Economics*, 45.

[24] 1 Corinthians 7:23: "You were bought at a price; do not become slaves of men." We see similar elements in the Old Testament—an example of the classic situation of redemption from slavery in Leviticus 25:48: "he retains the right of redemption after he has sold himself. One of his relatives may redeem him." Or 2 Samuel 7:23: "And who is like your people Israel—the one nation on earth that God went out to redeem as a people for himself, and to make a name for himself, and to perform great and awesome wonders by driving out nations and their gods from before your people, whom you redeemed from Egypt?" Or Psalms 107:2: "Let the redeemed of the LORD say this—those he redeemed from the hand of the foe." Or Psalms 111:9: "He provided redemption for his people."

[25] Mark 10:42 45; "ransom" refers to the covenant mechanism by which those who have fallen into debt-slavery could be ransomed (see Leviticus 25:25–28, 47–55). See Horsley, *Covenant Economics*, 123.

[26] Ephesians 1:7.

[27] Colossians 1:14.

For this reason Christ is the mediator of a new covenant, that those who are called may receive the promised eternal inheritance—now that he has died as a ransom to set them free from the sins committed under the first covenant."[28] In other words, he came to "proclaim the year of the Jubilee" the year of forgiveness of debts, sins.

REDEMPTION OF DEBTS TODAY

If this concept seems distant or irrelevant today, let's just remember the recent redemption of banks and large companies in the crisis years of 2008 and 2009.

Our modern society, paradoxically, cannot function without the institute of this unfair forgiveness of debt. Every here and now, we ourselves practice an unfair forgiveness of debt and unfair treatment. It would be hard to imagine the financial Armageddon that would follow if the government actually did not pay the ransom and redeem banks and some large companies. This, of course, goes against all principles of sound reason and of basic fairness. We also breached many rules of competition on which our capitalism is built. Why did the most indebted banks and companies, which did not compete very well, receive the largest forgiveness? So we see that the principle that Jesus uses is one which is (at least in times of crisis) quite common till this very day. It was not fair, to be sure, but it had to be done in order to redeem not only these particular troubled and highly indebted companies but also others who would fail if these few were not saved.

GIFT-GIVING AND TRANS-ACTION

In economic theory, the gift is among the anomalies that are hard to explain with existing models. At the same time, the concept of the gift (which we cannot repay) is the basic principle of the Christian salvation. "For it is by grace you have been saved, through faith—and this not from yourselves, it is the gift of God—not by works, so that no one can boast."[29] God's redemption is free; it cannot be paid for, not by deeds, merit or "good behavior." There simply is no exchange; it is a gift.

> This righteousness from God comes through faith in Jesus Christ to all who believe. There is no difference, for all have sinned and fall short of the glory of God, and are justified freely by his grace through the redemption that came by Christ Jesus.[30]

---

[28] Hebrews 9:12–15.
[29] Ephesians 2:8–9.
[30] Romans 3:22–24.

And further, "I am the Alpha and the Omega, the Beginning and the End. To him who is thirsty I will give to drink *without cost* from the spring of the water of life."[31] Although it is paradoxical, in transcendental issues (*trans-scandere*, exceeding, rising, permeation through) the monetary trans-action (or above- or intra-action) is not possible.[32] *Transcendance* cannot be bought; it must be given.

Not long after the establishment of the first church, a magician appeared who wanted to buy and pay for these gifts with money. The apostles' reaction could probably be expected. "Peter answered: May your money perish with you, because you thought you could buy the gift of God with money!"[33] Let's pause for a moment for an economic view on the gift and on things or areas that are price-*less* (in both meanings of the word).

A mutual or reciprocal gift is a much deeper and older method of transaction than purchase and sale with an explicit price. For many generations of human history, things simply did not have a price; people got by without pricing. People long ago gave things reciprocally or lived in communities where things were exchanged—even if the first example was more common. The first nonmonetary social systems were gift economies. When barter did occur, it was usually between either complete strangers or potential enemies.[34] We should realize that even today money is intended for contact in large societies, while older or smaller societies did not and do not use money as much (such as family).[35]

The phenomenon of the gift is a greatly discussed and controversial topic among economists to this day. Why do people give gifts? Tips in restaurants or other occasions (such as taxis) could be considered a form of voluntary giving.[36] Why is a voluntary tip given in motels in foreign countries where we will never return?[37]

The main characteristic of a gift is that it has no price. It certainly has value, but never a price. A gift can be reciprocal and mutual (and frequently tends to be), but their exchange value will always be imprecise, unclear, fuzzy (we are not exchanging same for same). In Christianity, we give trust and faith (many consider that to be "God's gift," too), and

---

[31] Revelation 21:6. Author's emphasis.

[32] From the Latin preposition *trans* ("across, on the far side, beyond"). The prefix *trans* means across, through, over, beyond, or to the other side of, outside of.

[33] Acts 8:20.

[34] Graeber, *Toward an Anthropological Theory of Value*, 154. See also Cheal, *The Gift Economy*.

[35] The Czech philosopher Jan Sokol likes to add that his grandmother needed money only several times per year, and that was to buy salt.

[36] It is interesting overall to monitor which areas and which cultures have become refuges of tipping. Tips are given in restaurants, but never in stores with service. They are given to taxi drivers, but not to bus drivers. They are given to repairmen in the Czech Republic, while in America they are not given to maids or janitors.

[37] Tips are hotly debated, and not just among economists. One of the most interesting discussions on this topic can be found at the beginning of *Reservoir Dogs*, Quentin Tarantino's film.

God gives salvation to those who accept the gift. The gift is not negoti-
ated; there is no possibility of a discount. As opposed to this, trade has a
precise-to-the-cent price that both parties agree to. We must be aware
that without the existence of a large and functioning market, setting a
precise price must have been rather complicated and ultimately a sensitive matter as well. Even Thomas Aquinas battled with this problem (as
do present-day antimonopoly offices, which frequently keep watch or set
prices in situations where a market does not function well). Contemporary
"speculative bubbles" are also an important imaginary "departure" of
prices from their values (and after a certain time they burst, which means
that prices "return" to their notional idea of value). To this day, gifts are
given in all kinds of marketing promotions—"free items"—whether they
are teddy bears at gas stations, 10 percent more ketchup, or "buy one, get
one free." This too can be considered a modern effort to sweep away an
exact price of goods in the framework of competition.

Another interesting thing is that we frequently hide prices or keep
them secret. We carefully remove prices from gifts, only the payer may
look at the bill in a restaurant, and in better restaurants the bill is even
elegantly hidden in various folders. In the best restaurants, the person
being invited apparently gets a menu where prices cannot be seen at all.[38]
We evidently have the feeling that the most valuable things should be
given for free, that they should not be available for purchase.[39] It is precisely the most valuable things in life that must not be sold or monetized.
The notion comes from somewhere within us that precise reciprocity is
undesirable for important things or for people close to us. You may have
noticed that nothing is bought or sold in the entire Lord of the Rings trilogy. The Fellowship gets everything it needs on its journey through gifts.[40]
The extremely careful J. R. R. Tolkien (who loved to immerse himself in
details) never mentions currency anywhere in the *Lord of the Rings*. In this
it is similar to most older tales, fairy tales, myths, and stories. Not even in
the Epic of Gilgamesh do we find out anything about money, and not
once does anyone sell anything. Important things are simply given, found, or
stolen (the Ring of Power, for example, uses all these methods of changing
owners—but it is never sold).[41]

---

[38] Note also the dynamics of mutual gifts in restaurants or bars. People are invited to dinner
or for a drink, but if you wanted to "treat" them by putting $8.50 in front of them, you will
not make him or her happy at all. But a drink worth $8.50 is something few of your friends
will refuse, even though this is de facto the same transaction (from the point of view of
"numerical" economics).

[39] This is captured in one Old Testament passage: "Come, all you who are thirsty, come
to the waters; and you who have no money, come, buy and eat! Come, buy wine and milk
without money and without cost." Isaiah 55:1.

[40] Bassham and Bronson, *The Lord of the Rings and Philosophy*. As Alison Milbank points out,
all goods are gifts and no financial trades occur.

[41] Even if it is somewhat disputable whether the person owns the ring or vice versa. Take
Gollum, for example: Did he once own the ring, or did he find it and was subsequently

While money is necessary for the functioning of today's society, among those close to us we frequently create situations where it is as if money were not there, or at least that it is not important (which is why we "buy rounds," or take turns paying at a restaurant). I once heard that friends are people who are so mutually indebted to each other that they forget how much they owe. On the other hand, if a friend wanted to pay for your help, it would probably offend you. "Paying back" by invitation for a dinner or drinks or doing a deed in return, on the other hand, is acceptable. But never payment that has a precise price and is exact. Marcel Mauss argues that this reciprocal gift-giving is "like a resurrection of a dominant motif long forgotten" and a "return to the old and elemental."[42] Some anthropologists tend to argue that gift economies are essential or elementary structures, and money or quid pro quo exchange, are only secondary issues.[43]

And really, for untradable things that cannot be exchanged (such as friendship), there is no way to trade them or swap them (you cannot buy a true friend or inner peace). But you can buy things that seem to be around it: proxies. You can buy a dinner in a restaurant for your friends, but there is no way you can buy true friends by doing so; or you can buy a cabin in the mountains and *try* to find peace there, but you cannot buy peace itself. Ultimately, advertising functions on this principle: They show you something that cannot be traded (a good night's sleep, a happy family at breakfast, or beauty) and offer you a tradeable proxy (an expensive bed, some kind of breakfast cereal, a mountain cabin, or shampoo). And even though we know this is an illusion and that actors and extras play in ads, we still start to desire a better pillow (mine is responsible for my troubled sleep), new yogurts and cereals (the happy family at breakfast), and shampoo (even if the model in the ad has probably never used the particular brand).

But back to prices. Is the Czech philosopher Zdeněk Neubauer right when he argues that "price is unholy"?[44] The prominent German sociologist Georg Simmel seems to hint that too when he calls money *common* (meaning vulgar): "Objects themselves are devalued of their higher significance ... Money is 'common' because it is the equivalent for anything

---

owned and controlled by it? Galadriel or even Gandalf worry similarly that they will not control the ring, but that the ring will control them and reshape them in its image. With this, I want to say that it is an extreme image of two-way ownership. Not only do we own things, but things own us. A similar theme is explored in Chuck Palahniuk's book and the cult film made from it, *Fight Club* (David Fincher, 1999); in it, Tyler Durden says to the main character in the film (who has no name and represents Everyman, the average American), "the things that you own end up owning you."

[42] Mauss, *The Gift*, 66, 67.

[43] Cheal, *The Gift Economy*, 2. Also see Durkheim, *The Division of Labor in Society*, 4–7, Levi-Strauss, *The Elementary Structures of Kingship*, and Bourdieu, *Outline of a Theory of Practice*.

[44] Neubauer, *O čem je věda* [What Science Is About], 145.

and everything. Only that which is unique is distinguished; whatever is equal for many is the same even for the lowest among them, and for that reason it pulls even the highest down to the level of the lowest. That is the tragedy of every levelling process: it leads directly to the position of the lowest element."[45] It even insults us when, for the most important things, someone accuses us of profit-seeking, or that we're "just in it for the money."

THE ECONOMICS OF THE KINGDOM

Aside from the paradox of the gift that you can never work off, Jesus's teachings are often based on paradoxes, just like many of his parables.[46] Jesus considers more valuable two mites that a poor widow drops into the collection than the golden gifts of the rich.[47] Aside from the fact that here he expresses sensitivity to marginal disutility, at the same time he grants the legitimate role of money. Christianity respects the material side of life, does not condemn it, and when Jesus is asked whether secular taxes should be paid at all, he looks at the likeness stamped on the coin and answers: "Give to Caesar what is Caesar's."[48] It is true that Jesus once chased out the "men selling cattle, sheep and doves, and others sitting at tables exchanging money"[49] from the temple…but he didn't chase them farther than that! His argument was not against their employment

---

[45] Simmel, *Peníze v moderní kultuře a jiné eseje* [Money in Modern Culture], 249.

[46] Even Jesus's life is ultimately a paradox: The king is born in a manger (Luke 2); the most fervent "believers" of his time refuse him (Matthew 21:45–46); he befriends tax collectors and prostitutes; his strength is demonstrated in weakness, and before the crucifixion; God, the most powerful being on Earth, is brutally nailed to the cross along with criminals. For all of this, let's cite only a few passages that portray these paradoxes: "Jesus said to them, 'I tell you the truth, the tax collectors and the prostitutes are entering the kingdom of God ahead of you. For John came to you to show you the way of righteousness, and you did not believe him, but the tax collectors and the prostitutes did. And even after you saw this, you did not repent and believe him.'" Matthew 21:31–32. "The Son of Man must be delivered into the hands of sinful men, be crucified, and on the third day be raised again." Luke 24:7. "You killed the author of life, but God raised him from the dead." Acts 3:15.

[47] Mark 12:42–44: "But a poor widow came and put in two very small copper coins, worth only a fraction of a penny. Calling his disciples to him, Jesus said, 'I tell you the truth, this poor widow has put more into the treasury than all the others. They all gave out of their wealth; but she, out of her poverty, put in everything—all she had to live on.'"

[48] Matthew 22:17: "'Tell us then, what is your opinion? Is it right to pay taxes to Caesar or not?' But Jesus, knowing their evil intent, said, 'You hypocrites, why are you trying to trap me? Show me the coin used for paying the tax.' They brought him a denarius, and he asked them, 'Whose portrait is this? And whose inscription?' 'Caesar's,' they replied. Then he said to them, 'Give to Caesar what is Caesar's, and to God what is God's.'" Also Luke 20:25.

[49] John 2:14.

(it wouldn't have been enough to drive them out of the temple) but that they mixed the sacred with the profane.[50]

Jesus, of course, frequently warned against and talked about a two-way relationship to property—it isn't one-way ownership, but a reciprocal ownership seems to exist, too. The biblical warning sounds appropriate: Earthly things (things of bread) are all right, but we should not care too much for them, should not cling too much to them, because they contain a trap:

> Do not store up for yourselves treasures on earth, where moth and rust destroy, and where thieves break in and steal. But store up for yourselves treasures in heaven, where moth and rust do not destroy, and where thieves do not break in and steal. For where your treasure is, there your heart will be also.[51]

We should present the following passage similarly:

> Therefore I tell you, do not worry about your life, what you will eat or drink; or about your body, what you will wear. Is not life more important than food, and the body more important than clothes? Look at the birds of the air; they do not sow or reap or store away in barns, and yet your heavenly Father feeds them. Are you not much more valuable than they? Who of you by worrying can add a single hour to his life?... But seek first his kingdom and his righteousness, and all these things will be given to you as well. Therefore do not worry about tomorrow, for tomorrow will worry about itself. Each day has enough trouble of its own.[52]

What is interesting is that these words speak to rich and poor times with the same force. Even if (or precisely because) we have too much to wear (and the problem is to choose, buy, or order them), these words make sense to us, just as they make sense (or made sense) to the society of the poor, or the society that *truly had nothing to wear*. The passage is interesting to read again with this viewpoint: It is also aimed at over-rich society, which does not suffer from shortage but from surplus. And out of this surplus we worry what to *eat or drink* (isn't it too greasy, too sweet?) and *what to wear* (what shall I wear?).

It is also certainly appropriate to add the following citation: "For the love of money is a root of all kinds of evil. Some people, eager for money, have wandered from the faith and pierced themselves with many griefs."[53] The expression is commonly misquoted as simply "money is the root of all evil," which is not what the text says. It is *love* of money that makes prudence a vice. Perhaps the next quote (also by Paul but in a different

---

[50] "So he made a whip out of cords, and drove all from the temple area, both sheep and cattle; he scattered the coins of the money changers and overturned their tables. To those who sold doves he said, 'Get these out of here! How dare you turn my Father's house into a market!' John 2:15–16. It should be noted that this is actually Jesus's second public act (after changing water into wine at Cana in Galilee), which John recorded in his gospel.

[51] Matthew 6:19–21.

[52] Matthew 6:25–34.

[53] 1 Timothy 6:10.

letter, where he also uses the term *love of money*) puts it better in perspective: "Keep your lives free from the love of money and be content with what you have."[54] In the parable of the sower, "worries and riches and pleasures" seem to be one of the key obstacles that do not allow the seed (of faith) to bring "fruit to maturity."[55]

GAME THEORY: LOVE THY ENEMY VERSUS AN EYE FOR AN EYE

We can look at certain results in the way offered by the modern approach of game theory. In the well-known Prisoner's Dilemma, two prisoners choose *their* dominant strategy, which maximizes their expected individual utility, but not the total utility. Both rationally choose the noncooperative option and thus ensure the worse result (non-pareto optimal). The system itself (the character of the game) "forces" us toward collectively unwanted results. Barry Nalebuff, one of the leading figures of contemporary game theory, notes that negotiations on the basis of the Christian maxim "do unto others as you would have them do unto you" knows how to overcome this conflict: "If people were to follow the golden rule, there would be no prisoner's dilemma."[56]

An anthropological approach indicates interesting historical development related to both game theory and to the history of morals. For a long time it was argued in game theory that in strategies of repeated simultaneous games, it pays to use a *tit-for-tat* strategy, or the equivalent measure in response during every following step. If two players play a game of fraud-cooperation, a highly effective strategy is to retaliate fraudulent moves with similarly fraudulent moves, and vice versa. In other words, to repay a slap with a slap, a smile with a smile, and a caress with a caress. This strategy was considered the best since the era of Axelrod's experiments in 1980, when leading game theory experts played against each other; Anatol Rapoport used the *tit-for-tat* method and won repeatedly. It is a simple, strict strategy that forces adherence to the rules, urges cooperative solutions, and knows how to forgive (proportionally and quickly, which ensures that the game is not finished after the first cheating of any kind). It is actually the Old Testament's eye for an eye and tooth for a tooth.

Only recently a strategy was found that works even more effectively. In a world of imperfect information and noise, it simply arrives at a disinterpretation of signals and a (frequently unnecessary) beginning of a retaliatory strategy.[57] In addition, this strategy has a recursive tendency

---

[54] Hebrews 13:5.

[55] Luke 8:14.

[56] Dixit and Nalebuff, *Thinking Strategically*, 106.

[57] Ultimately the great themes of Shakespeare's plays are the small misunderstandings at the beginning which over time become amplified to gigantic dimensions. His comedies tend

and tends to be connected with a spiraling effect of descending to the bottom. Nalebuff argues that the *kinder* is more effective in the end.

As in the history of Eastern civilization, the rule of *eye for an eye, tooth for a tooth* was first considered to be the most effective strategy.[58] For the first time, Jesus arrives at a more cooperative long-term strategy:

> You have heard that it was said, "Eye for eye, and tooth for tooth." But I tell you, Do not resist an evil person. If someone strikes you on the right cheek, turn to him the other also. And if someone wants to sue you and take your tunic, let him have your cloak as well. If someone forces you to go one mile, go with him two miles. Give to the one who asks you, and do not turn away from the one who wants to borrow from you.[59]

In a situation of repeated games, if both sides take a strategy of an eye for an eye, or repaying good with good and evil with evil, evil gains a much greater space. One single act of evil (perhaps even a random one) takes on recursive echoes over time. It isn't certain whether a small wave of evil will gradually fade away or whether it will grow into a devastating storm.[60] Our paying off of evil does not decrease it but multiplies it. Compared to Nalebuff's game, *the merciful* come to a much greater minimalization of evil than the tit-for-tat, eye-for-an-eye strategy—in a similar way to what Jesus spoke of:

> You have heard that it was said, "Love your neighbor and hate your enemy." But I tell you: Love your enemies and pray for those who persecute you, that you may be sons of your Father in heaven. He causes his sun to rise on the evil and the good, and sends rain on the righteous and the unrighteous. If you love those who love you, what reward will you get? Are not even the tax collectors doing that? And if you greet only your brothers, what are you doing more than others? Do not even pagans do that?[61]

At the same time, Christianity carried out a major revolution on this ethical question. As we have shown in previous chapters, evil may but does not have to take on a moral form; certain evils (a tree falling on a person) are bad, but it is not a moral evil for which someone should be found guilty. In this gospel, all evil, including *residual evil*, simply occurs— whether consciously or inadvertently, moral or outside morals—and all

---

to end with everyone laughing at themselves, while the tragedies end with everyone killing each other.

[58] Exodus 21:23–25: "But if there is serious injury, you are to take life for life, eye for eye, tooth for tooth, hand for hand, foot for foot, burn for burn, wound for wound, bruise for bruise."

[59] Matthew 5:38–42.

[60] In the book *Good Omens: The Nice and Accurate Prophecies of Agnes Nutter, Witch*, by N. Gaiman and T. Pratchett, one of the Riders of Apocalypse, War appears as a war correspondent and causality is turned around. Wars start wherever she goes. One slightly distorted interview with one party, the second again slightly shifted from the other side, and a war breaks out even among parties who originally got on well together.

[61] Matthew 5:43–47; and Dixit and Nalebuff, *Thinking Strategically*, 109.

this evil is placed on the shoulders of the Messiah, who is sacrificed for all the evil in the world. In these complicated systems, guilt is found only with difficulty, and precisely for this reason God is in this sense unfair, because He *forgives*. He is, so to say, "positively unfair," just as is the landholder who pays unfairly high wages to his laborers even though he does not have to.[62] Moral systems seeking guilt will get drowned in one go by grace in the New Testament.

THE ECONOMICS OF GOOD AND EVIL IN THE NEW TESTAMENT

> *Stop helping God across the road like a little old lady.*
> U2, "Stand Up Comedy"

Does good pay (economically)? The question of *why* to do good presented a problem for Jewish thought (as we have shown), and the New Testament resolves it to a great extent. And in a dual manner.

By introducing the new concept of the "Kingdom of God," which was quite foreign to Judaism, Christianity literally opened a "new space" where moral acts receive their payment. The earthly world does not have to be just (the just can suffer here, while the unjust live in surplus and abundance), but justice awaits every person in the coming kingdom. While Judaism must simply deal with the problem of just rewards in *this world*, Christianity shifts justice to another *world*, to the *world beyond*. Good and evil (outgoing) therefore have an economic logic in that the reward (incoming) occurs, but in heaven. So it pays to do good and to suffer evil, because the just will receive their reward in heaven.

This is an elegant solution, but even this solution has its price—and the price was this world. The world, which in the Old Testament was a world of good and the scene of history, has been shifted to the second track. Christianity has provided a satisfactory solution to the ancient economic-moral paradox of the just reward, but not for free—the solution to this paradox comes at the cost of sacrificing the world. To many Christians, the world seemed unjust and to a large extent evil. This is where some of the New Testament's distance, sometimes as far as resistance, to this world stems from: "Don't you know that friendship with the world is hatred toward God? Anyone who chooses to be a friend of the world becomes an enemy of God."[63] Because only in a thoroughly bad world can the just suffer and the unjust enjoy themselves; it would appear wisest to run away from such a world. Apostle Paul writes, "to die is gain…I desire to

---

[62] Matthew 20:1–16.
[63] James 4:4.

depart and be with Christ, which is better by far."[64] In the end, the personification of evil gains a more specific and more horrifying form than in
the Old Testament.[65] In the Old Testament, Satan is explicitly named in
four occasions[66] (if we count the snake in Genesis as his representation).
On the other hand, he is mentioned nearly fifty times in the New
Testament. What's more, he is said to be the "ruler of this world."[67] In this
sense, the economics of good and evil does not work *in this world*. The
reward for the just is not here (see the story of Lazarus) but in heaven.

The Christian detachment from the world originates from this point
especially. From this standpoint, the world appears evil, unfair, transitory,
unimportant. Let us not deal with the so-called world of Platonic shadows, let's not be tied up or tied down by them; the best is to ignore them
as much as possible (Augustine also thinks similarly, but this trend is overturned by Aquinas in later phases of Christianity).

The second, much deeper way in which the New Testament solved the
problem of economics of good and evil was by dismantling the *accounting*
of good and evil altogether. Salvation is an undeserved gift (as we have
seen above) that you cannot earn. In this sense, the economics of good and

---

[64] "For to me, to live is Christ and to die is gain. If I am to go on living in the body, this will
mean fruitful labor for me. Yet what shall I choose? I do not know! I am torn between the
two: I desire to depart and be with Christ, which is better by far; but it is more necessary
for you that I remain in the body. Convinced of this, I know that I will remain, and I will
continue with all of you for your progress and joy in the faith, so that through my being with
you again your joy in Christ Jesus will overflow on account of me." Philippians 1:21–26.

[65] "In the Old Testament, Satan is not represented as a fallen and malignant spirit, but as a
servant of Yahweh, performing a divine function and having his place in the heavenly train.
In the parallel accounts of David's numbering of Israel (1 Samuel 24:1; 1 Chronicles 21:1),
the tempting of David is attributed both to Yahweh and Satan. . . . The unveiling of Satan as
a rebellious world-power is reserved for the New Testament." *International Standard Bible
Encyclopedia*: "Satan" entry.

[66] 1 Chronicles 21:1: "Satan rose up against Israel and incited David to take a census of
Israel." (Incidentally, it is interesting to compare the same story captured in the historically
older 2 Samuel 24:1, where on the contrary "[a]gain the anger of the Lord burned against
Israel, and he incited David against them, saying, 'Go and take a census of Israel and Judah.'"
Then in Zechariah 3:1–2: "Then he showed me Joshua the high priest standing before the
angel of the Lord, and Satan standing at his right side to accuse him. The Lord said to Satan,
'The Lord rebuke you, Satan! The Lord, who has chosen Jerusalem, rebuke you! Is not this
man a burning stick snatched from the fire?'"Satan shows himself several times at the beginning of the book of Job (chapters 1 and 2). The fourth case, even if it has been discussed, is
the figure of the "serpent" in the Garden of Eden. This "snake" tends to be frequently published as Satan. Certain translations translate the prosecutor in Psalms 109:6 to be Satan.

[67] In John 14:30 Jesus speaks of Satan as the ruler of this world: "I will not speak with you
much longer, for the prince of this world is coming." Or in John 12:31: "Now is the time
for judgment on this world; now the prince of this world will be driven out." In Ephesians
6:11–12, Paul further writes, "Put on the full armor of God so that you can take your stand
against the devil's schemes. For our struggle is not against flesh and blood, but against the
rulers, against the authorities, against the powers of this dark world and against the spiritual
forces of evil in the heavenly realms."

evil ceased to exist. We shall come to this later, but first let's pause at the biggest commandment—the commandment of love.

YOU MUST LOVE

Here it would also be good to recall what the Old and New Testaments want primarily: to "love your neighbor as yourself." According to Jesus, this law immediately follows the commandment to love God and is the largest commandment of all:[68] "The entire law is summed up in a single command: 'Love your neighbor as yourself.'"[69]

This commandment is important for economists as well because it has to do with the regulation of egoism or self-love. One should not have unlimited self-love or zero self-love, but his or her interest in him- or herself should be as great as he or she feels toward those close to him or her. The one who loves greatly can greatly love him- or herself as well. Incidentally, we note that both count as love. Our self-love should be the same as love toward those close to us. No more, no less.

In addition, our outgoing love should be independent from the behavior of the other party, or the behavior toward us (incoming good). In other words, Jesus wants us to love each other at all costs. Let the other party love or hate us, but we should love those close to us the same as ourselves.

There is nothing bad about caring for oneself (prudence), but it must not become an obsessive love. Prudence is even one of the seven virtues, as McCloskey notices: "Thomas Aquinas in the middle of the thirteenth century, assigned a place of honor among the seven virtues to Prudence—that is, to know-how, competence, a thrifty self-interest, 'rationality' on a broad definition."[70] We should note here that the virtue of prudence is only one of seven, not the only one, and we should always keep that in perspective.

THE INDESTRUCTIBILITY OF EVIL: THE PARABLE
OF THE WEEDS

Evil is difficult, if not impossible, to get rid off. Even in the perfect state of the garden of Eden, the (latent) possibility of evil—the Tree of the

---

[68] "'Love the Lord your God with all your heart and with all your soul and with all your mind and with all your strength.' The second is this: 'Love your neighbor as yourself.' There is no commandment greater than these." Mark 12:29–30.

[69] Galatians 5:14. And then, "The entire law is summed up in a single command: 'Love your neighbor as yourself'" (Romans 13:9). James even marks this as the Royal Law. "If you really keep the royal law found in Scripture, 'Love your neighbor as yourself' you are doing right." James 2:8.

[70] McCloskey, The Bourgeois Virtues, 8.

Knowledge of Good and Evil—had to exist.[71] Evil had to be possible. This is something Christianity is completely aware of; we cannot be rid of evil through human effort. Once it exists, it grows through good like an omnipresent weed. This is why the world needs Christ's representative sacrifice; if we were able to achieve pure good through our own effort, this sacrifice would be unnecessary. In this context, the parable of the weeds in the Gospel of Matthew is interesting:

> Jesus told them another parable: "The kingdom of heaven is like a man who sowed good seed in his field." But while everyone was sleeping, his enemy came and sowed weeds among the wheat, and went away. When the wheat sprouted and formed heads, then the weeds also appeared. The owner's servants came to him and said, "Sir, didn't you sow good seed in your field? Where then did the weeds come from?" "An enemy did this," he replied. "The servants asked him, "Do you want us to go and pull them up?" "No," he answered, "because while you are pulling the weeds, you may root up the wheat with them. Let both grow together until the harvest. At that time I will tell the harvesters: First collect the weeds and tie them in bundles to be burned; then gather the wheat and bring it into my barn."[72]

We cannot get rid of evil absolutely; evil has a role to play. If we were to set about uprooting all evil, we would destroy a lot of good wheat. In the words of Thomas Aquinas, "for if all evil were prevented, much good would be absent from the universe."[73] Augustine seemed to be of similar opinion: "For He [God] judged it better to bring good out of evil, than not to permit any evil to exist"; and elsewhere he writes, "For if it were not a good that evil should exist, its existence would not be permitted by the omnipotent God."[74]

The parasitic weed (evil) should be pulled only in the context of the field; weeds are not pulled outside the field (for example, in a meadow or on a hillside).

The parable of the weeds has another dimension: We would certainly not be able to distinguish what is "good seed" and what is weed—until

---

[71] Genesis 2:16–17: "You are free to eat from any tree in the garden; but you must not eat from the tree of the knowledge of good and evil, for when you eat of it you will surely die."

[72] Matthew 13:24–30.

[73] Aquinas, *Summa Theologica* I. Q22, A.2, R.O.2:

"[O]ne who provides universally allows some little defect to remain, lest the good of the whole should be hindered...inasmuch as the defect in one thing yields to the good of another, or even to the universal good: for the corruption of one is the generation of another, and through this it is that a species is kept in existence. Since God, then, provides universally for all being, it belongs to His providence to permit certain defects in particular effects, that the perfect good of the universe may not be hindered, for if all evil were prevented, much good would be absent from the universe. A lion would cease to live, if there were no slaying of animals; and there would be no patience of martyrs if there were no tyrannical persecution."

[74] Augustine, *Enchiridion on Faith, Hope, and Love*, 33, 110.

it grows.[75] Our abstract-moral systems are also imperfect, not to mention their transfer into practice. There is no moral school that has proven to be completely consistent and without contradictions. Is it within man's power at all to distinguish between good and evil ("Do not judge, or you too will be judged."[76])? Incidentally, this parable is being fulfilled to this day, when mankind is not able to set up a satisfactory moral system, even though the greatest and most creative minds have attempted to do exactly that.

It is as if beams were stuck in our eyes through which we see the moral world distortedly—we do not perceive our own errors, and at the same time we are capable of pulling out "the speck of sawdust in your brother's eye."[77] We are trying to create sophisticated moral systems (one, for example, is the system of the Pharisees) with which we filter out the mosquitoes but swallow the camels.[78] Jesus defied such artificial moral systems in his time, and even mocked them.[79] Jesus left behind that no system of rules could be judged from the outside, only commandments to love. Jesus takes the position that all good or evil comes from within man, be it from his will or his heart.[80] But how should we judge those whose hearts we cannot see into? Paul adds another *non*rule to this: "The goal of this command is love, which comes from a pure heart and a good conscience and a sincere faith."[81] And even more plainly: "To the pure, all things are pure, but to those who are corrupted and do not believe, nothing is pure. In fact, both their minds and consciences are corrupted."[82] And finally, a crowning *non*rule: "Everything is permissible for me—but not everything is beneficial. Everything is permissible for me—but I will not be mastered by anything."[83]

But let's go back to the Garden of Eden, where, according to the Bible, the ability to know, to distinguish between good and evil, was born. From this standpoint, there remains an eternal paradox whereby all moral schools try to outdo each other on which of them can better *distinguish* the difference between good and evil (to *know* what is good and what is evil).[84] At the same time, according to Genesis, the fall of man from the

---

[75] Without evil, are we able to perceive good at all? Do we perceive that our teeth do not hurt until they actually start to hurt and later stop?

[76] Matthew 7:1; also Luke 6:37: "Do not judge, and you will not be judged. Do not condemn, and you will not be condemned. Forgive, and you will be forgiven."

[77] Matthew 7:3–5.

[78] Matthew 23:24: "You blind guides! You strain out a gnat but swallow a camel."

[79] Mark 2:27: "Then he said to them, 'The Sabbath was made for man, not man for the Sabbath. So the Son of Man is Lord even of the Sabbath.'"

[80] Payne, *Odkud zlo?* [Whence Evil?] 78.

[81] 1 Timothy 1:5.

[82] Titus 1:15.

[83] 1 Corinthians 6:12. Paul then repeats this four chapters later in 1 Corinthians 10:23: "Everything is permissible—but not everything is beneficial. Everything is permissible—but not everything is constructive."

[84] For more, see Bonhoeffer, *Ethics*.

Garden of Eden was precisely due to the desire to taste the fruits of the Tree of the *Knowledge* of Good and Evil. The desire to know, to distinguish between good and evil, therefore became the cause of the failure— and moral schools try (yet again) to excel in exactly that! Jesus's words shift morals from the area of acts to the area of thoughts and imaginings, desires. To commit a sin, it isn't necessary to kill; it's "enough" to hate.[85] The difference between hatred and murder is often one of nerve and opportunity, sometimes even mere logistics. Other sins were similarly shifted from external (carried out) to internal (desire for evil, intention), as can be seen in the Sermon on the Mount. A message of the Christian gospel is that when it comes to salvation, good and evil no longer count. As the apostle Paul writes, "Blessed is the man whose sin the Lord will never count against him."[86] For those who have been forgiven, their evil will now not be counted. This was a very radical (both practically and philosophically) way out of the labyrinth of rules of human morality. Christ atones for our guilt and its repayment, and by doing so he transforms morality and cancels the concepts of good and evil that existed up to that point. Christ cancels the economy of good and evil. The relationship to God is not similar to double-entry accounting, but to love and joy. Instead of this, he offers an unearned, unfair (positively unfair) grace, one that is unfair to our benefit.[87]

LABOR AS A BLESSING, LABOR AS A CURSE

We have seen how the concept of labor developed with the Hebrews and the Greeks. Man was placed in the Garden of Eden "to work it and take care of it."[88] Eden was not a place of idleness; even in a state of perfection and bliss, man worked.[89] Labor belongs to man as a means for fuller expression, self-realization, and ultimately as a permanent source of introspection—a recognition of one's own possibilities and limits, often even a partial role in this world. Man therefore does not work out of necessity

---

[85] Matthew 5:21–22: "You have heard that it was said to the people long ago, 'Do not murder and anyone who murders will be subject to judgment.' But I tell you that anyone who is angry with his brother will be subject to judgment. Again, anyone who says to his brother, 'Raca,' is answerable to the Sanhedrin. But anyone who says, 'You fool!' will be in danger of the fire of hell."

[86] Romans 4:8.

[87] The idea that all evil is redeemed and that man should, at the same time, remain responsible to God, himself, and those close to him precisely *because of* love and gratitude is truly not trivial. Augustine's "love and do what you want" might be better understood in this regard. A discussion of grace and the law is understandably deeper and more complicated. This dispute was dealt with by Paul, for example, in his letter to the Romans.

[88] "The LORD God took the man and put him in the Garden of Eden to work it and take care of it." Genesis 2:15.

[89] See more in *Summa Theologica* I. Q102, A.3.

but out of his nature.[90] Unpleasant work (*in the sweat of your face*) occurred only after the Fall.

We read similar stories in Greek legends. Labor long ago was pleasant, but because Pandora, the first woman created (and who was created as a punishment), opened her box, and aside from every possible evil, that which came out of the box was also the unpleasantness of labor—burdensome labor that mankind had not known previously.[91] It is as if labor itself was not cursed (it existed long ago in a blessed form), but suffering was added to its character: "Cursed is the ground because of you; through painful toil you will eat of it all the days of your life."[92] It is as if it said: "That which was created to give you pleasure and give meaning to your existence will now be frequently disagreeable and will fight with you."

This conception boldly complements the classical economic view of labor, which implicitly assumes a negative utility from labor from the first hour worked. Today we consider work to be a disutility and consumption utility (men work *just so* they can consume). However, we overlook the deeper, ontological sense of labor, or the fact that labor is unique for man and that people see a deep sense in their work and see it as a partial (yet important!) goal of their lives.

But back to the New Testament. Labor should provide man with pleasure and fulfillment. The Bible does not call for a life without manual labor, as opposed to certain Greek ideals. Labor is even a responsibility for man: "If a man will not work, he shall not eat."[93] The notion that a spiritual person should be clear of all drudgery and earthly hurrying is shaded by the simple reality that Jesus Christ came to Jerusalem as a trained carpenter. All his disciples worked, mostly as fishermen (manual), but also as tax collectors (nonmanual). None of them made their livings as philosophizing intellectuals, people who would spend all their time meditating. Even the Apostle Paul, who composed an astounding part of the New Testament and spread the gospel all the way to Rome, did not *specialize* in spiritual things, and worked any time he could—he built tents so as not to be a bother to others.[94]

Where is the balance between the physically active and contemplative life? Neither the New nor Old Testament sees any *either-or* between the two areas. On the contrary, those who want to live piously should work honestly and make the money for their livelihood, the Apostle Paul writes

---

[90] *Summa Theologica* I. Q97, A.3, Corpus.

[91] See Hesiod, *Theogony* 571nn.

[92] Genesis 3:17.

[93] 2 Thessalonians 3:10.

[94] Acts 18:1–4: "After this, Paul left Athens and went to Corinth. There he met a Jew named Aquila, a native of Pontus, who had recently come from Italy with his wife Priscilla, because Claudius had ordered all the Jews to leave Rome. Paul went to see them, and because he was a tentmaker as they were, he stayed and worked with them. Every Sabbath he reasoned in the synagogue, trying to persuade Jews and Greeks."

to the church in Thessalonia, where a growing number of people started to refuse manual labor under the guise of various spiritual reasons.

> In the name of the Lord Jesus Christ, we command you, brothers, to keep away from every brother who is idle and does not live according to the teaching you received from us. For you yourselves know how you ought to follow our example. We were not idle when we were with you, nor did we eat anyone's food without paying for it. On the contrary, we worked night and day, laboring and toiling so that we would not be a burden to any of you. We did this, not because we do not have the right to such help, but in order to make ourselves a model for you to follow. For even when we were with you, we gave you this rule: "If a man will not work, he shall not eat." We hear that some among you are idle. They are not busy; they are busybodies. Such people we command and urge in the Lord Jesus Christ to settle down and earn the bread they eat. And as for you, brothers, never tire of doing what is right. If anyone does not obey our instruction in this letter, take special note of him. Do not associate with him, in order that he may feel ashamed.[95]

Elsewhere, the Apostle Paul again emphasizes that not even he lived from the charity of his neighbors, even though he fully concentrated on his spiritual mission to spread the gospels to the pagans:

> I have not coveted anyone's silver or gold or clothing. You yourselves know that these hands of mine have supplied my own needs and the needs of my companions. In everything I did, I showed you that by this kind of hard work we must help the weak, remembering the words the Lord Jesus himself said: "It is more blessed to give than to receive."[96]

PRIVATE OWNERSHIP: WHO OWNS THE LAND?

Connected with labor is the earning that stems from it, own ownership. Now, is private ownership always valid? In a certain extreme sense, in times of existential need, Christianity doubts the absolute right to private property. Despite this, Thomas Aquinas argues that private ownership has a beneficial influence on social calm, proper order, and positive motivational impulses. Aquinas makes one important exception related to the right of private ownership: "In cases of need all things are common property.... So that there would seem to be no sin in taking another's property, for need has made it common."[97] This is based on the idea that *by nature* all earthly assets fall under common ownership. His idea has gained popularity not only from the time of the scholastics, but also in the era of classical economics. John Locke, one of the fathers of the Euro-Atlantic economic tradition, put forth a similar notion. He argues using both

---

[95] 2 Thessalonians 3:6–14.
[96] Acts 20:33–35.
[97] Aquinas, *Summa Theologica* IIa–IIae Q.66 A.7 Corpus.

reason and faith: "Whether we consider natural reason, which tells us that men, being once born, have a right to their preservation, and consequently to meat and drink and such other things as Nature affords for their subsistence, or 'revelation,' which gives us an account of those grants God made of the world to Adam, and to Noah and his sons, it is very clear that God, as King David says (Psalm 115:16), 'has given the earth to the children of men,' given it to mankind in common."[98] The classical economist John Stuart Mill considers this in a similar context: "No man made the land. It is the original inheritance of the whole species."[99]

Human law must never infringe on the eternal laws of God.[100] Not even private property laws can be placed above man as a member of human society. In other words, the institution of private property falls at the moment human life is at stake.

While Thomas Aquinas does not see anything bad about wealth as such (on the contrary, as we will still show, he greatly doubts traditional tendencies toward asceticism), he cannot imagine it in conditions of extreme shortages for one's neighbors (his view of society as a society of neighbors more or less predetermines this view). On the other hand, he is aware that there are many destitute and that it is impossible to satiate all of them. "Nevertheless, if the need be so manifest and urgent, that it is evident that the present need must be remedied by whatever means be at hand..., then it is lawful for a man to succor his own need by means of another's property, by taking it either openly or secretly: nor is this properly speaking theft or robbery."[101] This is because "this necessity diminishes or entirely removes sin."[102] The idea is also repeated in the *First Treatise on Civil Governments* by John Locke, a well-known defender of (almost absolute) property rights.[103]

The rich should be prepared to share with others in times of need.[104] Aquinas gives the example of the Old Testament instruction that it is not considered a crime for someone to feed themselves from the fruits of a vineyard that does not belong to them. The hungry may eat until full in others' vineyards, provided they do not take any grapes with them.

---

[98] Locke, *Two Second Treatise of Government*, 16.

[99] Mill, *Principles of Political Economy*, 142; For more see M. Novak in *The Catholic Ethic and the Spirit of Capitalism*, especially 151, 285, 287.

[100] Aquinas, *Summa Theologica* IIa-IIae Q.66 A.7 Corpus: "I answer that, things which are of human right cannot derogate from natural right or Divine right."

[101] Ibid., IIa-IIae Q.66 A.7 Corpus.

[102] Ibid., IIa-IIae Q. 66, A.6 R.O.1.

[103] John Locke: *First Treatise on Civil Governments*, 4.42. Also see secondary literature: Sigmund, *St. Thomas Aquinas on Politics and Ethics*, especially 73.

[104] "The second thing that is competent to man with regard to external things is their use. In this respect man ought to possess external things, not as his own, but as common, so that, to wit, he is ready to communicate them to others in their need. Hence the Apostle says [1 Timothy 6:17,18]: 'Charge the rich of this world [!] to give easily, to communicate to others, etc.'" *Summa Theologica* IIa–IIae Q. 66, A.2 Corpus.

Thomas Aquinas argues that this is not against the law of society's welfare (i.e., private ownership), because the law should be set up in such a way as to "teach people to be used to being prepared to give to others from their property."[105]

The law on gleaning is taken in a similar spirit as well. The rich had the responsibility not to send out a second round of harvesters to collect the first group's leftovers.[106] Everything that was left in the field belonged to the poor, widows, and orphans.[107] Anyone who has read the Old Testament must have noted how frequently the text lays out special orders to protect the socially weakest people.

SMALL LOVE: COMMUNITARIANISM, CHARITY, AND SOLIDARITY

From an economic viewpoint we cannot go without mentioning the reality that the first church lived in communes of sorts, which functioned on the basis of joint ownership, in the expectation that the end of days would be coming soon:

> All the believers were together and had everything in common. Selling their possessions and goods, they gave to anyone as he had need ... All the believers were one in heart and mind. No one claimed that any of his possessions was his own, but they shared everything they had. There were no needy persons among them. For from time to time those who owned lands or houses sold them, brought the money from the sales and put it at the apostles' feet, and it was distributed to anyone as he had need.[108]

A similar means of ownership would later shift to monasteries and occasionally to Christian cities as well, such as the Czech city of Tábor during the Hussite Wars in the fifteenth century. How the notions of a voluntary and deeply religious communitarianism became atheistic communism is a question unto itself. Regardless, communists owe Christianity for this notion. Nevertheless, as is seen from history, the Marxist communist vision was not capable of offering a functional alternative to capitalism.

We know similar reports of communitarianism from the numerous references to the "House of Prisca and Aquila."[109] The first generation of

---

[105] "The purpose of the law was to accustom men to give of their own to others readily" *Summa Theologica* Ia–IIae Q. 105, A.2 R.O.1.

[106] "If you enter your neighbor's vineyard, you may eat all the grapes you want, but do not put any in your basket." Deuteronomy 23:24–25.

[107] "When you reap the harvest of your land, do not reap to the very edges of your field or gather the gleanings of your harvest. Do not go over your vineyard a second time or pick up the grapes that have fallen. Leave them for the poor and the alien. I am the LORD your God." Leviticus 19:9–10.

[108] Acts 2:44–4:35.

[109] 1 Corinthians 16:19; Romans 16:5.

Christians wanted to create an "alternative society that separated itself from the dominant imperial society as much as possible."[110] These local assemblies[111] celebrated the Lord's Supper[112] and gathered money for the poor.[113]

In Latin, *charitas* means love. In the New Testament, several words for love are used instead of the one used today: The Greek *agapé* (divine love) was different from *erós* (sexual love, flames, attraction), *stergein* (family love), and *filia* (friendly love).[114] Charitas was a kind of social love, compassion. It could almost be said that "small love" is a kind of gravitational force which, while weak (and almost imperceptible in comparison with other forces), is similar to charity in that it is a weak love, difficult to detect in comparison with other loves (which are intense and concentrated on one or a couple of people). But just as with short but strong (nuclear) forces and distant and weak (gravitational) forces, charitas holds together large units, in our case society—in a similar way to how gravity keeps together objects at large distances but is not as "strong" as nuclear or electric forces.

The oldest charitative or solidarity customs or rules have been known since the Old Testament.[115] The New Testament further expands on this: "Surplus goods that one did not need were to be given as alms rather than to be stored up like a treasure."[116] And in some cases the New Testament goes even further: "Sell your possessions and give to the poor," says Jesus

---

[110] Horsley, *Covenant Economics*, 140.

[111] Ibid., 144. It was these local assemblies that Paul seems to have been visiting and writing letters to in his travels.

[112] 1 Corinthians 11:20.

[113] Galatians 2:1–10; Acts 15:6–41.

[114] For more, see Lewis, *The Four Loves*, or McCloskey, *The Bourgeois Virtues*; compare to *Letters of C. S. Lewis*, 225.

[115] According to Lowry, "the earliest suggestion or concept of social or economic justice comes from the book of Nehemiah 5:5 in the Old Testament." Lowry and Gordon, *Ancient and Medieval Economic Ideas and Concepts of Social Justice*, 5. The biblical citation is Nehemiah 5:1–8:
"Now the men and their wives raised a great outcry against their Jewish brothers. Some were saying, 'We and our sons and daughters are numerous; in order for us to eat and stay alive, we must get grain.' Others were saying, 'We are mortgaging our fields, our vineyards and our homes to get grain during the famine.' Still others were saying, 'We have had to borrow money to pay the king's tax on our fields and vineyards. Although we are of the same flesh and blood as our countrymen and though our sons are as good as theirs, yet we have to subject our sons and daughters to slavery. Some of our daughters have already been enslaved, but we are powerless, because our fields and our vineyards belong to others.' When I heard their outcry and these charges, I was very angry. I pondered them in my mind and then accused the nobles and officials. I told them, 'You are exacting usury from your own countrymen!' So I called together a large meeting to deal with them and said: 'As far as possible, we have bought back our Jewish brothers who were sold to the Gentiles. Now you are selling your brothers, only for them to be sold back to us!' They kept quiet, because they could find nothing to say."

[116] Horsley, *Covenant Economics*, 155.

to his disciples when he calls to them to "seek his kingdom, and all these things will be given to you as well."[117]

Nevertheless, redistribution should be carried out from goodwill and voluntarily. The Apostle Paul writes: "Whoever sows sparingly will also reap sparingly, and whoever sows generously will also reap generously. Each man should give what he has decided in his heart to give, not reluctantly or under compulsion, for God loves a cheerful giver."[118] The Apostle Paul describes equality in redistribution in the following citation about believers inside the church mutually helping each other out:

> Now finish the work, so that your eager willingness to do it may be matched by your completion of it, according to your means. For if the willingness is there, the gift is acceptable according to what one has, not according to what he does not have. Our desire is not that others might be relieved while you are hard pressed, but that there might be equality. At the present time your plenty will supply what they need, so that in turn their plenty will supply what you need. Then there will be equality, as it is written: "He who gathered much did not have too much, and he who gathered little did not have too little."[119]

> Now about the collection for God's people: Do what I told the Galatian churches to do. On the first day of every week, each one of you should set aside a sum of money in keeping with his income, saving it up, so that when I come no collections will have to be made. Then, when I arrive, I will give letters of introduction to the men you approve and send them with your gift to Jerusalem.[120]

The social safety net inside the church was supposed to function like that. But it was not about applying it to the entire society, where Paul had no guarantees that the money collected would be fairly handled. The money was only sent to places where there was an urgent need.

Now let's briefly look at the economic ethos developing in the dominantly Christian Europe later on.

LATER DEVELOPMENT: AUGUSTINE'S ASCETICISM AND AQUINAS'S GROUNDEDNESS

Augustine and Thomas Aquinas were among the key personalities who shaped Christian Europe and influenced its development. We can read about the tension between accepting the world and its marginalization in many parts of the New Testament, although Jesus's teachings do not stand as a priori negative against the world. One of the key messages of Jesus's gospel was made up of the news repeated many times that "the Kingdom

---

[117] Luke 12:31–33.
[118] 2 Corinthians 9:6–7.
[119] 2 Corinthians 8:11–15.
[120] 1 Corinthians 16:1–3.

of God is at hand."[121] In a certain sense it is already present in this material world, as if it were constantly arriving, breaking like waves on this world.[122]

Augustine ties, to a large degree, into Platonism,[123] and in the existing world he instead sees only a hallucination, a shadowplay which only tells of the *truly existing* world—for him, the visible does not represent reality (which in many ways is similar to the occasional extremes of a rational notion of the world, where abstractions are placed above the concrete). This is not directly about the dualism of body and spirit, but despite this Augustine understood the body as the "weight of the soul."[124] This notion itself meant that economics did not assign a great deal of importance to it. From an economic standpoint, it will be interesting for us to follow a later great personality, Thomas Aquinas, who reversed attention from the Augustine inwardness toward examining the external world.

Aristotle's writings, which reversed attention rather toward the external world, were discovered in Europe only in the time of Aquinas. At the end of the high Middle Ages, Aristotle was seen as a threat to Augustinian-oriented Christianity. Thomas Aquinas did not disdain an Aristotelian interpretation of earthly topics, but instead he endeavored them, so that slowly it would come to pass that "the world receives loving attention."[125] Just as Augustine connected the ideas of Platonism to Christianity, Thomas Aquinas did the same with the ideas of Aristotle (he refers to Aristotle almost constantly in his writings—what's more, he refers to him as a

---

[121] "The time is fulfilled, and the kingdom of God is at hand; repent and believe in the gospel." (English Standard Version, Mark 1:15). The kingdom of God is a strange concept, hard to identify; "nor will people say, 'Here it is,' or 'There it is,' because the kingdom of God is within you." (Luke 17:21). The fact that the kingdom is not *there* is also nicely described in the apocryphal Gospel of Thomas: "Jesus said, 'If your leaders say to you, "Look, the (Father's) kingdom is in the sky," then the birds of the sky will precede you. If they say to you, "It is in the sea," then the fish will precede you. Rather, the kingdom is within you and it is outside you.'" Sentence 3 from Patterson and Meyer, *The "Scholars' Translation" of the Gospel of Thomas*.

[122] C. S. Lewis probably best describes the coming of the kingdom of God: "At present we are on the outside of the world, the wrong side of the door. We discern Fresnel and purity of the meaning, but they do not make us fresh and pure. We cannot mingle with splendors we see. But all the leaves of the New Testament are rustling with the rumor that it will not always be so. Some day, God willing, we shall get in." *The Weight of Glory*, 16–17.

[123] Specifically, for example, in the book *Confessions*, book 7.

[124] Augustine, *City of God*, 19.17: "When we shall have reached that peace, this mortal life shall give place to one that is eternal, and our body shall be no more this animal body which by its corruption weighs down the soul, but a spiritual body feeling no want, and in all its members subjected to the will." On the other hand, we need to mention that Augustine tried to leave behind the extreme version of Plato's and especially Plotinus's duality of mind and matter, in which the flesh has a strongly negative connotation. A more detailed and finer distinction can be found in Augustine's narration on Psalm 142, eighth verse. For more detail, see for example Sipe, "Struggling with Flesh: Soul/Body Dualism in Porphyry and Augustine."

[125] Falckenberg and Drake, *History of Modern Philosophy*, 13.

Philosopher—with a capital P).[126] One of Thomas Aquinas's main contributions was that he served as an alternative to Augustinian neo-Platonism, which dominantly supported the teaching of the Western church for a thousand years.[127] By "christening" Aristotle, Aquinas created a system that viewed the created world through markedly friendlier eyes. One of the charges of the time against Thomas Aquinas (and Albert) that very well describes this was: "They claim divine wisdom, although worldliness is far more native to their minds."[128]

AQUINAS'S CELEBRATION OF REALITY

Neoplatonic thought favors the notion of an ascension toward God's *unchanging* existence through a gradational hierarchy, ranked more or less according to ties to matter. But Thomas Aquinas considers it differently: "Everything, whether alive or not, whether material or spiritual, whether perfected or wretched, and in fact whether good or evil—everything that has existence, confronts us with the very basic existence of God. This world is not only good—it is in a very precise sense holy."[129] Aquinas teaches us to behave with respect toward *all* creation, to take a positive position on everything that exists. In the words of Thomas Aquinas, "each thing is good because it possesses actual being . . . being itself must be called a good."[130] "God is in all things."[131] From an ontological standpoint, Thomas Aquinas understood the material world to be absolutely *real*.

---

[126] Despite Aquinas's accepting a large part of his teachings from Aristotle, he does not accept them uncritically, and it would be a strong simplification to argue that Thomism is just Aristotelianism in another guise, "re-christened." He cites Aristotle so that he does not have to unnecessarily repeat evidence already carried out, not out of blind honor for the word the Philosopher said. As opposed to his contemporary, Siger of Brabant, who let it be heard that more must be done to secure the opinion of the Philosopher than of the truth, for Aquinas, it was precisely about defending the truth, not Aristotle. On certain points Aquinas, on the contrary, points out Aristotle's erroneous argumentations, and on some questions he leans toward the opinion of Augustine or the neo-Platonic Dionysius Areopagita.

[127] "The truth is that the historical Catholic Church began by being Platonist; by being rather too Platonist." Chesterton, *St. Thomas Aquinas*, 36.

[128] Pieper, *Guide to Thomas Aquinas*, 121.

[129] Pieper, *Guide to Thomas Aquinas*, 142.

[130] Aquinas, *Contra Gentiles* III, Q.7, part 3. To explain the full logic goes like this: "From these considerations it becomes evident that no essence is evil in itself. In fact, evil is simply a privation of something which a subject is entitled by its origin to possess... Now, privation is not an essence; it is, rather, a negation in a substance. Therefore, evil is not an essence in things. Again, each thing has actual being in accord with its essence. To the extent that it possesses being, it has something good; for, if good is that which all desire, then being itself must be called a good, because all desire to be. As a consequence, then, each thing is good because it possesses actual being. Now, good and evil are contraries. So, nothing is evil by virtue of the fact that it has essence. Therefore, no essence is evil.... Therefore, nothing is evil by virtue of its essence.... Now, every being intends a good, when it is acting, as has been proved. Therefore, no being, as being, is evil."

[131] Aquinas, *Summa Theologica* I. Q8 (Whether God is in all things?) A.1, Corpus.

This world was not just a hallucination, a shadow, a trap, a test bed for evil, an imperfect forerunner to the real world—as could be found in the extreme Platonists and some notions of Augustine. For Aquinas, it made perfect sense to resolve the problems of this world.[132]

Thomas Aquinas went even further than Aristotle in his positive position toward *matter*. Aristotle argued that the world was formed by God from *pre*existing matter, which did not represent a subject of God's creation, but the material from which God only formed individual entities. Aquinas, entirely in keeping with the teachings of Judaism, remains convinced that even this primordial *matter* was created by God and that even that is the work of a *good* God's creation,[133] "for everything God created is good."[134] Aquinas counters Augustine's argument that "for the soul to be happy, it must be severed from everything corporeal,"[135] with the notion that the soul sequestered from the body is no more similar to God than the soul in the body. Corporeality therefore does not have to be negative; on the contrary, Aquinas defends it.

This question, which at first appears unspectacular, has immense consequences, especially for economics. If God created out of nothing, *ex nihilo*, then matter too must be the creation of a good God. From this viewpoint, matter, reality, and *this* world represent good—it is therefore worth dealing with, worth improving, and worth addressing. Today, it seems, we are at a somewhat different extreme, that of too much care of the material, exterior world and neglecting our interior, spiritual world, or neglecting the *care for the soul* (as one of the most influential Czech philosophers of the twentieth century, Jan Patočka, writes). Now, the era before Aquinas was biased in exactly the opposite direction. This swing of the pendulum is interesting, as both extremes are to be avoided. As Aquinas's biographer, G. K. Chesterton, wrote, "God made Man so that he was capable of coming in contact with reality; and those whom God hath joined, let no man put apart."[136] As presented by Thomas Aquinas, we look on something that could be called a blessing and emancipation of what today is a common perception of economic behavior.

ARCHETYPES OF THE INVISIBLE HAND

But what to do with the evil? Is it necessary to thoroughly punish and eradicate it through restraints and laws? Thomas Hobbes, for many the greatest philosopher of the modern era, offers a solution. According to

---

[132] Novak, *The Spirit of Democratic Capitalism*, 71, 96.
[133] Aquinas, *Summa Theologica* I. Q44, A.2, Corpus.
[134] 1 Timothy 4:4.
[135] Augustine's opinion quoted in the *Summa Theologica*, Ia-IIae. Q4, A.6, Corpus. Original citation from Augustine's *City of God*, 22.26.
[136] Chesterton, *St. Thomas Aquinas*, 91.

Hobbes, man is born infected by evil, and that is why his acts need to be firmly corrected and inspected. He offers the tough, firm hand of ruler-tyrant as a solution, someone with strong executive powers for suppressing all evil.[137]

If that does not occur, then wantonness will spread among free people, and soon thereafter will be a war with everyone against everyone (*bellum omnium contra omnes*) and chaos will start to grow. It isn't necessary to point out that this consideration has immense impacts for the notion of the economic freedom of individuals, however they are economically engaged. Aquinas stands against this notion: "Every evil is based on some good. Indeed, evil cannot exist by itself, since it has no essence…So, every evil is in a good thing."[138] Evil in and of itself (in and *for* itself) does not exist.[139] It is impossible to commit evil, unless there is some good for whose sake one does the evil deed.[140] Pure evil cannot be intended; it may occur only outside intent.[141] Evil things (evil decisions) do exist,[142] but they defy the basic orientation of human nature.[143] Human nature, and sound reason, tend toward good. Even Socrates had a similar opinion: "Anyone who does anything wrong or bad does so involuntarily."[144]

To avoid misunderstandings: I do not want to say here that man was or is good but only insofar as his nature, if you will, his core, is good. Man has a good core, a good essence, was created in good, but a distortion occurred and man actually does carry out evil deeds.[145] But he has a tendency toward good and is not altogether rotten to the core; man is, to put it in

---

[137] Hobbes, *Leviathan*, 129 : "Tie them by fear of punishment to the performance of their covenants… justice, equity, modesty, mercy, and, in sum, doing to others as we would be done to, of themselves, without the terror of some power… are contrary to our natural passions."

[138] Aquinas, *Contra Gentiles* III, chapter 11 (the title of the chapter is "That Evil Is Based on the Good"). "It can also be shown from the preceding considerations that every evil is based on some good. Indeed, evil cannot exist by itself, since it has no essence, as we have demonstrated."

[139] Ibid., chapter 12. In chapter 7 he concludes with some joy that, "it is impossible for any being, as a being, to be evil… Through this consideration, the error of the Manicheans is refuted, for they claimed that some things are evil in their very natures."

[140] Ibid., chapters 4, 6, and 7.

[141] Ibid., chapter 14: "Therefore, it is clear that evil is an accidental cause and cannot be a direct cause by itself." Or elsewhere, in III, chapter 71: "It is impossible for an agent to do something evil, unless by virtue of the fact that the agent intends something good."

[142] *Summa Theologica* Ia–IIae, Q18, A.1.

[143] Ibid., Q71, A2, OTC, here quotes Augustine (*De Lib.* Arb. III, 13): "Every vice, simply because it is a vice, is contrary to nature."

[144] "[A]s if there were anyone who willingly did bad things. I am pretty sure none of the wise men thinks that any human being willingly makes a mistake or willingly does anything wrong or bad. They know very well that anyone who does anything wrong or bad does so involuntarily." Plato, *Protagoras*, 345d–e.

[145] Mark 7:20–23; Jeremiah 17:9.

Christian terms, still salvable, including the "worst." If there is nothing, absolutely nothing good in mankind, what would be the point of saving them?[146] This is precisely the human core to which God can speak and address his challenges and calls. Bad things that are carried out are a subset of the good. Man can contemplate evil (murder), but it is carried out in a different intention (perhaps revenge, which is his subjective feeling of justice, and justice is good—he gets revenge out of [his feeling for] justice). Even the greatest evils (such as the Holocaust or witch-burning) are carried out under the pretense (rhetorically but also from the convictions of many) of a greater good, one which was behind this evil (the Nazis argued for a greater *Lebensraum* [living space, or the need to expand]; the Inquisitors that their acts would rid the world of evil). So man then carried out entirely mistakenly the greatest evil thinkable, but always did so in the (most self-warped) effort toward *some kind* of good. Intention is not enough for good; knowledge is also necessary.

Evil has its role here in this world, as mentioned before: "For if all evil were prevented, much good would be absent from the universe,"[147] Aquinas writes. Elsewhere he mentions that "many goods are present in things which would not occur unless there were evils."[148] And all in all [my emphasis]:

> It does not pertain to divine providence to prohibit evil entirely from things . . . good of the whole takes precedence over the good of a part. It is proper for a governor with foresight to neglect some lack of goodness in a part, so that there may be an increase of goodness in the whole. . . . If evil were removed from some parts of the universe, much perfection would perish from the universe, whose beauty arises from an ordered unification of evil and good things. In fact, while evil things originate from good things that are defective, still, **certain good things also result from them**, as a consequence of the providence of the governor. Thus, even a silent pause makes a hymn appealing. Therefore, evil should not have been excluded from things by divine providence.[149]

In some ways this starts to sound like the thesis that would later come out in Mandeville's *The Fable of the Bees: or, Private Vices, Publick Benefits*.[150] In his book *New Studies in Philosophy, Politics, Economics, and the History of Ideas*, F. A. Hayek perceives this context very well; he explicitly makes reference to the unoriginality of Mandeville's reflection: "Had not even Thomas Aquinas had to admit that *multitudae utilitates impedirentur si*

---

[146] "It is not the healthy who need a doctor, but the sick." Mark 2:17; "[W]ho wants all men to be saved and to come to a knowledge of the truth." 1 Timothy 2:4.

[147] Aquinas, *Summa Theologica* I. Q22, A.2, R.O.2.

[148] Aquinas, *Contra Gentiles* III, chapter 71.

[149] Ibid., chapter 71, part 7.

[150] At the time of its publication, the fable provoked a major scandal (Hayek, *New Studies in Philosophy, Politics, Economics, and the History of Ideas*, 252), and we will show why later.

omni peccata districte prohiberentur—that much that is useful would be prevented if all sins were strictly prohibited?"[151]

The idea of the invisible hand, or that an unsystematic and frequently evil effort from an individual in society leads to common benefit, is well known among the ancients as well. It was neither Adam Smith nor Bernard Mandeville, nor even Thomas Aquinas, who was the first to express this principle. The ancient poet Aristophanes writes:

> There is a legend of olden time
> That all our foolish plans and vain conceits
> Are overlured to work the public good.[152]

But Aquinas's conception is aimed elsewhere. Even if God does not want evil,[153] Aquinas puts the existence of evil into the context of *evidence* of God's existence and providence, and against those who see evidence of the nonexistence of God in evil acts. For the purposes of the welfare of the whole, partial evil must necessarily exist.[154] The good of the whole supercedes the good of its parts, as we have shown above. In support of these ideas, Aquinas presents two citations from the Bible:

> I form the light and create darkness,
> I bring prosperity and create disaster;
> I, the LORD, do all these things.[155]

And elsewhere:

> When a trumpet sounds in a city,
> do not the people tremble?
> When disaster comes to a city,
> has not the LORD caused it?[156]

If absolute good is to exist, it would certainly be a notion of God. Nevertheless, we see from the citation above that the Hebrews see things in a more complicated light: While it is God who causes peace, he also "causes disaster". Ultimately it is God who placed the Tree of the Knowledge of Good and Evil in the Garden of Eden, and when people ate of it He commented that "the man has now become like one of us,

---

[151] Hayek, *New Studies in Philosophy, Politics, Economics, and the History of Ideas*, 252. Citation from *Summa Theologica* IIa–IIae. Q78, A.2.

[152] Aristophanes, *Ecclesiazusae*, 289. Hayek cites in *The Trend of Economic Thinking: Essays on Political Economists and Economic Thinking*, vol. 3, 85, also in *New Studies in Philosophy, Politics, Economics, and the History of Ideas*, 254.

[153] Aquinas, *Contra Gentiles* I, chapter 95.

[154] Aquinas, *Summa Theologica* I. Q22, A.2, R.O.2.

[155] Isaiah 45:7.

[156] Amos 3:6. With this *Wesley's Notes* comment on this verse: "Evil... either immediately by his [God's] own hand, or by the hands of those he employs. Whatever are the instruments, God is the principal agent. Out of his mouth both good and evil proceed." Matthew Henry's concise *Commentary*: "The evil of sin is from ourselves, it is our own doing; but the evil trouble is from God, and is his doing, whoever are the instruments."

knowing good and evil."[157] On the other hand, we have again shown that even Satan, the embodiment of evil, plays a dual role; his evil role serves to contribute to *some* kind of good. But for moral categories of good and evil to exist, for morals to exist, freedom must exist, because we can only speak of morals within the context of free choice. In this sense, good cannot exist without (at least the possibility of) evil. The possibility of evil existed even in a perfect Eden.

Evil therefore cannot be wiped out from the world, nor is that desirable. This conception does not legitimize the idea of laissez-faire directly, but it significantly enriches it. We have already partially shown this in the parable of the weeds. In any case, we have moved far from the tough and thorough wiping out of vices by a governing power. God's providence does not rule out evil. "Nor was it fitting for the common good to be destroyed in order that individual evil be avoided, especially as God is so powerful that he can direct any evil to a good end."[158] Or, put even more bluntly: "I answer that it is by no means lawful to induce a man to sin, yet it is lawful to make use of another's sin for a good end, since even God uses all sin for some good, since He draws some good from every evil."[159]

Sometimes it is better to harness the devil to the plow than to fight against him. Instead of drawing up huge amounts of energy in the struggle against evil, it is better to use its own energy toward the desired goals; placing a mill on a raging river or harnessing the devil to a cart, as the Czech Saint Prokop did. If you cannot defeat him, trick him. It is wiser and more advantageous to make appropriate use of chaotic natural forces than to try vainly to suppress them in a Sisyphean manner. It is the same curse of evil we already know, thanks to the slip of the tongue of Goethe's Mephistopheles:

Part of that force which would
Do evil evermore, and yet creates the good.[160]

It is enough to direct and *regulate* the self-propelled energy of chaos, which nourishes itself and creates a feedback loop of causality, so that it serves our goals, as that saint did. Economics should then mean the art of helmsmanship. The interaction of chaos and free will should not be understood as an obstacle (even if it appears as a stormy sea) but as a resource. Instead of trying to calm the sea down and directing it by threats of violence, one should instead learn how to steer *on it*. Michael Novak writes interestingly about this problem in his book *The Spirit of Democratic Capitalism*. He argues that in all existing and historical systems, only the system of democratic capitalism has understood how deeply embedded "sin" is in the human spirit; however, it is not possible for any system to

---

[157] Genesis 3:22.

[158] Aquinas, *Summa Theologica* I. Q92, A.1, R.O.3.

[159] Ibid., IIa–IIae Q.78 A4 Corpus.

[160] Goethe, *Faust*, part one, scene 3. English translation: Goethe, *Goethe's Faust*, 159.

uproot this sin. For this reason, capitalism takes the "fallen world" as the base for reality, and in addition manages to "retransform its energy into creative power."[161]

Ultimately God also "plows with the Devil." He can use and uses this evil as His (albeit according to the interpretation of the passage in Ezekiel, stormy[162]) servant.

GOOD OR EVIL MAN

The question of whether man is good or evil is a key question for the social sciences. "Regulation" will develop from it. If man is evil by nature, then it is necessary to force him toward good (in the context and under the pretext of "social good") and limit his freedom. If it is a *dog-eat-dog world*, as Hobbes believes, we need a strong state, a powerful Leviathan that *forces* men toward (men's unnatural) good.

But if on the other hand human *nature* (or something of the ontological core of man's being, his very "I") is good, then more laissez-faire is possible. Man can be *left alone*, because human nature will automatically have a tendency to steer him toward good. State interventions, regulation, and limits to freedom need be applied only where man as part of a whole is not sufficiently (collectively) rational, where spontaneous social coordination works poorly or where *forced* coordination is capable of ensuring better results (in the case of externalities, for example). This is one of the key questions for economics: Can the free will of thousands of individuals be relied on, or does society need coordination from above? Which are the areas of human activity where the spontaneous market can achieve optimal results? When does the interaction of free (unregulated) human activity head spontaneously toward good and when does it head

---

[161] Novak, *The Spirit of Democratic Capitalism*, chapter 4: "Sin."

[162] Ezekiel 28:11–19. This prophecy against the King of Tyrus was so persuasive that it has become adapted to relate directly to the fallen angel Lucifer. Because of its persuasiveness and poetry, it is appropriate to cite it in full:

"You were the model of perfection, full of wisdom and perfect in beauty. You were in Eden, the garden of God; every precious stone adorned you: ruby, topaz and emerald, chrysolite, onyx and jasper, sapphire, turquoise and beryl. Your settings and mountings were made of gold; on the day you were created they were prepared. You were anointed as a guardian cherub, for so I ordained you. You were on the holy mount of God; you walked among the fiery stones. You were blameless in your ways from the day you were created till wickedness was found in you. Through your widespread trade you were filled with violence, and you sinned. So I drove you in disgrace from the mount of God, and I expelled you, O guardian cherub, from among the fiery stones. Your heart became proud on account of your beauty, and you corrupted your wisdom because of your splendor. So I threw you to the earth; I made a spectacle of you before kings. By your many sins and dishonest trade you have desecrated your sanctuaries. So I made a fire come out from you, and it consumed you, and I reduced you to ashes on the ground in the sight of all who were watching. All the nations who knew you are appalled at you; you have come to a horrible end and will be no more."

toward evil? It is precisely in this question of the good or evil of the human core where various schools' differing approaches lie. Are we a society of villains or of neighbors?

THE SOCIETY OF NEIGHBORS

Love toward one's neighbor is one of the key messages of Christianity. Man is born as a *zoon politikon*, a social being.[163] We do not come together into societies because of our shortcomings or necessity (this is not the primary reason) but due to our social character.[164] Not even the newly created and perfect Adam was supposed to remain in solitude: "The LORD God said: 'It is not good for the man to be alone.'"[165]

In the pages of *Summa Theologica*, Thomas Aquinas argues that man was supposed to live a "social life" even in the Garden of Eden—in a state of perfection and innocence.[166] But he goes even further. For him, man is naturally *the familiar and friend of every man*, which is the absolute opposite notion to Hobbes's *dog-eat-dog* world. Aquinas's man is good and, as a social being, is determined to do good even to others. This has a fundamental influence on the view of society and therefore also on the formation of the (economic) tools with which he operates.

> Besides, since "man is naturally a social animal," he needs to be helped by other men in order to attain his own end. This is most fittingly accomplished by mutual love, which obtains among men. Therefore, by the law of God, which directs men to their ultimate end, mutual love is prescribed for us.... Now, it is natural to all men to love each other. The mark of this is the fact that a man, by some natural prompting, comes to the aid of any man in need, even if he does not know him. For instance, he may call him back from the wrong road, help him up from a fall and other actions like that: "as if every man were naturally the familiar and friend of every man."[167]

---

[163] Aquinas, *Summa Theologica* I. Q97, A.4, Corpus; also Aquinas, *Contra Gentiles* III, chapter 117. The term and the idea of *zoon politikon* is taken, of course, from Aristotle. Also see Thomas Aquinas, *De Regno, On Kingship to the King of Cyprus:* "Yet it is natural for man, more than for any other animal, to be a social and political animal, to live in a group." 1.1.4.

[164] On the other hand, in order to avoid possible misinterpretations, it will be appropriate to note that Aquinas's man is an individual—that individuality exists (see *Contra Gentiles* III, chapter 113) and souls are specific (Sigmund, *St. Thomas Aquinas on Politics and Ethics*, 137). At the time not even this question was clear. A struggle with Islamic philosophers flamed up here as well; they believed that all people had a common *racios*, common reason.

[165] Genesis 2:18.

[166] "Because man is naturally a social animal and so in the state of innocence he would have led a social life." *Summa Theologica* I, Q97, A.4, Corpus.

[167] Aquinas, Contra Gentiles III, chapter 117 (this chapter is called "That We Are Ordained by Divine Law to the Love of Neighbor").

Aquinas further writes:

> For men are of mutual assistance to each other in the knowing of truth, and
> one man may stimulate another toward the good, and also restrain him
> from evil. Hence it is said: "As iron sharpens iron, so one man sharpens
> another." (Prov. 27:17). And it is said in Ecclesiastes (4:9–12): "Two are
> better than one, because they have a good return for their work: If one falls
> down, his friend can help him up. But pity the man who falls and has no one
> to help him up! Also, if two lie down together, they will keep warm. But
> how can one keep warm alone? Though one may be overpowered, two can
> defend themselves. A cord of three strands is not quickly broken."[168]

But with such knowledge, Aquinas still sees the existence of rulers as
necessary; rulers to correct the free movement of crowds, so that society
does not fall apart. Aquinas does not allow for anarchy. The following citation represents this reality in several sentences. In addition he considers
the coordination of public interests by a ruler, which creates the central
topic of economics.

> If, then, it is natural for man to live in the society of many, it is necessary
> that there exist among men some means by which the group may be gov-
> erned. For where there are many men together and each one is looking after
> his own interest, the multitude would be broken up and scattered unless
> there were also an agency to take care of what appertains to the common-
> weal. In like manner, the body of a man or any other animal would disinte-
> grate unless there were a general ruling force within the body which watches
> over the common good of all members. With this in mind, Solomon says
> (Prov. 11:14): "Where there is no governor, the people shall fall."[169]

Elsewhere Aquinas writes: "Men also adopt different methods in proceeding towards their proposed end, as the diversity of men's pursuits and
actions clearly indicates. Consequently man needs some directive principle to guide him towards his end."[170]

Society therefore requires neither a *tyrant* nor a *central planner* but a
regulator, a ruler-helmsman. So economics must also be epitomized by
the helmsman's art, instead of as a tool for turning rivers or completely
remaking them.

REASON AND FAITH

It would be a major misunderstanding to argue that the era of medieval
scholastics was a period of blind faith and that humanity had to wait until
the Enlightenment for the renewal of reason. If we read Thomas Aquinas
with this erroneous perspective, we will again and again be taken aback by

---

[168] Aquinas, *Contra Gentiles* III, chapter 128.
[169] Aquinas, *De Regno*, 1.1.8.
[170] Ibid., 1.1.

how much emphasis he places on the rational part of knowledge. In this regard he appears as one of the most devoted listeners to reason. Many other theologians before and after him appealed to pure revelation and disdained reason under the heading "lean not to your own understanding."[171] For example, Martin Luther later stated that faith is set up as the antithesis of reason, and he called reason "the devil's whore."[172] For the first time in this context, Aquinas's quote comes to the fore: "It is impossible that the truth of faith should be opposed to those principles that the human reason knows naturally . . . for God is the Author of our nature."[173] He requires a dialectic relationship between faith and reason in the sense that one needs the other, and he himself takes great pains that reason be developed as much as possible and that our faith not be misguided.

But Aquinas goes even further and insists that science is important for the teaching of faith, because if something can be undoubtedly proven which evidently resists dogma, then here science has revealed an item of faith which has either been badly interpreted or not understood.[174] Reason could not have received higher recognition. He designated the role of science in the following manner: If practical discoveries can be truly proven, the traditional explanation of the Bible must defer, because that interpretation was erroneous. Aquinas's biographer G. K. Chesterton is convinced that if the whole matter were left to Aquinas and the likes of him, there would have never been such a clash between religion and science.[175]

Reason is made nearly equal to virtue; revolting against reason was for Aquinas like revolting against God, for "in that field the reason has a right to rule, as a representative of God in Man."[176] According to Chesterton, Aquinas envisages divinity as pure intelligence. A person is as virtuous as the level on which they are able to listen to their reason and later act according to it. Not using reason where possible is a sin—"vincible ignorance is a sin," he writes.[177] In the chapter in which he discusses drunkenness, he classifies drunkenness as a sin precisely because man consciously gives up the use of reason.[178] We find an entire range of similar exaltations in Aquinas's writings. Aquinas was not able to imagine, as wasn't Descartes

---

[171] Proverbs 3:5.

[172] Luther, *Last Sermon in Wittenberg*, Band 51:126, Line 7ff. The entire citation reads, "But since the devil's bride, Reason, that pretty whore, comes in and thinks she's wise, and what she says, what she thinks, is from the Holy Spirit, who can help us, then? Not judges, not doctors, no king or emperor, because [reason] is the Devil's greatest whore." Also see Nelson: *Economics as Religion*, 131.

[173] Aquinas, *Contra Gentiles* I, chapter 7, part 1.

[174] Aquinas, *Contra Gentiles* II, chapter 3. Also see Pieper, *Guide to Thomas Aquinas*, 118–119.

[175] See Chesterton, *St. Thomas Aquinas*.

[176] Chesterton, *St. Thomas Aquinas*.

[177] *Summa Theologica* I, chapter 2, Q 76, A.2.

[178] "Thus drunkenness (of this kind) is a mortal sin because through it a man willingly and knowingly deprives himself of the use of reason which enables him to act virtuously and avoid sin." *Summa Theologica* IIa–IIae, Q150, A.2.

years later,[179] "God the Deceiver," who gave man reason and senses only so he could deceive him.

Aquinas revels in reason as far as it goes. In this he is very similar to Thomas H. Huxley, an agnostic who invented the word "agnosticism." In fact, Aquinas nearly literally accepts Huxley's definition of the agnostic method: *To stick to reason as far as it is possible*. The only question is *how far* is it possible? For at a certain point in argumentation, sooner or later, every rationalist falls back on intuition.[180]

THE CITY, NATURE, AND FREEDOM

Thomas Aquinas also runs into the trade-off between personal independence and social progress, which even Gilgamesh's civilized friend Enkidu knew. Aquinas writes:

> If man were intended to live alone, as many animals do, he would require no other guide to his end. Each man would be a king unto himself, under God, the highest King, inasmuch as he would direct himself in his acts by the light of reason given him from on high. Yet it is natural for man, more than for any other animal, to be a social and political animal, to live in a group. This is clearly a necessity of man's nature. For all other animals, nature has prepared food, hair as a covering, teeth, horns, claws as means of defence or at least speed in flight, while man alone was made without any natural provisions for these things. Instead of all these, man was endowed with reason . . . Now, one man alone is not able to procure them all for himself, for one man could not sufficiently provide for life, unassisted. It is therefore natural that man should live in the society of many.[181]

Specialization meant the necessity of social development from primitive being (just as the humanized Enkidu did) to a higher level. In this sense it is important to note that, as Georg Simmel puts it, "The metropolis has always been the seat of the money economy. Here the multiplicity and concentration of economic exchange gives an importance to the means of exchange which the scantiness of rural commerce would not have allowed."[182]

Man alone is unable to ensure all of the happiness society offers. If he lived alone in the desert or on a forgotten island, he would be the ruler of himself. Instead of the material well-being he receives in a specialized society, he would gain the freedom to govern himself and not be subordinate to anyone in a social structure. But if he lives in society and were to

---

[179] Descartes, *Discourse on Method*; similar topics also in *Meditations*.
[180] As G. K. Chesterton puts it: "I am a rationalist. I like to have some intellectual justification for my intuitions" (Chesterton, *Orthodoxy*, 203).
[181] Introduction to *De Regno*, 1.1.
[182] Simmel, *Simmel on Culture*, 176.

use its advantages, he must be naturally part of the order that enables society to head toward a common goal.

CONCLUSION: THE BIBLE AS AN ECONOMIC READING

Christianity is the leading religion of our Euro-American civilization. Most of our social and economic ideals come from Christianity or are derived from it. The economy is thus often believed or presented to be more of a social fabric than religious faith itself. If we have such high expectations of these commonly held beliefs (for example, in secularized economic progress, as we will see in the second part of this book), we must treat those beliefs with the same scrutiny as others.

It is surprising how much the economy has in common with the Old and New Testaments. The original sin can be also interpreted as a "sin of consumption," as Adam and Eve did actually consume something that they had no title to and did not need to consume; that consumption was connected with guilt (as we will see in second part of this book). Most of Jesus's parables use economic language or context. And the very key term of Christianity—redemption—originally had a purely economic meaning—to redeem, to purchase a slave, and to set him or her free. This undeserved forgiveness of debts, redemption, the forgiveness of sins, can be observed in our culture as well—when the government plays the role of the redeemer and redeems overindebted banks and companies. So did the word *sin*, which meant *debt* in Greek, originally have a purely economic meaning. In fact, the key concepts of Christianity would not make sense without economic terminology. And so it appears that the basic messages of Christianity can be better understood in our economic age much better if they are interpreted in the (original) economic terminology. They become much more specific and current. The prayer "forgive us our sins" meaning "cancel our debts" could be heard from the leading banks in the crisis of 2008 and 2009.

Christian thought highlights the concept of what could be called positive unfairness. It is unfair in a positive sense—such as redemption, or the parable of unjustly high wages for workers. It doesn't matter how hard you try—everyone gets the same reward. Christianity thus largely abolishes the accounting of good and evil. God forgives, which is positively unfair. Christianity introduces the concept of heaven into the great narrative and thus solves the Hebrew problem of divine justice and its manifestation (or lack of it) here on Earth.

We have also discussed gifts and prices, as some things that cannot be bought but must be given. We try to mimic that, often even today, when we pretend not to care about a price or intentionally dilute it. We have discussed the economics of salvation and love as the key binding principle of the universe. We have debated at some length the problem of evil and how evil plays a role in the good scheme of things—and how it can never be totally destroyed. We debated the issue of the invisible hand of the market—how our evil deeds can turn into benefits, but also how good intentions can turn sour. We debated the issue of whether we can truly have evil intentions and studied the concept of the relationship of good and evil. The economic thought of Augustine and Aquinas is also presented as very relevant for understanding of the fabric that makes up today's world. We debated the good or evil nature of human beings and the world. Finally, we have talked about the relationship between reason and emotions, and about nature versus civilization as the basic state of human existence.

5

Descartes the Mechanic

The standpoint of economic theory is Cartesian.
These are the roots of the homo oeconomicus,
as narrow a concept of man as can be imagined . . .
Piero Mini

Myths, faith, and religious teachings were thus far a determining key for explaining the surrounding world, including its "economic" characteristics. The arrival of the scientific era brought changes with it (or, as we will later see, should have brought changes). The era of scientific thought set a goal of pushing through a method of examining the world that would not allow doubt and would be free of any subjective, disputable dimension. Perhaps the most important characteristic of the modern era has been the change in emphasis from the question *why?* to the question *how?* This shift is, so to speak, from essence to method. The scientific era has tried to demystify the world around us, to present it in mechanical, mathematical, deterministic, and rational garments and to get rid of axioms that cannot be empirically confirmed, such as faith and religion. But alas, even in the dimension of *how?* the world around us to this day certainly keeps its secrets—and needs faith and belief to function.

While economics is classified as a social science, it relies the most (mainly mainstream economics) on a mechanical, mathematical, deterministic, and rational world. Thus, it is important to give appropriate attention to this tectonic maneuver. Understanding of the ideas of René Descartes has crucial importance for economists who consider these things, because "an economic position is Cartesian."[1]

MAN AS MACHINE

Descartes's scientific approach to perceiving the world unquestionably represented a huge breakthrough, and this is doubly true for economists. We have seen that the notion of the invisible hand of the market existed long before Smith. Homo economicus has gained his (a)moral side from

---

[1] Mini, *Philosophy and Economics*, 24.

Epicurus, but he acquired his mathematical and mechanical part from René Descartes. Mathematics was considered the original principle of all things as early as the Greek philosopher Pythagoras[2] (completely in the spirit of the postmodern era, where our current viewpoints are created only through recycling and combining past stories). Descartes's ideas, of course, became absolutely key, if not determining, for the methodology of economic science. Economics started to develop at the time when his legacy received widespread recognition. The first economists widely discussed theories of knowledge, and all have proven to be successors to Descartes. His ideas were brought to England by John Locke and David Hume. Through them, Descartes's teachings penetrated economics as well—and they have remained firmly built into it to this day. In no other social science were the Cartesian ideas accepted with as much enthusiasm as in economics. What did the greatness of Descartes consist of, and what was the fundamental significance of his theories for economists?

Descartes is widely and to a degree deservedly considered a key founder of modern science.[3] He changed seeing the world[4] and the anthropological understanding of the existence of man immediately in several areas. This scientific (re)construction had impacts on anthropology. Let Mill and Bentham's utilitarian calculus be an example of the effect on morals and economics; it would later, in modified form, become an inherent part of modern economics.

First, Descartes tried to get rid of tradition, myth, and superstition, but especially subjective nonsystematicness (understand this as a dependence on feelings and emotions). By doing so, he laid the foundations for a *new method* of systematic examination of the world on a firm (objective) basis. We will later get to how he managed to do this.

---

[2] "This rise of algebraic analysis was concurrent with Descartes's discovery of analytical geometry, and then with the invention of the infinitesimal calculus by Newton and Leibniz. Truly, Pythagoras, if he could have foreseen the issue of the train of thought which he had set going would have felt himself fully justified in his brotherhood with its excitement of mysterious rites. . . . The history of the seventeenth century science reads as though it were some vivid dream of Plato or Pythagoras." Whitehead, *Science and the Modern World*, 32–34.

[3] Some authors see Bishop Nicholas of Kues as the true founder of modern science. The first division of "modern philosophy from scholastic philosophy" can be dated to 1450 when Nicholas of Kues wrote his masterpiece *Idiota*. The process of "rebirth" was completed with Descartes's *Principles of Philosophy* in 1644. See Falckenberg, *History of Modern Philosophy*, 27.

[4] "But the revival of philosophy in the hands of Descartes and his successors was entirely coloured in its development by the acceptance of the scientific cosmology at its face value. The success of their ultimate ideas confirmed scientists in their refusal to modify them as the result of an enquiry into their rationality. Every philosophy was bound in some way or other to swallow them whole. Also the example of science affected other regions of thought. The historical revolt has thus been exaggerated into the exclusion of philosophy from its proper role of harmonising the various abstractions of methodological thought. Thought is abstract; and the intolerant use of abstractions is the major vice of the intellect." Whitehead, *Science and the Modern World*, 19.

Second, after the relatively Aristotelian-Thomistic medieval period, the ancient *dualistic* representation of the polarities of matter and spirit reentered the world—only the soul to a certain extent was replaced with intellect. So this new dualism was not as much ethical in nature as it was epistemological. Man is the only link between matter and intellect, just as in older dualistic concepts (of man hanging between good and evil). Even here the superiority of intellect over material holds—the rationalist position—which to this day enables economists to create their models without their necessarily having a fixed relationship to empirical reality.

Third, fascinated by the technical progress of the time, the new period introduces the concept of mathematical mechanics as the ontological texture of reality. Mechanics then is promoted from a relatively narrow use in machinery to the highest rung on the ontological ladder.[5] If morals are the main texture of reality in the notions of the Hebrews, mercy for the Christians, and love for Augustine, mechanics becomes the main building block in Descartes's hands. We will return to the difficulties of this notion, but here let us present Mini's noteworthy observation: "Despite his superficial emphasis on thinking, Descartes really assigned to thought only a very meager role. The roads to discovery are many, but he acknowledged only one—the mathematical one."[6]

The reduction of human anthropology relates to the reduction of intellect to mathematics. There is no room for emotion, chance, or any kind of unfilled space in such a world. Everything relates to each other with a deterministic hardness and the precision of a mechanical watch. Descartes and his heirs "conceived practically everything in mathematical terms—the universe, the body politic, the human body, even human impulses and morality."[7] Cartesian mechanics are excellently summarized in Descartes's own example in the *Treatise on Man*, where he perceives the body as "just a statue or a machine made of earth" and its function derived from simple mechanical principles, the same as "clocks, artificial fountains, mills and other machines."[8] This way of thinking allegedly knows how to

---

[5] "Also in his *Principles of Philosophy*, he [Descartes] says: 'That by our senses we know nothing of external objects beyond their figure [or station], magnitude, and motion.' Thus the bodies are perceived as with qualities which in reality do not belong to them, qualities which in fact are purely the offspring of the mind. Thus nature gets credit which should in truth be reserved for ourselves; the rose for its scent: the nightingale for his song: and the sun for his radiance. The poets are entirely mistaken. They should address their lyrics to themselves, and should turn them into odes of self-congratulation on the excellency of the human mind. Nature is a dull affair, soundless, scentless, colourless; merely the hurrying of material, endlessly, meaninglessly. However you disguise it, this is the practical outcome of the characteristic scientific philosophy which closed the seventeenth century." Whitehead, *Science and the Modern World*, 56.

[6] Mini, *Philosophy and Economics*, 24.

[7] Ibid., 18.

[8] Descartes, *Treatise on Man*, 99, AT XI, 120.

explain everything—even the things psychology has laboriously tried to do to this day: "Indeed one may compare the nerves of that machine I am describing with the pipes in the works of a fountain . . . with various devices and strings."[9] This faith is still strong in economics to this day—economic man is a mechanical construct that works on infallible mathematical principles and through pure mechanics, and economists are capable of explaining even his innermost motives.

In the spirit of the Ionian philosophers, Descartes transfers the entire world into one basic parameter of principles for one's own existence, which for him represents distribution in space, or *res extensa*, a kind of common denominator of all material things. For Descartes, only a single world exists: "Matter of the heavens and earth is the same."[10] His methodological monism (the effort to transfer or infer everything from one single principle) and the principal equivalence of the spiritual and material worlds play a leading role in economics to this day. The unifying, fundamental, and all-explaining principle to which economics is inclined at almost every opportunity is, understandably, self-interest.

COGITO ERGO SUM

Because René Descartes had a truly breakthrough influence on economic anthropology, it would be appropriate to at least briefly summarize his ideas. In the *Principles of Philosophy*, Descartes tries to throw out anything that could be even slightly doubted. Toward this purpose he forgets everything he knew, remembers what his senses say, and he concentrates solely on logical thinking. In the end, he comes to the conviction that something which makes up these thoughts—therefore he himself, who carries out these thoughts—must necessarily exist.[11] He comes to his famous conclusion *cogito ergo sum*. He bases his philosophy on this new and, according to his convictions, solid foundation. He later comes to evidence of the existence of God—because he finds his notion in thought—and continues further, until in the second part of the book he arrives at the principle of objective existence of material objects and space.

Because material objects, and therefore space as well, can apparently only be perceived by the senses, empiricism, in a philosophical sense, comes into conflict with rationalism. But Descartes tries to hold firmly to a rationalist methodology, one for which he himself clears a path. If, of course, the senses state something different than reason does, reason is right. Even if we do not see that reality, it is more reasonable to trust the logical explanation. Things also exist that are incomprehensible for our

---

[9] All from Descartes, *Treatise on Man*, 100, AT XI, 131.
[10] Descartes, *Principles of Philosophy*, paragraph 22.
[11] But he could have also carried this exercise in another way: "I feel, therefore I am," or "I love, therefore I am," etc.

senses; they are blind and mute in certain areas, and reason can go places where they cannot reach. Even if particles cannot be split infinitely "in reality," we are capable of this act in our thoughts (imagination). The real world therefore is a representation of the rational world rather than the world we know from "mere" experience.

But how can we be sure the external world of phenomena (and therefore also of space) exists at all if we cannot believe our own senses? How do we know it is not just a dream? But that would suppose that God is deceiving us and that everything we "see" is just an illusion of space, matter, and time. In certain places Descartes considers the exterior world as a continuous dream, one that objectively does not exist. As Descartes writes, this assumes a God that would want to deceive us. This is an unacceptable idea for him. He does not analyze where he gets his certainty from and relies only on a sort of theological evidence, one which is based on the Christian understanding of God as the giver of light.[12] If God is the most true and perfect, He cannot want to deceive us. If we are to assume that God is not intoxicating us with the opiate of dreams,[13] we must come to the conclusion that the external material world really exists and that we can examine it. What sort of "scientific proof" is this?

Of all material things, Descartes first deals with our bodies. While they lie in the realm of material world, they are an exception because they are in some way *joined* with our intellect, which is not subject to matter. Matter residing in space acts on our bodies, which function as a *medium*, and thus matter communicates with our reason through our senses. Another step leads to the examination of the essence of things that act on our bodies—material items whose principle Descartes seeks. This principle cannot be found in anything perceptible by the senses (such as color, hardness, temperature, matter), but only in their arrangement, which can be described in three mathematical characteristics: arrangement in width, length, and depth (in the basic Cartesian system these are represented by axes x, y, and z).[14] The reason why the nature of material things is

---

[12] "The first attribute of God which here falls to be considered, is that he is absolutely veracious and the source of all light, so that it is plainly repugnant for him to deceive us." Descartes, *Principles of Philosophy*, 27.

[13] "God would, without question, deserve to be regarded as a deceiver, if he directly and of himself presented to our mind the idea of this extended matter, or merely caused it to be presented to us by some object which possessed neither extension, figure, nor motion. For we clearly conceive this matter as entirely distinct from God, . . . since God cannot deceive us, for this is repugnant to his nature, as has been already remarked, we must unhesitatingly conclude that there exists a certain object extended in length, breadth, and thickness." Descartes, *Principles of Philosophy*, 42.

[14] "And indeed, as I perceive different sorts of colours, sounds, odours, tastes, heat, hardness, etc., I safely conclude that there are in the bodies from which the diverse perceptions of the senses proceed, certain varieties corresponding to them, although, perhaps, not in reality like them," Descartes, *A Discourse on Method*, 135; and "We perceive nothing out of us by our senses except light, colors, smells, tastes, sounds, and the tactile qualities; and these I have recently shown to be nothing more, at least so far as they are known to us, than

determined by arrangement in space is shown in the example of a stone. We can imagine that through grinding we can take the hardness away from a stone; we can also recall that a stone that has no color is clear; we can separate weight, the feeling of coldness and warmth, and all similar characteristics. The only substance that we cannot separate from a stone is its arrangement in three dimensions (*res extensa*). This substance is identical to space.[15]

MODELS AND MYTHS

In the hands of the rationalist Descartes, empirical perceptions (which were at the time of the later medieval scholastic tradition thought of as being in harmony with reason) suffered a defeat, and in the battle for closer proximity to "reality," reason won. Descartes closes his eyes and *meditates*: "I suppose, accordingly, that all the things which I see are false (fictitious); I believe that none of those objects which my fallacious memory represents ever existed; I suppose that I possess no senses; I believe that body, figure, extension, motion, and place are merely fictions of my mind. What is there, then, that can be esteemed true? Perhaps this only, that there is absolutely nothing certain."[16] The battle between rationalists and empiricists played out again in later periods, and the results varied; but it was Descartes who struck the historic key blow to the imperfection of our senses.

George Berkeley comments on this in the following way: "Prejudices and errors of sense do from all parts discover themselves to our view; and, endeavoring to correct these by reason, we are insensibly drawn into uncouth paradoxes, difficulties, and inconsistencies, which multiply and grow upon us as we advance in speculation, till at length, having wandered through many intricate mazes, we find ourselves just where we were, or, which is worse, sit down in a forlorn Scepticism."[17] And Galileo is even more blunt: "The new [Cartesian] science has carried out a rape of our perceptions."[18]

We can look at the philosophy of René Descartes as a leading example of what we could call *"paradox of inconsistency."* Despite the errors in its foundations, the Cartesian scientific method became the main *modus operandi* of today's mainstream economic thought. We have lived to see similar moments in economics as well. Systems containing internal inconsistencies,

---

certain dispositions of the objects, consisting of magnitude, figure and motion." Descartes, *The Principles of Philosophy*, 57.

[15] See Anzenbaucher, *Úvod do filozofie* [Introduction to Philosophy], 79.

[16] Descartes, *Meditations*, second meditation, first chapter.

[17] Berkeley, *A Treatise Concerning the Principles of Human Knowledge*, 9.

[18] Taken from Arendt, *The Human Condition*, 274, article n31 from Galileo's *Dialogues concerning the Two Great Systems of the World*.

which are partially in conflict with reality and frequently based on purely and *intentionally unrealistic* assumptions and which come to absurd conclusions in extremes, are nonetheless successfully applied. It would appear that the system has its lifespan not due to its infallibility or logical consistency, but because of the nonexistence of a competing system (these issues are discussed in greater detail by K. Popper, I. Lakatosh, P. Feyerabend, and finally also by T. S. Kuhn).[19] Economic models therefore are not accepted on the basis of greater or lesser truthfulness (even if a correspondence to reality certainly adds to their attractiveness), but rather on the basis of greater or lesser *believability, suitability, persuasive force,* or *correspondence with our internalized faith in the workings of the world* (i.e., with borrowed or inherited paradigms or, if you will, prejudices). Scientific and economic models play a similar role as myths when one system (or myth) replaces or destroys another. This is what occurred when theological myth was replaced by scientific myth. We should note when reading Descartes how inconspicuously and carefully he replaces the theological myth with the scientific myth and how he proceeds.[20]

DOUBTS ABOUT DOUBTING

It is paradoxical that Descartes, who wanted to separate pure logic and rationality, presents us with a pleiad of logically unfounded notions, prejudices, and ideologies that he himself believed. His path to pure reliance on reason then "surprisingly" leads *back* to an *affirmation of his previous ideas* (prejudices), or such a world as Descartes saw before he started to doubt at all (even if undoubtedly he had his doubts).

Descartes's "evidence" of God's existence can serve as an example. It builds on the idea that we bear the notion of God in our thoughts (read: as Descartes bore it); according to him this idea would not be possible if He were not real. Then what was the point of the exercise?

Descartes took the Bible and Thomas Aquinas's *Summa Theologica* with him on all his travels, and he also wrote of mystical appearances which he had.[21] Of course, if he were not a Christian he would find it

---

[19] Excellent secondary literature from this area comes from the Czech author B. Fajkus's *Současná filosofie a metodologie* [Contemporary Philosophy and the Methodology of Science], or Mini, *Philosophy and Economics: The Origins of Development of Economic Theory,* or Caldwell, *Beyond Positivism.*

[20] And so "reducing scientific knowledge to the collective beliefs of members of scientific disciplines." See Redman, *Economics and the Philosophy of Science,* 22, where she summarizes Kuhn's view using Suppe, *The Structure of Scientific Theories,* 647–648.

[21] For more on Cartesian "meditations" or the visions he had, see Yates, *The Rosicrucian Enlightenment,* 152: "Descartes went into winter quarters at a place on the Danube, where, warmed by a German stove, he fell into a series of profound meditations. On the night of 10 November 1619, he had dreams, which seem to have been a most important experience, leading him towards the conviction that mathematics were the sole key to the understanding

difficult to sometimes come to what he wishes to be universally valid conclusions. He makes an even more absurd judgment in the evidence of the existence of external things, or things found outside intellect—in the empirical "phenomenal" world. Put in a simplified fashion, it is unthinkable that our senses deceive, and from this he draws the conclusion that they do not deceive. Descartes, who developed his method precisely and mainly to be rid of traditions and prejudices, establishes them even more firmly.

We are very familiar with the same processes in economics, where on the basis of carefully selected assumptions we come to conclusions that are (understandably and, actually, unevitably) already contained in the assumptions. So, conclusions are really irrelevant (they are merely derived from assumptions); it is the *assumptions that are key*. (This is quite contrary to the exact opposite notion most hold of the popular versions of science—that assumptions are irrelevant and it is the *conclusions* that matter.) And so McCloskey notes that *Economics*, the bible-textbook of mainstream economics by Paul Samuelson, promises scientific "knowledge free of doubt, free from metaphysics, morals and personal conviction. What it is able to deliver renames as scientific methodology the . . . economic scientist's metaphysics, morals and personal convictions."[22] The anthropological difference between scientific and prescientific man is that prescientific man explicitly knew the assumptions referred to (articles of faith and myths) and actively accepted them (or rejected them). In contrast, modern man bears his (scientific) faith more or less unconsciously. Religion is accompanied by an explicit profession of faith[23] but not science (although it is clear that you must use belief in science as well).[24] It is as if modern man is ashamed of his (scientific) faith: This could very well be because it cannot be scientifically proven, which somehow does not correspond with our modern anthropology. The whole concept of "scientific faith" seems to a common ear to be an oxymoron, but it is not.

---

of nature." On the importance of hermeneutic writings in the Renaissance see Feyerabend, *Against Method*, 35: "After Aristotle and Ptolemy, the idea that the earth moves—that strange, ancient, and entirely "ridiculous" Pythagorean view—was thrown on the rubbish heap of history, only to be revived by Copernicus and to be forged by him into a weapon for the defeat of his defeaters. The Hermetic writings played an important part in this revival, which is still not sufficiently understood, and they were studied with care by the Great Newton himself." Also see Yates, *Giordano Bruno and the Hermetic Tradition*, especially chapter 8, "Renaissance Magic and Science": "For the new school of Cartesian philosophy, Renaissance animist philosophies, with their Hermetic basis, were utterly outmoded ways of approaching the world. Science replaced magic in the great seventeenth-century advance," 395.

[22] McCloskey, *The Rhetoric of Economics*, 16.

[23] For example, Apostolic professions of faith: "I believe in God the Almighty, Creator of the Heavens and the Earth."

[24] "It is the faith that at the base of things we shall not find mere arbitrary mystery. The faith in the order of nature which has made possible the growth of science is a particular example of a deeper faith. This faith cannot be justified by any inductive generalisation." Whitehead, *Science and the Modern World*, 20.

Prescientific man did not bother with scientific evidence and, therefore, did not have to be ashamed of his *articles of faith* (today we would say *prejudices*) and could confess them freely. They are nowadays hidden in *axioms* that are *postulated* (not confessed in terms of "I believe in . . ."), never proven; most of scientific faith, however, is laid even before such axioms are even mentioned; this faith rests deeper, so deep we don't even notice it. Thus, Alfred N. Whitehead criticizes Descartes's approaches as a "source of those quite unbelievable abstractions by which modern philosophy has been ruined."[25]

Through the *pretentious* (yes, *pretentious*) *doubting* of the existence of the real world, Descartes returns in a circle back to the existence of the real world (only this time it is "scientifically proven"). If he *truly doubted*, he could not pronounce (not even in his *dreams*) that he *believes* in an empirical world, one which must be real and not deceptive, and conduct his "evidence" on the basis of these rearrangements. Doubts can therefore be made about the integrity of Descartes's doubting: We can doubt his doubting. We must search for the meaning of his inquiry, because what use would this exercise be to us if it only confirmed everything we previously believed? In addition, it is actually ironic and paradoxical that Descartes began and gave birth to the foundation of the scientific method and scientific discourse in a *dream*.[26]

INFLATIONARY RATIONALITY IN A CIRCLE

Kant later raised the thesis that pure reason needs an external, empirical world to be able to *think* at all. In other words, in order for reason to be able to function, it needs to operate with *external* stimuli or their concepts. Language itself is a net of abstractions that are meaningless in and of themselves. *Rationality in and of itself* simply turns inflationarily in a circle; rationality is of itself hollow. On the other hand, empiricism in and of itself is bereft of interpretation; it is lacking meaning, is *sense*less, is *meaning*less, and therefore does not exist.[27] Facts do not work without a rational perceiver, a certain rational framework in which interpretation, name, and meaning are gained. As Caldwell writes, "at least for science, there are no brute facts."[28]

---

[25] Whitehead, *Science and the Modern World*, 82.

[26] "It is one of the more profound ironies of the history of thought that the growth of mechanical science, through which arose the idea of mechanism as a possible philosophy of nature, was itself an outcome of the Renaissance magical tradition." Yates, *The Rosicrucian Enlightenment*, 150. Frances Yates is a respected authority in this field.

[27] Meaning without an interpretational framework, without an explanatory theory—we cannot cognitively perceive facts without the framework, story, interpretation, meaning.

[28] Caldwell, *Beyond Positivism*, 48.

For economists, Descartes's reduction of man has additional key consequences. From his time, man is defined not by emotion but by logical reasoning. A perceptive individuality falls and is lost in the generality of an objective rationality identical for all. What cannot be calculated or at least proxied with numbers is treated as if it were not real, illusionary. A mathematical equation becomes the ideal of truth: cold, distant, the same for all individuals, historically and spatially constant. Man and reality are reduced to mechanical-mathematical calculus. If this reduction cannot be carried out, it is as if it only testified to a shortage of knowledge and of ignorance—such a preserve remains unchartered territory, mythic and scorned.

YOU WILL ALWAYS DREAM ALONE

With this we come to another conclusion, one that is important for economics. By doing this (reducing man and reality to mechanical-mathematical calculus), Descartes also carried out a less generally known step in the direction of the individualization of the individual. Descartes's man is not defined in the context of society—he does not accept social impulses. Descartes remains completely alone in his dreamworld. Even Plato, who carried out a similar exercise with the deception of the senses two thousand years before Descartes, finally got to the point when a man who has lived his whole life in a cave of dreams (*with his friends*, whom he later tries to free!) breaks free of his bonds in the end and comes out of the cave to behold bare reality. Plato's parable of the cave reaches its climax when he remembers those close to him and with his return to them. But Descartes is closed off in his world, completely alone. After all, rationality doesn't need others. As Edmund Husserl put it: "Descartes, in fact, inaugurates an entirely new kind of philosophy. Changing its total style, philosophy takes a radical turn: from naive Objectivism to transcendental subjectivism."[29]

It is precisely this sociopsychological position from which we can attack Descartes's first meditational step as well, when he comes to his famous *cogito ergo sum*. It can nevertheless be said just as well—and perhaps more convincingly—that man gained all his *cogitos* on the basis of social interaction (as Plato's story somewhat portrays).[30] Philosophers such as Immanuel Kant, Martin Buber, Emmanuel Levinas, and others stand on this side; they *define* human existence on the basis of individuals meeting with other individuals. According to them, only through meeting with another is the notion of the "I exist" born.

---

[29] Husserl, *Cartesian Meditations*, 4.
[30] Compare this with Marx's position in Mini, *Philosophy and Economics*, 174.

CONCLUSION: OBJECTIVITY AND MANY COLORS

In conclusion, let's mention another of Husserl's observations. Descartes struggled to set up new, unshakable foundations of science, so that scientific knowledge would be left unified, self-evident to all, and indisputable. Briefly put, he struggled for objectivity (unity, or the unification of points of view) so that he could rid the new philosophy (science) of disputes, doubt, subjectivity, and the disunity of explanations that stem from it. His new science was to be such that everyone would agree on—objectively. In other words, he wanted to remove all doubt.

If we look around ourselves, we can see that a unification of neither scientific viewpoints nor methods occurred and that the opinions of individual philosophers (or scientists, among whom economists, sociologists, or doctors could be counted) drastically differ. Specifically, in economics there is not even agreement on the most fundamental models, and methodology by far is not unified. It is more the agreement on a question that unites a field, not the answers.

Science has not succeeded in being built as Descartes wished. Science is overflowing with doubts. We find ourselves in a similar situation as before Descartes, when world opinion was set by religion. The only difference is that science has become the religion of the modern era. After an excursion into the area (more or less successful) of the transformation of myth in science, let us return to the main setting of economic thinking. Let us start with a man who has influenced economic thinking to the present day, despite the fact that only a couple of sentences are devoted to him in economic theory textbooks, Bernard Mandeville.

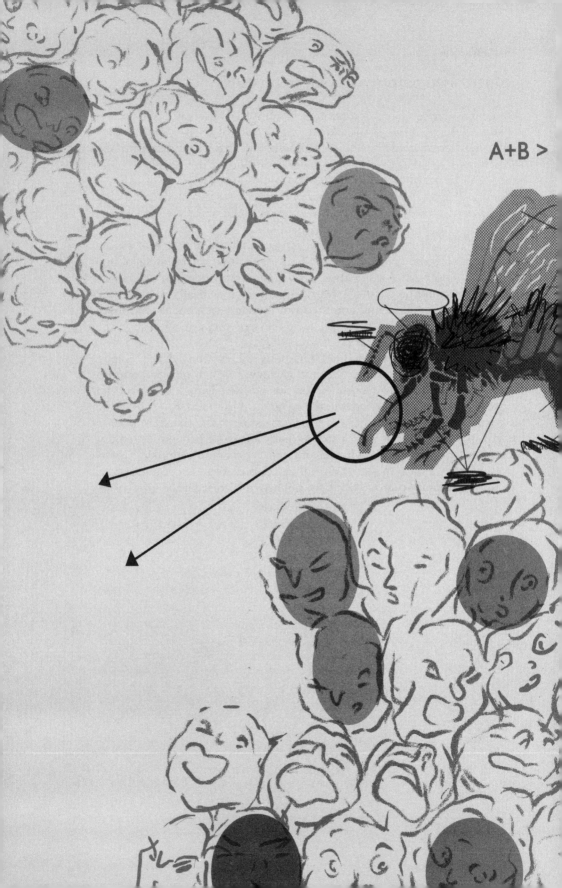

A+B >

6

Bernard Mandeville's Beehive of Vice

The Worst of all the Multitude did something
for the common Good.
Bernard Mandeville

As argued in the chapter about the Old Testament, ethics has disappeared from mainstream economic thought. A debate about morality was considered the somewhat luxurious icing on the cake of profitability and wealth. For economists, ethics became uninteresting and irrelevant. There was no need to talk about ethics—it sufficed to rely on the invisible hand of the market; it would automatically transform private vices (such as selfishness) into general welfare (such as growth in efficiency). Once again, we have a historic irony: As we will soon see, the idea of the invisible hand of the market is, in reality, born of moral inquiry, but about a hundred years later the issue of morality is lost and economics is completely emancipated from ethics. An unusual reversal has taken place. Adam Smith, Thomas Malthus, John S. Mill, John Locke—the great fathers of classical liberal economics—were foremost moral philosophers.[1] A century later, economics had become a mathematized and allocative science, full of graphs, equations, and tables, with no room for ethics.

How could this happen? We must search Bernard Mandeville for an important part of the answer; he may not be as well known as Adam Smith, but he is the true father of the idea of the invisible hand of the market as we know it today. The theory of the market's invisible hand, which today is erroneously attributed to Adam Smith, left a deep mark on the morality of economics: It postulated that private ethics do not matter; anything that happens, be it moral or amoral, contributes to the general welfare. It's not difficult to suspect that just at the moment when the principle of the invisible hand is simplified and popularized, ethics becomes seemingly irrelevant. The originally universal notion of the relationship between ethics and economics, which we have already encountered in the Old Testament, was turned on its head. Together with Mandeville, the argument began that the more vices there were, the more

---

[1] The topic is also examined by Amartya Sen, winner of the Nobel Prize in Economics. In the book *On Ethics and Economics*, he points out that economics until recently was taught as part of the moral sciences at the University of Cambridge. Sen, *On Ethics and Economics*, 2.

material well-being there could be. It's a certain historical irony that Adam Smith sharply and completely clearly distanced himself from the idea of the market's invisible hand as Bernard Mandeville presented it.

The attention of economists today is starting to return once again to ethics, and the internalization of norms is becoming an attractive field. It is beginning to be generally recognized that economics does better in an ethical environment where the actors abide by the rules of the game. Under various labels (quality of business environment, corporate governance, transparency, surveys of informal institutions, etc.), respected global institutions are starting to pay attention to research on the influence of ethics on the economy. Attention is going back to the beginning, to the Hebrew notion that more ethics is better for the economy. This is a notion with which Adam Smith would have agreed.[2] And the provocative poet Bernard Mandeville figured in that beginning.

THE BIRTH OF HOMO ECONOMICUS

> *Till now I imagined there had never appeared in the world such*
> *a book as the works of Machiavel. But de Mandeville goes far*
> *beyond it.*
> John Wesley[3]

Even if Mandeville remained somewhat in the shadow of other, more renowned names, it was he who was the first to be explicitly concerned with economics, economic well-being, and their ties to morality. He was the first to systematically perceive the unintended beneficial societal impacts of the actions of individuals and to openly postulate that societal welfare can (and must!) be based on egoism. He asserts his ideas in an absolutely audacious, provocative, and original way. Retrospectively, there are indications that some of his theses can be found in much older writings (as we have already shown in the Sumerians, in the Hebrews, and in the teachings of Thomas Aquinas). Nevertheless, it was clearly Mandeville who introduced the concept that moral vice in individuals can lead to the economic welfare of the whole into mainstream Western thought. From this standpoint, we must consider Mandeville, not Adam Smith, the very first modern economist.

---

[2] "Human society . . . appears like a great, an immense machine, whose regular and harmonious movements produce a thousand agreeable effects. . . . So virtue, which is, as it were, the fine polish to the wheels of society . . . while vice, like the vile rust which makes them jar and grate upon one another, is as necessarily offensive." Smith, *The Theory of Moral Sentiments*, 464.

[3] *The Journal of Rev. John Wesley*, London 1909–1916, IV, 157, note from 14 April 1756. Quoted in Harth's introduction to Mandeville, *The Fable of the Bees*, 8.

He was also unique to take on economic topics in verse. In short and lively poems, he creates an original thought complex, one completely beyond all moral and societal concepts published before him.

KNAVES TURN'D HONEST

Great ideas are very rarely encountered without accompanying controversy. Bernard Mandeville's stories provoked a fierce scandal at the time. Among those greatly offended, as we will see, was Adam Smith himself—the same Adam Smith whom economists generally consider to be an upholder of Bernard Mandeville's ideas.

Mandeville originally made a living by translating and writing fairy tales. He gained his renown through a single work that met with public acceptance, *The Fable of the Bees: or, Private Vices, Publick Benefits*. His fable in verse was first published in 1714, but it only provoked a scandal in reedition in 1723. He suddenly found himself at the center of one of the most heated debates of the eighteenth century. The number of Mandeville's critics grew quickly; joined by such distinguished figures as George Berkeley, Francis Hutcheson, Archibald Campbell, and John Dennis. Adam Smith branded Mandeville's teaching "in almost every respect erroneous."[4] The English theologian John Wesley likened Mandeville to Machiavelli in his depravity. Mandeville's ideas were banned in courts, and in France his book was burned in the streets by executioners. Many considered him to be the Antichrist, and even David Hume and Jean-Jacques Rousseau joined his opponents.

The poem starts with a description of a prospering society whose characteristics correspond to the social system in England at the time. Here, vice thrives under the mask of an apparently peaceful society. There is no trade without fraud, no authority without bribery and corruption:

> Thus every Part was full of Vice,
> Yet the whole Mass a Paradice;[5]

But the bees complain, and believe they would live better in a just and honest society. The god of the bees, Jove, hears their request and transforms the bees into honest and virtuous creatures.

> The Bar was silent from that Day;
> For now the willing Debtors pay,
> Ev'n what's by Creditors forgot,
> Who quitted them, that had it not.
> Those, that were in the Wrong, stood mute,
> And drops the patch'd vexatious Suit.[6]

---

[4] Smith, *The Theory of Moral Sentiments*, 451.
[5] Mandeville, *The Fable of the Bees*, 9 (in the Penguin edition, 67).
[6] Ibid., 70.

But this is what happens: Instead of the beehive prospering and the bees living better, the exact opposite occurs. Many bees lose their jobs because only a handful of blacksmiths can earn a living in a society where neither bars on windows nor ironwork on doors is necessary. Judges, lawyers, and defenders lose their jobs, and bureaucrats overseeing the enforcement of the law cease to be necessary. Because luxury and gluttony disappear, ordinary people—farmers, servants, shoemakers, and dressmakers—suffer due to decreased demand for goods. The bee nation becomes peace-loving, so it stops arming itself as well. The fable comes to an inglorious end. The beehive dies out and only a small part survive, because the other bees were not needed and could not support themselves. In the end, another swarm drives them from the hive, and the bees find shelter in the remains of a fallen tree.

ODE TO VICE: THE SOURCE OF THE WEALTH OF NATIONS

Pride and Vanity have built more Hospitals than all the Virtues together
Bernard Mandeville[7]

Mandeville becomes a bitter mirror of his time with a single goal: in his own words, to point out our hypocrisy.[8] We rail against vice and try at all costs to wipe it out—and nevertheless our welfare flows from it. If Mandeville lived in a society where it was appropriate to curse and swear against vice, he himself pointed out that we owe a great deal exactly to these same (hated) vices. For this reason, instead of cursing vice, he decided to devote a hymn to it. The bee god sends virtue as a punishment for the beehive's hypocrisy, because the bees' sin was not vice but hypocrisy. At the same time, Mandeville does not turn to an apology for vice—he continues to consider vice as vice. Despite all its attempts, society will never get rid of vice:

> If People were to be made better by any thing that could be said to them; but Mankind having for so many Ages remain'd still the same, notwithstanding the many instructive and elaborate Writings, by which their Amendment has been endeavour'd, I am not so vain as to hope for better Success from so inconsiderable a Trifle.[9]

Mandeville even argues that "vices are inseparable from great and potent Societies."[10] Vice is compared to trash on the street—yes, it is unpleasant, it dirties one's shoes and clothing, slows one down, and harms

---

[7] Mandeville, *An Essay on Charity, and Charity-Schools*, 164.
[8] Mandeville, *The Fable of the Bees*, 55.
[9] Ibid., 56.
[10] Ibid., 57.

the aesthetic, but it is an indivisible part of every city. "Dirty streets are a necessary Evil"[11] and "every Moment must produce new Filth."[12] But if someone were to decide to uproot evil (Mandeville isn't able to imagine such a change without a miracle and direct—and, it must be pointed out, maleficent—divine intervention), they must pay a high price. To wit, vice is advantageous for the economy.

> Such were the Blessings of that State;
> Their Crimes conspired to make 'em Great.[13]

According to Mandeville, we should be grateful to vice and amorality for full employment, lively trade, and the de facto basis of the wealth of nations. Put in more modern language, vice is a multiplier of effective demand, which becomes a driver for the economy. Adam Smith was looking for the cause of the wealth of nations; Mandeville found it in linking vices to an economic system.

> That strange ridic'lous Vice, was made
> The very Wheel, that turn'd the Trade.[14]

If we were to allow the existence of an honest society, we would have to say farewell to economic prosperity and give up an important position in history. Mandeville himself does not give preference to the creation of the former or the latter, but merely points out what every regime amounts to. "Religion is one thing and Trade is another."[15] If the ideals of a religion were to be realized in a specific society, a poor and "stupidly innocent"[16] community would be created. People must choose between morality and prosperity, and according to the poet-economist, herein lies the trade-off: "And so [they wrongly] conclude, that without Pride or Luxury, the same Things might be eat, wore, and consumed; the same Number of Handicrafts and Artificers employ'd, and a Nation be every way as flourishing as where those Vices are the most predominant."[17] Mandeville really ascribes the wealth of nations to vice:

> Let us examine then what things are requisite to aggrandise and enrich a Nation. The first desirable Blessings for any Society of Men are a fertile Soil and a happy Climate, a mild Government. . . . In this Condition they may be as Virtuous as they can, without the least Injury to the Publick, and consequently as happy as they please themselves. But they shall have no Arts or Sciences, or be quiet longer than their Neighbours will let them; they must be poor, ignorant, and almost wholly destitute of what we call the Comforts of Life, and all the Cardinal Virtues together won't so much as procure a

---

[11] Mandeville, *The Fable of the Bees*, Preface, 57.
[12] Ibid., Preface, 57.
[13] Ibid., 68.
[14] Ibid., 68.
[15] Mandeville, *Search into the Nature of Society*, 197.
[16] Mandeville, *The Fable of the Bees*, 23.
[17] Ibid., note M on 149.

tolerable Coat or a Porridge-Pot among them: For in this State of slothful Ease and stupid Innocence, as you need not fear great Vices, so you must not expect any considerable Virtues.

Would you render a Society of Men strong and powerful, you must touch their Passions. . . . Pride will set them to work in earnest: Teach them Trades and Handicrafts, and you'll bring Envy and Emulation among them: To increase their Numbers, set up a Variety of Manufactures, and leave no Ground uncultivated; . . . Suffer no body to act but what is lawful, and every body to think what he pleases . . . make good use of their Fear, and flatter their Vanity with Art and Assiduity . . . teach 'em Commerce with Foreign Countries, . . . this will bring Riches, and where they are, Arts and Sciences will soon follow . . . .

But would you have a frugal and honest Society, the best Policy is to preserve Men in their Native Simplicity, . . . remove and keep from them every thing that might raise their Desires, or improve their Understanding.[18]

In his fable, Mandeville proposes a uniquely provocative description of causes of an economic cycle. Their god lets the beehive slide into recession because the bees became honest. In this way, he gets to the opposite pole of thought than the one we described with the Hebrews, which is that nations do better economically if they act honestly. According to Mandeville, wiping out evil in all its particulars results in a much greater evil—the dying out of most of the hive and the general demise of the whole. Removing partial evil results in even greater evil, because

The Worst of all the Multitude
Did something for the common good.[19]

As is the custom with fables, we find a "moral" at the end:

Then leave Complaints: Fools only strive
To make a Great and honest Hive.
T'enjoy the World's Conveniences,
Befamed in War, yet live in Ease
Without great Vices is a vain
Eutopia seated in the Brain.
Fraud, Luxury and Pride must live;
Whilst we the Benefits receive.
. . .

Nay, where the People would be great,
As necessary to the State,
As Hunger is to make 'em eat.
Bare Vertue can't make Nations live
In Splendour; they, that would revive A Golden Age, must be as free,
For Acorns, as for Honesty.[20]

---

[18] Mandeville, *The Fable of the Bees*, note Q on 200–201.
[19] Ibid., 68.
[20] Ibid., 76.

THE INVISIBLE HAND OF THE MARKET AND
ITS PROTOTYPES

Mandeville bases his social philosophy explicitly on the principle of self-love, egoism—exactly that from which Adam Smith distances himself in the very first sentence of his book *The Theory of Moral Sentiments* (as we will soon see). If we were to remove evil from ourselves (our selfishness), Mandeville argues, prosperity would soon end. The mechanism is as follows. Each vice means at the same time an effective demand, either for goods (luxury clothing, food, buildings, etc.) or services (police, regulation, lawyers, etc.). A developed society, Mandeville argues, lives mainly from the economical satisfaction of these needs.

The thesis that partial evil contributes to the good of the whole and therefore is not advisable to remove is one we have repeatedly encountered in much older writings. We already know how Gilgamesh as well as St. Prokop made friends with forces they could not tame, and transformed evil into something beneficial to society. Jesus discourages his disciples from pulling out weeds, "because while you are pulling the weeds, you may root up the wheat with them. Let both grow together until the harvest."[21] And Thomas Aquinas reminds us: "Many goods are present in things which would not occur unless there were evils."[22]

It may have been unfortunate for Mandeville that he was not aware of these sources, because referring to them would have certainly saved him much of the controversy his fable provoked.

CONCLUSION: MANDEVILLE, THE FIRST
MODERN ECONOMIST

Mandeville was the key proponent of the *need for greed* philosophy. In this sense, greed is the necessary condition for progress of a society; without greed there would be no or little progress. For where would we be without greed and without vices, he asks? The society would reach a very basic level of development only and would not be able to stand in the international competition. He was a clear proponent of the hedonistic program: If there is a discrepancy between what we want and what we already possess, then we should aim at increasing our possessions, until it meets our demand(s). And he goes even further than the hedonist did: He advocates for our demand to grow further and further as this is the only way to progress in his view. In that regard, modern economics is a descendant of his thinking. Economics as a science assumes that human needs are unlimited (ever-growing demand), while resources are scarce.

---

[21] Matthew 13:29–30.
[22] Aquinas, *Contra Gentiles* III, chapter 71.

We should therefore try to utilize these scarce resources in a way that demand is met.

Does it mean that the only way forward would be catering to new demands, and does it mean that in order to do that we need newer and newer sets of tempting vices? If a society decided to be content with what it has (as the Stoics seem to suggest for their program), would that eventually mean the end of that particular society?

As for the economics of good and evil, Mandeville clearly believes that private vices contribute to public good and are therefore beneficial. He holds an opposite view from the Hebrews (and Adam Smith) who believed that virtue is economically beneficial and vice is not. As for the concept of the invisible hand of the market, to Mandeville the markets could turn vice to virtue and the markets were not just mere coordinators of human interaction but also convertors from personal evil to public good.

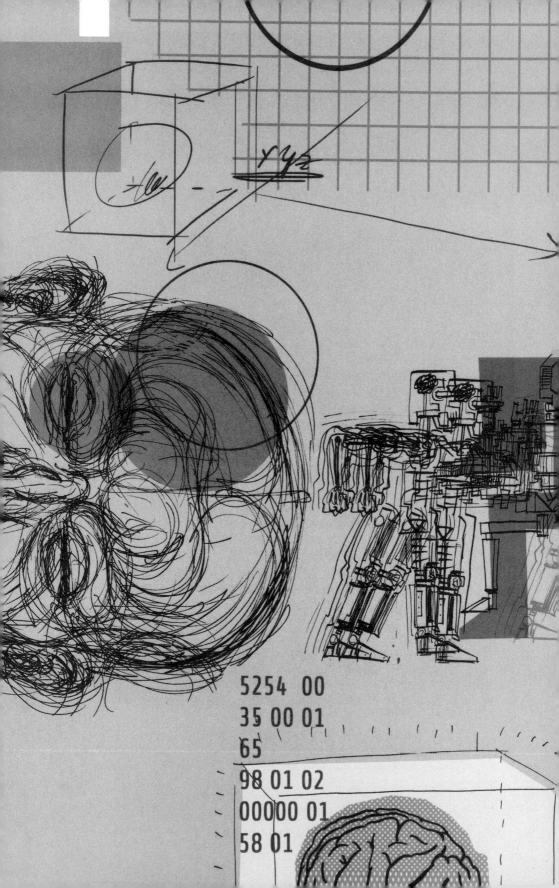

5254 00
35 00 01
65
98 01 02
00000 01
58 01

7

Adam Smith, Blacksmith of Economics

> *Adam, Adam, Adam Smith*
> *Listen what I charge you with!*
> *Didn't you say*
> *In the class one day*
> *That selfishness was bound to pay?*
> *Of all doctrines that was the Pith.*
> *Wasn't it, wasn't it, wasn't it, Smith?*[1]
> Stephen Leacock

In his novel *Immortality*, Milan Kundera, a French author of Czech origin, notes the paradoxical and cruel reality accompanying the life after death of great figures. The legends created around them after their deaths often completely miss their main message and concentrate on secondary issues (often erroneously). A good example is the astronomer Tycho Brahe, who served in the court of Emperor Rudolf II at the time when the ruler made Prague into the center of the Habsburg Empire. The astrologer— one of the figures who symbolize this extraordinary period for Czechs—is known by nearly everyone, not because of his discoveries, but because of his bladder. The legend in the Czech Republic goes that Tycho de Brahe would not dare to get up from a ceremonial dinner before the emperor, and he waited to urinate so long that his bladder burst at the table. This secondary and almost certainly untrue story ran completely roughshod over his truly *immortal* message.

Adam Smith, an exceptional Scottish thinker from the eighteenth century who is universally considered the father of modern economics, met a similar fate. The thesis that the wealth of nations and individuals is based on selfishness, self-interest, and the invisible hand of the market is universally ascribed to him. This is also illustrated by this chapter's introductory quote, where Stephen Leacock pillories Smith for the argument that "selfishness was bound to pay."[2]

It is as if already with a name like his, Adam Smith was predestined to a role as the father-economist of the scientific era, a man who brought older,

---

[1] Leacock, *Hellements of Hickonomics*, in Sen, *On Ethics and Economics*, 21.
[2] Ibid., 75. Also in Sen, *On Ethics and Economics*, 21.

unestablished ideas down to earth and gave economic inquiry a fixed framework. The name *Smith* speaks for itself, and in Old Testament Hebrew language, *Cain* translates as "smith." On the other hand, *Abel* in Hebrew means breeze, breath, or futility. When Cain, the smith and farmer, kills the unanchored shepherd, he sends him to "the winds." *Adam* means nothing less than the name of the first man (in Hebrew, *Adam* means "man"). Thus even in his name, Adam Smith, the man-smith, etymologically connects a rare combination of meanings.³

The notion that Adam Smith is the blacksmith of classical *egoistic* economics is, of course, somewhat more complicated. For example, an ordinary reader of the history of economic thought might be soundly shocked by the first sentence of Smith's *The Theory of Moral Sentiments*: "How selfish soever man may be supposed, there are evidently some principles in his nature, which interest him in the fortune of others, and render their happiness necessary to him, though he derives nothing from it except the pleasure of seeing it."⁴

The irony is such that Smith never stated what Stephen Leacock (and popular historical consciousness with him) ascribes to him. On the contrary, and precisely in the spirit of Kundera's message, Smith's name is written into economic history due to a principle that he himself did not invent, did not popularize, and generally de facto distanced himself from. A similar fate occurred to him with his second key contribution: specialization. As we have shown, the ancient Greeks examined specialization in detail; it could even be said that Xenophon devoted more attention to it and understood it more deeply than Adam Smith.

Smith did not exactly receive kind words from many commentators. For example, Schumpeter, one of the greatest authorities in the field of the history of economic thinking, writes: "no woman, except for his mother, ever played a role in his existence: in this as in other respects the glamors and passions of life were just literature to him."⁵ Similarly, the historian Norman Davies labels Smith "the ultimate absent-minded professor" and recalls a story where "he became one of the sights of Edinburgh, where he was given to rating the streets in a trance, half-dressed and twitching all over, heatedly debating with himself in a peculiar affected voice . . . Virtually unmarriageable, he always lived with his mother. It is nice to

---

³ Similar plays on names occur relatively frequently, and in ancient as well as modern stories. The main hero of the film *The Matrix* is named Neo (an anagram of the word "one," a reference to the Messiah, while Neo in Greek means "new.") In the illusory Matrix, the same character is named Thomas Anderson. The name Anderson is very common (it is the ninth most common name in the United States) and thus stands in direct conflict with the original and new name of Neo. Anderson has its origin in *Andrew's son*. Andrew means in Greek the same as the Hebrew Adam, or man. Anderson thus means the *son of man*, which is a marking that Jesus frequently chose for himself. And while we are on the topic of *The Matrix*, we should remember that Neo's main enemy is none other than (agent) Smith.

⁴ Smith, *The Theory of Moral Sentiments*, 1853, 3.

⁵ Schumpeter, *History of Economic Analysis*, 177.

think that this charmingly chaotic character should have set about putting intellectual order into the workings of everyday life."[6]

THE WEALTH VERSUS ETHICS

The misunderstanding is based on the fact that Smith left a dual (and in many ways contradictory) heritage, one that today is frequently reduced to his most famous book, *Wealth of Nations*.

It is, of course, generally known that Adam Smith did not write only one book; aside from the cult favorite *Wealth of Nations* (1776), he previously wrote *The Theory of Moral Sentiments* (1759). Simply put: At first glance his two books could not be more different from each other. *Wealth of Nations* became the beginning of an entire economic discipline, while in *The Theory of Moral Sentiments*, Smith looks at ethics, and he sharply distances himself from such economic concepts as the now-classic invisible hand of the market. "Smith himself is said to have thought it [*The Theory of Moral Sentiments*] superior to *Wealth of Nations*."[7] As we could be convinced, the very first sentence of his four-hundred-page book unequivocally objects to any kind of attempt to transfer all human activity to (more or less hidden) egoism.[8]

Those connecting Smith with the invisible hand of the market could easily consider him a successor to the Hedonists, who were focused on reason, calculation, and self-interest. This, of course, would be a grave mistake. Let us recall that the Hedonists found the meaning of all earthly activities in enjoyment. If it was necessary to resist pleasure or undergo pain, then it was only because of the greater "utility" (or lesser evil) that followed. Whether acts are good or evil, they do not bear their own inherent value, which is judged from the viewpoint of their results and impacts on utility, on enjoyment. Good does not have its own value aside from its resultant utility. Good is not the goal of behavior and it only represents a means toward enjoyment. This system not only preceded utilitarianism but also became the basis for our contemporary economic dogmatics.

Most commentators certainly agree that Smith's teachings are, on the contrary, built to a certain extent on the philosophy of the Stoics.[9] Smith divides moral schools into three lines, which are defined as the terms *propriety*, *prudence*, and *benevolence*. Epicurus is broken down in relation

---

[6] Davies, *Europe: A History*, 604.

[7] Raphael, *The Impartial Spectator*, 1.

[8] See Kerkhof, "A Fatal Attraction?" and Force, *Self-Interest before Adam Smith*, 14. See also Hurtado-Prieto, *Adam Smith and the Mandevillean Heritage: The Mercantilist Foundations of Dr. Mandeville's Licentious System*.

[9] "Stoic philosophy is the primary influence on Smith's ethical thought. It also fundamentally affects his economic theory." Raphael and Macfie in the Introduction to the Glasgow edition of Theory of Moral Sentiments. Smith, *The Theory of Moral Sentiments*, 1982, 5.

to the term *prudence* and his heritage is unequivocally condemned: "This system is, no doubt, altogether inconsistent with that which I have been endeavouring to establish."[10] He continues: "By running up all the different virtues, too, to this one species of propriety, Epicurus indulged a propensity, which is natural to all men, but which philosophers in particular are apt to cultivate with a peculiar fondness, as the great means of displaying their ingenuity—the propensity to account for all appearances from as few principles as possible."[11]

Smith classified the Stoics under the chapter *propriety* and devoted more space and acknowledgment to them. Despite undergoing his criticism and the fact that he does not consider their teachings feasible, this school probably remains the closest to him, and his admiration is frequently evident directly from his text: "The spirit and manhood of their [Stoics'] doctrine make a wonderful contrast with the desponding, plaintive, and whining tone of some modern systems."[12] Even though Smith admires the Stoic school, what he dislikes about the Stoics is their indifference, apathy, lack of interest in anything. At the same time he is aware of how complicated it is to achieve the Stoic ideal, and he is not able to identify completely with the idea that *no relationship* between cause and effect can be observed in nature, as the Stoics believed.

For Smith, moral teachings based on mutual kindness (*benevolence*) and *restraint* (self-command) were more inspiring as the main building blocks of society.[13] He refers to Augustine and Plato and to the church teachings of Dr. Hutcheson, and Thomas Aquinas would also belong in the same category. According to these schools, any benefit destroys morality. In other words, if we are rewarded for our good deed, the given deed has lost its moral dimension and has become, simply put, a tool for benefit. "If an action, supposed to proceed from gratitude, should be discovered to have arisen from an expectation of some new favor, or if what was apprehended to proceed from public spirit, should be found out to have taken its origin from the hope of pecuniary reward, such a discovery would entirely destroy all notion of merit or praise-worthiness in either of these actions."[14] Smith writes that this school believes that "self-love was a principle which could never be virtuous in any degree or in any direction."[15] Smith evaluates this stream favorably ("a system which has a peculiar tendency to nourish and support in the human heart the noblest and the most agreeable of all affections"[16]); however, despite this he does not agree with it in

---

[10] Smith, *The Theory of Moral Sentiments*, 1853, 438.

[11] Ibid., 438.

[12] Ibid., 283.

[13] "The more extensive treatment given to self-command in edition 6 suggests that Smith had now acquired an even warmer regard for Stoicism than he felt in earlier days." Ibid., 18.

[14] Ibid., 302.

[15] Ibid., 444.

[16] Ibid., 445.

its isolated form: He does not consider the motive of kindness and charity out of love to be strong enough to hold the entire society together and to explain our basest instincts.

Smith further supports this construct by connecting it to the institution of the impartial spectator—a man within, an imagined concept according to which one impersonally yet emphatically judges and commits one's deeds.

> We suppose ourselves the spectators of our own behaviour, and endeavour to imagine what effect it would, in this light, produce upon us. This is the only looking-glass by which we can, in some measure, with the eyes of other people, scrutinize the propriety of our own conduct.[17]

A similar concept is used also by Hutcheson, Hume, and later by Mill. In his theory of nonindividualistic utilitarianism, Mill constructs an ethic according to which one should make sure he or she maximizes the utility of the whole. That is not personal or individualistic but collective perception of utility. If, as a true total utilitarian, I feel that giving up a hundred units of my wealth increases somebody else's utility more than it decreases mine, in an extreme understanding, I should give it up for his sake, for it is not my utility but the utility of the whole that is of concern to a true follower of Mill's utilitarianism. And this should be done voluntarily. Society guided by the "impartial spectator" would be a happier society than the one guided by individual maximalization of utility only. He understood well that there is a role for other factors in the economy than just a market, even though he was right—and for the period of his writing also brave—to stress and justify that the market must be at the core of every economic system. To conclude, using Smith's philosophy to support a pure laissez-faire economic system is simply not accurate. Smith never asserted that every market allocation benefits society.

MEET AND SHAKE THE INVISIBLE HAND

The fact that society holds together due to sympathy and the concept of an *impartial spectator* are two important contributions that Smith actually did make. Today it seems that he implied that it is the invisible hand that prevents our society from falling apart. Yet, Adam Smith himself used the term "invisible hand" only three times—once in each of his two major books and once in *Astronomy*. Therefore it is not clear why these things caused so much commotion.[18]

---

[17] Smith, *The Theory of Moral Sentiments*, 1853, 164.
[18] Raphael and Macfie argue that "Commentators have laid too much stress on the 'invisible hand,' which appears only once in each of Smith's two books. On both occasions the context is the Stoic idea of harmonious system, seen in the working of society" (in Smith, *The Theory of*

The first occurrence is in perhaps Smith's most famous passage, which describes a butcher's motives to do business and which has served until now as a frequently used explanation of free-market forces [my emphasis]:

> It is not from the benevolence of the butcher, the brewer, or the baker, that we expect our dinner, but from their regard to their own interest. We address ourselves, not to their humanity but to their self-love, and never talk to them of our own necessities but of their advantages. He [the butcher] generally, indeed, neither intends to promote the public interest, nor knows how much he is promoting it. By preferring the support of domestic to that of foreign industry, he intends only his own security; and by directing that industry in such a manner as its produce may be of the greatest value, he intends only his own gain, and he is in this, as in many other cases, led by an **invisible hand** to promote an end which was no part of his intention. Nor is it always the worse for the society that it was no part of it. By pursuing his own interest he frequently promotes that of the society more effectually than when he really intends to promote it. I have never known much good done by those who affected to trade for the public good. It is an affectation, indeed, not very common among merchants, and very few words need be employed in dissuading them from it.[19]

Compare this with the second occurrence in *The Theory of Moral Sentiments*, where the context seems to be quite contrary to the previous one. In this case, the invisible hand seems to be the distributive hand, the role which is often called the visible hand (of the redistributing government):

> … they divide with the poor the produce of all their improvements. They are led by an **invisible hand** to make nearly the same distribution of the necessaries of life, which would have been made, had the earth been divided into equal portions among all its inhabitants, and thus without intending it, without knowing it, advance the interest of the society, and afford means to the multiplication of the species. When providence divided the earth among a few lordly masters, it neither forgot nor abandoned those who seemed to have been left out in the partition. These last, too, enjoy their share of all that it produces… . The same principle, the same love of system, the same regard to the beauty of order, of art and contrivance, frequently serves to recommend those institutions which tend to promote the public welfare.[20]

To give a full account, there is actually one more occurrence of the "invisible hand" in Smith's books, but it is irrelevant for our debate about economics and ethics. In his earlier piece *Astronomy*, when writing of early religious thought, he talks of a supernatural agency:

> Fire burns, and water refreshes; heavy bodies descend, and lighter substances fly upwards, by the necessity of their own nature; nor was the

Moral Sentiments, 1982, 7), and continue: "In the Wealth of Nations the Stoic concept of natural harmony appears, especially in 'the obvious and simple system of natural liberty' (IV.ix.51)."
[19] Smith, *An Inquiry into the Nature and Causes of the Wealth of Nations*, 266 (1.2.2; 4.2.9).
[20] Smith, *The Theory of Moral Sentiments*, 1853, 264–265, emphasis mine.

invisible hand of Jupiter ever apprehended to be employed in those matters.[21]

So we see here that Smith used the notion of the invisible hand in three contexts: as a coordinator of the individual pursuit of self-love, as the collective hand of redistribution, and as a mystical, godlike power (of Jupiter). He simply could not have given the term he coined a larger and more confusing span of meaning.

And so it occurred that Smith's *The Wealth of Nations* remained misunderstood. Smith is frequently presented as a successor not only of Mandeville's thoughts, but also of Thomas Hobbes's as a propagator of ideas of human nature's egoistic motivation. Because free individual egoism is sufficient for the direction of society, morals are superfluous, for the market recasts everything (both good and bad, but especially the bad) into general welfare. That society could (or must) be built on selfishness. Briefly put, a person gets the feeling that instead of Smith we hear others cited—such as Hobbes (the battle of everyone against everyone), Mandeville (the sins in society will be recast into virtue by the invisible hand of the market), Herbert Spencer (defender of market Darwinism and a minimal state), or Ayn Rand (reductionism and radical egoism). Now, Adam Smith did not think in this way at all, and not even in one direction. We cannot even read such conclusions in the economic *Wealth of Nations*, even if we overlook *The Theory of Moral Sentiments*, which he directly contradicts nearly everything described above.

SMITH VERSUS MANDEVILLE

In *The Theory of Moral Sentiments*, aside from the three main schools described above, Smith also devotes special attention to the "debauched teachings" (*Of Licentious Systems*), characterized in that they erase the differences between vice and virtues. Here Smith also classifies Mandeville, a person for whose teachings he had no understanding at all:

> There is, however, another system which seems to take away altogether the distinction between vice and virtue, and of which the tendency is, upon that account, wholly pernicious: I mean the system of Dr. Mandeville. Though the notions of this author are in almost every respect erroneous, there are, however, some appearances in human nature, which, when viewed in a certain manner, seem at first sight to favour them. These, described and exaggerated by the lively and humorous, though coarse and rustic eloquence of Dr Mandeville, have thrown upon his doctrines an air of truth and probability which is very apt to impose upon the unskilful.[22]

---

21 Smith, *Essays on Philosophical Subjects*, 49. See Macfie, "The Invisible Hand of Jupiter."
22 Smith, *The Theory of Moral Sentiments*, 1853, 451.

Adam Smith comes out strongly against the idea that we erroneously ascribe to him. If we were to discuss the beginnings of economics and the thesis that the wealth of nations stands on selfishness and self-interest, most of us would immediately mark Adam Smith as the father of this teaching. But this is peculiar. For even though Smith was familiar in detail with Mandeville's work, it isn't cited anywhere in *The Wealth of Nations*. The only place he quotes it is in *The Theory of Moral Sentiments*, where he clearly and repeatedly distances himself from the "dissolute" Mandeville and his attempt to reduce everything to (vicious) egoism. What's more, Mandeville is the only one whom Smith so directly criticizes, ridicules, and caricatures—and does so in several places. It sometimes gives the impression that the entire book was written with the intention to argue against Mandeville. So there is no way Smith considers himself Mandeville's successor, as popular history, on the contrary, has it.

Above all, Smith was not willing to come to terms with the thesis that there is no difference between vice and virtue (which was certainly not something Mandeville ever argued, even if Smith rebuked him for it). In reality, we instead witness how the definition of good and bad character-istics shifts slightly for Smith. Mandeville considers selfishness and self-love to be vices on which (aside from a multitude of other vices) the bees' kingdom stands. This is why he came to the conclusion that *vices* lead to good. But Adam Smith *did not consider* self-love to be a vice. He renames "self-love" as "self-interest" (he freely swaps both terms), and despite not basing the *principle of the functioning of society* on it, he considers it impor-tant in the conduct of business. With this he can place himself as being against Mandeville (who was so condemned at the time), while at the same time basing his economic theories on a similar basis. With a silent redefinition of vice into virtue, Smith managed to draw from the logic of Mandeville's argument without having to face derisive criticism. With Smith, Mandeville's scornful "self-love" becomes the virtuous "self-interest"—a word we find (as opposed to the term "egoism") in *The Wealth of Nations* or *The Theory of Moral Sentiments*.

This is a surprising approach from a teacher of morals. One can only look on in wonder at how Smith could silently redefine vice into virtue without appropriate discourse, and how he could fail to concede at least a bit of acknowledgment for Mandeville.

DAS ADAM SMITH PROBLEM

Entire libraries could be filled with publications about the issue of the "two Smiths."[23] Joseph Schumpeter named the topic *Das Adam Smith*

---

[23] For example, Heilbroner, *The Worldly Philosophers*; Smith, *Adam Smith's Moral and Political Philosophy*; Morrow, "Adam Smith: Moralist and Philosopher"; Gaede, *Politics and Ethics: Machiavelli to Niebuhr*.

Problem, and despite all of the discussions (whose main lines we will summarize), a satisfactory answer has not been found to this day to the question of what Smith actually thought about self-interest and sympathy.[24] Whatever Adam Smith's anthropological perception of economic man is (whether it is about the individual or society, let it be built on self-love or not), what certainly remains is that the "father of economics" endowed the young field with a contradictory, unclear, and ambiguous view.

With a certain degree of exaggeration, it could be said that the dispute has dragged into the current day, and it divides current economic schools in many ways. For example, the dispute between methodological individualism and collectivism to a certain extent relates to the unclear definition of the problem of the "two Smiths." Adam Smith did not decide what economic anthropology would be like in coming eras. In *The Wealth of Nations*, man appears as an individual whose motives are given by self-interest. Smith, although a professor of ethics, doesn't discuss the moral issues at all at this point, and he does not look at how man functions in society outside the refuge of the conduct of business. Here self-love is the sole and apparently sufficient link between members of society, and not a single word appears on the necessity of mutual sympathy: "He will be more likely to prevail if he can interest their self-love in his favour, and show them, that it is for their own advantage to do for him what he requires of them."[25]

The above-mentioned passage with the butcher teaches us about the invisible hand, which harmonically, elegantly, and nonviolently governs, and, it would appear, no other helping hand is necessary. As opposed to this, the human beings in *The Theory of Moral Sentiments* look completely different. The governing principle of human behavior is loving benevolence, fondness; man is not a rational actor but is primarily led by emotion, and Smith's friend, David Hume, believed similarly. Man is not an individual actor torn away from society, but he is on the contrary its indivisible part. Schools that teach otherwise undergo sharp criticism by Smith. His sharpest words are reserved precisely for Mandeville's system, which later researchers erroneously ascribed as his (greatest?) contribution to the history of economic thought. In *The Theory of Moral Sentiments*, Adam Smith shines as a philosopher and a very capable moral teacher (acclaimed to this day), not as an economist. He creates very courageous,

---

[24] Among the countless volumes, I would like to especially point out Witzum's article (1998), in which the author summarizes in detail and psychologically analyzes the possible conflict or on the contrary harmony between self-love and benevolence, or the (apparent) conflict between *The Wealth of Nations* and *The Theory of Moral Sentiments*. The following are worth pointing out: Doomen ("Smith's Analysis of Human Actions"), Hurtado ("Pity, Sympathy and Self-interest: Review of Pierre Force's Self-interest before Adam Smith"), Friedman ("Adam Smith's Relevance for 1976") or Evensky ("Adam Smith on the Human Foundation of a Successful Liberal Society").

[25] Smith, *An Inquiry into the Nature and Causes of the Wealth of Nations*, 1869, 15.

original, and complicated psychological-societal constructs, only to fully and most rigorously show that the approach that seeks to find self-interest in every deed is erroneous. Sometimes one even gets the impression that Smith schizophrenically confronts himself and that one book casts doubt on the other.

NOT ONE, BUT MORE MOTIVES

According to Smith, the key to the correct view is a combination of motives. For this reason, he also criticizes Epicurus. Smith eludes efforts to seek a *single* explanatory principle behind *all* human acts, and he proposes more guiding principles instead. On one hand, kindness represents the finest and most beautiful principle, but it is not strong enough in and of itself. There is nothing wrong with mixing kindness with self-love; Smith sees nothing vicious or contemptible in it.

> The mixture of a selfish motive, it is true, seems often to sully the beauty of those actions which ought to arise from a benevolent affection. (...) Benevolence may, perhaps, be the sole principle of action in the Deity (...) so imperfect a creature as man, the support of whole existence requires so many things external to him, must often act from many other motives.[26]

We can find an entire range of efforts to resolve and consolidate what at first glance appears to be Adam Smith's schizophrenic position. First, some scholars openly admit the incongruity of both of the author's theories (this approach has been given the difficult-to-pronounce term *Umschwungstheorie*).[27] For example, H. T. Buckle[28] argues that: "They are, in reality, the two divisions of a single subject. In the *Moral Sentiments*, he investigates the sympathetic part of human nature; in *The Wealth of Nations*, he investigates its selfish part." And later: "In the *Moral Sentiments*, he ascribes our actions to sympathy; in his *Wealth of Nations* he ascribes them to selfishness. A short view of these two works will prove the existence of this fundamental difference, and will enable us to perceive that each is supplementary to the other; so that, in order to understand

---

[26] Smith, *The Theory of Moral Sentiments*, 1853, 446–447.

[27] Hildebrand in *Die Nationalökonomie der Gegenwart und Zukunft* [The National Economy of the Present and the Future] charges Smith with "materialism" (meaning an egoistic theory of human nature), Knies in *Die Politische Oekonomie vom Standpunkte der geschichtlichen Methode* [Political Economy from the Standpoint of the Historical Method] argues that Smith changed his views between writing *The Theory of Moral Sentiments* and *The Wealth of Nations*, and that the change was a result of his visit to France. See also von Skarżyński in *Adam Smith als Moralphilosoph und Schoepfer der Nationaloekonomie* [Adam Smith as a Moral Philosopher and Creator of National Economy]. According to von Skarżyński, Smith learned all his moral philosophy from Hutcheson and Hume, and all his economics from French scholars. See Introduction to Smith, *The Theory of Moral Sentiments*, 1982, 20.

[28] Volume 2 of Buckle, *History of Civilization in England*, 432–433, 437.

either, it is necessary to study both." Second, there have been many attempts to link these two sides of Smith, sometimes more, sometimes less elegantly.[29]

One of the solutions can be found in the next passages of *The Theory of Moral Sentiments*.:

> All the members of human society stand in need of each other's assistance, and are likewise exposed to mutual injuries. Where the necessary assistance is reciprocally afforded from love, from gratitude, from friendship, and esteem, the society flourishes and is happy. (…) though among the different members of the society there should be no mutual love and affection, the society, though less happy and agreeable, will not necessarily be dissolved. Society may subsist among different men, as among different merchants, from a sense of its utility, without any mutual love or affection. (…) it [society] may still be upheld by a mercenary exchange of good offices according to an agreed valuation. Society, however, cannot subsist among those who are at all times ready to hurt and injure one another. (…) Justice, on the contrary, is the main pillar that upholds the whole edifice.[30]

From this viewpoint it appears that Adam Smith respected both basic principles and was only acting to distinguish how important a role this or that motive had in every action. Although both great emotions—love and self-love—frequently appear in their pure forms, mostly they mix together in our motives. Martin Buber speaks beautifully about this when he divides human relations between expedient relations and those that are purely and completely removed from utility.[31] So, it is possible that Adam Smith considered the principle of self-love to be the dominant motive of societal relations as a whole, where complete strangers are joined together. However, this motive alone would only lead to a minimalist functioning of a humanly

---

[29] In the edited version of *The Theory of Moral Sentiments* scholars argue that

"The so-called "Adam Smith problem" was a pseudo-problem based on ignorance and misunderstanding. Anybody who reads *The Theory of Moral Sentiments*, first in one of the earlier editions and then in edition 6, will not have the slightest inclination to be puzzled that the same man wrote this book and *The Wealth of Nations*, or to suppose that he underwent any radical change of view about human conduct. Smith's account of ethics and of human behaviour is basically the same in Edition 6 from 1790 as in Edition 1 from 1759. There is development but no fundamental alteration. It is also perfectly obvious that *The Theory of Moral Sentiments* is not isolated from *The Wealth of Nations*." In Smith, *The Theory of Moral Sentiments*, 1982, 20.

Other scholars who see no problem between the two views are Hasbach, *Untersuchungen über Adam Smith und die Entwicklung der Politischen Ökonomie*; Limentani, *La morale della simpatia*; Eckstein in the Introduction to his translation (1926) or Campbell, *Adam Smith's Science of Morals*. To these can be added, for acute treatment of the *Umschwungstheorie*: Zeyss, *Adam Smith und der Eigennutz*, and Oncken, "The Consistency of Adam Smith," and in more detail, Wolf, ed., "Das Adam Smith–Problem," *Zeitschrift für Sozialwissenschaft*, 25–33, 101–8, 276–87. See also Macfie, *The Individual in Society*.

[30] Smith, *The Theory of Moral Sentiments*, 1853, 124–125.

[31] See Buber, *I and Thou*.

poor society. So, we have to add Smith's second basic principle of loving benevolence. This principle can be found especially in interpersonal relations. It is what makes a society of people into a de facto society.

SMITH'S SOCIAL MAN AND HUME'S HERITAGE

In *The Theory of Moral Sentiments*, Smith presents a very "unselfish" thesis, which states that individuals are joined by a natural bond he calls *sympathy.* He is thinking not only about mutual favor (liking) but of a universal human tendency, solidarity, and the ability to understand the motives of the other, empathy. He relies on people having an ability coded in them to feel for one another and, due to this, to behave fairly a priori. In order for Adam Smith to avoid the objection that a willingness to respect the motives of others is actually only self-love in a different guise (for example, we are afraid that a similar pain will happen to us), he creates his own system: According to him, man does not imagine that the given state could occur to him himself, but he *adapts* himself to the role of the other person. He gives as an example a man who puts himself in the place of a woman undergoing labor pains, even though he knows that such pain will never happen to him and that he doesn't even have to worry about it. There is an important difference in this, and Smith insists on this seeming detail and spends a lot of time and energy to raise it up beyond any doubt. With the help of "putting one's self into another's situation," Smith created a psychological defense against the individualism of his time. "Sympathy, however, cannot, in any sense, be regarded as a selfish principle."[32]

Smith builds his social ethics on the principle of mutual sympathy. Man is a social creature, and his nature is rooted in a need to feel empathy and to be part of his surroundings. This is also why morality has a valuable role across society: "Virtue is the great support, and vice the great disturber of human society."[33] We could not imagine a greater conflict between Smith and Mandeville, who on the contrary considers vice to be the source of society's wealth; on the other hand, at the moment the society becomes virtuous (as Smith would have it), it falls into poverty and is soon destroyed. For Smith, "virtue, which is, as it were, the fine polish to the wheels of society (…) while vice, like the vile rust, which makes them jar and grate upon one another, is as necessarily offensive. (…) If virtue, therefore, be desirable for its own sake, and if vice be, in the same manner, the object of aversion, it cannot be reason which originally distinguishes those different qualities, but immediate sense and feeling."[34]

---

[32] Smith, *The Theory of Moral Sentiments*, 1853, 465.
[33] Ibid., 463.
[34] Ibid., 464.

SOCIETY AS A RATIONAL CHOICE?

Does society hold together based on the choice of rational reasons of an individual, a notion the modern economy seems to presuppose? Is it rational calculus that keeps a man a (good) member of a given society? Or is something else at play?

Smith's contemporary David Hume contributed in great measure to the search for answers to these questions and to the understanding of economic anthropology overall. He commented on key topics of economic interest such as the origin of social order, the theory of utility and self-love, and also the relationship between rationality and extrarationality. Hume is important for us, since Smith and Hume held very many similar views, and they were very close friends.

Hume comes out against the conception of a social contract promoted by people such as Thomas Hobbes. According to Hobbes' theory, man "exchanges" his freedom for social order by voluntarily (rationally) subjecting himself to social rules and at the same time expects that others will do the same. Society is therefore held together on the basis of the principle of self-love; it is therefore nothing more than hedonist calculus. Hume does not agree with this theory and writes:

> The most obvious objection to the selfish hypothesis is, that, as it is contrary to common feeling and our most unprejudiced notions, there is required the highest stretch of philosophy to establish so extraordinary a paradox. To the most careless observer there appear to be such dispositions as love, friendship, compassion, gratitude ... [which are] plainly distinguished from those of the selfish passions ... All attempts of this kind [to prove all from self-love] have hitherto proved fruitless, and seem to have proceeded entirely from that love of simplicity which has been the source of much false reasoning in philosophy.[35]

Here he uses an argument that Adam Smith uses later. According to Hume, it is in our nature to carry out and praise acts "where the utmost subtilty of imagination would not discover any appearance of self-interest, or find any connexion of our present happiness and security with events so widely separated from us."[36] It is in our nature to celebrate acts that have no relationship at all to ourselves or the level of our utility, either in time or in space. According to Hume, the reason why we consider such acts as moral and good despite having no relationship to our utility is simple: These acts resonate with our moral *sentiment* (and therefore not with calculus). Private utility, Hume argues, cannot serve as a building block of society. We can still give many examples where "We have found instances, in which private interest was separate from public; in which it was even contrary: And yet we observed the moral sentiment to continue,

---

[35] Hume, *An Enquiry Concerning the Principles of Morals*, from Hume, *Selections*, 245.
[36] Ibid., 213.

notwithstanding this disjunction of interests."[37] As regards self-love and private utility, he does not consider it as an exclusive and all-explaining emotion but includes a wider utility as well, the utility of society: "Usefulness is agreeable, and engages our approbation. This is a matter of fact, confirmed by daily observation. But, *useful?* For what? For some-body's interest, surely. Whose interest then? Not our own only: For our approbation frequently extends farther."[38]

This is a key idea, one that can also help us to understand Smith's con-cept of societal coexistence. Hume believed that human moral *sentiment* is stronger and deeper than the principle of utility. (Emotional) sentiment is stronger than (rational) calculus. The norms of human behavior existed *before* the creation of the state (the state did not create them in a Hobbesian way) and it is impossible to explain it from the position of social contract theory. "Compelled by these instances, we must renounce the theory, which accounts for every moral sentiment by the principle of self-love,"[39] Hume concludes. Social morals are the domain of emotions, feelings—not rationality. "Unlike modern economists Adam Smith assumes that people are highly interdependent as they consider the alternatives they face. Because people share similar feelings and passions, they can identify with others as others express their passions in behaviour."[40]

Like Aristotle and Aquinas, Hume considers human beings to be a *zoon politikon* and argues that it is *natural* for a person to be part of a society. In other words, the individual does not rationally "choose" to be a part of a society because it would bring a calculable utility, but because it is in his nature; at the end of the day the society is something he is (literally) born into. Human beings have a *natural* tendency toward good and a strongly inherent *social* sympathy, even empathy. "Everything, which contributes to the happiness of society, recommends itself directly to our approbation and good-will. Here is a principle, which accounts, in great part, for the origin of morality."[41] He simply considers this characteristic as a "principle of human nature."[42]

"The human heart (…) will never be wholly indifferent to public good."[43] He writes elsewhere: "No character can be so remote as to be, in this light, wholly indifferent to me. What is beneficial to society or to the person himself must still be preferred."[44] Hume probably summarizes this idea best in the following passage: "It appears that a tendency to public

---

[37] Hume, *An Enquiry Concerning the Principles of Morals*, from Hume, *Selections*, 215.

[38] Ibid., 214. Stress on the word "useful" in original text.

[39] Ibid., 215.

[40] Halteman, "Is Adam Smith's Moral Philosophy an Adequate Foundation for the Market Economy?"

[41] Hume, *An Enquiry Concerning the Principles of Morals*, from Hume, *Selections*, 215.

[42] Ibid., 216.

[43] Ibid., 229.

[44] Ibid., 230.

good, and to the promoting of peace, harmony, and order in society, does always (…) engage us on the side of the social virtues (…) principles of humanity and sympathy enter so deeply into all our sentiments, and have so powerful an influence, as may enable them to excite the strongest censure and applause."[45] Here again the motive emerges that we know from Adam Smith, the motive of the individual who not only depends on himself, but whose strongest emotions bind him to others and to the entire society. It is appropriate to note again that Hume is speaking not of a rational calculus but about the *feelings* that lead us to *social virtue*. According to Hume, these virtues are not rationally justifiable, as the theory of the social contract argues.

Neither Smith nor Hume would agree that society is founded on hedonistic principles and on the principle of rational choice, as the rationalists and Rousseau's theory of the social contract postulate. Human anthropology is different—man associates on the basis of innate feelings. The mystery of how society holds together shines through here as well. We are born with it, and we cannot say more about it.

REASON AS A SLAVE OF THE PASSIONS

Smith's view on the rationality of human behavior appears interesting as well. Here he was also strongly influenced by David Hume. Adam Smith writes:

> But though reason is undoubtedly the source of the general rules of morality, and of all the moral judgments which we form by means of them; it is altogether absurd and unintelligible to suppose that the first perceptions of right and wrong can be derived from reason (…) These first perceptions (…) cannot be the object of reason, but of immediate sense and feeling. (…) But reason cannot render any particular object either agreeable or disagreeable (…) Reason may show that this object is the means of obtaining some other which is naturally either pleasing or displeasing and in this manner may render it either agreeable or disagreeable for the sake of something else. But nothing can be agreeable or disagreeable for its own sake, which is not rendered such by immediate sense and feeling.[46]

Hume was made famous by the passage that sets rationalistic anthropology on its head: "Reason is, and ought only to be the slave of the passions, and can never pretend to any other office than to serve and obey them."[47] (Incidentally, on this point he stands very close to the ideas of Bernard Mandeville,[48] whom he criticizes so heartily together with Smith.) The passage more or less summarizes his philosophy—reason and feelings

---

[45] Hume, *An Enquiry Concerning the Principles of Morals*, from Hume, *Selections*, 219.
[46] Smith, *The Theory of Moral Sentiments*, 1853, 470.
[47] Hume, *A Treatise of Human Nature*, 297.
[48] Compare Mandeville, *The Fable of the Bees*, 56.

do not fight against each other and one is not set against the other. They are not lying on the same level so as to compete with each other. Human actions are led by feelings, passions, and affects, and reason plays its role only on a secondary level, in the process of rationalization.[49] John Locke uses a similar argument: "Reason does not so much establish and pronounce this law of nature as search for it and discover it ... Neither is reason so much the maker of that law as its interpreter."[50]

Our actions are not the result of careful calculations of convenience or inconvenience, utility, and cost. Our actions instead allow themselves to be carried by forces that we do not understand, emotions that motivate us to action. Keynes's *animal spirits* also has a similar irrational character.

David Hume would have defied the contemporary anthropology of homo economicus from the following angle: Feelings, not rationality, are the moving force behind human behavior. Put more simply, rationality itself is not enough to motivate a human being to action. According to Hume, interests of society "are not, even on their own account, entirely indifferent to us. Usefulness is only a tendency to a certain end; and it is a contradiction in terms, that anything pleases as means to an end, where the end itself no wise affects us."[51] Reason itself does not know how to order our preferences in such a way as to act; reason does not know how to motivate us to action. "What is honourable, what is fair, what is becoming, what is noble, what is generous, takes possession of the heart, and animates us to embrace and maintain it. What is intelligible, what is evident, what is probable, what is true, procures only the cool assent of the understanding; and gratifying a speculative curiosity, puts an end to our researches."[52]

Immanuel Kant seems to take a similar position. "Pure reason, however, cannot command any ends a priori."[53] Reason plays only a secondary role—when it finds the best path to a goal.[54] We find in our acts a cooperation between reason and feeling.[55] We shall come to this in the second part of this book. Reason alone produces paradoxes: "It is not contrary to reason to prefer the destruction of the whole world to the scratching of my finger."[56]

---

[49] Rawls, *Lectures on the History of Moral Philosophy*, 29, 30.
[50] Citation from Hayek, *Law, Legislation, and Liberty*, 151.
[51] Hume, *An Enquiry Concerning the Principles of Morals*, from Hume, *Selections*, 239.
[52] Ibid., 197.
[53] Kant, *The Metaphysical Elements of Ethics*, 41. (Chapter 9: "What Is a Duty of Virtue?")
[54] Rawls, *Lectures on the History of Moral Philosophy*, 31–32.
[55] Hume, *An Enquiry Concerning the Principles of Morals*, from Hume, *Selections*, 198.
[56] Hume, *A Treatise of Human Understanding*, 298: "It is not contrary to reason to prefer the destruction of the whole world to the scratching of my finger. 'Tis not contrary to reason for me to chuse my total ruin, to prevent the least uneasiness of an Indian or person wholly unknown to me.... In short a passion must be accompanied by some false judgement, in order to its being unreasonable; and even then it is not the passion, properly speaking, which is unreasonable, but the judgement."

CONSOLIDATION OF THE TWO SMITHS?

It is a paradox that important economic authorities deny economic originality to both Mandeville[57] and Smith,[58] while they praise both as important thinkers in the areas of psychology, ethics, and philosophy. So how is it possible that these two built the foundations of economics? Is it because psychology, philosophy, and ethics *are* in reality at the core of economics and precisely because, more than anyone else before them, Mandeville and Smith were at the climax of the economic debate which has lasted from time immemorial to this day? Why do we not consider the mercantilists as the fathers of economics? Or the mathematics-oriented physiocrats? It was the French physiocrat Vincent de Gournay (1712–1759) who—a generation before Smith—pronounced the proverbial catchphrase used to this day, *laissez faire, laissez passer*. But today we don't hear much about him—or about others—while *Das Adam Smith Problem* (i.e., the problem of egoism in the theories of Smith) is still lively and discussed to this day.

The problem is the definition of the breadth of "egoism," or everything that we intend to include in this term. If the acts of Jan Hus, the famous Czech reformist preacher, who chose to be burned to death rather than deny his truth, or Francis of Assisi, who gave away his property, are defined as egoistical acts, then everyone behaves egoistically, but the term "egoism" visibly loses its meaning because it becomes an untestable, all-inclusive term that can be used to explain any—even completely opposite—acts.

CONCLUSION: MR. SMITH RELOADED

In this chapter we have followed the misunderstanding that occurred in connection with the concept of the invisible hand of the market, which was ascribed to Smith. We have discussed the problem of his ties to Bernard Mandeville and the concept of social contracts as a rational construct overall. We have opened the issue of *Das Adam Smith Problem*, and pointed out that human behavior cannot likely be explained by a single (egoistic) principle. At the same time we have paused to consider the philosophy of his close friend David Hume, from whom Smith took many ideas. Hume, for example, diminished the role of reason and placed emotion and feeling at a key location. Adam Smith, then, talks of a basic social

---

[57] See Hayek: "I am not going to represent him as a great economist ... I should be much more inclined to praise him as a really great Psychologist." *The Trend of Economic Thinking: Essays on Political Economists and Economic History; The Collected Works of F. A. Hayek*, 74–75, chapter "Dr. Mandeville."

[58] Schumpeter: "He never uncovered the footprints of his predecessors with Darwinian frankness. In criticism he was narrow and ungenerous... But no matter what he learned or failed to learn from his predecessors, the fact is, that *The Wealth of Nations* does not contain a single *analytic* idea, principle, or method that was entirely new in 1776." *History of Economic Analysis*, 177–179.

principle of *sympathy*, which holds society together. Both perceived man as an essentially social being, one who feels connected even to the most distant member of the human family.

The modern mainstream, which claims to be a descendant of classical Smith economics, has neglected ethics. The issue of good and evil was dominant in the classical debates, yet today it is almost heretical to even talk about it. As I have tried to show, I further argue that the popular reading of Adam Smith is a misunderstanding. Smith's contribution to economics is much broader than just the (dubious) concept of the invisible hand of the market and, birth of the egoistic, self-centered homo economicus.

The popular reading of Smith makes economics lopsided. For an understanding of the current state of economics it is therefore necessary to read both Smiths. Because if one focuses only on the popular side of Smith's *Wealth of Nations* without having the broader context of *The Theory of Moral Sentiments*, one can easily reach conclusions that were not of Smith's intentions.

Smith did understand the crucial importance of ethics and gave it a major role and place in society, although his legacy is a bit confusing. For us economists, I believe Smith's legacy is that moral questions must be included in economics—that it is the key question of economics. To me, his most influential contribution to economics was ethical. The debate on good and evil did not begin but culminated with Smith.

Part II

BLASPHEMOUS THOUGHTS

Without suffering, nothing changes, the least of all human nature.
C. G. Jung

What are all these old stories, Babylonian myths, or New Testament parables good for? What does the (post)modern era, especially economics, have to learn from these ancient symbols? What good can this thinking do for us, especially in a time of debt-crisis, when we have enough worries as it is?

The psychologist Carl Gustav Jung believed that human thinking and worldview moves in archetypes that remain valid over millennia. This is why it is worthwhile to study these archetypes and know about them. And it is simplest and best to study them in their raw early forms, in a sort of bareness, when our civilization was young(er)—and then to follow their transformations in the context of historical development.

What we have stored somewhere in our unconscious can be recognized best in times of crisis. "It is in the most unexpected, the most terrifying chaotic things that reveal a deeper meaning,"[1] Jung writes. For him, the breaking point was what he often built on.

An economy also tells us much more about itself when it expresses its weakness, not when it is at full strength. We can get to know it much better when it is bare and humble than when it overflows with pride and despises everything other than itself. Strength frequently hides the essence of things, while weakness reveals it.

---

[1] Jung, "The Archetypes and the Collective Unconscious," 33–34.

8

Need for Greed

The History of Want

We wanted to find love,
We wanted success,
Until nothing was enough
Until my middle name was excess.
P. J. Harvey, "We Float"

Whenever Pandora's box opens, there tends to be a lot of trouble. But who was Pandora and what exactly was in the box? In this chapter we will study the very advent of human desire, or in economic terms, the birth of want, or demand for things that are not necessary (for survival). This is the point where the utility that comes from external goods which we "don't need," began. As economics puts so much emphasis on the concept of satisfying needs (desires), this should be of interest.

According to Greek mythology, Pandora was the first woman (something of a counterpart to Eve in the Old Testament), but she (as opposed to Eve, who was created to be Adam's "suitable helper") came into the world as a form of the gods' revenge on man. She carried a box (or more precisely a jar) with her that stored every possible suffering and evil, things which had not existed on Earth before this. After she opens it out of curiosity, evil, sickness, and (what now interests us the most) the *curse of labor* entered into the world. Labor, which before this had been pleasant, now became hard and tiring work. Pandora quickly closed her box, but it was too late.

THE CURSE OF THE GODS: THAT HIDEOUS DEMAND

We can read something similar in the story of Eve and Adam (Adam plays such a passive role in the story of the Garden of Eden that I have a tendency to put him in second place). Eve, after the intellectual clash with the serpent (which Adam completely avoided), tasted the forbidden fruit (also out of curiosity?), and the result was banishment from paradise and at the same time the entrance of evil into the world. After banishment from paradise, Adam relates a single curse *expresis verbis*: The Curse of Labor:[2] "Cursed is the ground because of you; through painful toil you will eat of it all the days of your life. . . . By the sweat of your brow you will eat your food."[3]

Several interesting things for us come out of this. First, humankind in its stories remembers a time when labor was pleasant. Man had to work, even in the Garden of Eden: God put man into the Garden of Eden so he could "work it and take care of it."[4] For first cultures, the original perfect state was not a state of inactivity, but of *pleasant* labor.

Second, in both stories it was a desire, curiosity, especially an exaggerated demand and an insatiability, or, if you will, inadequacy that *brought evil* to the earth. Eve and Adam could eat in abundance of "every tree in the garden,"[5] but that was still *not enough* for them. We do not know what it was that led the first people to such immodest inadequacy. What were they lacking in the perfect state in paradise? In this sense, the story is similar to the story of Pandora. These stories reveal something to us: Even if we have enough of everything and live in paradise, it will still not be enough for us, and we will have a constant tendency (completely unnecessarily) to consume what we do not need to consume (or even are forbidden to consume) and to open Pandora's boxes.

As Agent Smith tells Morpheus at the end of the first film in the *Matrix* trilogy: "Did you know that the first Matrix was designed to be a perfect human world? Where none suffered, where everyone would be happy. It was a disaster. No one would accept the program." Agent Smith continues, speculating on the reason for this anomaly: "Some believed we lacked the programming language to describe your perfect world. But I believe that, as a species, human beings define themselves in reality through suffering and misery."[6] Lowry derives similar lessons from the story of the Garden of Eden: "When Adam and Eve ate the forbidden fruit of the tree of knowledge and asserted the right to choose for themselves, they were cast out of the world of abundance into scarcity; to 'eat bread in the sweat of their faces.' The moral theme is that knowledge and the exercise of choice are burdens in a world of divinely imposed or natural scarcity."[7]

Third, the character of the divine curse is not direct; instead, divinity opens ways, allows people to go to their misfortunes themselves. This applies to the forbidden tree in the Garden of Eden as well as to the

---

[2] Compare with Lowry, *Ancient and Medieval Economic Ideas*, 15.

[3] Genesis 3:17–19. It is interesting that people were not cursed. *Only the serpent* was cursed; woman and man were not. The woman was punished with birth pangs, and was told "your desire will be to your husband, and he will rule over you ... Because of Adam, the Earth was cursed."

[4] Genesis 2:15.

[5] Genesis 2:16: "God made all kinds of trees grow out of the ground—trees that were pleasing to the eye and good for food. In the middle of the garden were the tree of life and the tree of the knowledge of good and evil."

[6] Irwin, *The Matrix and Philosophy*, 139.

[7] Lowry, "Ancient and Medieval Economics," 14.

forbidden fruit in the form of Pandora's box. Desire and curiosity are sisters. Even the fruit of the forbidden tree was "pleasing to the eye"[8]—like advertising, which must also be pleasing to the eye. In addition, advertising frequently appeals to our extrarational (one wants to say *animal*) aspects.[9] One way or another, the serpent (animal) awakens a desire in Eve, a desire that she did not have before and a desire for things that she did not, by any means, *need*. The term *awake desire* in this context is most appropriate, because it activates something that was already inside us but was dormant. The serpent did not create desire but awakened it.

The medieval notion frequently prevails that the first sin in the Garden of Eden was sexual, that the form of the original sin had sexual character. But this is missing convincing argumentation. I offer another possible angle: It would appear to be much more likely that the original sin had the character of (over)*consumption*. After all, in the story of the Garden of Eden, Eve and Adam *literally* consume (the word "ate" is repeated two times) the fruit. "She took some and ate it. She also gave some to her husband, who was with her, and he ate it."[10]

According to the historian Norman Davies, Adam Smith "entered the realm of economics by asking himself about the implications of human greed."[11] According to this quite sensible reading of the reasons for writing the inquiry into the source of the wealth of nations, it would be *greed* that stands not only practically at the birth of theoretical economics but also at the cradle of our history, with the very concept of original sin.

THE ECONOMICS OF DESIRE: GETTING RID OF SUFFICIENCY

Aside from the Hebrews and Greeks, let's bring in a third ancient culture, the Sumerians. As we showed in the Epic of Gilgamesh, Enkidu was originally sent by the gods as a punishment, just like Pandora. And in the end, Enkidu became a lifelong companion to Gilgamesh, just as Adam and Eve were meant to be.

Enkidu originally lives in the forest like an animal. And it is a woman, the temple prostitute Shamhat, who brings him to the city, symbolically making a human out of him by doing so. Now, we can look at the issue in two ways, which, in the end, appear to complement each other.

---

[8] Genesis 3:6.

[9] Advertisements "forge links between the consumer (a derivative of the sacred individual) and the values embodied in the goods. Tellingly, advertising emphasizes not so much rationalized (monetary) value as qualities whose value has not been metricized (cf. Lears 1983) . . . Advertising thus gives . . . a mechanism for settling on temporarily dominant modes (fashions) for the enactment of the sacred in everyday life." Boli, "The Economic Absorption of the Sacred," 104.

[10] Genesis 3:6.

[11] Davies, *Europe: A History*, 604.

To a certain extent in the Epic of Gilgamesh, a woman (the prostitute) was Enkidu's downfall. Until then Enkidu was satisfied, he had no desires, only basic needs—food, shelter, security. He was even able to satisfy these himself, without civilization, like an animal. But along came Shamhat and she *showed* him *what* to desire. As Slavoj Žižek says,[12] we need to be shown what to desire (in this respect, advertisements are very crucial for our society[13]). For the first time, this action was accompanied by the desire for more. As he lived like an animal, there was no discontent, no desire; Enkidu had everything he needed, because he did not need much. As Alfred Marshall writes, "The uncivilized man indeed has not many more than the wants of brute animal; but every step in his progress upwards increases the variety of his needs together with the variety in his methods of satisfying them."[14]

Now that he needed more, desire was born. Here we witness the advent of desire, the advent of want (i.e., desire for something I don't have and don't really need). At the same time, Shamhat estranged Enkidu from animals, from nature, from his natural environment. She brought him to the city, the home of people.

The second way we can look at the story is that Shamhat is Enkidu's redeemer. The woman showed him *what* to desire. Thus she made him into a human being. She gave him a higher goal, gave him dissatisfaction, discontent. She was a bearer of culture. It was she who brought him to the city, civilized him, and gave him beer to drink. For Enkidu, Shamhat was the bearer of progress.

We have shown the first awakenings of desire. It appears that the effort to constantly be dissatisfied and want more is a natural phenomenon— and lies at the very heart of our civilization, of being human (and the ancients realized this very well). We can even go as far as to say that discontent is the engine of progress and of market capitalism. Frank Knight, probably the most important Chicago economist of the last generation, noted: "[I]t is human nature to be more dissatisfied the better off one is."[15] George Stigler, Knight's student, even wrote: "The chief thing which the common-sense individual wants is not satisfactions for the wants he had, but more, and better wants."[16]

In our constant desire to have more and more, we have sacrificed the pleasantness of labor. We want too much and so we work too much. We are by far the richest civilization that has ever existed, but we are just as

---

[12] Žižek, *Pervert's Guide to Cinema*, movie.

[13] In this, the need for and the usefulness of advertising are mutual. Not only does advertising need consumers, but consumers need advertising—to tell them what they should want. For more, see Boli, "The Economic Absorption of the Sacred," 105. In this context, Rushdie comments, "No wonder advertising was popular. It made things better. It showed you the road." Rushdie, *Fury*, 29.

[14] Marshall, *Principles of Economics*, 86.

[15] Nelson, *The New Holy Wars*, 293.

[16] Stigler, "Frank Hyneman Knight," 58. See also Nelson, *Economics as Religion*, 294–295.

far from the word "enough" or from satisfaction, if not further, than at any time in the distinct "primitive" past. In one sentence: If we ourselves did not have to constantly increase GDP and productivity at all costs, we would not have to also constantly overwork ourselves in "the sweat of our faces."

MALTHUS REBORN FOR THE THIRD TIME: CONSUMPTION AS A DRUG

> *And you can never get enough of what you don't really need.*
> U2, "Stuck in a Moment"

Reverend Thomas Malthus was an economist living at the end of the eighteenth and beginning of the nineteenth centuries. Many of his theories were disputed, but to this day he is remembered for his book *Principles of Population*, in which he elaborated the theory which argues that: "The power of population is so superior to the power of the earth to produce subsistence for man."[17] In other words, the planet cannot support the growth in human population.[18] Here he actually is arguing that human demand (as a whole) is infinite, while the planet's (agricultural) resources are limited. It was later shown that due to developments in agrarian technology, fertilizers and pesticides, the earth is several hundredfold more productive than it appeared at the time, and our planet thus far does not have this problem. Malthus has been overcome: There is enough food, but the problems are only with its distribution or with implementing of new technologies.

Later, a neo-Malthusian argument appeared which said that the increasing fertility of the earth, technology, and productivity of labor must have their limits, but nevertheless, not even this second derivation of Malthusian catastrophe has yet to come to pass. So I would like to propose a third derivation: Our needs grow faster than their fulfillment.

Some time ago we thought that the more we will have, the less we will need or want. But here is where we made a major mistake. Needs grow with what we have. We will never be satiated. In other words, growth in supply will never catch up to growth in new demand. But it takes us further, as Malthus himself noticed[19] (I am not using the word "forward" here

---

[17] Malthus, *An Essay on the Principle of Population*, chapter 7, 6.

[18] Therefore, reproduction must be limited. Respectively, if laborers are paid a higher salary than the living minimum, they start to reproduce and again there will not be enough food. In Malthus's dismal outlook, laborers will never earn significantly more than the living minimum in the long run.

[19] "Had population and food increased in the same ratio, it is probable that man might never have emerged from the savage state . . . Evil exists in the world not to create despair, but activity." Malthus, *An Essay on the Principle of Population*, 158.

intentionally, because we can only go forward when there is a certain goal.) In this regard Don Patinkin argues, "history has shown that Western society created new wants just as fast as (if not faster than)! it expanded the means of satisfying them."[20] In other words, desire can never be satisfied, or as Slavoj Žižek puts it "desire's raison d'être is not to realize its goal, to find full satisfaction, but to reproduce itself as desire."[21] The author of Ecclesiastes even noted it: "The eye never has enough of seeing, nor the ear its fill with hearing."[22]

When confronted with today's reality, Alfred Marshall appears to be less accurate in his forecast: "Human wants and desires are countless in number and very various in kind: but they are generally limited and capable of being satisfied."[23] Needs perhaps, but not wants and not desires. They seem to be endless. On the contrary, the more we have, the more we seem to want. If we need more and more consumption, like an alcoholic maintains his inebriation, does consumption show the same characteristics as an addictive substance? If we have a depression from GDP stagnation, or zero or low growth, haven't we become addicted? Why don't we know how to be reasonable? Because consumption behaves like a drug.

In her book *Women Who Run with the Wolves*, Clarissa Estes offers an interesting description of addiction: "Addiction is anything that depletes life while making it 'appear' better."[24] In his book *Fury*, Salman Rushdie writes that every sin is a sin of impropriety—in other words, an inadequacy where we stake claims on things we have no right to.[25] Aristotle also sees things similarly: "[E]vil belongs to the class of the unlimited."[26]

We thought that satisfying our wants would lead to their being satisfied. But, alas, as we can see today from our historically overrich yet overindebted society, this was a nontrivial mistake. Demand simply creates

---

[20] Patinkin, *Essays on and in the Chicago Tradition*, 34.

[21] Žizek, *The Plague of Fantasies*, 39. In "The Signification of the Phallus," Lacan distinguishes desire from need and demand. Need is a biological instinct that is articulated in demand, yet demand has a double function. On one hand it articulates need, and on the other it acts as a demand for love. So, even after the need articulated in demand is satisfied, the demand for love remains unsatisfied, and this leftover is desire. For Lacan "desire is neither the appetite for satisfaction nor the demand for love, but the difference that results from the subtraction of the first from the second." Lacan, *The Four Fundamental Concepts of Psychoanalysis*, 318. Desire then is the surplus produced by the articulation of need in demand. Lacan adds that "desire begins to take shape in the margin in which demand becomes separated from need." Lacan, *The Four Fundamental Concepts of Psychoanalysis*, 344. The Czech biologist Josef Šmajs calls this abiotic demand (or abiotic needs, abiotic consumption). See Šmajs, *Filozofie: obrat k zemi* [Philosophy: Back to Earth], 356–392.

[22] Ecclesiastes 1:8.

[23] Marshall, *Principles of Economics*, 86.

[24] Estes, *Women Who Run with the Wolves*, 492.

[25] Rushdie, *Fury*, 28.

[26] Aristotle, *Nicomachean Ethics*, 1106b29–30: "[E]xcellence is a kind of a mean, since it aims at what is intermediate ... evil belongs to the class of the unlimited ... and good to that of the limited."

new demand. Supply does not satisfy this demand but creates it anew. Furthermore, demand (want, lust, craving) grows larger and larger with every new supply—until, out of oversaturation, we could get into the situation described in Psalm 107: "They loathed all food."[27] Milan Kundera points out in his book *Laughable Loves*, especially in the story "The Golden Apple of Eternal Desire," there is a certain happiness in the pure *pursuit* of happiness, although the final bliss point is never met. In his opening quote to the story, Kundera points to Pascal's observation that some hunters "do not know that it is the chase, and not the quarry, which they seek."[28] As the economist Knight puts it: "[T]he experienced reward is more the joy of pursuit than of possession ... man is doomed ... to strive towards goals which recede more rapidly than he as an individual, or even society, advances toward them. Thus life is finally, if one chooses, or if one's temperament so dictates, a sort of labour of Sisyphus."[29]

In this view, man does not know his or her bliss or saturation point. We grope around it and we seek for it as if with eyes closed, and we see it only in retrospect. "I will never be happy *again*" is the typical sentence that one hears, not "I will never be happy." We know that there was a point when we were happy, but we notice it only when our utility has been decreased. As Simmel puts it, the closer we are to happiness, the more the desire for it grows. The hottest desire is not brought about by that which is absolutely distant and unattainable but by the things that we don't have, and yet it seems—and this illusion is strengthened by the monetization of our society—to be just within our reach.[30] It behaves like the mythical treasure at the end of the rainbow. The further you walk toward the rainbow, the further the rainbow, and the treasure, advance. "Enough is just always over the horizon, and like the horizon it recedes as we approach it."[31] There always will be a distance, a gap between our supply of possessions and demand thereof. The failure of equilibrium economics becomes even more obvious. "The nearer your destination, the more you're slip slidin' away," as Paul Simon sings.

CAN SUPPLY EVER MEET DEMAND?

How to bridge this gap? There seem to be two ways to minimize the discrepancy between demand and supply. One is to increase the supply of goods (in personal lives as well as in permanent GDP increase) until it satisfies our demand—to have, so to speak, all that we want to have.

---

[27] Psalms 107:18–17: "Some became fools through their rebellious ways and suffered affliction because of their iniquities. They loathed all food and drew near the gates of death."
[28] The original comes from Pascal's *Pensées*, 70.
[29] Knight, "Liberalism and Christianity," 71.
[30] See Simmel, *Money in Modern Culture*, 19–20.
[31] As Paul L. Wachtel writes, cited in Volf, "In the Cage of Vanities," 177.

This is the Hedonist program: Find out what you want (this itself is a difficult exercise, as I attempted to show above) and then strive toward it. This is a never-ending story, as is the case of a carrot on a stick. However, this is the program that we have chosen from the Greek era until today. That is one reason why our GDP has grown as it has—because we wanted it very, very much.

The other reply to the problem of demand versus supply is an opposite one, and it can be found in the ideas of the Stoics: If there is a mismatch, a gap between demand and supply, then *decrease demand* to meet your existing *supply*. While it looks easy on paper, this is a tough psychological exercise that the Stoics had to train a lifetime for. A common reply to this was: "It is better to be a human being dissatisfied than a pig satisfied; better to be a Socrates dissatisfied than a fool satisfied."[32] This is true, but it is even better to be a Socrates *satisfied* (at least in terms of consumption). For it was Socrates himself, by the way, who said "in that case stones and corpses [who have no wants nor desires] would be happiest."[33] Ultimately, Plato does not ascribe positive values to the desires and needs of the human body—for they are deceptive—as we have already shown in the first part of this book.

In this view, a truly "rich" man is someone who wants nothing (more), while the needs of a poor man are many. Thus, technically speaking, an unsatisfied millionaire can be much poorer a man than a man with low income.

CARE FOR EXTERNAL GOODS

At the end of *The Protestant Ethic and the Spirit of Capitalism*, Weber argues that "care for the external goods should only lie on the shoulders of the saint like a light cloak, which can be thrown aside at any moment. But fate decreed that the cloak should become an iron cage."[34] Knowing that we are not saints and that "care for external goods" can become "an iron cage" no matter how prosperous our civilization is, what are we to do? Either we limit our wants (as the Stoics advise) or we shall be never happy (this is the paradox of Hedonists).[35] If we pursue happiness and happiness alone, we will never be happy. Happiness seems to come as a by-product of doing something good, not as an end in itself. But should this be a topic for economics? Of course—a field that tries to maximize utility all the time should be at least fully aware of this.

Today it is believed that the more we have the happier and freer we are. Some Stoics had it exactly the other way. A good example of this is

---

[32] Mill, *Utilitarianism*, 12.
[33] Plato, *Gorgias*, 492e.
[34] Weber, *The Protestant Ethic and the Spirit of Capitalism*, 123.
[35] A controversial paradox in literature known as the problem of Hedonistic adaptation.

the well-known case of Diogenes of Sinope, better known as Diogenes the Cynic. He believed that the *less* he had the *freer* he was. Today, we believe the *exact* opposite.

To avoid misunderstanding, I do not want to propose here that we give up our possessions but to show that this is a never-ending story. We are naturally discontented—as we have seen, insaturability is something that has been in human nature from its very beginning; Diogenes is a rare exception. It goes against human nature, Kant writes, "to stop possessing and enjoying at some point and be satisfied."[36] The question is *to what extent* should we give in to this inborn meta-property of human beings and how should we limit ourselves? We should not want everything that we can want.

TAUTOUTILITY, MAXU

> *Oh Happiness! Our being's end and aim!*
> Alexander Pope, *Essay on Man*

Economics believes that every person, no matter what they do, maximizes their utility. We call it the economic approach. This goes back to Gary Becker, who in his imperial claim says that "the economic approach is a comprehensive one that is applicable to all human behavior, be it behavior involving money prices or imputed shadow prices, repeated or infrequent decisions, large or minor decisions, emotional or mechanical ends, rich or poor persons, men or women, adults or children, brilliant or stupid persons, patients or therapists, businessmen or politicians, teachers or students."[37]

But what does this word "utility" mean? We have many models for the maximalization of utility and can spend years studying optimization calculations. In the flood of all mathematical definitions and proofs, our "rigorous" textbooks have forgotten to define what the term "utility" actually *means*. It is no wonder, because they know very well what they are doing: If they defined it, students would quickly lose interest in the textbook. It is better to be quiet about this and draw attention to the abundant mathematical apparatus. "Utility" is supposed to be the goal of all human activity, so let's examine this word and let's see how far we can go with it: "In order to shake a hypothesis, it is sometimes not necessary to do anything more than push it as far as it will go."[38]

---

[36] Volf, "In the Cage of Vanities," 172. Kant, *Critique of Judgement*. Or "Insatiability belongs to the basic makeup of human beings."

[37] Becker, *The Economic Approach to Human Behavior*, 8. Also see Force, *Self-Interest before Adam Smith*, 8.

[38] Diderot, *Diderot's Selected Writings*, 77.

We can find the following definition of utility in the *Collins Dictionary of Economics*:[39]

> Utility: Satisfaction or pleasure that an individual derives from the consumption of a good or service.

Of course, utility, satisfaction, and pleasure are synonyms—in the aforementioned citations they can be freely switched. This is about a definition of the type A = A, where utility is satisfaction or happiness or pleasure. For this reason, if we were to rewrite this sentence, we get:

> Utility is the utility an individual gains through the consumption of a good or service.[40]

Of course, it is not true that an individual constantly maximizes his or her utility through goods and services only. Sometimes, for example, he or she sleeps, stands idle, sleeps longer than is necessary for regeneration, or chats with children and friends. A reasonable person would consider none of this to be the consumption of goods or services. At this moment, a noteworthy thing usually happens: The definition of utility expands to include sleep, talking with children, and so forth. If we want to remain consistent in that a person constantly maximizes his utility no matter what, we must give up the unequivocal, "narrow" definition. We get:

> Utility is the utility (satisfaction or pleasure) which an individual gains through the consumption of a good or service, rest, labor, etc. (understand this to mean anything that subjectively makes a person happy, or in other words, increases utility).

Another solution is to expand the term "consumption" to any other activity that increases the consumer's utility. Of course, the result is the same:

> Utility is gained by an individual through the consumption (or making) of that which increases utility.

It isn't necessary to continue with this exercise—it is clear that any sentence on the maximalization of such utility is naturally valid. We gain a tautology:

> Utility is gained by an individual through activities that increase utility.

And because each person has utility from something else, we get:

> An individual does what he wants to do.

---

[39] The term "utility" does not even appear in the index of some economics textbooks. For Mankiw, *Principles of Economics*, it appears on page 442—utility is at the same time happiness and the satisfaction that a person has with regard to their life situation. Utility is the measure of prosperity. This is again about defining synonyms, because it is also very possible to say that happiness is the level of utility or satisfaction, or that satisfaction is the level of happiness and utility.

[40] If we translate "the consumption of assets or services" into normal language, we find out that utility is the utility an individual gains through consumption.

We can see that this sentence is vacuous—and for this reason it can be constantly "valid" because it says that A = A. In this way it is possible to try to economically explain, for example, the love of a mother for her child and say that the mother gains utility from loving her child. And anything she sacrifices for her child is because it maximizes her utility—this is why, for example, she nurses her child, because she gains utility from it. This of course means the same as saying that a mother nurses her child because she wants to nurse him. But an economist would get caught in a circle without saying anything new. If a mother did not nurse her child, an economist would deftly explain *that the mother did not nurse, because she gains utility from not nursing.*[41]

Alternatively, we define utility narrowly, such as the utility stemming from tradable assets, but then we come to the conclusion that the homo economicus model does not know how to explain *all* human behavior.[42] Nevertheless, economists were not satisfied with this (testable) conclusion, and redefined the term "utility" in such a way as to include everything—including (presumptive, expected) utility from rewards in the afterlife. When we include everything under the term "utility," even martyrs or St. Francis become selfish maximizers of their own (albeit posthumous) utility. With this, economics fell into the Marxist snare of Popperian falsification[43] and the untestability of models that de facto say that man does what he wants to do. If an individual maximizes utility, which everyone defines themselves, Popper would immediately ask: How would an individual have to act in order *not to* maximize their utility? In other

---

[41] "The assumption that all behavior is selfish is the most parsimonious we can make, and scientists always like to explain much with little. But we cannot conclude, neither in general nor on any given occasion, that selfishness is the more widespread motivation. Sometimes the world is messy, and the most parsimonious explanation is wrong. The idea that self-interest makes the world go round is refuted by a few familiar facts. Some forms of helping behavior are not reciprocated and so cannot be explained by long-term self-interest. Parents have a selfish interest in helping their children, assuming that children will care for parents in their old age—but it is not in the selfish interest of children to provide such care. And many still do." Elster, *Nuts and Bolts for the Social Sciences,* 54. Also in Force, *Self-Interest before Adam Smith,* 10.

[42] Instead of the word "utility," Albert O. Hirschman uses the word "interest." The implications, however, are the same; while he seems to praise the principle, he himself admits: "[I]t became a real fad as well as a paradigm (à la Kuhn) and most of human action was suddenly explained by self-interest, sometimes to the point of tautology." Hirschman, *The Passion and the Interests,* 42.

[43] Sir Karl Popper proposed to recognize scientific arguments according to whether their postulates were falsifiable. What would have had to happen for a given theory to be proven false? If such realistic variants exist, but despite this were unproven, the given theory may be considered scientific. But on the other hand, if the given theory explains all possible behavior, then it becomes pseudoscience. Popper, for example, describes why the Marxist approach to history seemed unscientific to him: Marx was capable of explaining absolutely everything about his theory, and even the seemingly opposite situation. If a given theory manages to explain all imaginable situations, for example, in the context of the theory of class warfare, then something is wrong somewhere. If the theory can explain everything, that is not its strength, but its weakness.

words: Can one go in an opposite direction to their optimization function? If it is not possible to present a thinkable example, then the theory
is not falsifiable and is de facto pointless.

But back to the main line of the argument. As Caldwell notes, elaborating on a point by Hutchison:

> [S]cience contains statements which are either conceivably falsifiable by
> empirical observation or are not. Those which are not so falsifiable are tau-
> tologies, and are thus devoid of empirical content. It follows then, that the
> propositions of pure theory have no empirical content. (. . .)[44]

Caldwell further writes: "The pursuit of self-interest, it is claimed, is useless if defined too narrowly, (...) and empty if defined too broadly, for
then all behaviour becomes maximizing behaviour".[45]

We can learn from mistakes, but rarely from tautologies. Tautologies
are a useful exercise in logical methods. They do not allow, by definition,
any errors, but are nonetheless always valid and "true." They are not *nonsense*, but they are without *sense*, without *content*. "The tautology has no
truth-conditions, since it is unconditionally true: and a contradiction is
true on no condition. Tautologies and contradiction lack sense. (. . .)
Tautologies and contradictions are not pictures of the reality. They do not
represent any possible situations. For the former admit all possible situations, the latter none."[46]

And here we come to a key paradox: The pride of economists, that the
homo economicus model *includes all possibilities* and therefore can explain
everything, should in reality be our greatest shame. If we can explain everything with a term or principle, the meaning of which we do not know,
then we must ask what we are actually explaining.

Incidentally: It is not true that abstract thinking always makes things
simple. Sometimes we can really complicate them as well. This was noted
by Friedrich Nietzsche, who spoke of how theoretical cognition can make
us blind to obvious things. This is illustrated, for example, by the Greek
story of Oedipus. Although (or precisely because) Oedipus is the wisest
of his people (he manages to solve the riddle), he remains completely
blind to the obvious. Not only that he does not know the basic thing every
child knows (who his mother and father are), but even that he (unknowingly!) committed patricide and incest.

THE AGE OF THE ECONOMIST: THE DEBT AGE AND
THE FALL OF ICARUS

Aristotle considered *excessiveness* to be people's main weakness. Each
characteristic (even good ones), if taken to extremes, becomes harmful.

---

[44] Caldwell, *Beyond Positivism*, 108
[45] Ibid., 146.
[46] Wittgenstein, *Tractatus Logico-Philosophicus*, 4.461–4.462.

Thus overwhelming love threatens to become suffocating jealousy, healthy care for oneself can become unbearable selfishness, where everything except for me and my interests loses legitimacy. For this reason, Aristotle is frequently called the philosopher of the golden middle way. The only characteristic, Aristotle writes, that cannot in any way be taken to extremes or overdone is *moderation*. It is moderation, however, that we lack; in recent times we have been too tempted by wealth, just as Icarus was tempted to fly too close to the sun.

Perhaps our era will go down in history as the Debt Age. In recent decades, our debt has risen not out of shortage but out of surplus, excessiveness. Our society is not suffering from famine, but it must solve another problem—how to host a meal for someone who is full. A saying used in Slovakia expresses this well: *The eye would eat, but the belly is full.* In ancient Rome, when riches and tastes overcame the capacity of the stomach, the conflict between the hungry eye and the physically over-full stomach was solved by their legendary vomitoriums. In our society, this is considered unaesthetic—so we created new provisions to solve that problem.

The problem of our part of the world is *how to eat and at the same time not to eat* (while, of course, for the fundamental part of our history and today, part of the world goes hungry). We created fat-free cream, butter without butter. We remove the most nutritious parts from our meals.[47] In this context, it is also interesting to mark Jesus's words:

> Do not worry about your life, what you will eat or drink; or about your body, what you will wear. Is not life more important than food, and the body more important than clothes?[48]

These words speak with the same audibility to our overfed generation as they did in the times when there was worry over what to eat—the worry that one will have *too little* to eat. Our worry today is also what to eat—but the worry comes from exactly the opposite side—we worry we will have *too much* to eat.

The more we have, the more we want. Why? Perhaps we thought (and this sounds truly intuitive) that the more we have, the less we will need. The more things move from the set of *need to have* into the set of *I have*, the more the set of *I need to have* should shrink. We thought that consumption leads to saturation, the satiation of our needs. But the opposite has proven to be true. The more we have, the more additional things we need. It's enough to compare all that we did not need

---

[47] In previous cultures, where the dominant characteristic was a real shortage, the most valuable part of the meat was considered the fat (hence the Biblical "fat of the land": "I will give you the best of the land of Egypt and you can enjoy the fat of the land," Genesis 45:18) and tallow, while lean meat was thrown to the dogs. Also Prometheus fooled Zeus by having one packet of meat that appeared fat; precisely this packet was chosen by Zeus. Today, our approach to meat is the opposite.

[48] Matthew 6:25.

twenty years ago (computers, mobile telephones) with that which we objectively need today (ultralight laptops, new mobile phones every two years, permanent and fast connection to the mobile internet). While the rich should have fewer unfulfilled needs than the poor, the reality is turning out to be absolutely the opposite. Keynes once said that wages are sticky downward. Well, it is really consumption that is sticky downward. It's easy to go up the consumption ladder but asymmetrically more unpleasant to go back down. Every new satisfied want will beget a new one and will leave us wanting. So beware of every new desire that you acquire—it is a new addiction. For consumption is like a drug.

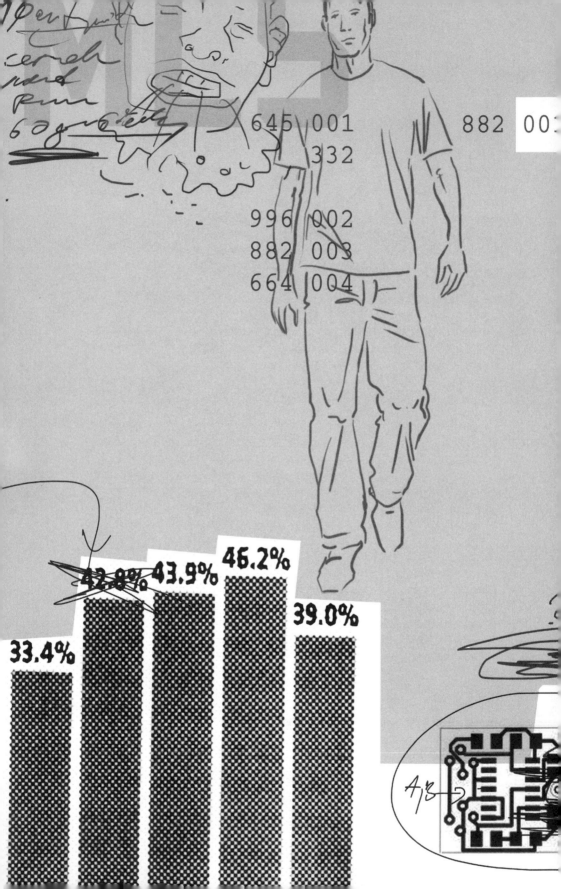

9

Progress, New Adam, and Sabbath Economics

We cannot see anything until we are possessed with the idea of it, take it into our heads,—and then we can hardly see anything else.
Henry David Thoreau[1]

PROGRESS

In the same way that Queen Elizabeth in 2008 asked economists why they were unable to predict the coming economic crisis, Václav Havel, in reaction to the crisis, asked about the meaning of growth. "Why must everything constantly grow? Why must industry, manufacturing, and production grow? Why must cities unconceptually grow in all directions, until not even a bit of the landscape remains, not even a bit of grass?"[2] As Havel himself remembers, during his more than five years in prison under the communist regime he also had to constantly work, but in the vast majority of cases it was completely nonsensical work—it was "work for work's sake." Does economic growth always have a meaning, or is it just growth for growth's sake?

When there is too much of something, we often do not notice it. And it tends to be the most important things that we overlook—precisely because we seem to be so certain of them. One of these is the idea of progress. It constantly surrounds us. On television, in ads, in political announcements, and from economists' mouths. It is the undiscussed imperative of our time, something that is simply so automatic that we do not see it. We can also look at our system as being a bit like the illusion in the *Matrix* trilogy. Specifically, the idea of growth has the power to control us and in a way turn us into slaves. In Morpheus's words, we are "kept inside a prison that [we] cannot smell, taste, or touch."[3]

---

[1] Thoreau, *Civil Disobedience and Other Essays*, 96.
[2] Havel, interview with R. Kalenská, "*Někdy se mě zmocňuje pocit* … [I sometimes have this vain feeling …]," in Lidové noviny, Kalenská, November 15, 2008.
[3] For further commentary see Irwin, *The Matrix and Philosophy*, chapter by Daniel Barwick, "Neo-Materialism and the Death of the Subject," 258. And furthermore: "The intelligences

The recent global economic crisis has shown how dependent we are on growth, and how we accept a drop in GDP with almost religious disappointment, when we take stands on tenths of a percentage point.

But where did this anticipation of never-ending growth come from? Everything suggests it is only the idea of progress in different clothing—first in religious (heaven) and later in secular forms (heaven on earth). It is the concern (alas, duty!) of markets, the state, science, and sometimes all of them together to *ensure* progress, or growth, as if economic growth were supposed to bring us closer to heaven on earth. Any stumble in GDP takes us farther from our goal and is considered evil. Growth is the greatest good; it is the maxim not only of economics, but often of our entire social and political lives.

Before the industrial revolution, we did not expect much of growth. Then we were impressed with its speed, and today we consider it to be completely automatic.[4] What's more, today we think of progress in economic and technical terms. Progress was previously perceived more or less spiritually and internally, but today we have secularized the idea and connected it to the *external* world. Consistent measurement of GDP statistics was first implemented in the United States in 1790, although humanity had gotten by without it until then. We did not need to know by how many percentage points or tenths of a point we were richer than the previous year, nor how we were doing compared with other countries. Incidentally, in 1790 the real GDP per capita was $1,025 in today's prices, almost 40 times lower than today.[5] In the past twenty years, real U.S. GDP per capita has risen by 37 percent. Impressed? Perhaps. But are we appreciative or satisfied? Hardly.

The History of Progress: The Golden (c)Age

As we have seen with Gilgamesh and the early ancient Greeks, in the beginning the notion of progress barely existed. A cyclical notion of time held reign, with no development; everything turned in a circle, like the seasons. Their role is to change and return, nothing more. This cyclicality was also frequently accompanied by rituals that were supposed to enable seasons' return. In addition, stories took place in indefinite time, in a kind of loop (which never happened but was constantly taking place). And thirdly, many of these cultures believed that the Golden Age of mankind had already passed, not that it had yet to come. Man was created better

---

that imprison human beings in the Matrix must control their captives according to the captives' own wishes." In Irwin, *The Matrix and Philosophy*, chapter by James Lawler, "We Are (the) One! Kant Explains How to Manipulate the Matrix," 139.

[4] It is striking to realize that kids played with the same type of wooden toys for practically all generations until the last two. No big progress here, no big change in the standard equipment of households until now.

[5] Johnston and Williamson, *What Was the U.S. GDP Then?*

than he was then, and the farther from the beginning, the more deterioration, the worse off we were—the exact opposite of how our civilization thinks today. Today we are grateful that progress has extricated us from ancient, "primitive" times.

The Hebrews and, later, Greek thinkers came up with a linear concept of time that incorporates historical development. The sociologist Robert Nisbet finds that "No single idea has been more important than … the Idea of Progress in Western civilization for three thousand years."[6] Despite the fact that the concept of progress cannot be considered a modern idea,[7] its secularized and economized version became a raison d'être for economics, science, and politics and is something our civilization grew up with and simply counts on.[8] Goodness seems to always be just around the corner. The British thinker C. S. Lewis once ironically expressed this even more tersely: "goodness = what comes next."[9] And we are so obsessed with this idea of permanent maximum growth that we are willing to sacrifice our indebtedness at its feet. Not just in times of recession and crisis, but also in times of relatively generous economic growth. So much growth was induced by debt steroids that much of the expansion in recent years was not Gross Domestic Product, but Gross Debt Product. We have become overobsessed with the idea of growth. We are not exactly sure what we are growing toward, but we compensate for this shortcoming by accelerating.[10]

But is this really natural? The debate on whether progress of *techne* leads toward or away from the Golden Age spans many civilizations. Not even the ancient Greeks were clear on it. For example, Hesiod claims, "the Golden Age was when there was no knowledge but, at the same time, no contaminants to moral virtue and universal happiness."[11] We see something of a warning sign that progress and knowledge often come at the expense of happiness, calm, and harmony.[12]

The Enlightenment later came up with the notion that the beginnings of mankind, its natural state, was, in the words of Thomas Hobbes,

---

[6] Nisbet, "Idea of Progress," 4.

[7] Today, a nearly century-old classic on the topic is Bury, *The Idea of Progress*, which begins with the Enlightenment. Nisbet, both in his book *The History of the Idea of Progress*, and in the article *The Idea of Progress: A Bibliographical Essay*, starts with (we could say *only with*) the Greeks. And although he mentions the Hebrews in passing, he does not devote them a proper study; "We begin with Hesiod (ca. 700 B.C.) and his Works and Days," he writes in his article.

[8] Volf says, "for many in the seventeenth century and after, mammon seemed an increasingly attractive lord, however." Volf, "In the Cage of Vanities," 170.

[9] Lewis, C. S., *Evolutionary Hymn*, 55–56.

[10] This is a paraphrase of the aphorism by the witty Polish author Stanisław Jerzy Lec: "We know we are on the wrong track, but we are compensating for this shortcoming by accelerating."

[11] Nisbet, *History of the Idea of Progress*, 9.

[12] See also Nussbaum, *The Fragility of Goodness*. In Protagoras, the Greeks realize that "Science both saves us and transforms us, helps us attain our ends and reshape the ends themselves," 91. For a more detailed anthropological analysis, see Eliade, *Cosmos and History*.

"nasty, brutish, and short."[13] This theory holds that paradise is in the *future* and, furthermore, a technical, scientific (i.e., not spiritual) *task of men*. So, in the mid–nineteenth century, "Fichte proclaimed that true paradise was not a gift of grace that humanity enjoyed in the distant past, but a promised land to be conquered by humanity's efforts in the not-too-distant future."[14]

But we can also trace this line of thought back to ancient Greece, where a similar notion later prevailed: "Not long afterward Protagoras, first and greatest of the Sophists, made emphatic his conviction that man's history is one of escape from primeval ignorance, fear, and barrenness of culture, and of gradual ascent to ever-better conditions of life, the consequence of the steady advancement of knowledge."[15] Xenophanes, late in the sixth century B.C., believed that "the gods did not reveal to men all things in the beginning, but men through their own search find in the course of time that which is better."[16]

Plato describes in Protagoras a touching scene in which "Prometheus bewails the terrible punishment he has received from Zeus for the 'crime' of having brought to mankind fire and thus stimulated men to rise intellectually and culturally to emulate the gods themselves. There is no more moving passage in all literature than that in which Prometheus, consigned to an eternity of punishment, tells how he had found mankind on earth in a pitiful condition—subject to every kind of deprivation, ever-fearful, ignorant, and living like animals in caves. He brought to man the gift of fire, enabling mankind through its own efforts to slowly ascend the scale of culture, learning language, arts and crafts, technology, and how to live amicably in groups and federations."[17]

We see here a somewhat similar point as in the story of Eden. In both cases, it was *knowledge* that brought a fundamental change of human condition, be it the Tree of Knowledge of Good and Evil or Prometheus' technological *knowledge*. Knowledge seems to bring progress, but at the same time causes anger of God or gods and deterioration of His or their relationship with humans.

The End of the Future and Modern Priests

Material progress has become, in many ways, the secular religion and a major hope of our times. As Robert Nelson, an economist who has studied in great detail and written two books about this topic, puts it, "many

---

[13] Hobbes, *Leviathan*, xliii.

[14] Volf, "In the Cage of Vanities," 175.

[15] Nisbet, "Idea of Progress," in the section "Greek Poets, Sophists, and Historians on Progress."

[16] Nisbet, *History of the Idea of Progress*, 11.

[17] Nisbet, "Idea of Progress." He continues: "Thucydides, in his history of the Peloponnesian War, devotes the first few paragraphs to pointing out that in ancient times the Greeks lived just as did contemporary barbarians and savages, but that over a long period of time they had risen to greatness through their own efforts."

economists believe in progress in a religious way, as something that is significantly improving the basic human condition for the better."[18] The economist Robert Samuelson represented it as follows: "[E]very age has its illusions. Ours has been this fervent belief in the power of prosperity."[19]

We economists are of course somewhat aware, or at least Frank Knight was, that we live in a "milieu in which science, as such, is a religion."[20] Now, religion does not have to have a (pre)defined deity. The generally accepted definition adopted by the U.S. Supreme Court (inspired by Paul Tillich, perhaps the most prominent Protestant theologian of the twentieth century) accepts "a wide range of 'belief systems' as valid religions even when they 'avoided any reference to supernatural entities or forces.'"[21] Originally a religious idea of progress has become secularized into a technical belief that science can save us and that riches can not only make us happy (personal, individualistic heaven on earth), but also make society, as such, better off (general heaven on earth).

Dreams of the End of Avarice

Not only do we automatically connect high material hopes with progress, but we also have ethical and social dreams of the end of avarice, connected with progress. The notion that *progress can save the world* has taken a form of social hope par excellence. David Hume believed that "if nature gifted us with a surplus of material possessions and everyone had enough of everything, then it would be certain that every virtue would blossom in that blessed state."[22] Injustice would disappear and "judicature would henceforth be unnecessary." John Stuart Mill, one of the fathers of economics,[23] believed that "mutual trampling, destruction, pressing with sharp elbows and stepping on heels" are only the syndrome of a transitional era.[24] When it ends, we will achieve a *steady age*, when "no one

---

[18] Nelson, *Economics as Religion*, xix. The other book of interest would be Nelson, *Reaching for Heaven on Earth*.

[19] Ibid., 81.

[20] Knight, *Freedom and Reform*, 46.

[21] Nelson, *Economics as Religion*, xxiv.

[22] Hume, *Selections*, 203–204.

[23] First published in 1848, Mill's work quickly became the bible of nineteenth-century English economics. The editor of a recent reedition titles it: *Principles of Political Economy with Some of Their Applications to Social Philosophy*, ix.

[24] Mill, *Principles of Political Economy*, 4.6.2:
"I confess I am not charmed with the ideal of life held out by those who think that the normal state of human beings is that of struggling to get on; that the trampling, crushing, elbowing, and treading on each other's heels, which form the existing type of social life, are the most desirable lot of human kind, or anything but the disagreeable symptoms of one of the phases of industrial progress. It may be a necessary stage in the progress of civilization, and those European nations which have hitherto been so fortunate as to be preserved from it, may have it yet to undergo." Mill, *Principles of Political Economy*, 88.

desires to be richer."[25] Mill, however, writes in a chapter called "Of the Stationary State":

> But in contemplating any progressive movement, not in its nature unlimited, the mind is not satisfied with merely tracing the laws of the movement; it cannot but ask the further question, to what goal? Towards what ultimate point is society tending by its industrial progress? When the progress ceases, in what condition are we to expect that it will leave mankind? It must always have been seen, more or less distinctly, by political economists, that the increase of wealth is not boundless.[26]

We should not forget that economics was, for a long time from its beginning, a "dismal science." In the beginning, largely thanks to Thomas Malthus, economic progress tended to produce a dismal *stationary state*. As if, so to say, we were aiming for a hell on earth. How exactly a dismal science became a happy and optimistic science, one believing in progress, is a question worth studying. To a certain extent we can divide economists into optimists (heaven on earth awaits us) or pessimists (economic Armageddon is to come). Mill and Hume seem to be the first optimists. Keynes joined them in the 1930s, when he expressed the hope that such a heaven on Earth would be within reach in the coming hundred years. Then the "greatest change our material development has ever had" would take place: The greatest change in man's material (and, as it would appear below, not only in material) development would occur and a new man would arise—a new, different Adam, who would lie back and not have to constantly hurry:

> I draw the conclusion that ... the economic problem may be solved, or be at least within sight of a solution, within a hundred years ... the struggle for subsistence, always has been hitherto the primary, most pressing problem of the human race—not only of the human race, but of the whole of the biological kingdom from the beginnings of life in its most primitive forms. Thus we have been expressly evolved by nature—with all our impulses and deepest instincts—for the purpose of solving the economic problem. If the economic problem is solved, mankind will be deprived of its traditional purpose ... For many ages to come the old Adam will be so strong in us that everybody will need to do some work if he is to be contented ... for three hours a day [of work] is quite enough to satisfy the old Adam in most of us![27]

As can be seen, Keynes is probably one of the greatest optimists regarding economic progress. He saw not only material salvation in economic growth but, as with David Hume, moral rebirth as well, a great change "in the code of morals":

> When the accumulation of wealth is no longer of high social importance, there will be great changes in the code of morals. We shall be able to rid ourselves of many of the pseudo-moral principles which have hag-ridden us

---

[25] Mill, *Principles of Political Economy*, 4.6.2.
[26] Ibid., 188, in 4.6.
[27] Keynes, *Essays in Persuasion*, 358–373.

for two hundred years, by which we have exalted some of the most distasteful of human qualities into the position of the highest virtues ... I see us free, therefore, to return to some of the most sure and certain principles of religion and traditional virtue—that avarice is a vice, that the exaction of usury is a misdemeanor, and the love of money is detestable, that those walk most truly in the paths of virtue and sane wisdom who take least thought for the morrow. We shall once more value ends above means and prefer the good to the useful. We shall honour those who can teach us how to pluck the hour and the day virtuously and well, the delightful people who are capable of taking direct enjoyment in things, the lilies of the field who toil not, neither do they spin.[28]

The only four things we need, to reach this state, which Keynes calls "economic bliss," except for about a hundred years of time, are:

Our power to control population, our determination to avoid wars and civil dissensions, our willingness to entrust to science the direction of those matters which are properly the concern of science, and the rate of accumulation as fixed by the margin between our production and our consumption; of which the last will easily look after itself, given the first three.[29]

Keynes probably expressed faith in the economic satisfaction of our needs the strongest; faith in the beneficial action of material progress is professed by a majority of the figures of economic thought of our time. This is why we must permanently grow—because we are headed toward a paradise on Earth.

Economists as Priests

Because care for the soul has been replaced today by care for external things, economists have become figures of great importance in our time. They are expected to perform interpretations of reality (as if capricious Olympus has been replaced by capricious Wall Street), give prophetic services (macroeconomic forecasts), reshape reality (mitigate the impacts of the crisis, speed up growth), and, in the long run, provide leadership on the way to the promised land. Samuelson, Friedman, Becker, Knight, and many others have become passionate evangelists of economic progress, used not only within their own country but also toward other cultures. Nelson calls this Economic Zeal—economists are "compelled to do it."[30] As Gary Becker would write in a personal tribute, Friedman had "a missionary's zeal in the worship of truth ... and enormous zeal to convince the heathen."[31]

---

[28] Keynes, *Essays in Persuasion*, 369.
[29] Keynes, *Economic Possibilities for Our Grandchildren*, 373.
[30] Nelson, *Economics as Religion*, 162.
[31] Becker, "Milton Friedman," 138–146.

In the end, Fukuyama's faith in the *End of History* through the victory of democratic capitalism is telling. The only challenge now becomes convincing all citizens of the right (economic) faith and exporting it to other cultures, or pagans, who have not yet "matured" economically. We have economic heaven within reach and want to grant it to others. And, as with most religions, the more adherents it has, the better off its original proclaimers are. International trade seems to be advantageous for the poor countries, but surely much more for developed ones.

As we know, economic heaven has not been that easy to achieve, and it probably won't be for some time. We should ultimately realize that overvaluing the role of economics is a rather widespread discipline these days.[32] Nevertheless, it is good to be aware that Marx himself started it. It was Marx who (paradoxically) de facto believed that the economy and economics is the foundation of everything, the foundation of society, which then determines everything else, and that everything else (including morals and culture) is a superstructure above an economic foundation. Everything else is, in his view, *false conscience*—a society-wide illusion, *an opiate of the masses*. Economic development becomes the main explanatory factor of history. As the economic historian Niall Ferguson persuasively writes:

> When I was a schoolboy, the history textbooks offered a variety of explanations for twentieth-century violence. Sometimes they related it to economic crises, as if depressions and recessions could explain political conflict. A favourite device was to relate the rise of unemployment in Weimar Germany to the rise of the Nazi vote and Adolf Hitler's "seizure" of power, which in turn was supposed to explain the Second World War.... Then there was the theory that the century was all about class conflict.
>
> ... Let me now reformulate those preliminary schoolboy thoughts in rather more rigorous terms.... some severe economic crises did not lead to wars. Certainly, it is now impossible to argue (though Marxists long tried to) that the First World War was the result of a crisis of capitalism; on the contrary, it abruptly terminated a period of extraordinary global economic integration with relatively high growth and low inflation.[33]

A Slap in the Face of Progress

Let me make one more final note on scientific progress as such and the blow inflicted on it in the first half of the twentieth century. Incidentally, let us note that it was Marxism-Leninism and finally racism as well (based on an extreme version of scientific Darwinism) that staked claims to the adjective "scientific," emphasizing their scientific nature at every opportunity.

---

[32] See also, for example, Stigler, "Economics: The Imperial Science?" Stigler argues: "So economics is an imperial science: it has been addressing central problems in a considerable number of neighbouring social disciplines, with and without invitations," 311.

[33] Ferguson, *War of the World*, xxxvii–xxxviii.

At that time there was no way to "objectively" cast doubt on the given theory; somehow we only know it today, now that the ethos has changed. And the problem is that if a certain approach is recognized as scientific by the scientific community, then it becomes a scientific topic.[34] The opposite is understandably true; scientific truth is not, then, a matter of some kind of objective appraisal, but a matter of appraisal by its own academic community. Here, too, it is certainly possible to suspect the scientific community of a tendency leaning toward the political or scientific fashion. In this respect, we should be careful with trendy ideas. And we are not at all discussing how it is the scientific community that "creates" the truth and "arbitrates" it at the same time. Those who "create" the truth and those who "appraise" it are one and the same. In the scientific world there is none of the division of power we know and carefully watch over in the world of politics. For this reason, Marxism-Leninism and, in the long run, even racism were entitled (at the time) to appropriate the title of "scientific." The fact that our scientific era is among the bloodiest in history was one of the serious cracks in the religion of secular progress. The sociologist Zygmunt Baumann argues that the Holocaust was not a mistake or a misstep of modernity, but its direct result.[35]

I Can't Get No Satiation—Still Haven't Found What I'm Greeding For

For modern economics, this discussion should be of interest because the idea of progress is a double-edged sword. On one hand, the pursuit of progress has enabled real progress. The reason why we have grown so much (in GDP) in the recent past is that *we wanted it very, very much*. On the other hand, the question is, are we more satisfied? Not only do we not know how to achieve satisfaction, but it is not even all that desirable: "Satiation is undesirable for modern believers in progress."[36]

From an objective standpoint, we are living in the richest period in the history of the planet. Despite this, it is not enough for us; affluence brings new problems. Picking only one of the seven cakes in the sweetshop when one has both a sweet tooth and the money for all of them can be psychologically painful. At the moment you decide, you give up the other six flavors and are in doubt as to whether you shouldn't have had the hazelnut instead of the pistachio, or even better yet, the chocolate. Best would be to taste them all, and then you could either leave the sweetshop in a quandary or with a stuffed belly, because you were unable to fight off choice.

---

[34] For more, see Kuhn, *Structure of Scientific Revolutions*, or Redman, *Economics and the Philosophy of Science*, 16–22.

[35] See Baumann, *Modernity and the Holocaust*.

[36] Volf, "In the Cage of Vanities," 176.

For economists, such a situation is hard to grasp. Economics mainly counts on situations when a person is unsaturated and would like to consume more (and also make more money). What would economics look like without this? Our resources have grown so much that we can allow much more than full satiation. Economics is the study of "allocation of scarce resources," but what happens when they are in abundance? Our bliss point is actually somewhere *inside* the set of what we can allow; it is within our budgetary limitations. But finding it is just as difficult. It may simply happen that we overcome material surplus, and that could lead to oversaturation. Neither is a blissful state, and it could also happen that we curse the weight of our own purchases.

Tyler Durden, the main character in the novel *Fight Club*, describes the modus vivendi of consumer society very persuasively: "Generations have been working in jobs they hate, just so they can buy what they don't really need."[37] The postwar period was characterized by its rapid rise in wealth, which sparked the first wave of criticism of consumer life in the 1960s. The hope of the Hippie generation, of course, turned out to be false. Our society became dependent not only on its wealth but also on debt. To this day a debate is raging between psychologists, economists, and sociologists as to whether wealth contributes meaningfully to our feelings of happiness.[38] After many years of studying the phenomenon of happiness in many countries, the sociologist Ronald Inglehart[39] came to the conclusion that a feeling of well-being increases somewhat with growing wealth, but the increases become smaller and smaller—the function of well-being is concave. In a rich world, happiness rises only minimally with accumulating wealth. There's nowhere to rise to. According to Inglehart, in rich countries, the correlation between income and happiness is "surprisingly weak (indeed, virtually negligible)."[40] We call this Easterlin's paradox.

David G. Myers finds that "as far as happiness is concerned, it hardly matters whether one drives a BMW or, like so many of the Scots, walks or rides a bus."[41] Research among the wealthiest people (*Forbes's* 100 wealthiest Americans surveyed by the University of Illinois psychologist Ed Diener) showed they are "only slightly happier than average."[42] Myers further contemplates the temporary joy of wealth: "Lottery winners appear to gain but a temporary jolt of joy from their winnings. The euphoria doesn't last. In fact, activities previously enjoyed, such as reading, may become less pleasurable. Compared to the high of winning a million

---

[37] Palahniuck, *Fight Club*, 1996, 141.

[38] The question of whether economic growth increases a person's well-being at all is not that clear. See, e.g., Tibor Scitovsky's older classic *The Joyless Economy*, or Luigino Bruni's quite recent and outstanding book *Civil Happiness—Economics and Human Flourishing in Historical Perspective*.

[39] Inglehart, *World Values Survey*.

[40] Inglehart, *Culture Shift*, 242.

[41] Myers, "Does Economic Growth Improve Human Morale?"

[42] Diener, Horwitz, and Emmons, "Happiness of the Very Wealthy."

dollars, ordinary pleasures pale."[43] Aristotle[44] also speaks of a similar *deafening effect* of sharp joy compared with normal joy (normal joy vanishes at the presence of sharp joy [drugs] and this new joy takes its place, so to speak).

In a society in which everyone lives in four-thousand-square-foot houses, people are likely to be no happier than in a society in which everyone lives in two-thousand-square-foot houses.[45] It would appear that in the long run, it is all the same how much we have or do not have, while even this statistic has become a fresh topic for discussion.[46] Even if we found the imaginary bliss point, would we know how to rest at it and not trudge onward? How do we actually recognize such a point? And: aren't we at it right now? Beckett's citation from *Waiting for Godot* is expressive:

VLADIMIR: Say you are, even if it's not true.
ESTRAGON: What am I to say?
VLADIMIR: Say, I am happy.
ESTRAGON: I am happy.
VLADIMIR: So am I.
ESTRAGON: So am I.
VLADIMIR: We are happy.
ESTRAGON: We are happy. (Silence.) What do we do now, now that we are happy?
VLADIMIR: Wait for Godot.[47]

It would appear then that there are two ways to be happy in consumption: to permanently escalate consumption (to reach the next unit of happiness, we need ever more consumption material) or to *become aware* that we have enough. The only thing we have a real shortage of is shortage itself.

If economics loses its goal, the only thing remaining for us is growth—growth which knows nothing but itself, because it has no goal to measure. A feeling of aimlessness[48] binds it to meaninglessness[49] and homelessness. Racing to a goal differs from racing for the sake of racing. If we are racing for the race itself (jogging), then we are running in a circle, which is okay, but then we cannot be surprised that we have "run nowhere."

---

[43] See also Brickman, Coates, and Janoff-Bulman, "Lottery Winners and Accident Victims"; and Argyle, *The Psychology of Happiness*.

[44] Aristotle, *Nicomachean Ethics*, 1154a27–1154b9.

[45] Example suggested by the Cornell University economist Robert Frank at a conference on "Understanding Quality of Life: Scientific Perspectives on Enjoyment and Suffering."

[46] Stevenson and Wolfers, *Economic Growth and Subjective Well-Being*.

[47] Beckett, *Waiting for Godot*, 66. Also see Bell, "The Cultural Contradictions of Capitalism," 22.

[48] Aristotle argued that all activity must have a direction and meaning, *telos*. For a more modern version of this, see for example MacIntyre, *After Virtue*.

[49] Key psychologist Viktor Frankl writes about meaninglessness in *Man's Search for Meaning*, especially in the chapter "The Existential Vacuum," 106.

The sentence "I don't have much time for my personal life" used to be considered a loss, an expression of inability. Today it is often evidence of engagement and is often pronounced with an expectation of respect for the activities of the person in question. Thus, while Gilgamesh had taken away personal lives of the workers by violence, today we often give them away voluntarily. It's like Gilgamesh and his (today, voluntary and still unnecessary) wall.

The Shortage of Shortage

The paradox is that we must—often artificially—create shortage. Only in shortage is there adventure, and therefore entertainment and meaning of life as well. It is symptomatic that an entire industrial sector has been created for this purpose: The entertainment industry—factory-created entertainment and diversion, which frequently lies in the *simulation of shortage*. Why? It is because real shortage does not occur in our everyday lives. And so it happens that we the oversatiated watch, from the warmth of our homes, televised adventures in which the heroes suffer from hunger and cold. We are entertained by the danger we would be glad to experience ourselves. It is a paradox: The more satiated and safe we become, the more we demand artificial entertainment and plastic danger. And there is a second paradox: We can *only* watch filmed simulations of suffering of cold and hunger from a position of surplus, in the warmth of our homes and with popcorn in hand. Watching such films while also experiencing the same type of shortage (hungry, cold) would be hard to imagine.

Perhaps it is the shortage, the hunt, that we desire. It is desire we desire. The inflation of needs was described by Xenophon in his dialogue *Hiero*, where the tyrant argues that he is worse off than anyone else because he has so many available pleasures that he enjoys none of them at all. "The more viands set before a man at table (beyond what are sufficient), the more quickly will satiety of eating overtake him. So that in actual duration of pleasure, he with his many dishes has less to boast of than the moderate liver."[50]

This mercurial inconstancy in our times is compounded by deficit economics, which we would most prefer to constantly be at the edge of overheating. If maximum growth is the imperative of our time, at any cost, then true rest and satisfaction are not possible. And if the meaning is lost, Jan Patočka, a leading Czech philosopher and Havel's fellow inmate in a communist jail, calls this state "boredom as an ontological status of mankind."[51] This leads to a need for *orgiasticy*, a sort of universal freeing in an ecstatic happening. The emptying of everyday moderation drives us

---

[50] Xenophon, *Hiero.*
[51] Patočka, *Kacířské eseje o filosofii dějin* [Heretical Essays on Philosophy and History], 98.

out from our dwellings-but-not-homes to an orgiastic excess, where we know no limits.

Patočka's explanation in the dialectic of human behavior is possible to apply to the causes of the current crisis—too large a consumption party on credit.

The Residuum of Insufficiency

Insufficiency is inherent to man; it is our characteristic, which, according to the story of the Garden of Eden, existed even before the Fall and de facto led to expulsion from Paradise. "The human race did not need to wait for capitalism to infect it with the virus of insatiability ... the virus was there all along ... the inactive virus just needed a change in socioeconomic and cultural conditions to provide it a friendly environment."[52]

But we can influence *what* we begin to lack. And we should pay closer attention to what we choose. As Aristotle puts it, one passion overcomes another. Despite the sharp growth in wealth in recent years, we still do not have enough. As if all the new "production fills a void that it has itself created."[53] How much must we have in order to not have too little? What is that mercurial element in us that cannot manage to find satisfaction? Why can't we find peace?

On the one hand, this volatility and shortage is useful. It forces us toward new discoveries, new activities, and it is precisely due to these new shortages that we owe constant economic growth. In this creative destruction, in which something new constantly replaces yesterday's completely functional things, an economist sees the pulling principle of capitalism and freedom.

On the other hand, this is how the economist Fred Hirsch[54] explains the paradoxical situation in which we are not the happiest with growing wealth.

If you're sitting at a concert and someone suddenly gets up, they gain a comparative advantage, but at the expense of the other person whom he or she is blocking. When others follow and also stand up, the comparative advantage disappears—all are again in a similar situation, only with the difference that everyone's feet hurt more. Then someone gets on their tiptoes and the entire spiral starts again. Then people start to sit on others' shoulders while standing on their tiptoes, and so on.

Our satisfaction is simply comparative; it is not absolute and we feel like the greatest paupers if our neighbor buys a new car, despite our being satisfied with our own. Is there an escape from this spiral? Well it would seem, perhaps, that it is possible to run away from this consumption curse into the paradise of the heart, where there is calm and rest. Let us not find

---

52 Volf, "In the Cage of Vanities," 172.
53 Ibid., 171.
54 See Hirsch, *Social Limits to Growth*.

rest in the material, but in the spiritual. Even Jesus never greeted his disciples with the greeting "happiness be with you," but with "peace be with you".

In his book *Confessions*, Augustine offers the memorable phrase "restless is our heart until it comes to rest in Thee."[55] But did his heart rest during his life? Did he find what he was looking for, and didn't he search for more? Just like the Old Testament Jews, when they finally got to the Promised Land, they had to continue to fight, without a trace of the desired peace and rest. Ultimately, "Jerusalem" means, in translation, "City of Peace." Even if it has such a promising name, it is not at peace to this day. It would appear that in this, the material world is similar to the spiritual world. In both we want ever more and nothing is ever enough for us. It is as if there were an indestructible residual element of insufficiency in us which creates in us neverending tension.

In his Stoic legacy, Aristotle tends toward the idea that we have to be satisfied with what we have, and that happiness can be found precisely in that. Otherwise we are caught in the trap of the deceptive "vanity-fair" syndrome, and because appetite grows with food, we will never be satisfied. "All things are wearisome, more than one can say. The eye never has enough of seeing, nor the ear its fill of hearing,"[56] as Ecclesiastes wrote thousands of years ago. Aristotle's advice is good, but it is hard to live by, especially if we have in ourselves the residual element of insufficiency, which, what's more, has been so pampered in recent years. Despite this, we should make an effort toward gratitude and satisfaction, especially in situations where we have—crisis or not—at least materially one hundred times more than the incredibly poor Philosopher.

SABBATH ECONOMICS

The solution we might seek is therefore not asceticism, but rather Sabbath economics. Relaxing appears to be a delightful agenda. Nevertheless, one of the most broken of the Ten Commandments today is—paradoxically— not observing the Sabbath. Mankind is caught between the tendency to change the reality around it and to be satisfied with what it has, the progress it has made. In the Torah, man was to change the world around him for six days, but then pause. Man should rest, contemplate, and *enjoy* the work of his hands. It is paradoxical that this had to be a commandment; it would appear that it would be enough for God to *recommend* rest, and not (frequently under threat of death[57]) forbid work. But there is probably something in our nature that has a tendency to permanently

---

[55] Augustine, *Confessions of St. Augustine*, 1.1.
[56] Ecclesiastes 1:8.
[57] Exodus 31:15.

work—to maximize—and this is why this commandment had to be a commandment.

In the Old Testament, it was commanded that once every seven years the soil had to be left to rest. Aside from letting the ground lie fallow having certain beneficial agrarian impacts, the meaning of this commandment is deeper. Once every seven years, debt slaves (Hebrews who were indebted so much they fell into slavery) were freed from their slave labor. Once every forty-nine years, debts were forgiven, and the land returned to its original tribal families. Simply, once in a while the accumulation of wealth was erased. There was, so to speak, a systemic reset, restart, or, more modernly, reboot.

If we are to look at ourselves, we can see we have really achieved an awful lot in the past decades. My country has pulled away from its communist legacy and has become a more or less standard "Western-style" economy. The West itself has delved into even deeper progress, both in terms of technology and prosperity. But it is as if the horse has been ridden too hard. The economic and social imperative is commanded by maximalizing, not by being content—maximize performance, maximize consumption. And although the new technologies come disguised in the promise of saving our time, we are not granted (we don't grant ourselves) more rest.

And incidentally, is it necessary to invest all the new energy from technological progress into consumption and growth? Energy can be invested elsewhere; other wells of joy exist.

Opposed to this is the commandment of the Sabbath: *Do not always optimize.* Utility from consumption may be almost exhausted; that well is already dry, and it might not be possible to further maximize it.

The question, then, is what to do with this manna, this energy. It appears to me that we put all of the time savings back into production. We do not enjoy the manna, but again return it to the system so that it may bring "more manna." In other words, the United States could have devoted the technological development of the last twenty years to saving time. In other words, if the United States remained at the standard of living it had twenty years ago, and were to invest technological progress into free time, maintaining this standard would require 40 percent less work, or a three-day workweek, exactly as Keynes forecasted seventy years ago (here we are using, let's admit it, the (in)famous *ceteris paribus* trick).

This is similar for the differences in competitiveness between the United States and France. The United States is more productive, expressed annually (in a year an average American produces more than an average Frenchman), but expressed hourly the Frenchman produces more in that one hour (in which the Frenchman actually works). The difference is given especially in the number of vacation days and days off. And here is the U.S.-European trade-off: Do we, as Europeans, want higher GDP? Then cross out half of our days off, work during them, and the problem is resolved. But the question is whether the additional growth in GDP is worth it.

Is there an alternative to MaxGDP at all times? There is a question as to whether we should announce for ourselves a sort of year of Jubilee a time of rest, a time of content. If the Hebrews living in the Old Testament times, a society many times poorer, could *afford* to do something like this, why not us? Our contemporary society is, nevertheless, very far from this. Until now, we have not dared to take even the first necessary step—to become free of the artificial stimulation of growth through debt. Slowing down does not sound as foolish if we look into economic thoughts before the period of fascination with GDP growth.

Joseph, the Pharaoh, and Bastard Keynesianism

The economy moves in cycles since time unknown. The first historically recorded story of business cycles we perhaps still remember from our Sunday school. About 4,000 years ago, the Pharaoh of Egypt had a dream in which he saw a macroeconomic prediction fourteen years ahead of time: seven fat cows and seven poor cows, seven years of abundance and seven of despair. There are really no reasons for this explained in the Bible: The cycle (the abundance and the famine) was neither a punishment nor a reward for a deed. It was more of a test. A test of wisdom of how to deal with this propensity of reality.

The advice the Pharaoh got from Joseph, who interpreted the dream for him, was Keynesian. Build surpluses during the good times and don't consume all that grows in the years that it grows but save it for the seven bad years. This approach helped Egypt prosper and actually enslave many surrounding nations (including the descendants of Joseph), at least according to the story from Genesis, chapter 41.

The beauty of the story is that it is so simple that a small child understands. The scary part is how far we have wandered from the basic wisdom of the story. Now, let's fast-forward to our age. Our age has built beautiful mathematical models to deal with the details, but we have overlooked the basic line. Keynes has been reloaded as a recipe for the weak economies after the 2008 crises. However, the economic policy we are used to today is not the least bit Keynesian. The best term I can think of to describe our current fiscal philosophy is Bastard Keynesianism. We took only one part of the teaching (deficits are allowed) but forgot the second part (surpluses must be built), and we allow and accept (need?) deficits even during surplus times. Compared to today's perspective, we are far *left of* Keynes. Today not only do we not build store houses for storing grain for worse times, but the only thing they are full of is IOUs.

The EU rules underpinning the euro set a cap on annual budget deficits at 3 percent of GDP, but the pattern quickly changed from "3% is max" to "3% is OK." We psychologically treated 3-percent deficits "as if" balanced.

Anything that was less than 3 percent was applauded as a success.[58] Where do we get with this mentality? And why do all talk about deficit reduction, when the appropriate discourse should be about a budget surplus? In most cases, deficit reduction means just slower pace of falling into debt—but what we really need is not to increase debt slower, but to reduce it as soon as possible, so that we have made at least some fiscal reserves before the next crisis hits us. In the future, we simply must sacrifice a part of our GDP growth and slow the economy artificially down so that we recuperate this energy and devote it to debt reduction. This is called restrictive fiscal policy. And we have largely forgotten about the fact that if at times we want to stimulate the economy to higher growth (fiscal expansion), we must also be ready to have a payback time (fiscal restriction).

So far, there is no rule that forces anyone to create surpluses during good years. This could be a first step. Keeping this rule will not make us avoid recessions (nothing will!) but it will create room for solutions. This room is what we are slowly running low on.

As far as the debt crisis is concerned, an easy suggestion for a functional fiscal rule would be something along the lines of a new "Joseph's" rule: GDP growth plus general budget deficits must be no larger than, say, 3 percent of GDP. In other words, if your economy grows by 6 percent, you must have a budget surplus of at least 3 percent. If your economy shrinks by 3 percent, you can have deficits as large as 6 percent GDP. Deficits would be allowed during the bad years, but they must be compensated for during good ones.

We have gained unimaginable riches during the last growth period from 2001 to 2008 (alas seven years!), and yet we put very little or none aside to cover old debts or make room for worse times. On the contrary, many countries generated further debt.

Baby Slow Down

That which we should have reserved and carefully guarded for bad times only (deficit fiscal policy) is that which we ate in the good times. In the summer, when wood is dry and is easy to collect, it is wise to collect supplies for winter. But we have burned the wood in the summertime—and we not only have not collected any new wood, we have burned (during the summer) additional debt-wood borrowed from our neighbor. What we need is the same principle Joseph suggested: Have surpluses so that you can have deficits. If you have deficits, pay them back quickly.

---

[58] The Slovak Republic, which had GDP growth of 10 percent in 2007, had a deficit of 1.9% of GDP and was highly praised for what was generally considered and applauded as a responsible fiscal policy. This begs the question: How strong growth must we have to allow for a budget surplus?

This crisis has not destroyed us (although some countries in our civilization did go bankrupt or got near to it), but if we enter the next crisis as debt-burdened as we are now as a civilization, the next crisis, which may come in a generation or two, could be truly lethal.[59]

We have to change the general target of economic policy—from MaxGDP to MinDebt. The often-undisputed mantra of our generation was MaxGrowth—at any cost, be it debt, overheating, or overworking. Instead of MaxGDP we should aim for *targeting reasonable* levels of growth. An advanced country should "aim" for reasonable levels of growth, and if the winds of growth tend to be stronger and offer a faster growth, we should fiscally consolidate and use that energy to create fiscal surpluses that would decrease the level of debt. When the car goes quickly down the hill, we would apply the brakes, slow down, and recuperate energy as in an electric car. Speeding up while going down the hill, as we have in recent years, has no meaning. The key message is this: We should change the way we drive from MaxSpeed to MinDebt, and slow down to *Economy drive*.

---

[59] We have gained unimaginable riches during the past growth period. Incidentally, just around seven fat years elapsed between the dot-com bubble and the collapse of Lehman Brothers. And yet we put very little, or nothing, aside to cover old debts or prepare for worse times. On the contrary, many countries generated further debt. A civilization like this needs to change itself, or it must not be surprised that it deserves seven years of thin cows.

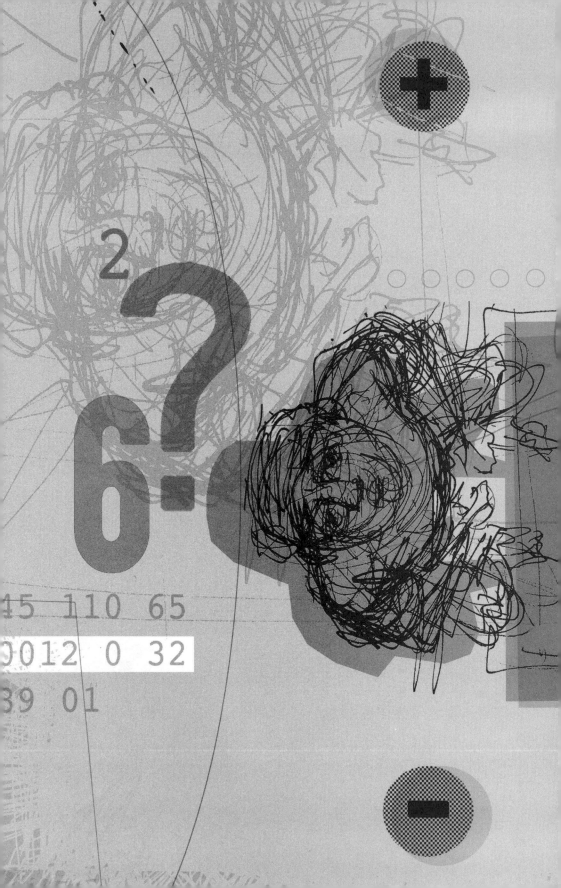

10

The Axis of Good and Evil and the Bibles of Economics

In the introduction I wrote that all economics is essentially about good and evil and the economics of that relationship.[1] Despite modern mainstream economics' efforts to avoid the categories of good and evil at all costs, or any kind of value judgments or subjective opinions or faith, it is still an open question as to whether we have succeeded—or whether it is even possible to succeed in this effort. Incidentally, the desire of economics (or of science in general) to be separate from good and evil, the effort toward positivism and value neutrality (to be outside good and evil) strongly brings to mind the time when mankind knew no difference between good and evil. Didn't Adam and Eve lose that state by biting into the fruit of the Tree of Knowledge of Good and Evil? Before that, they *were* value-neutral; they did not know the difference between good and evil, and were unaware in this regard. Economics (and science in general) therefore wants to know much *in certain things*, but in the moral area it wants to know *nothing*.

But we cannot run away from knowing good and evil anymore; it is now embedded in all our activity, including science. Despite this desire to be value-free, a fundamental part of our science of economics is based on normative judgments that such things as suffering,[2] inefficiency, poverty, ignorance, social inequality, and so forth are bad and that they should be removed (by science). Isn't all of science and our progress built on our hope to escape evils?

For a large part of history, the idea that ethics and economics are firmly joined together, that one has an influence on the other, has dominated. The Hebrews, Greeks, Christians, Adam Smith, David Hume, J. S. Mill, and others considered the interdynamics of economics and ethics to be a

---

[1] Wuthnow, *Rethinking Materialism*, in the chapter "The Economic Absorption of the Sacred": "As a moral force, the economy is a primary source of good and evil. The good is the very essence of the economy; it produces 'goods' that have 'value,'" 103.

[2] Not even this "obvious truth" is so obvious (our civilization could have taken a completely different normative development), as St. John of the Cross has a different opinion about suffering: "Because in suffering the soul continues to acquire virtues and becomes purer, wiser, and more cautious." St. John of the Cross, *Dark Night of the Soul*, 84.

crucial topic. Whatever conclusion they reached, they all believed that the study of ethics *is important* to economics. Distinctions between economic and ethical questions were rarely ever made.

THE AXIS OF GOOD AND EVIL

In our pilgrimage through history, we have repeatedly met with the cardinal question of whether goodness pays, whether it is "economical" to behave well, and whether any utility or economic reward stems from it. Let's begin with a brief summary of economic systems of good and evil. Among the main moral schools to deal with "economics" (or reward) for good or evil, we will also include the current mainstream economic thought. Even if we must move at the very edge of acceptable simplification, for better illustration we will order individual schools on a notional axis according to how much they say goodness pays. Let's start with the schools of thought that separate morality and utility the most and that are the most skeptical toward the economics of good and evil. We will finish with those who place an equals sign between morality and utility.

The Strict Immanuel Kant

We will start with the most extreme moral school. Kant wants a morality in which any (economic) reward in this world is criticized and considered a degradation of the morality of the given act. Kant considers as moral acts only those that are *not* rewarded. If we save someone's life at the risk of our own, and our act leads to a reward or is carried out with a vision of gain or other utility, the morality of our act is annulled. With this, Kant approaches the Christian understanding of reward for morality, which is best described in the parable of Lazarus: The rich man goes to hell because he has already enjoyed himself in this world, while the poor man goes to heaven because he has suffered.

For Kant, a moral act can only be carried out unselfishly, or therefore out of pure responsibility toward moral imperative. Kantian ethics are completely antiutilitarian. They say that a moral person pays no heed to increases or decreases in utility; if one wants to carry out a moral act, it must, so to speak, go against one's indifference curves and one must, in Kant's words, "overcome one's self" and go against the dictates of the pursuit of maximization of one's own utility. With this, Kant becomes the strictest moral teacher.

The Abstracted Stoics

Kant appears even stricter than the Stoics, who do not refuse rewards for good deeds—the reward only must not be the *motive* for the act. The Stoics remain indifferent to the results of their actions; they do not pay attention to whether they will be rewarded or punished for it. Their responsibility is to act according to the rules, come what may, and not to be interested in the results of their actions. They are interested in the motive, in the act itself. The economic impact on individuals, an increase or decrease in utility, remains off the Stoics' playing field and is not supposed to be considered at all.

Both Plato and Aristotle are close to the Stoics. Despite their disagreement on whether pleasure is always bad (as, according to Aristotle, Plato argued), both agreed that it is essential to live a good life. Aristotle argued that while pleasure does not always have to be bad, it should be subordinate to a good life.

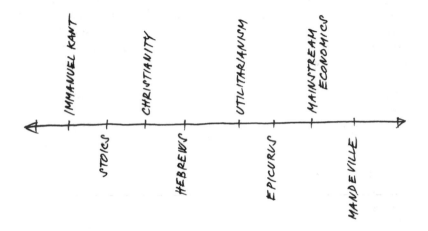

Christianity

In its ascetic tradition, Christianity is close to the Stoic ideals of indifference to utility, pleasure, and sorrow. It also disdains sensual motives and delights, and it portrays them as the characteristics of the fallen human body—as a physicality that must be tamed, subjugated, and (to use the Christian vocabulary) crucified. The Christians break with the Stoics over the prescription on how to do this. Christians postulate that man himself is not able to achieve these ideals. The Christian ideal is at the same time more demanding than the Stoic ideal because Christianity finds sin in thoughts as well, not just in physical execution, as is the case with the Stoics. The emphasis in an honorable life is to depend not as much on strong will and self-denial (as the Stoics do) as on help from above (change of heart, will, thought). As opposed to the Stoics, a new transcendental dimension appears.

Thomas Aquinas also gave reason a similar role; ultimately it was he who took what was until then emotive Christianity and placed it on rational foundations. Aquinas put reason equal to virtue because God is conceived of as pure intelligence. A person is as virtuous as the level they are able to listen to their reason and later act according to it. Aquinas writes and literally chastises anyone who would hesitate to use their reason, because "ignorance is sin."

A different, more emotive direction for Christianity leads believers to deep interior transformations, after which all motives and yearnings automatically come into conformance with good. The Bible speaks in this context about a "changed heart" and a "new man."

Hebrew Teachings

From the point of view of utility and morals, it would appear that the teachings of the ancient Hebrews can be placed somewhere between the teachings of the Stoics and the utilitarians. They are more allied with a positive perception of utility than the Christians. The Old Testament attributes clearly positive marks to pleasure; man should "rejoice in his days." The teachings of the Old Testament do not object to the maximization of utility as such. But this maximization must not go beyond certain (God-given) rules. The Hebrews therefore believed in the maximization of utility in the framework of certain limited sets. This is beautifully described in a citation from the Book of Ecclesiastes: "Be happy, young man, while you are young, and let your heart give you joy in the days of your youth. Follow the ways of your heart and whatever your eyes see, but know that for all these things God will bring you to judgment."[3]

The Old Testament Hebrews were not against pleasure. They definitely do not condemn a good deed because it was rewarded. They do not share with the Stoics an indifference (more or less sincere) to utility. As opposed to many Christians, they do not decry bodily desires but take them as a natural part of God's endowment. Rewards for their deeds (and therefore pleasure from utility) are not moved from this world, as they are for Christians, but placed in this world. But, as opposed to the Hedonists, the Hebrews believed that pleasure is subordinate to rules, and so the pursuit of utility has its clear boundaries.

Utilitarianism

Before we get to the Epicureans on our notional axis, we must rank utilitarianism ahead of it. While it is based on similar foundations, as presented by J. S. Mill, it tries to overcome human egoism by implementing the institution of the impartial observer.

Total utilitarianism is *not* selfish; it prioritizes the *good of the whole* and sets it (uninterestedly) above the good of the individual. If the decreased utility for individual Y is less than the proportional utility increase for the whole (or a second individual), then individual Y himself (pleasurably and voluntarily) accedes to the decrease of his own utility in the interest

---

[3] Ecclesiastes 11:9.

of the whole (or the second individual). Mandeville's bees would never do that.

Nevertheless, Mill is much less selfish in his search for the morality of utility than the Hedonists. The difference is simple: The Hedonists consider the maximization of *personal* utility to be the summum bonum, while Mill's maximization is that of the *entire system*. According to Mill, in the given act one must consider not the maximization of *his or her* utility (as one does in the realism of the Hedonists, who mirror the teachings of Machiavelli) but the maximization of the entire system.

Epicurus

As intellectual rivals to the Stoics, the Epicureans (Hedonists) value the morality of their acts exclusively according to the utility achieved; they became the pioneers of the famous credo "the ends justify the means." On our notional axis of good and evil, then, we are heading into territory where evil and vice are tolerated. Of course, the Epicureans need the sinful means for their sanctified goals. If the goal is good, if it maximizes the well-being of the whole more than any other alternative, it becomes a legitimate means. Epicureans are—in our list—the first school that avoids the needs of external, exogenously given rules. This is a considerable argumentative advantage, because defending the general validity of abstract rules good for everyone and for all time would mean a pitfall for every school, from the Stoics to Kant. Hedonism (like its modern form—utilitarianism) does not need any abstract system. Good is observable, literally calculable, endogenous, from the system and situation itself.

We would be doing the Epicureans and their successors an injustice if we failed to emphasize that they too were trying for the minimalization of evil—as opposed to Mandeville, who considered evil as necessary for proper functioning of an advanced society. He did not try to minimalize it because by doing so it would threaten the stability and prosperity of his beehive.

Mainstream Economics

If we were to classify the teachings of the economic mainstream, then we would have to classify modern economics behind the Hedonists. Even Epicurus admitted that not *all* of our actions were led by self-love. He presents friendship as an example of a nonselfish relationship. Modern economics is even capable of seeing self-love in maternal love, partners' relationships, and so forth.

Efforts by modern economics to reduce *everything* to self-love and calculus are so strong that not even Epicurus would have dared to have similar thoughts. In addition, modern economic schools have taken over Mill's utilitarianism, but they have not acceded to his main principle of personal morality, that of the impartial observer. The principle of voluntary renouncement of utility (which Mill's orthodox utilitarianists are obliged to carry out) for the benefit of the whole is completely foreign in today's economics. Today's economic anthropology is an unusual jumble. It does not involve itself with personal morals, because the invisible hand of the market will recast personal vices into general welfare.

Mandeville

At best, Mandeville displaced care for morals onto an irrelevant track. But he also carried out something more: He introduced an implicitly reverse, indirectly proportional relationship between morals and economics. The less honest an individual was in a given state or system, the better the whole would do. This is the most extreme view on the relationship between economics and ethics. Private vices cause public welfare. From this viewpoint, Mandeville believes that while the dependence between benefit and ethics is valid, he considers it reversed. As opposed to other schools, he seems to argue that more vices create room for the greater happiness for the whole.

With this, we close our notional axis of questioning about the economics of good and evil: from Kant, who required unselfish good, to Mandeville, for whom omnipresent good leads to societal decline.

"BIBLES" OF ECONOMICS: FROM SMITH TO SAMUELSON

Adam Smith, and most classical economists with him, perceive the question of ethics and economics to be closely tied. Many of them were moral philosophers (Mill, Bentham, Hume) or priests (Malthus). To a certain extent it could be said that, in this regard, Adam Smith was not the founder of economics but the person with whom the discussion of ethics and economics reached its culmination. With later explorers in the field of economics, interest in ethics fell. The last important classical mainstream economist to be seriously involved in ethical questions was Alfred Marshall. At the same time, he brought mathematics into the mainstream of economic thought, despite the fact that before him we had seen mathematization in marginalist schools and certain French economists.

The first standard economics textbook was *The Wealth of Nations* by the moral teacher Adam Smith, published in 1776; in 1848 (the same year that Marx published the *Communist Manifesto*) it was replaced by J. S. Mill's *Principles of Political Economy* with the expressive subtitle *with Some of Their Applications to Social Philosophy*. Not one of these textbooks contains a single graph or equation. Aside from the chapter "Numbers," numbers almost do not appear, and there is neither sight nor sound of mathematical models. Both works were, rather, philosophical texts and, in any case, were narrative. In 1890, Marshall's *Principles of Economics* became the bible of economics; it included several simple graphs (there are 39 on

788 pages, or one graph for every 20 pages), and in the conclusion Marshall added an Appendix of Mathematical Notes. The book, of course, contained an introduction to the history of economic thought as well as the history of management and several ethical-economic debates.

John Maynard Keynes also placed great emphasis on the ethical dimension in economics. And although Keynes was skilled in mathematics, his major work, *General Theory*, contained only a few graphs or equations. Nevertheless, the following economics Bible, the notoriously well-known textbook *Economics* by Paul Samuelson, who developed Keynes's legacy, already looked like a physics textbook: On nearly every two-page spread there was a graph, equation, or table. No doubts, no ethical-economic debates. Everything was clear: We present to you the mechanical machine *Economics*.

11

The History of the Invisible Hand of the Market and Homo Economicus

They say seeing is believing. This is odd; how can we believe something we see—how do we believe something that is (or seems to be) evident? Don't we have to *believe* what we have not seen? It is impossible to see something that is invisible, such as the invisible hand of the market, which is why even we as economists have to *believe in it (or not).*

The belief in the invisible hand of the market has had a tough life. Either people believe too blindly in its omnipotence and omnipresence and view it as a (disguised, thus invisible) solution to almost all of life's (and global) problems, or they believe it is the root of all evil. We are in a similar situation with another key concept of economics: the notion of homo economicus.

As the classic in the field, Albert Hirschman notes[1] that Saint Augustine believed in the following three principal vices (or lusts): lust for power (*libido dominandi*[2]), sexual lust (*libido carnalis*), and lust for money. Each of the three vices has been given a key position in the writings of influential thinkers as the instrumental driving force of mankind or society. And all of these (personal) vices have eventually turned at the hands of other thinkers (each in its own way and own time) into virtues and principles that drive mankind and society forward.

Take power, for example. "Augustine's *libido dominandi* is comparable with Nietzsche's *der Wille zur Macht,* 'will to power' . . . the essential difference between Nietzsche and Augustine is that the former considered the 'will to power' a virtue, but the latter deemed the 'lust for power' a vice."[3]

---

[1] As Hirschman notes in his classic *The Passion and the Interest,* 15. It must be pointed out, however, and Hirschman seems not to be aware of this, that for Augustine *love is the basic human impulse.* Love is behind everything, good or bad. In these three areas Augustine describes a situation where love has gone out of control, or, if you will, has gone out of proportion, or has gone in a bad direction. For more see Hare, Barnes, and Chadwick, *Zakladatelé myšlení* [Founders of Thought], chapter 9 on Augustine.

[2] According to Augustine, the principal characteristic of Babylon, the city of man, is libido dominandi, "the lust for power" (City of God 1, praef. 1.30; 3.14; 5.13, etc.) Also see Fitzgerald et al., *Augustine through the Ages: An Encyclopedia,* 84.

[3] Fitzgerald et al., *Augustine through the Ages: An Encyclopedia,* 84. As Thomas Lewis puts it, "domination is not an end in itself; it is a means to the end of recognition for being powerful." (Lewis, T., "Persuasion, Domination and Exchange: Adam Smith on Political Consequences

The topic of sexual libido in early psychology (especially in the writings of Sigmund Freud) as a driving force behind *every* action would also deserve a study of its own.

Each one of these main drivers has a sort of an invisible hand of its own— each of these three "personal driving vices," if well calibrated in institutions, can be turned into social benefits. Augustine sarcastically adds that Roman society has become characteristic by having many private benefits and many public vices.[4] In other words, he reverses the key principle of the invisible hand of the market, as stated more than a thousand years later by Bernard Mandeville: that individual vices cause common good.

Faith in the supernatural abilities of the invisible hand of the market is one of the fundamental economic beliefs. It is one of the key mysteries, which is nicely captured in the following quote: "The invisible hand is a mystical god, working in mysterious (or at least unexplained) ways with more than a touch of miracle to produce a holistic beneficence that is not predictable from the unholy motivations of the self-interested actors."[5]

At the same time, it is one of the key elements of economic argumentation, one that has lasted centuries: To what extent can the invisible hand of the market be relied on? How can we trust that the chaos of free wills will in the end create order (for all of society)? What areas of the economy are better off when planned and influenced by the government, and which are better off left to laissez-faire? So, one extreme solution is central planning—here the fear of spontaneous chaos is so strong that it leads to governing almost everything—and the other extreme is anarchy.

To what extent can we depend on the invisible hand of the market recasting selfishness (and other private vices, to use Bernard Mandeville's words) into general welfare? In this chapter we will not go so much into answers to these eternal questions[6] but follow history and the implications of these notions, faiths, theories, or myths.

THE HISTORY OF PRECEDENTS

The topic of the invisible hand that transforms sin into good across society runs like a thread through all of the historical chapters of

---

of Markets," 287.) The driving principle here is not self-love (in the sense of Rousseau's *amour de soi*) but sympathy and the desire for sympathy. See also Force, *Self-Interest before Adam Smith*, 46.

[4] Hare, Barnes, and Chadwick, *Zakladatelé myšlení* [Founders of Thought], chapter 9 on Augustine: "'[A]fter the destruction of Carthage there came the highest pitch of discord, greed. Ambition and all the evils which generally spring up in times of prosperity.' [Augustine quotes Sallust] We infer from this that those evils generally spring up and increase even before such times".

[5] Boli, The Economic Absorption of the Sacred, 97.

[6] For further study, see Hirschman, *The Passion and the Interests*; or Force, *Self-Interest before Adam Smith*.

this book. The term itself comes from Adam Smith, who only raised it up fleetingly, as if incidentally. This is similar to Keynes and his very brief usage of his term *animal spirits*. Both authors have left both of the terms they coined shrouded in great mystery, only to leave tremendous room for later disputes, quarrels, and misunderstandings that lasted for many generations. Till today these topics fill vast library spaces.

Put generally, it appears that the main power of the invisible hand of the market lies in the following key characteristics. First, the reversal of private evil into general goodness (Mandeville: Private vices become public benefits). Second, the social glue that binds the basic structures of the economy and society together, creating order out of chaos (Smith: The butcher who provides meat because he himself gains utility from it).

TAMING OF EVIL

Although Adam Smith named the phenomenon[7] which Mandeville thoroughly developed before him, the foreshadowing of this principle can be seen from the beginnings of our civilization's history. We have seen as early as the Epic of Gilgamesh that a domestication, taming of evil that first harmed mankind (civilization) occurred; but this wild natural evil (Enkidu) in the end was used to society's benefit. It was impossible to win against this force in a face-to-face fight; it had to be outwitted using tricks in order to harness this wild, chaotic, natural, harmful evil to society's benefit.

As F. A. Hayek[8] notes, the ancient Greeks, specifically Aristophanes, also knew of the principle of the invisible hand of the market:

> There is a legend of the olden time
> That all our foolish pains and vain conceits
> Are overlured to work the public good.[9]

We later discussed the Christian concept of the (co)activity of good and evil. We have presented the parable of the weed, in which Jesus said it was not advisable to pull out the weeds and risk pulling out the wheat from its roots as well.[10] It is neither advisable nor possible (in this world) to be rid of evil; much good would be damaged by doing so.

---

[7] Here the importance of naming can be seen: If the naming does not take place, it is as if the topic does not exist. Had Bernard Mandeville thought up the term, he surely would be now generally considered its father. He described the principle of the invisible hand better and in more detail, but he did not think of a fitting name.

[8] Hayek cites in *The Trend of Economic Thinking*, 85; also in *New Studies in Philosophy, Politics, Economics, and the History of Ideas*, p. 254.

[9] Aristophanes, *Ecclesiazusae*, 289.

[10] Matthew 13:29.

Thomas Aquinas later dealt with this topic in more detail, and the following lines make it clear that he was familiar with the problem long before Mandeville: "Nor was it fitting for the common good to be destroyed in order that individual evil be avoided, especially as God is so powerful that he can direct any evil to a good end."[11] Or: "Human laws leave certain things unpunished, on account of the condition of those who are imperfect, and who would be deprived of many advantages, if all sins were strictly forbidden and punishments appointed for them."[12]

The thought is far from new. Even the Enlightenment thinkers have acknowledged it many times, as Hirschman nicely points out: "All the heroic virtues were shown to be forms of self-preservation by Hobbes, of self-love by La Rochefoucauld, of vanity and of frantic escape from real self-knowledge by Pascal."[13] So political science also has its own invisible hand, as Montesquieu names it: "Each person works for the common good, believing he works for his individual interests . . . it is true that the honor that guides all the parts of the state is a false honor, but this false honor is useful to the public."[14] He elaborates this point further: "You could say that it is like the system of the universe, where there is a force constantly repelling all bodies from the center and a force of gravitation attracting them to it. Honor makes all the parts of the body politic move."[15] It must have seemed this way to the enlightened economists too: One man's self-love checks and balances another's. Ultimately, Pascal (almost half a century before Mandeville) writes that "the greatness of man even in his lust, to have known how to extract from it a wonderful code, and to draw from it a picture of benevolence. Greatness—the reasons of effect indicate the greatness of man, in having extracted so fair an order from lust."[16] So we see the invisible hand had a vast number of forefathers.

At the end of the day, "much of Mandeville's philosophy might be summarized as an elaboration of La Rochefoucauld's maxim 'Nos vertus ne sont le plus souvent que des vices déguisés.'"[17] Meaning: *Our virtues are most often nothing more than vices in disguise.* There are a lot of other thoughts behind the "economic" application of the "invisible hand." Theology has its own, as do politics and ethics. The invisible hand does not belong to economics (or the economy) alone.

---

[11] Aquinas, *Summa Theologica* I, Q92, A1, R.O.3.

[12] Ibid., Ia–IIae, Q79, A.1. See also *Summa Contra Gentiles* III, chapter 71.

[13] Hirschman, *The Passion and the Interests: Political Arguments for Capitalism before Its Triumph*, 11. In this he sees the "demolition of the hero." This (sad or laughable) collapse of the hero "left behind" can be shown in Miguel de Cervantes's delusional "last hero" Don Quixote.

[14] Montesquieu, *Spirit of Laws*, 70.

[15] Ibid., 72.

[16] Pascal: *Pensées*, numbers 402, 403, 416.

[17] Kaye, Introduction to *The Fable of the Bees*, by Bernard Mandeville, 48.

SOCIAL DARWINISM: NATURAL SELECTION AND
TAUTOLOGY THEREOF

It is not difficult to see the old Stoic faith in the harmony of nature behind the idea that the markets will handle everything best themselves: that the nature of the market is to will itself into balance, so to speak—but *why* on earth should things get into balance by themselves? The idea of the invisible hand of the market is therefore also connected to the concept that the market selects the best (most adaptable) players and sorts out the bad ones. Or, in other words, the idea of Social Darwinism.

Actually, it happened the other way around: Darwin was inspired by social processes, to apply this principle to biology. The sociologist Herbert Spencer wrote about the "survival of the fittest" long before Darwin—and he also popularized the term. Jonathan Turner humorously notes:[18] "It is not that Spencer was a social Darwinist; rather one should more properly say that Darwin was a 'biological Spencerian.'" Darwin was greatly influenced by the economic theories of David Ricardo, Adam Smith, and Thomas Malthus. This "invisible hand of selection," as the Czech biologist and philosopher Stanislav Komárek writes, created in biology the concept of "survival of the fitter, the dying out of the more poorly adapted . . . the notion that animals and plants were born with no other intent than to reproduce and survive."[19]

And truly, Darwin's Natural Selection (which he personalized by writing with capital letters) very strongly recalls the "invisible hand of the market." It is Adam Smith—and his predecessors and followers—from whom this sociomorphic notion comes; Darwin later applied and developed it in biology.[20]

The problem with the theory of Natural Selection is similar to the concept of utility—both claim to be an all-explaining cause of human behavior or social and natural development. Even in the case of natural selection—be it biological or social—are we not able to say in advance what would have to happen for this theory to *not* be valid? In other words, how would it look if the market (nature) did not select the most adaptable? It is actually a bit of a tautology: Those who survive are always those who are the most adaptable. But who actually are (how can we tell?) the most adaptable? Well, those who survive. We can only know this expost, from hindsight. So, if we only paraphrased this famous saying slightly, it would say only this: Those who survive are the most capable of surviving

---

[18] Turner, *Herbert Spencer: A Renewed Appreciation*, 107; also see Werhane, "Business Ethics and the Origins of Contemporary Capitalism: Economics and Ethics in the Work of Adam Smith and Herbert Spencer," 19–20.

[19] Komárek, *Obraz člověka a přírody v zrcadle biologie* [Image of Man and Nature in the Mirror of Biology], 80.

[20] For more see Komárek, *Obraz člověka a přírody v zrcadle biologie* [Image of Man and Nature in the Mirror of Biology], 14.

(instead of the word adaptable). In other words: Those who survive are those who survive. And so it happens that *everyone* who survives is pronounced the most adaptable. It is therefore necessary to agree with this "theory" because it cannot be disagreed with. So Social Darwinism is a truism.

ST. PAUL AND THE INVISIBLE HANDS OF THE MARKET: RESIDUAL GOOD AND EVIL

Within economic thought, a good deal of ink has been devoted to the topic of unintended good, which classical economics has grown up on as well. Smith's selfish butcher goes toward his goals as homo economicus and creates social good as a somewhat peripheral, unintended by-product. "It is not from the benevolence of the butcher, the brewer, or the baker, that we expect our dinner, but from their regard to their own interest,"[21] goes the famous line from Adam Smith. For Mandeville, but also in a flattened popular reading of Smith, goodness becomes something of an automatically generated positive externality springing forth from self-interest. The invisible hand of the market has the ability to reshape, convert, and recast selfishness into general benefit. As the subtitle of Mandeville's *Fable of the Bees* states, *private vices* spontaneously become *public benefits* completely, unintentionally, and spontaneously, thanks to the invisible hand of the market.

The Apostle Paul dealt with a similar topic. He also considered the relationship between intended and unintended good and evil and its impacts. But, interestingly, from the complete opposite angle:

> So I find this law at work: When I want to do good, evil is right there with me... What a wretched man I am! Who will rescue me from this body of death?[22]

Or as the New Living Translation puts it:

> I have discovered this principle of life—that when I want to do what is right, I inevitably do what is wrong... Oh, what a miserable person I am! Who will free me from this life that is dominated by sin and death?

So, exactly unlike Mandeville's bees, Paul *intends* to do good, but it ends up *evil*. With this he also, to a point, uncovers the meaning of the

---

[21] Smith, *Wealth of Nations*, 1.2.2, or page 30. The longer quote: "Give me that which I want, and you shall have this which you want, is the meaning of every such offer; . . . It is not from the benevolence of the butcher, the brewer, or the baker that we expect our dinner, but from their regard to their own interest. We address ourselves not to their humanity but to their self-love, and never talk to them of our own necessities but of their advantages. Nobody but a beggar chooses to depend chiefly upon the benevolence of his fellow-citizens" (30–31).
[22] Romans 7:21–25.

story of the first wrongdoing in the Garden of Eden. Adam and Eve, who have, having tasted from the forbidden Tree of the *Knowledge* of Good and Evil, become similar to God,[23] capable of *somehow feeling* the difference between good and evil, but unable to abstractly categorize it, let alone to carry out the good. So humanity has the *concept* of good and evil—we are capable of perceiving the difference (and in this we are *similar* to God), but we are not capable of precisely identifying it (as in the parable of the weeds previously mentioned) and we are incapable of *carrying out* good. Furthermore, we often end up committing *evil* while we *desire* the *good*. We are speaking of unintended evil with good intentions. This can be seen in the sense of a folk saying: The road to hell is paved with good intentions.

Mandeville's theory of the invisible hand looks at the issue from the completely opposite point of view. The vices of individuals are somehow transformed (for free!) into general (unintended) welfare. Whatever that individual's intention was, however selfish, the result springs forth as general welfare—which in modern economics has frequently led to moral cynicism. First, it does not depend on private morals; second, vices are automatically, unintentionally transformed into the general welfare, of which (third) it somewhat implicitly follows that private vices fall into the category of good. Therefore: Whatever man does is, from this angle, irrelevant, because even vices contribute to the general welfare of the economy.

THE CLASSICAL UNINTENDED

The classical problem of the invisible hand of the market deals with only a single aspect of the *unintended*: the unintended results of egoistic acts, which make up only one subset of social interactions. It does not discuss the unintended evil results of acts of good. It does not discuss the unintended good results of acts of good. Or the evil results of evil acts. The situation can be described with the following sketch:

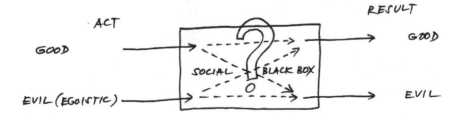

---

[23] Genesis 3:22: "And the LORD God said, 'The man has now become like one of us, knowing good and evil.'"

Christian thinkers later developed another conceptual apparatus that examined unwanted social evil: A system in which no one wants to do evil but in which social institutions nonetheless generated it—this was called a *sinful structure* in papal social encyclicals.[24] Certain institutions have a structure, in which individual actors do not carry out evil, but despite this at the end of the process something evil tends to be created (environmental damage, for example, which no one *intends*). Ultimately something similar was perhaps intended by the old Roman folk saying that goes: *Senatores boni viri, senatus autem mala bestia*, or *Senators are good men, but the Senate is an evil beast.*[25]

It would appear that the division of labor represents a relatively simple concept compared to the division of responsibility or guilt. We are able to perceive and sort the division of labor relatively precisely, but it is problematic to divide the guilt or responsibility for the product that results. The problem of these structures is that we recognize their *sinfulness* only ex post—while evil is never the goal, it is difficult to recognize in the construction of the institution itself. It only emerges retrospectively in the results.[26] The second problem lies in how complicated it is to specify and precisely assign guilt. With the division of labor, we can relatively simply recognize the added value of each actor; it is nearly impossible, however, to specify guilt in the same way. In a highly specialized society evil can well be born and live between the cracks of specialization, so to speak.

Old Testament culture dealt with this residual evil, which was created somewhere in social institutions' gray areas, by an annual symbolic sacrifice. It simply was not possible to assign certain guilt to a specific person, but despite this, inhabitants agreed on the general necessity of getting rid of it. In Christianity, the symbolic sacrifice for those who "do not know what they are doing"[27] and are "blind guides"[28] is resolved once and for all by Christ's sacrifice, the sacrifice of the ceremonial sheep that he became. In a more and more complex society it is easier and easier to be blind. Alas, we don't even know (or have never even cared to ask) who made the very shirt that we now wear and count our own. And this is a

---

[24] Social encyclicals are papal encyclicals that react to social questions. More on this topic see: Rich, *Business and Economic Ethics*.

[25] Morgenthau, *Truth and Power: Essays of a Decade*, 159. Also see "The Economic Review: Edition 13,"189.

[26] Let's add an even more systematic application of sinful structures to this consideration (rather incidentally and intentionally in the footnotes). A relatively frightening conclusion stems from the aforementioned; although it appears to us now to be miraculous and advantageous, the entire system of market capitalism could itself later prove to be a sinful structure. While it is the most efficient system so far that mankind has used for its common coexistence, it is possible that it will lead us up a dead-end street, one whose end will have catastrophic results. But this subconscious residual systemic fear of the unknown will subliminally exist in every system and we will never be completely rid of it.

[27] Luke 23:34.

[28] Matthew 15:14.

simple matter—just consider how blind we are in more complex social interactions.

EVIL: SUBORDINATE TO GOOD

Let us pause for a moment at the term "evil." Where does it come from? In the Hebrew notion, evil is always in a subordinate relationship with good. During the time of early Christianity, dualistic currents existed which argued that good and evil are on the same ontological level, that therefore God and Satan are antagonists, antipoles which are on the same ontological level, so to speak. Augustine, who himself belonged at some point to this belief, deals with this issue carefully and in some depth—he labels this thesis a *Manichean trap.*[29] But, he argues, Satan and evil are not on the same level as God and good. Satan is one of God's angels (even if according to legend he is an insurgent) and constantly remains a servant who cannot carry out anything outside God's (or human) permission or consent.[30] This is shown well in the Book of Job: While (technically speaking) Job's pain is committed by Satan, all of it is permitted by God, which is why Job addresses all of his complaints[31] to God: "The arrows of the Almighty are in me, my spirit drinks in their poison; God's terrors are marshalled against me"[32] and "why do you [God] hide your face and consider me your enemy?"[33] Evil cannot do anything God does not allow, which is why Job doesn't even deal with Satan (it almost seems that he was not even aware of his existence), instead addressing all his reproofs and lamentations directly to God.

Evil must borrow its goals from good because it never has its own.[34] Good creates goals of its own accord. Evil never does. Evil does not have its own ontological entity at its disposition. *Pure* evil itself does not exist; it always acts as a sort of parasite on good.[35] If we carry out something evil, then we do it with an *excuse*. The reason for evil is always something good (however distortedly the evildoer views the world). For example, if a person steals something, he or she does so with the goal of being richer.

---

[29] Manicheism was dualistic teaching of equal ontological power of good and evil and has its beginnings in Persian Zoroastrianism.

[30] "Satan is God's great enemy in the cosmic sphere, but he is God's creation, exists by divine will, and his power is relatively no more commensurate with God's than that of men." *International Standard Bible Encyclopedia*: "Satan" entry.

[31] Job 7:11: "Therefore I will not keep silent; I will speak out in the anguish of my spirit, I will complain in the bitterness of my soul."

[32] Job 6:4.

[33] Job 13:24.

[34] An interesting reading on this, albeit with a somewhat different notion of the purpose of evil, is Terry Eagletton's *On Evil*.

[35] "The well known Augustinian notion of Evil as having no positive substance of its own." Žižek, *The Parallax View*, 152.

But there is nothing evil about wealth. Nobody steals just for the stealing. They may steal for things like the experience and adventure, thrill—but again, adventure and thrill are *good* things, which is the reason why some choose to steal. In both cases, evil means are chosen to achieve something that could be achieved *without evil*. Only we choose an inappropriate shortcut toward that end.

Anyway, the general principle is that evil is in a subordinate position to good. Therefore, that evil must always serve a kind of higher good is an ancient principle. An alternative to this point of view is a certain moral Manicheism, or a faith that good and evil are on the same ontological level. Put mildly mathematically, it is the belief that the absolute value of good equals the absolute value of evil. Now, the refusal of moral Manicheism was carried out by most monotheistic religions—I tried to show that according to, for example, St. Augustine or Thomas Aquinas, evil, to a certain extent, is always in a subordinate position to good. So, in an ontological and theological sense, the principle of transformation of evil into good is defensible.[36]

ETHICS OF HOMO ECONOMICUS AND THE STATE OF THE (ECONOMIC) ART

How did morality disappear from economics, which was originally a branch of moral science? Let us start with one of the hopeful expectations of Alfred Marshall [emphasis added]:

> It is a strong proof of the marvelous growth in recent times of a **spirit of honesty and uprightness** in commercial matters, that the leading officers of great public companies yield as little as they do to the vast temptations of fraud which lie in their way . . . there is every reason to hope the progress of trade and morality will continue . . . and thus collective and democratic forms of business management may be able to extend themselves safely in many directions in which they have hitherto failed . . .[37]

It was an optimistic expectation that *the rise of the spirit of honesty* would provide the necessary conditions for growth. The development of the theory has, however, chosen a different angle of view: reversed.

Marx's teaching of the economic base of society seems to have been accepted by economic theory. He believed that it was the economy that would bring about a spirit of honesty, so to speak. That would be one feasible explanation of the shift of interests of economists from moral

---

[36] "By casting both humanity and the Devil in the role of Servants of God, he [Bernhard of Clairvaux at the end of the first and beginning of the second millennium] implies that God is lord over all beings, including the Devil." Marx, *The Devil's Rights and the Redemption in the Literature of Medieval England*, 22.

[37] Marshall, *Principles of Economics*, 253. See also Simon, *Empirically-Based Microeconomics*, 12.

inquiries as basis of human action to the notion that economics is *really* the basis of a society and that all movement and action of the individuals stems from it (including its own ethics). Smith's warning has come true— economics is trying to explain everything by a one single factor: economics.

There are many streams of economics that call for the return of economics to its origins: morals.[38] Even Lord Keynes gives his voice to this request, as professor Milan Sojka writes: "Keynes was calling for a return to the original perception of economics as a moral science and criticized the scientific approach typical for neoclassic economics, which tries to imitate the exact natural sciences."[39] The many critiques of mainstream economics attack it mainly from the standpoint of, as Etzioni calls it, *wrong reduction of a man.*[40] This reduction of man into a rational agent who optimizes his utility under the given budget constraint has led into the alleys of mathematization of economics. The state of the art of today's base philosophy behind mainstream economic science is not even utilitarian, although it is believed and proclaimed to be so. According to today's prevailing theory, an individual *cannot* move *against* his utility function. The theory is, at its best, Hedonistic. Sometimes, however, it is not even that, considering the difference that the Hedonists placed on the importance and relevance of morals. The difference is as follows: The Hedonists admitted that *not everything* could be explained by the principle of self-love, and that areas such as friendship are *exceptions*.

The situation as of today rules out any relevance of ethics due to a misinterpretation of Adam Smith. What economics has actually developed is Bernard Mandeville's system of thought, which Smith refused. The study of economics has shifted from a moral science to merely a mathematically allocative science. I am convinced that it should have developed the latter but not neglected the former. Had it continued to devote the same amount of mental energy to ethical questions, it would be plausible to believe that some of the "dead end" questions that appear

---

[38] Of special interest to us are the concepts of James Buchanan. In his book *Economics and the Ethics of Constitutional Order*, he classifies three different systems of ethics: The "Cost of Violating Rules"—i.e., the extreme liberal approach, which leaves no room for nonopportunistic behavior. Buchanan distances himself from it. The second model is "Overriding Transcendental Norms," which he calls Augustinian—the origin of morals in external, transcendental norms. This explains some nonopportunistic behavior. The third model is "Enlightened Self-Interest," which is based on the ethics of David Hume—the individual is aware of the feedback effect of his actions. The last model is David Gauthier's model of "extended rationality" which uses the concept of the Prisoner's Dilemma as a basis for cooperative behavior. See Buchanan, *Economics and the Ethics of Constitutional Order*, the chapter "Economical Origins of Ethical Constraints," 179. Let us mention here only the main representatives of other alternative attempts: A. Sen, F. Fukuyama, A. Etzioni, H. Simon, and others.

[39] Sojka, *John Maynard Keynes a současná ekonomie* [John Maynard Keynes and Contemporary Economics], 89. See also Simon, *Empirically-based Microeconomics*, 15–16.

[40] See Etzioni, *Moral Dimension*, chapters 1 to 6, for an elaborate description of this problem.

in the study of economics, and in the study of political economy in particular, would be clearer. Economics in general has been surprisingly uncommunicative with the ethical sciences it originated from.

THE MORALITY OF EGOISM: EVEN SELF-LOVE IS LOVE

Whether or not egoism is morally condemnable is a major question. Adam Smith himself defended it to a certain extent but did not carry out a detailed discussion.

Now, even the most important commandment, the "Golden Rule," says:

Love your neighbor as yourself.[41]

This rule sets self-love at the level of love of those around us. It should not be set any higher or lower. If it brings a person pleasure (increases utility) to bring pleasure to those he or she loves (increasing utility), then it can be classified as (i) hidden egoism or (ii) kindness and sympathy. If, instead of eating ice cream myself, I selflessly give it to my child or friend, I am carrying out an act of kindness. It could also be phrased in the following way: *Because* I gave it away willingly, I did it in order to increase my own selfish utility. In common language, such an act would not be classified as egotistical, but on the contrary deserves thanks, acknowledgment, and praise. Yet it is not appropriate to praise egotistical acts. In a strictly economic sense of the term, if I have from option (i) greater utility from giving than from personal consumption, then no thanks are necessary, and the giver should be doing the thanking, not the receiver, because the giver increases his own utility through the act of giving. This, obviously, is absurd.

On the other hand, it is human nature to wish failure and pain to people one hates, whom one considers enemies. This case appears, for example, in one of the Psalms.

O Daughter of Babylon, doomed to destruction, happy is he who repays you for what you have done to us.[42]

In a milder form, an equals sign has been placed between decreasing my own utility and the utility of the other:

If anyone injures his neighbor, whatever he has done must be done to him: fracture for fracture, eye for eye, tooth for tooth. As he has injured the other, so he is to be injured.[43]

---

[41] Mark 12:29–31: "The most important one," answered Jesus, "is this: 'Hear, O Israel, the Lord our God, the Lord is one. Love the Lord your God with all your heart and with all your soul and with all your mind and with all your strength.' The second is this: 'Love your neighbor as yourself.' There is no commandment greater than these." This commandment already appears in Leviticus 19:18.

[42] Psalm 137:8.

[43] Leviticus 24:19–20.

Therefore, in the Old Testament, the price for decreasing my utility is the same (no more, no less) as decreasing the utility of the person who caused the decrease. It is as if this were true: You will love your neighbor as yourself and hate your enemy as he hates you. One's own utility and that of others is therefore even.

Jesus discussed this in his famous Sermon on the Mount:

> You have heard that it was said, "Love your neighbor and hate your enemy." But I tell you: Love your enemies and pray for those who persecute you, that you may be sons of your Father in heaven. He causes his sun to rise on the evil and the good, and sends rain on the righteous and the unrighteous. If you love those who love you, what reward will you get? Are not even the tax collectors doing that? And if you greet only your brothers, what are you doing more than others? Do not even pagans do that? Be perfect, therefore, as your heavenly Father is perfect.[44]

To love and wish good things on one's enemies is therefore unnatural (as opposed to wishing good things for those close to us and wishing bad things on enemies). But Christianity wants us to love even enemies. This virtue is unnatural.

If both principles (individual egoism and sympathy to others) are real and powerful, which principle is dominant? On one hand it can be said that in a greeting to a stranger we wish them (when it costs us nothing) to "fare well" or "have a good day"; rarely do we hear "have a bad day." If it costs us nothing, and we could have it our way, we would wish others well without having any direct utility from it. It is the same as how it pains us to merely hear of the destruction of something beautiful—be it a picture or landscape which we would barely ever have the chance of seeing (again), to have any personal (aesthetic or other) utility from it.

Nevertheless, it would be utopic to rely on this form of pure altruism as the *main* mover of society, as Adam Smith notes:

> We address ourselves, not to their humanity but to their self-love, and never talk to them of our necessities but of their advantages. Nobody but a beggar chuses to depend chiefly upon the benevolence of his fellow-citizens.[45]

Even Aristotle expressed something in a similar spirit, surprisingly contemporarily [emphasis added]:

> Again, how immeasurably greater is the pleasure, when a man feels a thing to be his own; for surely the love of self is a feeling implanted by nature and not given in vain, although selfishness is rightly censured; this, however, is not the mere love of self, **but the love of self in excess**, like the miser's love of money; for all, or almost all, men love money and other such objects in a measure. And further, there is the greatest pleasure in doing a kindness or

---

[44] Matthew 5:43–48.
[45] Smith, *Wealth of Nations*, 1.2.2, 31.

service to friends or guests or companions, which can only be rendered when a man has private property.[46]

It would therefore appear that egoism is the dominant behavior in all of society, but behavior which must be moderated (held within reasonable borders, as Aristotle points out) and complemented with love (sympathy, participation) to those close to us (as Christianity or Smith discuss).

Man seeks the society of others, and he cannot live (does not *want to* live) completely egotistically. Robert Nelson, in his provocative book *Economics as Religion: From Samuelson to Chicago and Beyond*, notes the fundamental paradox of the market economy: According to many economists, we owe the running of the market economy to self-interest. If, however, this power of self-interest "crosses certain boundaries," it can threaten the functioning of the market economy itself.

---

[46] Aristotle, *Politics*, Book II, Part V.

001 002 000

12

The History of Animal Spirits

The Dream Never Sleeps

In every one of us there lives a piece of Gilgamesh, something of Plato, a piece of an ancient prince or Aragorn. And we are most often not even aware of it. There is something in us that is strong and out of our control, which seems to control us more than the other way around. "Dreams, they talk to you, dreams they walk with you," to use a phrase from the movie *Blue Velvet*. It could be said that we do not have dreams; dreams have us. There is something that moves us forward, stimulates our rationality, gives our lives purpose, meaning. This mystical residue, if you will, in the rationalistic-causal equation of the matrix of the world was what Keynes called Animal Spirits. And as Akerlof and Shiller put it, "we will never understand important economic events unless we confront the fact that their causes are largely mental in nature ... [theory] has ignored the role of animal spirits. And it has also ignored the fact that people could be unaware of having boarded a rollercoaster."[1]

In this chapter I will attempt to support one of my main arguments in this book: Although economics presents itself as a science that highly values rationality, there are surprisingly many unexplained factors behind the scenes, and a religious and emotional zeal that accompanies many schools of economic thought. The study of meta-economics is important: We should go beyond economics and study what its beliefs are, what's "behind the scenes." There is at least as much economic wisdom to be learned from our own philosophers, myths, religions, and poets as from exact and strict mathematical models of economic behavior.

For this reason it is good to examine the phenomenon of animal spirits as a kind of counterpoint to the frequently mentioned homo economicus. Perhaps due to this it will be better shown how extreme and misleading it is to rely on this strictly rational and mechanical model that mainstream economics bases itself on.

---

[1] Akerlof and Shiller, *Animal Spirits*, 1.

MAN'S SPONTANEOUS URGE

What was originally meant by the term "animal spirits" is as unclear and muddy as the case of Adam Smith's *invisible hand*. Adam Smith used the term *invisible hand* only three times in his writing; so did Keynes in his *General Theory*—he also used the term animal spirits only three times: He did not devote more than a brief passage to something that was later on considered his trademark contribution, one that others have written books about. Keynes used it in the following context:

> [T]here is the instability due to the characteristic of human nature that a large proportion of our positive activities depend on spontaneous optimism rather than mathematical expectations, whether moral or hedonistic or economic. Most, probably, of our decisions to do something positive, the full consequences of which will be drawn out over many days to come, can only be taken as the result of animal spirits—of a spontaneous urge to action rather than inaction, and not as the outcome of a weighted average of quantitative benefits multiplied by quantitative probabilities. . . . Thus if the animal spirits are dimmed and the spontaneous optimism falters, leaving us to depend on nothing more but a mathematical expectation, enterprise will fade and die . . . individual initiative will only be adequate when reasonable calculation is supplemented and supported by animal spirits. . . .[2]

Animal spirits, as the term itself, are mystical in nature: "Where these animal spirits come from is something of a mystery," as Bishop's dictionary[3] puts it. In common interpretations it is embodied trust and has nothing to do with animals; it is merely animating "urge to action." Here I would like to stretch the concept perhaps even further and wi(l)der and take it in an unorthodox and most embracing way: As true animal spirits or remnants of our ancient past. Humans may have left the wild and moved into civilized and more predictable cities, which seem under control, but wildness has not left us. It has moved to cities with us; it is in us. We have, so to speak, taken our Enkidu with us to the city.

Animal spirits seem to mean that which motivates us, animates us, somewhat irrationally; that which gives us our aims, hopes, purposes, dreams. It is unpredictable and does not easily lend itself to mathematical analysis. "John Maynard Keynes once defined 'animal spirits' as precisely those unpredictable human drives that influence stock markets and push economic cycles."[4] Or, to use the words of two great economists, when they speak of animal spirits, they speak of "the extent to which people are also guided by noneconomic motivations. And it fails to take into account the extent to which they are irrational or misguided."[5]

---

[2] Keynes, *The General Theory of Employment, Interest, and Money*, 273–274.
[3] Bishop, *Economics: An A–Z Guide*, "animal spirits" entry.
[4] Pasquinelli, *Animal Spirits*, 13.
[5] Akerlof and Shiller, *Animal Spirits*, 3.

NATURALLY UNNATURAL

From whatever angle you take it, be it Darwinian, creationistic, or otherwise, human beings are close to animals. Yet they are something different. In most languages, likening one to an animal is a basic and most common form of an insult (pig, worm, rat . . .) but, alas, also of praise (lion, tiger, dove . . .). Other forms of insults include our hidden parts, sexual and reproductive organs. One has to wonder whether there is a connection. Do we point to that which is hidden? The animal in us and the nakedness we hide? What is the connection between our shame and animals? We insult and ridicule things that are taboo and that we feel ashamed about. Our sexuality seems to provide that. And now, what on earth is the possible connection to economics?

In any case, on the scale of things, we humans seem to be the only creations for whom it is natural to be unnatural. And conversely, it is unnatural for us to be natural. Take nakedness, for example: Although it is literally our natural state, it is unnatural for us to be naked. Some authors consider nakedness a sacred taboo of our society.[6] C. S. Lewis says, "You could almost say they put on nakedness as a ceremonial robe."[7] I think he names a common notion that we all have: "We think simply of a happy, naked savage sitting on the grass."[8] Nakedness is connected with being savage, and the notion of being a savage is connected with the notion of being satisfied.

But in the story of Genesis, both Adam and Eve were naked in a perfect state in the Garden of Eden. After they partook of the fruit of the Tree of Knowledge of Good and Evil, the first emotion they felt was shame and nakedness.[9] Adam and Eve felt the need to cover themselves. In other words, important for economists, the leaves that hid their private parts were the first *external possessions* that man ever owned—they felt that they by *themselves* were not enough, as if they missed something without the cover. They needed something more. If we were to paraphrase Fromm's dilemma, "To Have or to Be," they needed to have, not only to be.[10] They felt more natural with an external possession. The very first use of an external possession was to cover their shame. Before the

---

[6] For example, Frazer, *Golden Bough*.

[7] Lewis, *The Four Loves*, 147. Lewis further writes, "Are we not our true selves when naked? In a sense, no . . . we are 'more ourselves' when clothed," 146.

[8] Lewis, *A Preface to Paradise Lost*, 112.

[9] It is also important to note that the common denominator here was shame. Children are not ashamed to be naked; they are, however, ashamed of meeting strangers. When a naked child is ashamed, it wants to hide itself, and if it cannot, covers its eyes with his hands; an adult hides his genitals but not eyes. A child seems to be ashamed of strangers, but we are ashamed of our sexual organs. Does it hint at us being estranged from our naturalness, our nakedness?

[10] See Fromm, *To Have or to Be*, 13: "The alternative of having *versus* being does not appeal to common sense. To *have*, so it would seem, is a natural function of our life."

Fall, they were content (naked) as they were. Later on, the first transaction in the Book of Genesis was a *gift* that God gave them: animal skin for clothes. And so here and ever since, an unnatural thing happened: Animal skin was put on our human skin. We feel (much) better that way.

This desire to be shielded by something, a desire to own (to protect oneself through ownership), to protect oneself (not to be *alone in this world*, not to be naked), to not be so easily wounded, led to our losing our freedom and becoming dependent on things because we started to need them. This is beautifully captured in a quote from Rousseau:

> The savage breathes nothing but liberty and repose; he desires only to live and be at leisure; and the ataraxia of the Stoic does not approach his indifference for every other object. The citizen, on the contrary, toils, bestirs and torments himself without end, to obtain employments which are still more laborious; he labors on till his death, he even hastens it, in order to put himself in a condition to live, or renounces life to acquire immortality . . . For such in reality is the true cause of all those differences: the savage lives in himself; the man of society, always out of himself, cannot live but in the opinions of others, and it is, if I may say so, from their judgment alone that he derives the sentiment of his own existence.[11]

This was similar to Enkidu—he also lived like an animal; he lacked nothing. Shamhat awoke insufficiency within him. In the city he became a citizen; he tasted beer, which is unnatural (it is not found in the "natural state of nature"). Quite generally, as Slavoj Žižek points out, there is *nothing natural, spontaneous about our desires*. The question is not how to fulfill our desires, but how to know what we desire. *Our desires are artificial, we have to be taught how to desire* and be shown what to desire. Instrumental to this process are stories, movies, and advertisements, as well as political and economic ideology (as we have seen, for example, with the idea of progress). From this perspective, rationality becomes a mere tool in the hands of our dreams.

HUMANS AND ANIMA(L)S

The history of the relationship between the rational and the irrational is a lively one. In this context C. G. Jung writes: "From the myth of Gilgamesh it is clear that the attack of subconscious [Enkidu] becomes the very source of power of a heroic battle; and it is so impressive that one has to ask, if this alleged animosity of this motherly archetype [anima] is not the very trick of Mater Natura (Mother Nature) how to induce her favourite child to the highest performance."[12] In Jung's version, Enkidu represents

---

[11] Rousseau, *Discourse on the Origin of Inequality*, 96. Also see Force, *Self-Interest before Adam Smith*, 45.

[12] Jung, *Hrdina a archetyp matky* [Hero and the Archetype of a Mother, from the German original *Heros und Mutterarchetyp*]. *Výbor z díla* [Collected Works of C. G. Jung], vol. 8, 197.

the first of Gilgamesh's anima—something that came from the forest and that was supposed to attack him, but which he in the end took with him to the city and befriended. What actually took place, instead of a fight, was a reconciliation of two principles and a great life story.

Nevertheless, what Jung thought of the trickery of Mother Nature is first explained several pages later. In this story, he reveals to us that the "Shining Peaks" are unreachable by mortals.[13] These eternal goals we set out for ourselves—for example, the utilitarian bliss point—take on the form of the mythical Olympus, an effort to return to the (already forbidden) Garden of Eden.

But back to our concept of irrational animal spirits. In Greek thought there was a major dialectic between the ideal of reliability and constancy vis-à-vis the world of variability, inconstancy, instability. Plato revels in a very negative concept of the variable, irrational components of one's self:

> "Irrational parts of the soul" . . . our bodily and sensuous nature, our passions, our sexuality, all serve as powerful links to the world of risk and mutability . . . [t]o nourish them at all is thus to expose oneself to a risk of disorder or "madness."[14]

Aristotle seems to have a friendlier view, and in any case he is aware of its supplementary, complementary character:

> [O]ne element in the soul is irrational and one has a rational principle.... Of the irrational element one division seems to be widely distributed and **vegetative in its nature**. . . . Now the excellence of this seems to be **common to all species and not specifically human**; for this part or faculty seems to function most in sleep. . . There seems to be also another irrational element in the soul—one which in a sense, however, shares in a rational principle. . . . **it urges** them [humans] aright and towards the best objects; but there is found in them also another element **naturally opposed to the rational principle**, which fights against and resists that principle.[15]

This irrational (partly *vegetative*) animal-spirit (which we *partly* share with all living creatures) element moves, animates us even if we most likely will never understand how. After all, how could it be possible to *rationally* understand the *irrational* element of the soul? In any event, the animal spirit is something that moves us, a sort of primary mover. Aristotle is of the conviction that the soul is implicated in motion.[16]

Many thinkers who followed spoke of how the desires of passion were astonishingly strong, almost determinant. This was succinctly expressed by the Hugenot statesman Duke of Rohan (1579–1638), who said,

---

[13] See Jung, *Hrdina a archetyp matky* [Hero and the Archetype of a Mother, from the German original *Heros und Mutterarchetyp*]. *Výbor z díla* [Collected Works of C. G. Jung], vol. 8, 201.

[14] Nussbaum, *The Fragility of Goodness*, 7.

[15] Aristotle, *Nicomachean Ethics*, 1102a, 27–1102b7. Author's emphasis

[16] Aristotle, *On the Soul*, 405b11; 409b19–24.

"Princes order their people around and interest orders princes around."[17] Several centuries after him, David Hume judges reason as being a slave of *passion*. The importance of passion (he actually reverses the logic of Plato that we quoted above) is defended by Helvetius: "[O]ne becomes stupid as soon as one ceases to be passionate."[18] To what extent these dreams, emotions, and passions are controllable, if at all, is a different question, one which Hirschman deals with at great length, so I refer the reader to him. For our purposes it suffices that we are aware how much and how strong our desires, our animal spirits are, or can prove to be.

ANIMAL-NONHUMAN

> *[T]he greater the spirit, the greater the beast[.]*
> an old Dutch-Jewish saying[19]

That which we are afraid of, *which we run from*, frequently reveals the most about us and our time and age, possibly more than what we desire, or *that which* (we think) we are running to. In the last chapter, we dealt with irrational attractors; here I want to talk about repellents, fears. It appears that as humans we existentially fear two things—too much animality (too spontaneous, too alive) and too much mechanics (too cadaverously, deadly cold). Ultimately even "Aristotelian philosophy . . . exists in a continual oscillation between too much order and disorder . . . excess and deficiency, the super-human and the merely animal."[20]

Let us notice that most horror characters are a combination of animal and human (for example, the devil has horns like a he-goat, a vampire is like a bat, and the werewolf combines human beings with wolves). The other horror figures consist of separation of the body from the spirit. So, for example, we are haunted by zombies that look like our beloved (ex)members of our family (or they have their bodies), but are really merely animals (vegetative principle) in human shell, they are devoid of soul or sprit. They have nothing in common with human beings except for their (animal) body. The other case is the fear of spirits, ghosts that no longer have a body. We fear either of the parts when body and spirit are separated.

---

[17] I owe my Rohan citation to Hirschman, *The Passion and the Interests*, 34.

[18] Hirschman, *The Passion and the Interests*, 27. Smith, D., *Helvetius*, 55–56.

[19] Pasquinelli, *Animal Spirits*, 9. This popular saying is probably of Jewish origin: see the *Talmud*, Tractate Sukkah 52a: "The greater the person, the greater his Yetzer Hara (evil inclination)" (Pasquinelli, *Animal Spirits*, 211).

[20] Nussbaum, *The Fragility of Goodness*, 262. Also see page 238: "We have been brought back repeatedly to the question, how far is a human being like a plant (or a nonrational animal), how far like a God or a solid immutable form?"

This is not a new fear. There is a general fear of human beings becoming animals. "Nations outside Europe on the other hand explain the origin of monkeys, especially apes, with a 'decline' and a 'savagery' of people, their departure into the forest and (often intentionally) forgetting how to talk is either caused by some curse or a wish not to have to work."[21] This was the popular belief before Charles Darwin completely reversed the notion of an animal to a human predecessor. To return to the example of the werewolf, the fear is that raw nature enters a human body and drives us to do things that no human being would. The werewolves usually fight and try to resist their transformation, but something else, something animal, takes over (when the moon is full . . .) and is in control.

FEAR OF ROBOTS, SYMBOLS OF PURE RATIONALITY

On the other hand, a large number of modern stories and myths captured today mostly on film point to how robots (i.e., something mechanical that we once created to serve us) pose the greatest threat to humanity. The machines, the creation of our own hands, go terribly out of control, as if we called forth a kind of mechanical demon from Aladdin's scientific lamp. The Genie was also primarily ready to serve us, yet he later takes control. In this scenario, humanity is not threatened by its animality, but rather by an inhuman, somehow revived dead machine (recall, for example, *The Matrix*, but also in older classics, such as the Czech science fiction drama *R.U.R.* from 1920). Cyberpunk overturns the long-optimistic view of progress (be it consumer or scientific-technical) and turns it into a nightmare. Machines also become uncontrollable, but from the opposite side; they behave as if possessed by pure rationality and have no compassion, no feelings (as is beautifully depicted in Kubrick's *2001: A Space Odyssey*). And the machines have a tendency to re-create the world in their image:[22] the destruction of the human *animal* and replacement with the robotic. This cyberpunk postindustrial armageddonist genre, quite popular in recent years, could be described as being *high-tech* and *low-life*.[23]

In the first scenario animals destroy us, in the second it is the robots that we ourselves have crafted. In both cases we fight the same thing: the apathy with which they tear us (humans) to bits. In both cases, humanity means less than the napkin served with a hot dog. And they tear it equally readily.

---

[21] Komárek, *Obraz člověka a přírody v zrcadle biologie* [Image of Man and Nature in the Mirror of Biology], 144–145.

[22] Marx ascribes this characteristic to industrial bourgeois society: "In one word, it creates a world after its own image." Marx and Engels, *Manifesto of the Communist Party*, 46.

[23] See Punt, "The Prodigal Son and *Blade Runner*, Fathers and Sons, and Animosity."

But how on earth does this relate to economics? First, a person does not have to be a psychologist to see that in both extremes man is afraid of his own psychic traits. These (horror) movies, of course, are a mirror reflection of our internal (infernal?) self—it is not the image on the screen that is scary, but the things that it points to within us. We fear both extremes of our self: the merely animal and merely rational. Now, we humans must stay precisely in the middle, within these two extremes, between cadaverous rationality and animality of uncontrollable emotions. Second, horror film humano-animals as well as dead mechanical machines (or dead souls) are missing what the economist Adam Smith considers the key human characteristic, which is: *sympathy*. If we lose it, we will become either animals or machines. That depends on which extreme we tend toward, whether the animal in us or the mechanical-rational. We have ontological fear of both. Third, we subconsciously fear scientific-technical progress. We fear that we may have summoned something that has become out of control, lives a "life" of its own, something which, instead of being controlled by us, controls us and tears apart the world we knew and loved.

But we have only brought something animal and spontaneous from the forest, from the time when we lived naturally. We may live civilizedly in the city, wear ties and read statistics, but we all carry our animal spirits within us. We live from them, but we are afraid of their elemental force. The opposite is true for the rationally mechanistic robots. We need technology (are even existentially dependent on it), but, on the other hand, we are afraid of it. It would appear that both extremes have become, in a way, our nightmare. But, alas, both make us human. Perhaps peace will come only when we manage to live in harmony with them. "The task is to integrate the subconscious, that means in synthesis of the cognitive with the sub-cognitive."[24] Or not, for the biggest mistake of psychoanalysis could be the fervent belief that psychological peace is possible. We might be just eternally torn between the two extremes, hanging in between two forces that we will never master.

Our place, as human beings, is somewhere in the middle. We cannot fall captive to the rational, explainable homo economicus, nor can we completely give way to our animal spirits.

DREAMS NEVER SLEEP: OR, THE HERO IN US

In the film *Watchmen*,[25] there is a scene that looks like it is from an urban Armageddon—streets on fire, people dying on the barricades. One of the film's heroes, terrified, asks his friend, who is holding a revolver in his

---

[24] Jung, *Hrdina a archetyp matky* [Hero and the Archetype of a Mother from German original *Heros und Mutterarchetyp*]. *Výbor z díla* [Collected Works of C. G. Jung], vol. 8, 194.
[25] The film *Watchmen*, 2009, directed by Zack Synder. Writers (screenplay) David Hayter, Alex Tse. More information in the Internet Movie Database (IMDb, www.imdb.com).

hand, beating and shooting these people: "What the hell happened to us? What happened to the American dream?" And the other hero, the one with the revolver, replies: "What happened to the American dream? It came true. You are looking at it." If what you want is fulfilled, and you are still not satisfied with it and have a tendency to want something more, it is more than probable that things could go as far as is portrayed in this apocalyptic scene.

Our dreams are still with us—and influence us more than we think. Not just in dreams, but during the day as well. If we were to indulge a dream of progress, and if we were to believe in the imperative of constant increases in the standard of living, then it is precisely this dream that forces us to get out of bed every Monday morning and work on things we do not enjoy, which we do not find fulfillment and meaning in, or which we literally find repugnant. Such notions then make us a prison, one we cannot see or feel, but which nevertheless controls us; dreams never sleep, whether we are sleeping or awake.

But such a dream influences us in other senses as well. One day we want to be the adventurous Aragorn, so we head out into the forest (or more likely urban-jungle, a domesticated wild: the bar); on another day the dream of the seductive rich man takes us over, so we head out to a candlelight dinner. Where these heroes-in-us come from, and when each of them speaks, is a great mystery. We have taken some heroes from our grandmothers' fairy tales and others from our story-making media—film, books, advertisements. These media(!) have (unwittingly) mediated stories retold for centuries: Archetypes of heroes that may be thousands of years old are handed onward, modernized, and adapted.[26] In the words of C. G. Jung: "The hero as a character-anima acts in the stead of the cognitive person which means that it does what the subject in question would not have to do, could or wanted to do, but consciously neglects it . . . what takes place in phantasy is a compensation to the state or aim of the cognitive self. When it comes to dreams, this is a rule."[27]

Once films were made in such a way as to look like they are "from a real life"; today, I feel, we try to live our lives so that they look like they were "from a movie." Dreams simply never sleep—and they are hard to control. In multiple meanings of the word: The one who learns to control his or her dreams will be able to control his or her reality.[28]

---

[26] See Campbell, *Hero with a Thousand Faces*.

[27] Jung, *Hrdina a archetyp matky* [Hero and the Archetype of a Mother from German original *Heros und Mutterarchetyp*]. *Výbor z díla* [Collected Works of C. G. Jung], vol. 8, 204–205.

[28] For all this I believe that studying economics without studying *beyond* economics can never lead to the fuller understanding of human behavior. And as such, neglecting these metaphysical issues can lead to a dismal economic science. I am afraid that mainstream economics is close to it.

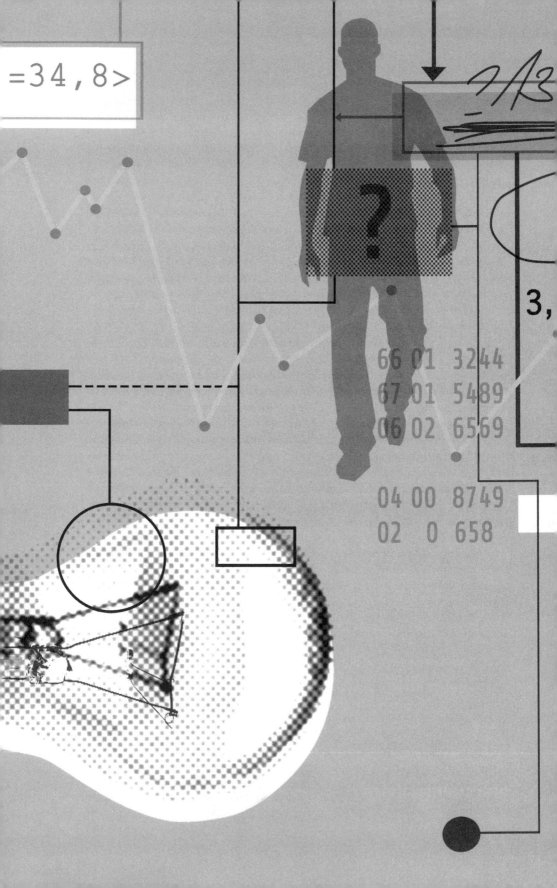

13

Metamathematics

. . . and to expect that by any multiplication or enlargement of our faculties we may be able to know a spirit as we do a triangle, seems so absurd as if we should hope to see a sound.
George Berkeley[1]

Almost all real numbers are irrational.
Wikipedia[2]

Without a doubt, mathematics has become the main language of modern economics. This was already described by George Stigler in 1965: "The age of quantification is now full upon us. We are now armed with a bulging arsenal of techniques of quantitative analysis, and of power—as compared to untrained common sense—comparable to the displacements of archers by cannon."[3] And economics has caught these opportunities as it could. Today economics is clearly the most mathematical social science, and if it has a scientific example of sorts, it would be physics (not a social science field, as one would expect). And really: If you were to open an advanced economics textbook (or most academic economics journals) and hold it far enough away to be readable, it would look like a page of a physics textbook.

In the first part of this book I have tried to show that economic thought in the course of history was always meaningfully influenced by philosophical and religious currents, and it always had ethical content. Economics, as we have come to know it from the work of its founding fathers, was like this.

Later, though, mostly in the twentieth century, economic thought was influenced especially by determinism, mechanical Cartesianism, mathematical rationalism, and simplified individualistic utilitarianism. The emergence of these influences changed economics into the form we know from today's textbooks. It is economics full of equations, graphs, numbers, formulas . . . well, mathematics. In economics, we now find little of history, psychology, philosophy, or a wider social science approach.

---

[1] Berkeley, *A Treatise Concerning the Principles of Human Knowledge*, part 3, 97.
[2] http://en.wikipedia.org/wiki/Irrational_number.
[3] Stigler, *Essence of Stigler*, 113.

BURN THE MATHEMATICS?

The arrival of modern computer technology—which can work with amazing quantities of data and enables the testing of new hypotheses—brought a real revolution to economics. Interestingly, it was the centrally planned economy of the Soviet bloc believing that with increasing computer and mathematical capabilities, central planners would be able to substitute market mechanisms with "optimal" price setting. For these Soviet-type central planners, mathematics was meant to be the tool to plan the economy, to rule the economy.

Surprisingly, at the beginning of the twenty-first century, the mathematization of human behavior is inherent not to the centrally planned economy (one of the factors behind its collapse was not being able to design "optimal" human behavior) but to the free-market economy. Today, it is the most developed market system that puts so much emphasis on the mathematical modeling and economic prediction. How did economics get from a field of moral philosophy to a largely mathematical science?

Alfred Marshall, one of the founding fathers of mathematical economics, nearly a hundred years ago stressed the role of mathematics as *language only*, not as the "engine of enquiry." Let us quote the full text of the man who was at the beginning of the whole epoch of mathematization of mainstream economics:

> In later years I went more and more on the rules: (1) use mathematics as a short-hand language, rather than as an engine of inquiry. (2) Keep to them till you have done. (3) Translate into English. (4) Then illustrate by examples that are important in real life. (5) Burn the mathematics. (6) If you can't succeed in four, burn three. This last I did often . . . I think you should do all you can to prevent people from using mathematics in cases in which the English language is as short as the mathematical.[4]

So, in his monumental textbook *Principles of Economics*, which became an economic bible for the early twentieth century, "Marshall relegated his formal systems to the appendix. But, as his pupil Keynes explains, . . . he did so as to avoid giving the impression that mathematics provides answers to real life problems just by itself."[5] Now look—one hundred years after Marshall, this is exactly what happened.

MATHEMATICS IN ECONOMICS

Despite Marshall's warnings during the last century, the mathematization of economics and human behavior is being advocated more and more.

---

[4] Groenewegen, P., *A Soaring Eagle: Alfred Marshall 1842–1924*, 413; cited in Weintraub, *How Economics Became a Mathematical Science*, 22.
[5] Emmer, *Mathematics and Culture*, 105.

In 1900, the French mathematician Louis Bachelier wrote his dissertation on share price movements on the Paris stock exchange. Bachelier found out that it is possible to consider the influence of all small participants on the exchange as independent influences, and to apply to them the laws of random phenomena by normal division—Gaussian curves.[6] These ideas were picked up by economist and mathematician Irving Fisher, and in his book *The Nature of Capital and Income* he laid the foundations for what was later called "The Random Walk" in explaining share price fluctuations on markets.[7] Fisher founded a consulting company, which collected data on shares, created indexes, and gave recommendations to investors. In the 1920s he gained great renown as well as financial success. He also became famous for his comments ten days before the crash on the New York stock exchange, saying that shares had reached a permanently high level.[8] Ironically, statistics did not help him to predict the crisis of Black Friday in 1929, when he lost all of his invested assets in shares.

In 1965, Eugene Fama formulated the rational markets hypothesis. The conviction that the market is rational, quantifiable, became the mainstream of financial economics for forty years. But this free-market math-based ideology was somehow disrupted by the last big financial crisis. Even Alan Greenspan, long the head of the American Federal Reserve and a big supporter of free markets and the "laissez-faire" approach, announced in October 2008 that his free-market position (and the minimization of any kind of regulation) was erroneous.[9] No mathematical modeling could help the market participants avoid the market crash. Models will always be imperfect, and one of the reasons for this mathematical imperfection is that human behavior cannot be put in equations in full. There is some behavior that we will never be able to model, to predict.

Again, this is not a criticism of mathematics, nor one of mathematical economics. Rather, this is a reminder, an appeal, not to forget that economic thought is much richer than just applied math and that we should try to understand it all if we want to talk about all human behavior. For that, math is useful but not sufficient. It is only the tip of the iceberg. Below it lie much more fundamental issues, issues we have tried to debate throughout this whole book.

So where did mathematics come from, and how did mainstream economics part from the tenets of ethics? In no way can I include the entire issue,[10] so I will limit myself only to several examples and ideas that

---

[6] Fox, *The Myth of Rational Markets*, 6.

[7] Ibid., 13.

[8] "Fisher Sees Stocks Permanently High," *The New York Times*, 16 October 1929, 8.

[9] Lanman and Matthews, (23 October 2008). "Greenspan Concedes to 'Flaw' in His Market Ideology." Bloomberg.com.

[10] For this there are authors who are much better qualified, such as E. R. Weintraub: *How Economics Became a Mathematical Science*; Mirowsky, *More Heat Than Light: Economics as a Social Physics, Physics as Nature's Economics* and *Machine Dreams: Economics Becomes*

I consider interesting (partially making reference to selected problems of the misinterpretation of mathematical research in economics). I do not want to "fight" against mathematics, which I consider a very powerful and useful tool, as well as an interesting and demanding topic of research. I would, however, like to express my reservations against the belief among economists that mathematics is able to contain and describe the whole real world. We economists are frequently not even really aware of what we say with our models. This is caused by devoting more attention to (mathematical) methods than to the problems these models are being applied to.

NUMBERS AS METAPHYSICS

Discoveries in the field of geometry, especially in ancient Greece, are considered the beginnings of modern mathematics. Their contribution to modern mathematics is undisputed, especially due to the large amount of preserved works.[11] Nevertheless, a number of civilizations had developed mathematical proficiency long before them. A number of abstract constructions we use to this day come, for example, from ancient Babylon. "The division of the circle into 360 units originated in the Babylonian astronomy . . . The astronomer Ptolemy (2nd cent. AD) followed the Babylonians in this practice."[12] The Babylonians used both Base 6 and Base 10 systems and freely mixed them (as we do today; a minute has 60 seconds, just as an hour has 60 minutes, but a second has 1,000 milliseconds, etc.); they knew fractions, exponentials, and roots; solved algebraic as well as geometric equations; and in one table solved a set of 10 equations (mostly linear) with 10 unknowns.[13] As regards geometry, they knew π and rounded it to 3, or, more precisely, to 3 1/8.

The ancient Egyptians, from whom the Greeks often drew, had a very advanced knowledge of mathematics and geometry, as can be judged from their buildings. Now, in all of these cultures, mathematics was nearly inseparably connected with philosophy and mysticism.

In the case of the Hebrews, the history of a number also had an extraordinary development. Despite many Old Testament constructions being described in detailed numbers (the instructions to Noah's Ark[14] or the

---

a Cyborg Science; Blaug, *The Methodology of Economics*; and last but not least, Deirdre McCloskey in her book *The Secret Sins of Economics*.

[11] We could mark *conceptual thinking* to be one of Greek civilization's greatest contributions to modern mathematics. The idea of assigning only a certain part of something's meaning, defining it as precisely as possible so that we can continue to work with it, is not trivial, and without it neither contemporary mathematics nor science would be possible.

[12] Kline, *Mathematical Thought from Ancient to Modern Times*, vol. 1, 13.

[13] Ibid., 9.

[14] Genesis 6:15–16.

first temple[15]), other numbers seem to be very fuzzy. For example, during the creation of the world, God constantly alternates between singular and plural form. Similarly, during the visit of the three beings to Abraham before the destruction of Sodom and Gomorrah, singular and plural forms of the visitors are constantly oscillating. And while we are discussing Abraham: Despite his arduous negotiations with God about the number of righteous people large enough to save Sodom, the result seems to be almost a picturesque example of the fact that it is not about numbers—no actual *counting* of 10 righteous ultimately took place in the story, as if the entire numerical negotiation was completely beside the point.[16] Nevertheless, as regards numbers, "the Hebrew 'science' of gematria (a form of cabbalistic mysticism) was based on a fact that each letter of the alphabet had a number value because the Hebrews used letters to represent numbers . . . In the prophecy of Isaiah (21:8), the lion proclaims the fall of Babylon because the letters in the Hebrew word for lion and those in the word for Babylon add up to the same sum."[17] We know of something similar from the time of the New Testament as well: In the Book of Revelation the number of the Beast is *calculated*: "This calls for wisdom. If anyone has insight, let him calculate the number of the beast, for it is man's number. His number is 666."[18]

But back to ancient Greece. "Numbers, chiefest of sciences, I invented for them,"[19] Aeschylus proclaims in the fourth century BC, from the mouth of the title character of his play *Prometheus*. The Greeks truly considered mathematics as an important *philosophical* tool for exploring the world. For the Pythagorean school, it is the most important tool; the number was even considered to be the most basic principle of the cosmos itself. "Number was their first principle in the explanation of nature. . . . Hence the Pythagorean doctrine 'All things are numbers.' Says Philolaus, a famous fifth-century Pythagorean, 'Were it not for number and its nature, nothing that exists would be clear to anybody either in itself or in its relation to other things . . . You can observe the power of number exercising itself not only in the affairs of demons and gods but in all the acts and the thoughts of men, in all handicrafts and music.'"[20] Plato tied in to the Pythagoreans, who saw a contemplative overview of mathematical-philosophical truths to be the best activity leading to truly mystic *knowledge*. As we know from previous chapters, this is almost the same reasoning that the founder of modern science, Descartes, had as well, only with the difference that he did not see mystic knowledge behind

---

[15] Exodus 20.
[16] Genesis 18:23–33.
[17] Kline, *Mathematical Thought from Ancient to Modern Times*, vol. 1, 13.
[18] Revelation 13:18.
[19] Aeschylus, *Prometheus*, 459.
[20] Kline, *Mathematical Thought from Ancient to Modern Times*, vol. 1, 147–148.

mathematics, while he himself was not free of mystic experiences, as we have tried to show earlier.

POETICALLY MAN DWELLS

Through Descartes, mathematics and mechanics became perceived as the personification of reason and rationality, and, what's more, perfect truth. Mathematics has become the language that we must use when we want to express a scientific truth, model, or principle. In today's economics, models of society must be woven with mathematics. Economic man is a module that constantly calculates marginal utility and cost, evaluates the opportunity cost of leisure, and cares about the optimal allocation of his resources. In this sense, Heidegger's "poetically man dwells"[21] has long since ceased to be valid; today man dwells mathematically. An implicit conviction prevails today: that the more mathematical a given problem (or answer) is, the more exact, the more real, and "better" on a sort of pedestal of knowledge it stands. Such answers are perceived to be more relevant and so also, so to speak, "truer."

The economist Piero Mini notices the following: Newton needed to solve a physical problem, so he set up his own calculus. He developed his mathematics as a tool—to accommodate the observed facts so as to simplify his work. Economics, it would appear, frequently does the exact opposite: It creates models of world (and man) in such a way that they fit mathematics.[22] But what is it about mathematics that we find to be so beautiful as to be seductive?[23]

BEAUTIFUL MATHEMATICS: SHE IS NOT TO BLAME

Much of what we want to know about economic phenomena can be discovered and stated without any technical, let alone mathematical, refinements upon ordinary modes of thought, and without elaborate treatment of statistical figures.[24]
Joseph Schumpeter

---

[21] Heidegger, *Philosophical and Political Writings*, 265.

[22] Mini, *Philosophy and Economics*, 84, 88.

[23] The advantages of mathematics as a tool are undisputed. Among the characteristics has always been clarity: One was always one (and therefore not 0.999999 nor 1.00001). Mathematics itself is exact, clear—it is not *fuzzy*. Its advantage is that it, in itself, provides clear results, is consistent, and is universal. Mathematics can go through abstract areas of thought where our senses are not enough. Because it is strictly precise, it sharpens our minds.

[24] Schumpeter, "The Common Sense of Econometrics," 5; this was the first issue of *Econometrica*. However, other texts advocated a mathematical approach to a certain extent. See Shionoya, *Schumpeter and the Idea of Social Science: A Metatheoretical Study*, 44.

In relation to the previous quote from one of the greatest economists, Joseph Schumpeter, I want to add that abstraction paradoxically does not know how to handle the simplest operations. George Berkeley has expressed this concisely: "The plainest things in the world, those we are most intimately acquainted with and perfectly know, when they are considered in an abstract way, appear strangely difficult and incomprehensible."[25]

The greatest miracle of mathematical thought is that *some parts* of the physical world in which we live behave to a certain extent according to that abstract, purely human creation: mathematics. Or at least it creates such an impression.[26] The Greeks were aware of these mysteries and paid great attention to how to connect these two worlds—or how not to. For mathematics displays the following characteristics: "Numeric entities exist in and of themselves. They have their existences within themselves, make no reference to anything, point to nothing, represent nothing, stand for nothing, indicate nothing, and mean nothing except themselves. They exist in the mind . . . they create a world of their own, a world one must learn to enter, be sanctified, consecrated into."[27]

But later there was an "identification of the natural world with the geometric world . . . until then scorned, earthly . . . occupations—calculations and accounting . . . technology and mechanics—were elevated not only from low trades to high art, but directly to the noble status of the royal science of mathematics."[28] Mathematics is truly not to be blamed for incorrect applications. It is poorly selected proxies, representing numbers or the poor application of inappropriate methods to reality, that are responsible. If a bridge falls, it is not an error of mathematics but of the builder who incorrectly applied it—at the same time, he may not have made a single mathematical error. The error tends not to be in mathematics, but in its usage.

Mathematics is *universal*, but just as with a new language, we must learn mathematics' rules. Herein lies mathematics' great power, but also its dangerous seductiveness—when it starts to claim more than belongs to it. Frequently, pride in the positive aspects of mathematics leads to a sort of "mathematical purism," or even "mathematical extremism," which goes as far as refusing anything with any inexactness or subjectivity.

To say that mathematics is universal is not to say that mathematics is unchanging. As with every artificial construct, it needs to be changed when its time is up. If a construct is not "up to the task" of what we want to do with it, we think up a new one. Of course, parts of mathematics such as algebra are only languages, a helpful tautology, a tool, and there we will probably not see any surprises. The situation, however, is completely

---

[25] Berkeley, *Treatise Concerning the Principles of Human Knowledge*, 127.

[26] Plato asks: How is it possible that in this changing, liquid world, something unchanging, invariant can be found? See *Philebus*, 15b.

[27] Neubauer, *O čem je věda* [What Science Is About], 72–73. Author's translation.

[28] Ibid., 74.

different at the foundations on which these constructions are based. As can easily be shown, from time to time we need a "new" mathematics. Take, for example, Russell's paradox. Bertrand Russell showed that the thinking on sets at the time led to unwanted (!) results. Because of this it was necessary to create a new theory of sets in which only certain groups of objects could be sets.[29] So we rebuild them in such a way as to get the conclusions we want. The theory had to change so that we could get rid of the paradox.

It is simply the same with mathematics, as it is with all of our sciences. We consider it true unless we run into an insufficiency/unresolvable problem/paradox; then we create/invent a new approach.

SEDUCTIVE MATHEMATICS

A fascination with the elegance of mathematics has found a safe haven in economics. Probably the greatest disadvantage or weakness of mathematics is precisely its attractiveness, which seduces us into using it too often— because it seems to be so elegant, robust, precise, and objective.

On the other hand, the elegance of mathematics is neither that surprising nor that miraculous, if we are aware that mathematics is a purely human creation, and that in reality it does not exist. It has no connection to the outside world—that connection must be added externally, for example through physics or civil engineering. Mathematics is a purely abstract creation of our minds—nothing more, nothing less. It is so elegant and perfect precisely because it was engineered to be so; mathematics is *de facto* not real.

Mathematics is pure tautology. In this regard, it is but an abstract construct, a language, a system of (useful) formulas that mutually refer to each other. This is why Ludwig Wittgenstein, one of the greatest logicians of the previous century, says that "[t]he propositions of logic are tautologies,"[30] and that "[l]ogic is transcendental . . . [m]athematics is a logical method . . . [i]ndeed in real life a mathematical proposition is never what we want".[31] Yes, mathematics remains only a method, and pure mathematics is without content. Bertrand Russell, one of the best-known thinkers in the area of logic, mathematics, and philosophy, described it best: "Thus mathematics may be defined as the subject in which we never know what we are talking about, nor whether what we are saying is true."[32]

---

[29] At the beginning of the twentieth century, it was common that any defined group of objects could be considered a set. Due to the *Russell's paradox*, this was shown to be unsustainable. Modern concepts of set theory, aside from the notion of sets, also knows the notion of classes.

[30] Wittgenstein, *Tractatus Logico-Philosophicus*, 6.1.

[31] Ibid., 6.2.

[32] Russell, *Mysticism and Logic*, 76.

It cannot be denied that economists they have found a number of practical applications for abstract mathematical languages; but a good servant
can also be a bad master. Wittgenstein's comment unfortunately also
holds true here: "The limits of my language mean the limits of my world."[33]
If mathematics has become the language of economists, we must also
count on the results: that by doing so we have duly limited our world.

Theoretical economics has only two possible "footings" in reality. The
first is the assumption mechanism, and the second is empirical testing of
the models' results. Yet, an unpleasant thing often happens in economics:
The model does not have realistic assumptions and its results often do not
agree with reality, or can be explained by both competing models. What,
then, remains of economics? Only the middle, the smiling subset of mathematics and high statistics.[34] Mathematics has the tendency to push out
any kind of mental competition and be uncontrolled if not guarded. This
is beautifully shown in the following story: "Plato shows us how Glaucon,
an ordinary gentleman, discovers in himself, through conversation with
Socrates, an intense love for the pure and stable activity of mathematical
reasoning, a love that requires the denigration of much that he had previously valued."[35] If we think mathematically, we can accomplish many
things, but we can also lose access to many other valuable facets of life.
Thinking about the soul (or love) mathematically is certainly possible,
but it can bring more harm than good. If we are to call truly scientific only
things translatable into mathematics, things like emotions and the soul
(and love) fall into something of a lower ontological category.

And while we are on the topic of emotions, as was indicated by the
aforementioned example with Glaucon, mathematics itself stirs the emotions ("an intense love for the pure and stable activity of mathematical
reasoning"), and so one can, at least according to Plato's account, love
mathematics, and even passionately. (It can be also hated, as is known
from school desks.)

If mathematics is not based on reality, it has a tendency to lead us
astray. We have to be careful so that abstraction is confronted with reality.
In theoretical economics, this is often impossible. In her book *The Secret
Sins of Economics*, Deirdre McCloskey points out the fact that a large part
of contemporary theoretical economics is nothing more than an intellectual game with assumptions. "A typical statement in economic 'theory' is,
'if information is symmetric, an equilibrium of the game exists' or,
'if people are rational in their expectations in the following sense, buzz,
buzz, buzz, then there exists an equilibrium of the economy in which
government policy is useless' . . . Okay, now imagine an alternative set

---

[33] Wittgenstein, *Tractatus Logico-Philosophicus*, 5.6.
[34] See also Mini, *Philosophy and Economics*, 8.
[35] Nussbaum, *The Fragility of Goodness*, 5.

of assumptions[36] . . . There's nothing deep or surprising about this: Changing your assumptions changes your conclusions . . . And on and on and on and on, until the economists get tired and go home. . . . I have expressed admiration for pure mathematics and for Mozart's concertos. Fine. But economics is supposed to be an inquiry into the world, not pure thinking."[37]

ECONOMETRIC(K)S

Many economists (and a large part of the lay public) today narrow economics to econometrics.[38] But it appears that economic (and other) *model prophecies* work "well" when reality (randomly or coincidentally?) behaves according to models (therefore if they do not vary too much from the previous observations the models are based on).

The exaggerated application of mathematics paradoxically has, at least in the case of econometrics, a tendency to obscure reality. As Wassily Leontief, winner of the Nobel Prize in Economics, writes: "Unfortunately, (. . .) uncritical enthusiasm for mathematical formulation tends often to conceal the ephemeral substantive content of the argument behind the formidable front of algebraic signs (. . .) In no other field of empirical inquiry [than economics] has so massive and sophisticated a statistical machinery been used with such indifferent results. (. . .) Most of these [models] are relegated to the stockpile without any practical application."[39] Some time-series econometrics even, according to the prominent Czech-American economist Jan Kmenta, "pushes econometrics away from economics. For instance, it is hard to believe that all that a person trained in economics can say about the generation of GDP is that it is determined by a time trend and a stochastic disturbance."[40]

David Hendry[41] wittily criticizes this approach in his analysis of the influence of rainstorms on inflation in Great Britain. The influence came out as *very significant*. The result was even *more significant* than attempts to explain inflation through the amount of money in the economy. Humorous, isn't it? Unfortunately, with econometric analysis we frequently can get the same valueless results, but for less obvious

---

36 What's more, the field for changing assumptions is also truly unlimited. It's usually enough to add any kind of human motivation other than self-interest or this or that reason for why someone has or does not have all the information (or symmetrical information, or random information, etc.).

37 McCloskey, *The Secret Sins of Economics*, 43–44.

38 In principle, econometrics tries to get all non-deterministic, random ingredients into a residue.

39 Leontief, "Theoretical Assumptions and Nonobserved Facts," 1, 3.

40 Kmenta, Review of *A Guide to Econometrics* by Peter Kennedy, 2003.

41 Hendry, "Econometrics: Alchemy or Science?" 387–406.

absurdities; and how can we then see that they are intuitively wrong if our intuition is silent (or if we have asked the wrong question)? For this reason, mathematics is only an important subtool for economics scientists; an economist must be equipped with wider social and historic knowledge. Only then can an economist distinguish between such absurdities and "more believable" causalities. It is the human in us that distinguishes us from computers.

However, perhaps the sharpest criticism of econometrics came in 1980 by Jeffrey Sachs, Christopher Sims, and Stephen Goldfeld, who declared that "One might go further and say that among academic macro-economists the conventional methods (of macro-econometric modeling) have not just been attacked, they have been discredited. The practice of using econometric models to project the likely outcome of different policy choices . . . is widely believed to be unjustifiable or even the primary source of recent problems."[42]

THE TRUTH IS LARGER THAN MATHEMATICS

But back to mathematics from our excursion into econometrics. It is frequently stated that mathematics is complete and consistent, objective, that it contains no contradictions. The lethal blow to this objective notion (i.e., to describe all reality only through several generally acceptable axioms and rules on how to handle them) was put forth in 1931 by the Czech, Brno native, and key mathematician Kurt Gödel. In his famous incompleteness theorem, he proved that no consistent theory containing elementary arithmetic can prove or disprove all the arguments it wishes to. Simply put, not all mathematical questions are computable or answerable. Ever since, we have heard a lot of talk of "true but not provable," even in mathematics. One of the direct implications is that we can never prove all that we *know* to be true. In other words, our natural thinking has a wider scale of a sense for truth of how to exhaust the (un)truthfulness of sentences than the formal approaches we can invent. Gödel's result is unique in that nobody expected it, and mathematicians and philosophers are still dealing with the results of his theorem to this day. According to Gödel, a system can be either consistent or complete—both is not possible and we have to make a choice. In this day and age, knowledge is confusedly returning to a combination of intellect and emotion/intuition, or at least to the necessity of reevaluating the notion of reason.

Interestingly, Kierkegaard also speaks about the impossibility of grasping the real world in abstract systemic form: "A logical system is possible; an existential system is impossible."[43]

---

[42] Sims, Goldfeld, Sachs, *Policy Analysis with Econometric Models*, 107.
[43] Kierkegaard, *Concluding Unscientific Postscript to Philosophical Fragments*, 99.

DETERMINISM AND SIMPLE IS NOT BEAUTIFUL

The nineteenth century was dominated by determinism, or the conviction that the development of the world is mechanically given by its current and previous states. For determinism, it is difficult to come to grips with randomness, chance, and it instead explains these phenomena by a lack of knowledge of the causes of these phenomena. Newtonian physics is a symbol of determinism. Although quantum physics markedly weakened it, determinism remains firmly anchored in economics. Expressions of the world as a collection of equations, with initial conditions and the faith that if we avoid external shocks we can describe the development of the world infinitely are typical of a large part of modern economics.

Human behavior, of course, is often badly predictable. Determinism then belongs in economics on only a limited basis, and that is precisely one of the fundamental differences between economics and Newtonian physics. Unfortunately, the expectations of the lay public are different. With their thick books, equations, derivations, Nobel prizes, and degrees from prestigious universities, economists must, so the belief goes, be able to say when an economic crisis will end and which means—which medicines— to use so that it ends as quickly as possible. But that is a big mistake. Economics is still a social science, not, as it sometimes pretends to be, a natural science. Just because we use *a lot of mathematics* doesn't mean we are an exact science (numerologists use a lot of mathematics, too).

Keynes predicted: "The day is not far off when the economic problem will take the back seat where it belongs, and the arena of the heart and the head will be occupied or reoccupied by our real problems—the problems of life and of human relations, of creation and behaviour and religion."[44] This day seems to be quite far off still, despite the unbelievable growth in wealth. For all that, mathematics is not to blame. But I am persuaded that economics which—due the strong focus on mathematics *only*—often neglects the wider social science approach to society (society is *not just the economy*), and pretends we understand the economy and the whole social context, and even can predict the future . . . this concept is to be blamed.

---

[44] Keynes, *First Annual Report of the Arts Council (1945–1946)*.

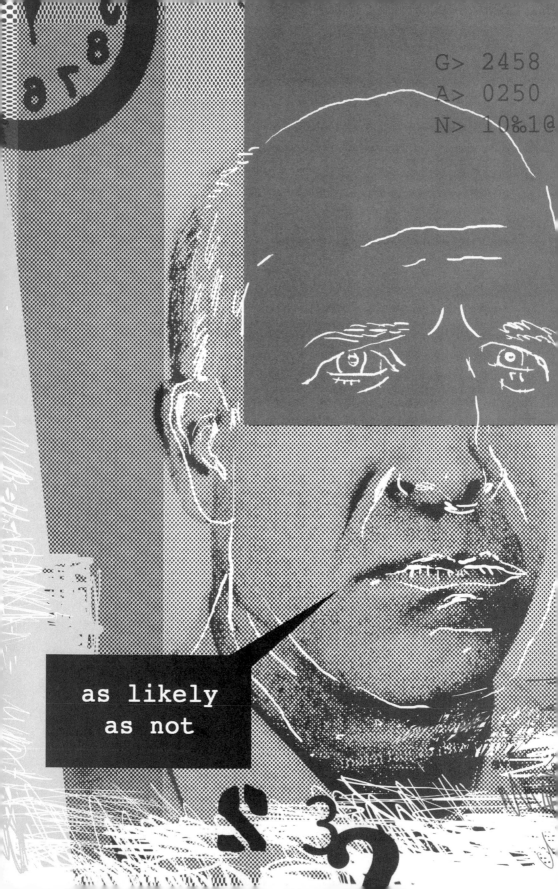

14

Masters of Truth

Science, Myths, and Faith[1]

> *The reasonable man adapts himself to the world.*
> *The unreasonable man persists in trying*
> *to adapt the world to himself.*
> *Therefore, all progress depends*
> *on the unreasonable man.*[2]
> George Bernard Shaw

What is truth? What is the nature of truth? Does truth lend itself more readily to scientific inquiry or is truth more of a poetic issue? In the words of Lévi-Strauss: "[T]he most wonderful and most challenging fact is that science does not and cannot pretend to be 'true' in any absolute sense ... it is a tentative organization of working hypotheses."[3]

The truth can be difficult. Nowadays, economics uses mostly analytical tools to understand it. But the truth is not always analytical. There are many secrets surrounding us, which we try to understand, but our analytical apparatus does not enable us to. For this reason we must give up the desire to know the entire truth using scientific analytical methods. And this should lead us to a much higher level of modesty than the economic science often exhibits. Nevertheless, economics has an admirable mathematical apparatus, which has been built over the last century. Because of it, it was possible to rewrite a major part of economics from pure verbal language into mathematical language. Using math has made economics more coherent, more precise. But mathematics is also only a language. A language which—like any other language—cannot express everything. And apart from that, what is even more important: If we start to speak in another language, should we start to ask ourselves different questions? Should the focus of our attention change just because we start to use this different language?

Mainstream economics in recent years has abandoned the original topics of economics such as ethics, morals, and on the contrary became

---

[1] The co-author of this chapter is Martin Pospíšil, who also co-edited this book as well as the previous Czech version.
[2] Shaw, *Man and Superman*, 189.
[3] Lévi-Strauss, *Myth and Meaning, Cracking the Code of Culture*, 16.

somewhat lost in the refuge of analytical-technical apparatus. We have changed—or extremely shifted—the attention of the science just because we have started to use a new language. In short, economics has overemphasized the mathematical and neglected the non-mathematical humanity in us. Normative economics has been suppressed by positive (descriptive) economics. If at all possible, positive and descriptive economic science *only* can be quite dangerous. It makes people abstract from important points, it makes us consider value judgments non-existing or unimportant, and it can by itself lead into blind and dangerous alleys; what is worse, it neglects important parts of life, the parts that do not lend themselves readily to (only) mathematical inquiry.

MODELS "R" US

> *We don't see things as they are;*
> *we see them as we are.*[4]
> Talmud

The introduction of certain abstractions (such as gravitation), that become generally accepted changes our world itself as well. A theory, if it is believed, will inevitably lead us to view the world through its own prism. The philosopher of mathematics Kolman comes in the conclusion that "as rational, self-confident beings we are not only products, but also co-creators of reality. Scientists, including mathematicians, systematically forget about the qualifications in their arguments."[5] Scientific theories, models of reality, become an indivisible part of reality themselves. Each theory is an ideology (I use the term ideology here without the negative connotation). Or, in other words, each interpretative framework forms an ideology (which, naturally, does not have to be political at all). And most successful ideologies are those that we take so naturally, so ideologically, that we do not even notice, let alone question, them. In the battleground of ideas, the home run of any ideology or idea is to become so deep-rooted as to seem natural and "always there."

In this sense we are the perfectors of creation, similar to what is indicated in the Book of Genesis, when Adam is given the task of naming the animals and, by doing so, arranges the world into orderly categories. We are not even able to perceive the world without an interpretational framework. So we can use Wittgenstein's simile: Even the seeing eye remains part of the world, and in our meaning that eye is the interpretational

---

[4] Kofman, *Conscious Business*, introduction to chapter 4 in Czech *Vědomý business*, 97. Nin, *The Diary of Anaïs Nin 1939–1944*, 220.

[5] Kolman, *Filozofie čísla* [The Philosophy of Numbers], 592. The citation continues, "and frequently issue various meta-statements related to inherited, and therefore a priori structure, as proven facts."

frame through which we see the world. As Kolman put it: "It can be seen precisely in mathematics that there exists, neither in the world nor in language, any kind of pre-provided, immediate, or natural facts if we do not first set a theory upon which we can discover, which means that everything may also be otherwise."[6] Facts and "objective reality" are fuzzy, that is, they offer themselves to various interpretations. And so it happens that economists using the same data sets, the same statistics, derive very different conclusions.

In science, we use the existing framework—with an awareness of its insufficiencies—until we manage to coherently construct a new framework, to create a "new world" (its new interpretation), so to speak. For example, over several centuries, the world "behaved" according to gravitation. This abstraction (gravitation) found neither competition nor dispute because (on a certain level of necessary simplification) it functioned sufficiently. We have asked the reality why items fall to the ground, and we have answered ourselves with the term "gravitation." Our answer was (for a certain time) sufficient. In Hegel's words: "If one looks at the world rationally the world looks rationally back."[7]

Similar laws are valid for economics. Assumptions (here we must point out that an overwhelming majority of our initial assumptions will remain unstated) are de facto only *means* of thinking about or observing the world. Without observers, in and of itself, the world is chaotic, until our ability for model thinking, or models within us (not in the world), enable us to view the world reasonably. The construct (mathematical equation, principle, law) according to which the world "behaves" does not rest in the world itself, but rather within us. It is our thinking, our imagination, that organizes the world into theories and models. Every great model that places as its ambition to become a worldview (to explain how and why the world functions as it does) always remains only a construct, a point of view, a standpoint, an opinion. Every theory therefore is a more or less useful fiction, or, if you prefer, a story, a myth. A myth we know not to be true (our assumptions are not realistic), but we still believe the theory to say *something true* about us and the world.

Models are usually an image of something (a model of a castle, a computer model of water simulation, the big bang model of the universe). Or are they models in the sense of models for statues or fashion? In other words, which models do we use to model reality? Do we shape the economy according to our models or do we create our models according to reality? The difference here is clear: The real castle, real water, and/or the entire physical world is not influenced by the models of physical science. However, the real economy is influenced by economic science. For example, economic theory influences the expectations of individuals as well as

---

[6] Kolman, *Filozofie čísla* [The Philosophy of Numbers], 592.
[7] Cited in Mini, *Philosophy and Economics*, 40.

their behavior. That is one more reason why the choice of economic theory matters.

CHOOSE YOUR BELIEF

Models *an sich* (in and of themselves) are not able to convince us; nearly every worldview has a legion of sufficiently functional models at its disposal. The choice of particular economic theory therefore depends much more on the a priori worldview the individual is equipped with. This is already given by the fact that a paradigm, a standpoint, the axioms of the given model are not proven, but that an individual selects a school of thought that best corresponds to his or her *worldview* in the assumptions or conclusions for the given model—a fashion model, if you will. This choice can be completely irrational and emotive, based on a priori sympathy with its assumptions or the expected results of the model. Models are therefore often accepted not on the basis of conformity to reality (none of them are realistic) but on the basis of *harmony* with a concept of the world, a sort of rhyme to a worldview, of how we believe or (often) want to believe. Even positive (meaning descriptive) models are, at their base, normative. In this regard, economics is also a faith—in axioms that are unproven, we must only believe. In an extreme approach, even economics becomes a religion.[8]

It is similar with models as it is with parables. If Jesus is described in the Bible as the "Lion of Judah," this obviously means something completely different than that he has a yellow mane, is carnivorous, and has an average life span of ten years. Every abstraction must take heed of its context; it becomes dangerous without it. Theoretical economics is a set of stories told in a scientific (adult) manner that differs in many ways from fairy tales and myths, but also has many features in common. We know that there is *some* truth in both,[9] but we also know they are fiction.

The story of Newton's gravitation gave way to the theory of relativity.[10] The same occurs with schools of economics. Who knows how economic thought will change in the future? Therefore, economists should approach reality humbly. But this humility stands in direct conflict with

---

[8] I have presented the deification of economic growth and scientific progress as examples.

[9] Patočka closes his discourse on mythological deities with the question: "Is this view, in its essence, true? Is human life grasped in its essence here?" Patočka, *Kacířské eseje o filosofii dějin* [Heretical Essays on the Philosophy of History], in the chapter "Pre-historické úvahy" ["Prehistoric thinking"], 270.

[10] "With Planck and Einstein there was a birth of a new physics ... Just as the objects of the physical world appeared changed—gone were billiard balls, newly present were quanta— the universe of mathematical objects changed ... we need to attend to the changing features of the mathematical landscape as a background against which we might understand how economics was reshaped, over the first two thirds of the twentieth century, as a mathematical discipline." Weintraub, *How Economics Became a Mathematical Science*, 11.

an effort to explain all human behavior with a single principle, which modern economics has frequently attempted. Economic models often hang in an abstract world that does not take into account differing context (cultural, social, historical, or religious). This context is often completely missing in economics. But can you study human behavior without an understanding of the context?

A CATHEDRAL OF SCAFFOLDING

As we have spoken so often of physics—which economics often sees as its example—it will be relevant to note the essential methodological differences between the two sciences. Physics uses a completely different hypothetical logic: Hypotheses are built like scaffolding, which helps to construct the building, and later, with the help of these artificial guideposts and aids, the scaffolding is torn down. For example, to ignore the friction of air in the measurement of free fall was a stroke of genius—a useful abstraction, which simplified much. But in a *real* calculation we must take air resistance into account if we *really* want to find whether a feather falls to earth faster than a stone. In a real application, their simplified assumptions must be disregarded and brought back to earth. In constructing models, we must look away from reality, and in applying these models to reality, we must instead look away from the models. We must, so to speak, tear down the scaffolding to see if there is anything left standing beneath it.

But in economics, assumptions, it often seems, cannot be torn down, not even ex post—the entire construction would be destroyed. So we are building a cathedral of scaffolding, one which remains de facto hollow. What would happen with mainstream theoretical economics if the model assumption of homo economicus were to be abandoned? If we tear down our scaffolding of assumptions, our whole cathedral would fall apart—or the magnificent cathedral would show not to exist in the first place, like in the story of the Emperor's new clothes.

Even Wittgenstein talks about scaffolding (a kind of tool that helps us get to a height): "A proposition constructs a world with the help of a logical scaffolding, so that one can actually see from the proposition how everything stands logically if it is true. One can draw inferences from a false proposition."[11] This is only about the scaffolding and not at all about the building itself. It only depends on how we use this scaffolding. The scaffolding is meaningless in and of itself. Strikingly, one of the fathers of modern economics, Alfred Marshall, called for the (scaffolding of) mathematics to be burned once the work was done.[12]

---

[11] Wittgenstein, *Tractatus Logico-Philosophicus*, 4.003.
[12] As we have shown in the chapter Metamathematics.

But an unpleasant thing often happens in economics. What happens if models have unrealistic assumptions and the results are not testable or falsifiable (for example, the model of homo economicus)? This effect can frequently be found in models whose conclusions agree de facto with the assumptions (how else . . .). We choose the assumptions and axioms according to what kind of results we want to get.

BEYOND METHODOLOGIES: TOWARD THE MYSTERY OF INSPIRATION

If one wants to, however, create a new paradigm, he or she must do as Einstein did—free ourselves from the old constructs. A new methodical approach requires more than the correct application of methodology, of course. We must first *completely get rid of the original methodology* and dare to think about something *completely new*.

The path to a new perception of the world leads through the abandonment of the current one. Wittgenstein's ladder must be used; we must climb on it and then throw it away.[13] No method exists to find a new method. Method (and with it all of scientific discourse) represents only a *secondary process* of learning. Original breakthrough discoveries in knowledge come through exactly and precisely refusing, breaking away and violating the old method(s). And how does this completely new thing happen? Through inspiration. And this takes place in the refuge of the muses, dreams, art, or revelations. In other words, in the emotive area, not in the rational. It is not for nothing that we say we are struck with an idea (in the sense that we are struck by lightning or a stick). When ideas strike us, a "lightbulb" turns on in our heads. Heffernanová notes that "we don't say we built an idea but that we got[!] an idea."[14] She continues with a humorous observation describing the experiences of many scientists who talk of inspiration coming to them in the form of the *three B's*: Bus, Bath, and Bed.[15] Only in the *secondary* process are the ideas given over to reason. If we do not know how to deliver the new thought in the context of other thoughts (with other systems of knowledge), it is refused either through the author of the idea himself or the scientific community. (Through discovery, an idea is brought into harmony with other ideas. The new phenomenon must be brought into the context of other, previously discovered phenomena.)[16] "A proposition must use old expressions to communicate a new sense," in Wittgenstein's words.[17]

---

13 Wittgenstein, *Tractatus Logico-Philosophicus*, 6.54.
14 Heffernanová, *Tajemství dvou partnerů* [The Secret of Two Partners], 71.
15 Ibid., 73.
16 Compare with Neubauer, *Respondeo dicendum*.
17 Wittgenstein, *Tractatus Logico-Philosophicus*, 4.03.

The perspective of "hardening" what once was an emotion into rational thought can also be seen in the process of discovery. The initial quiver of a new theory is the strength that moves the economic theory forward, and only afterward a new discovery is hardened into method (which is very often carried out only by the given thinker's successors). It is even plausible to say that new ideas occur to us constantly—but we refuse them because we do not consider them reasonable, they don't *fit*. Seeds fall on infertile ground. In other words, the idea that time is relative may have occurred to many of us on many occasions, but only Einstein was capable of turning this "nonsense" (in a Newtonian framework) into a construct that was able to tie in to the other, more sensible ones.

If we are to use a parable, with all of its limitations, we could compare emotive inspiration to being a kind of an engine in the automobile of discovery, and reason is its brakes and body. These two poles of soft and hardened (new and established) experience live in symbiosis, just as no functional automobile can exist without a functioning motor and brakes. An engine alone will never get us anywhere; nor will the construct of a car without an engine. In order to be willing to get an automobile running, we must believe that we can control the *brakes* as well. One hand cannot clap alone. Reason must be complemented (revived) by inspiration, just as inspiration must be corrected (kept on the ground, held back) by reason. As Evans puts it: "Knowledge is to be advanced by the invention of new concepts. But what makes a concept significant? ... It is brilliance of imagination which makes the glory of science."[18] As Wittgenstein argues in his foreword, he can be "understood only by someone who has himself already had the thoughts that are expressed in it—or at least similar thoughts."[19]

Logic must be complemented by the mysticism of inspiration (which, for example, Russell discusses[20]). For the anchoring and communication of inspiration, we need method. We must *saddle* inspiration with method, not bring it about with a method. The binding of research methodology can (and must) occur only secondarily within the framework of a *new system*, which the system always creates itself again and unpredictably. No *a priori methodology* of scientific research exists. If one were to be created, it would only be destructive. There is no scientific approach to science.

---

[18] Weintraub, *How Economics Became a Mathematical Science*, 75.

[19] Wittgenstein, *Tractatus Logico-Philosophicus*, 7.

[20] See Russell, *Mysticism and Logic*: "It is common to speak of an opposition between instinct and reason ... But in fact the opposition of instinct and reason is mainly illusory. Instinct, intuition, or insight is what first leads to the beliefs which subsequent reason confirms or confutes ... Reason is a harmonising, controlling force rather than a creative one. Even in the most purely logical realm, it is insight that first arrives at what is new." 30.

THE POVERTY OF FUTURISM: ECONOMISTS AS MODERN-DAY PROPHETS

> *The purpose of any science is the forecasting.*[21]
>
> Auguste Comte

> *If it were possible to calculate the future state of the market, the future would not be uncertain. There would be neither entrepreneurial loss nor profit. What people expect from the economists is beyond the power of any mortal man.*[22]
>
> Ludwig von Mises

If we were to search for the prophets of the twentieth and twenty-first centuries, we would have to look among economists. It is they who today most often predict the future and fulfill the role played in the ancient world by oracles. The trouble is that their predictions don't come true too often, and they cannot predict truly important things. But why do we fail so much? And can this change someday?

In ancient Greece, truth was long the domain of the poet. Homer's *Iliad* and *Odyssey* offered some of the many possible answers to questions such as: *What is man? What are gods? Whence from and what are the rules?* The behavior of characters in these stories and poetic interpretations of their acts are in large part set by a universal opinion on the character of god and man. With the arrival of Thales, truth became to a great extent the domain of philosophers and, after Aristotle, scientists as well, but nevertheless the poem and story maintained their role at least in the explanation of the world for millennia, up until the twentieth century. In Czechoslovakia's First Republic (1918–1938), the most-read newspapers published poems and stories, and their authors had a real influence on the formation of the public's political opinions. Today, terms such as *lack of scientific precision*, *subjectivity*, or *story* have nearly become epithets with which we very quickly write off a large part of the possible descriptions of reality. Economists occupy a privileged position between those descriptors. Why?

The last economic crisis has shown again that economists simply do not know how to predict the future. We cannot predict either the onset of a crisis or its scope. Despite such failures occurring relatively frequently among economists, it is still economists who are most active of all the social sciences to predict the future. Sociologists, political scientists, lawyers, psychologists, and philosophers do not rush to predict the future; at most they offer some kind of vision. Why aren't economists similarly reserved? Aside from demand simply existing for such predictions, there

---

[21] Comte, *Cours de philosophie positive* [Course of Positive Philosophy], 28.
[22] Mises, *Human Action: A Treatise on Economics*, chapter 38, "The Place of Economics in Learning."

is another explanation: Economics makes a clear effort to get as close as it can to physics, which is a natural science about "dead" objects; one which is probably closest to predicting the future events.

Despite the fact that we want to explain the future, we often cannot even explain the past. Philosopher Karl Popper wrote a book titled *The Poverty of Historicism*, in which he comes to the conclusion that explaining past events is practically impossible. Respectively: It is possible to provide an almost arbitrary number of "explanations." One does not have to go far for illustration: For example, economists cannot even agree what caused the great economic crisis in 1929, nor can they agree on what ended it. Likewise, we are not able to determine what precisely caused the current crisis, despite experiencing it firsthand.

PROGNOSIS: THE SELF-EXCLUDING PROPHECIES

The first major—and completely obvious—difficulty lies in the fact that it is impossible to predict the unpredictable. It's a direct contradiction. If it were possible to predict the event, the event would simply not be unpredictable. Careful observers of events (be they physicists or economists) can reveal a trend and extend it. But we cannot predict events. All we can say is what should happen in *model cases*, but the world is not a model.

We also have a magical incantation for predicting the future; we say *ceteris paribus* every time—"with the assumption that all else will not change," or "all else being equal." Aside from it sounding like "abracadabra," we must admit that reality tends not to be *ceteris paribus*.

On top of that, every true prophet carries a curse of his or her own. Consider the phenomenon of the curse of the prophet Jonah: biblical prophet Jonah did not want to prophesy, so a large fish swallowed him on his voyage at sea and after several days spat him up on the shore of Nineveh, the city he should have had predicted doom for. So Jonah reluctantly predicted a dark future for the city. But note that people took his warnings to heart (who would have expected it?) and carried out acts of repentance. The conclusion of the story was a happy end for everyone, except for Jonah: Instead of doom, in fact, nothing happened! Exactly *because* Jonah's message was believable, and people took his warnings to heart, the prophecy was not fulfilled, and the city was not destroyed. And Jonah then felt like the king of the madmen.

The point of the story is clear: We do not appreciate most of the truly good prophets. The reason why is beautifully explained by Nassim Taleb in the book *The Black Swan*: If there had been someone in 2001 who was such a good analyst of international affairs and an expert on terrorism that he or she were able to reveal the type of attack being prepared on the United States, and were he also able to convince his superiors, what would have happened? Nothing—because his information would have prevented the prediction from being fulfilled. And, in the best case, this (true) prophet would have fallen into obscurity. In the worst case, he would have gone down in history as a warmonger, a pessimist, and the least necessary regulator of all time. After all, because of him we would have had years of taking off our shoes at airports and undergoing degrading security inspections. It is a sort of principle of "self-excluding prophecy:" If a prophecy is "true," accurate, it frequently does not come true at all. If we are simply capable of anticipating problems, they do not have to come true at all. This is in fact the exact opposite of the "self-fulfilling prophecy" principle known in social sciences. Now the trick is that we will never know which principle will prevail. Sometimes warnings bring about the things that they warn about; sometimes they make them disappear.

If someone trustworthy starts in normal times to shout "crisis! crisis!" it can cause a psychological avalanche effect, and this alone could *bring about* crisis. Or the crisis can on the contrary be avoided because he or she pointed it out and people changed their behavior. The problem is that we can barely tell in advance which kind of case we are dealing with. And while we are on the prophets: The future is most probably not even known by God, otherwise theologians would not have been battling about this issue to this day.

It appears that the most probable conclusion comes from Alfred Whitehead, one of the most important philosophers and theologians (and also mathematicians) of the last century: The future is simply radically open, even for God. If God knew that Eve and Adam would taste the forbidden fruit, why would he have been so enraged? The prophecies in the Old Testament were not any deterministic look into the future, but were warnings and strategic variations of possible developments, especially those that required some kind of reaction. If the reaction was adequate, what was prophesied would frequently not occur at all. We cannot be opti- or pessi-mystic about the future all we can do is to remain mystic.

THE POVERTY OF FUTURISM

If we truly could know the future, would we want to? Would you love someone if you knew that in a few years you would come to hate them, and you had those events in full view? Aren't we grateful to uncertainty for many of our careers? I recall a beautiful scene in *The Hitchhiker's Guide to the Galaxy* when the philosophers went on strike because a genius computer was about to resolve the problem of the "Question of Life, the Universe and Everything" and the thinkers started to fear for their jobs.[23]

---

23 Adams, *The Hitchhiker's Guide to the Galaxy*, chapter 25.

It's like that with uncertainty. Would markets exist at all if we knew in advance what the developments in prices would be? Or, to take another example: Just how much money (how many billions of dollars) has been invested into researching the future development of oil prices? The ones who guess correctly are bound to get rich. Despite this, one can only "hit a bull's-eye" by chance.

I understand that everyone wants to know which horse in the race will win. But if it were known, we could close all racetracks down immediately. We frequently curse the uncertain future, but it is precisely because of it that we experience many beautiful things.

It is evident that there is no glory in knowing the future. Wouldn't it be better to leave the future to the future and concentrate on the "here and now"? It wouldn't. Thoughts about the future are the sine qua non of human life. Without a future, life would have no meaning. Without a future, not even the present would have a meaning. As one of the greatest Czech philosophers, Ladislav Hejdánek, wrote in his text: "A view ahead, to the nearest and to the farthest future, is necessary for truly seeing the present, whose real meaning appears first in the contexts which arrive and are coming."[24] If we want to know the present, the need returns to have a view to the future. Without a future and a past, the present would make no sense.

We face a radically open future and are trying to somehow deal with our fate. The apostles of permanent economic growth as well as the prophets of economic Armageddon have the same statistical numbers at their disposal. Except that according to their natures, one derives hope and the other the exact opposite.

THE THEORY OF A COGNITIVE NET: THE CONTINUUM OF REASON AND EMOTIONS

The difference between reason and emotion barely exists in practice.[25]
Jana Heffernanová

It has always puzzled me how we ascribe certain mental movements to emotion and others to rationality. Aren't both based on the same principle? Is there a way to bridge the (possibly apparent) gap between reason and emotion? How can we overcome the difference between subjective and objective facts? How can we reunite religion, faith, and myth on one side and science, evidence, and paradigm on the other side?

The first step in our closing meditation (in keeping with Descartes's methodology) is to abandon the clear dualistic divide between the rational

---

[24] Hejdánek, "Básník a slovo" ["The Poet and the Word"], 57.
[25] Heffernanová, *Tajemství dvou partnerů* [The Secret of Two Partners], 61.

and the emotive. Let us leave behind for now Hume's discourse on whether "reason is slave to the passions" or vice versa. But at the same time let us rethink the construct of homo economicus, whose maximization of utility leads to continuous rational optimization. Let us return to homo sapiens.

Can a system exist in which reason does not stand *against* perceptions, feelings, and emotions—a unified system, a continuum, in which reason and emotion mutually need and complement each other? In reality, nothing exists as pure perception without a framework of reason and abstraction, just as no rational construct exists without a perceptual impulse. Everything makes up only a part of a single, rational-emotional continuum. The only difference between the rational parts of the lines and their perceptual counterparts is the level of confirmed recursiveness, a sort of empirical or generally social confirmation of the given perception. New, original, and nontrivially classifiable perceptions appear to us as "soft" emotions, while repeatedly successfully (socially) confirmed emotions appear to us as rational constructs. In the early eras of culture, when there were few acknowledged hard emotions, this difference was not as steep as it is today, when humanity has gone far in its self-confirmation of certain stories or constructs.

Let's take an extreme example of mathematics as the generally recognized peak of rationality (which de facto has no empirical content, because mathematics is ultimately a system of completely abstract symbols, devoid of empirical opponents). At the moment of our first interaction with this fact (in childhood, or in the discovery of this construct), the equation in which one plus one equals two appears just as emotively unsubstantiated and unintelligible as any other perception. *Even mathematics was only emotion initially.* We had to *learn* this emotion (just as students in the first grade have learned to this day). Only through constant repetition and due to successful social confirmations of the given facts (that one plus one truly and constantly equals two), this *emotion* is gradually *hardened*, until it becomes a firm and reliable construction that we have learned to use safely and without the necessity of repeatedly confirming or verifying it. Through repeated confirmations, an emotional perception is "hardened," *rationalized*.

Due to this (useful) abstraction, the concept of two ones, the plus sign, the number two, and the equals sign gain real meaning. But the world itself does not contain these terms (as it contains no other abstractions). None of us have essentially seen *number* one or a two. We may have seen two apples and two pears, and one of the things that joins these two sets together is the number two. But two itself does not exist in the world. This is even more true for other mathematical symbols (think of minus two to start with). They are only symbols whose meaning and rules we must learn. We perceive the impulses of the real world safely in the terms of abstract units, pluses, and equals signs (the number of pears or apples and their resultant sum). The perceiving subject then creates an interpretational framework (in our example a mathematical one), through which he or she is able to see the world, simplify it, and then also *resolve* it. Rationality is nothing more than *hardened* emotion.

An example from the opposite pole of experience represents something fundamentally concrete and unique, subjective. Take flaming love or friendship as an example. In the first moments we do not know how to classify these strong emotions because we are going through the experience of something *radically new and different*, and we do not—literally—have words for; in the deepest sense of the word, we are speech*less* (like animals). (Words are possible only in a system of generalized-social experience, which is lived by at least two members who at the same time find out that their unique experience is *similar*, respectively that it has certain common expressions. Words cannot be made for one-off experiences.) Only later in our experience do we find elements we have heard of or have read, and are willing (or forced) to generalize our individual, unrepeatable, and unspeakable experience on the level of terms that exist and which other members of society have met with. No love or friendship is the same; none of the subjects experiencing it take in similar perceptions or feelings (nor are they comparable). Nevertheless, if people experience feelings in which they find a harmony with others, they can find abstract *words* expressing something similar for their unrepeatable experiences. Thus a subjective experience is rounded off to the nearest all-social denominator. Not even one sunset is the same as another; each is unique, and we are of course able to indicate our experience with a single term that expresses the sunset being watched through all human eyes. The frequency of events together with the need to communicate our experiences forms *in some respects* (never in all!) a repeated experience that gains its own name and becomes an abstract concept. Or something harder which it is possible to operate with. This leads to an abstract (because it is language) and objective rounding off of a unique subjective experience. Our language is nothing other than "lingual rounding off" of subjective emotions to the closest term available.

Even an emotive experience such as love or friendship hardens over time, and after repeated mutual confirmations of experiences becomes somewhat an automatic part of our lives. It hardens to a rational form that we simply count on. We could talk of an *inflation of experiences*, in which the same stimuli do not bring the same "rush of blood to the head" as in its initial virgin state. They harden, and become rational-like, something that we can count on. A hardened love is no worse or better than a young one. It is different; it displays rational properties.

Emotion is a young experience that has not yet found the rational form (which, perhaps later, awaits it). Something that is born from unconscious perception and in an original moment *does not exist*, because we cannot find a corresponding abstract term for the experience, later becomes something we know how to classify, communicate, and operate with. A construct of the world (in an individual or in society) then emerges from these perceptions, a net in our mind that weaves reality. Order is born from the chaos of unnamed solidity, which expresses itself through repetitive characteristics (which we mark or consider rational).

What if reason and emotions are made of the same matter? What if these are two poles of the same continuum? Psychologist Jana Heffernanová puts it in the following way: "The quarrel between reason and emotions is practically non-existent; for we will not once in life utter a sentence that would be built purely on rational reasoning alone and would have no emotional spark in it; behind the most reasonable statements there is some feeling, some opinion embedded in positive or negative emotions (…) In our daily lives it is one emotion standing against another, for example fear against compassion, where fear or lack of compassion is masked, explained, or defended by rational arguments as the reasonable thing to do, the right thing to do, the only thing to do."[26]

Some thinkers differentiate between stable and unstable emotions. The stable ones are so stable that they are often even considered rational—to the point that it becomes really confusing. So, for example, economic interest, care for oneself, etc. seem a "reasonable thing to do," although they are just stable emotions. To put it differently, the biblical warning of the *love for money* is primarily *love*. And love is an emotion par excellence. It may be a form of love that is foul, overemphasized, or pointed at the wrong directions … but it is still love, and love it will remain.[27]

IN PRAISE OF ERRORS

There is a crack in everything, that's how the light gets in.[28]
Leonard Cohen

Reason and emotion (old and new perceptions) come into conflict only rarely. Conflicts occur at moments when new (unconsolidated, unexplained) experiences collide with those (consolidated and explained) older ones, and when our subcognitive perceptions and emotions cannot be explained by seen or felt existing, cognitive concepts. If the unexplained subcognitive reality is repeated, if it remains in time and we are not capable of explaining it through any existing framework, two phenomena could occur: Either our cognitive system suppresses the new perception (whether consciously or unconsciously) into a sort of residue of the anomaly, of

---

[26] Heffernanová, *Tajemství dvou partnerů* [The Secret of Two Partners], 61.

[27] See also Bernard of Clairvaux: "There are only two evils—or two chief evils—which war against the soul: an empty love of the world and too much self-love (1 Pt 2.11)," (from *Sermon on the Song of Songs*, 211). It is helpful to realize that, despite the fact that we are dealing with (chief) evils, they are still, at root, *loves* (similar to the case of love of money which in the New Testament's 1.Timothy 6:10 is considered to be "root of all kinds of evil").

[28] Cohen, "Anthem."

which we are (somewhat unconsciously) aware, but are not willing, forced, or able to process into a system (or to devote attention to these deviations), this could even lead to a total suppression on an ontological level, when we do not notice the reality that *doesn't fit in*. The other option that could occur, of course, is that these "errors" break the old system.

Minor errors (when the observation does not correspond to the framework, or deviations from the expected, which do not correspond to existing theory) sometimes have the ability to unveil the imperfections of the theory and completely break it. These are precisely the "glitches in the Matrix" that reveal to us the mental matrix-lie construct of our worldview. So it happened, for example, that in observing the orbit of Mercury at the end of the nineteenth century, two minor deviations were observed that contradicted the Newtonian worldview. The issue was resolved (it sparked the very quest) in 1915 with Einstein's *general theory of relativity*, which managed to explain these minor discrepancies and which eventually replaced Newton's system.

A model is nothing more than a story (or, as the economist Weintraub puts it, an autobiography),[29] and through errors in current (otherwise well-functioning) models and abstractions we find ways to new stories. The residue that does not fall into the equations of current theories often holds in itself a hidden key to new horizons. Scientists therefore should not round off their errors but, on the contrary should devote maximum attention to them, because it is probably within them that it is possible to find the rudiments of a completely new (perhaps better) axiomatic system. This holds similarly true in personal lives as well.

The residue (whether named or unconscious) creates a kind of schizophrenic dialectic in scientific knowledge (and with it the human *psyche* as well). The unconsolidatedness of experiences can create in man a split personality (on a certain level this is generally true, because every situation in life requires an application of other paradigmatic systems—and it is no secret that these systems can be, and frequently tend to be, inconsistent; in every life role, which can alternate in rapid time intervals, we must apply different concepts of self and the world[30]). This is similar in science as well. No economic model is applicable in all situations—if the contrast is shown to be axiomatic, a new economic school is created. The new school then has the potential to overcome the current one and to establish itself as a general mainstream interpretational framework.

---

[29] "As James Olney once wrote, quoting Paul Valery, 'All theory is autobiography.'" Weintraub, *How Economics Became a Mathematical Science*, 6.

[30] If the human psyche absorbs (or is forced to absorb) too great an amount of inconsistent and unconsolidated observations, which it cannot explain or connect to one world, the psyche defends itself by creating two characters or two worlds which each react differently in the given situation (and are different!). The contrast in *roles* has become so radical that they are no longer sustainable and alternating roles alone is not enough, so the defensive alternating of *personalities* is necessary.

THE DEAD WORLD AND THE WORLD OF THE LIVING

Mathematics is appropriate for the study of the world only as long as we are aware of its limits. The objects of mathematical study must first be "killed" and set in place. Nelson argues: "[A]s economists in the recent years have been coming to understand, a static world has little to do with the essence of any real-world economic situation."[31]

Sören Kierkegaard once wrote: "Existence transcends logic."[32] It is as if the effort to model reality has hardened us into seeing two worlds. One of these is the abstract world (or the *un*real) model constructs, through which we perceive the world, and the other is the world *an sich, the real,* empirical *world,* unmodelable (because it is alive and real and cannot be moved around, as is the case with our mental constructs—they were created, it seems, exactly for the purpose of being freely moved, or "bossed" around). The same conflict is reflected in economics as well. On one side stand economic models that try to describe the behavior of individuals or the entire society, and where everything fits beautifully into itself. But these models are often based on unrealistic foundations or can lead to conclusions that can rarely be applied in practice. Unfortunately, frequently both happen.

Machlup was aware of this problem in it's full scale: "[E]conomic science is a system of a priori truths, a product of pure reason, an exact science reaching laws as universal as those of mathematics, a purely axiomatic discipline, a system of pure deductions from a series of postulates, not open to any verification or refutation on the grounds of experience."[33] Piero Mini goes even further: "[T]he world of logic is a dead world."[34]

The Dead World

Only the static, nonspontaneous, predictable, and therefore *non*living can be scientifically grasped. This is the price that Descartes and all scientists with him must pay for exactness. The price to pay for scientific precision and elegance is the fact that life eludes science. A replacement may be the world of logic and abstraction, which *works* in its own world. As if anything mathematically inconceivable has lost its right to real (scientific) existence. Mathematics works in this passive world, as does mechanics, causality, and all of our (internally consistent) constructs. Abstract models can be elegant and can fit beautifully into one another. But they can also be in pursuit of the faraway world of the living. Economics carries out a euthanasia of the living world, for example, through the incantation

---

[31] Nelson, *Economics as Religion,* 58.
[32] *Sören Kierkegaard's Journals and Papers,* 1054, cited in Mini, *Philosophy and Economics,* 211. Perhaps he had in mind the same thing that Wittgenstein wanted to show.
[33] Caldwell, *Beyond Positivism,* 140.
[34] Mini, *Philosophy and Economics,* 213.

ceteris paribus—with which the models are disconnected from reality. In such an artificial world we can create almost arbitrary models. In economics it frequently occurs that it is rather a *science about economics* than about economy. The trick with *ceteris paribus* is even pointed out by Terence Hutchison. According to him, it is one of the main ways that economic theory prevents empirical verifiability (the second way is the already-mentioned disconnection of the logical-deductive models from empirical content). Because in the real world *ceteris* is not *paribus*, economists have a lot of room for fantasizing without reality placing any limits on them or standing in their way.[35]

The Middle Ages overflowed with the numbers of dancing angels on the head of a pin … and our era is possessed by the idea of counting marginal optimization. In this light, however, the medieval discussion on how many angels could fit on the head of a pin appears more realistic only because, as opposed to the secret terminology of theoretical economics, the head of a pin is real and the concept of an angel is accessible to everyone. Nevertheless, both ways of theoretizing are not empirically measurable, and outside their own discourse they are nonsensical and inapplicable. They make sense only when locked in the given discourse—in their own world.

Silence and the World of the 65th Square

In the second world, the world of the living (vis-à-vis the Dead World), science is silent. This is best described by the last sentence of Wittgenstein's monumental *Tractatus*, which has at the same time become the climax of all his work: "[W]hat we cannot talk about we must pass over in silence."[36] Wittgenstein de facto gets to the paradox of non-sense (not nonsense!) in models. It is content-free but a useful scaffolding on which we can climb. The problems of the world are shown but cannot be enunciated; they allow neither questions nor answers. The real world of the living cannot be grasped abstractly. There is no model that would know how to take hold of its unadjusted and unabridged form—in its living complexity.

A chessboard has sixty-four squares. They are black and white, regular and square; any movement on them is firmly guarded by fixed and undisputed rules. It is de facto easily possible to reconstruct the game even backward;[37] we understand chess, we made the rules. My friends who play chess put their drinks on the next table, which they call *the 65th square*. And so the 65th square soon became the entire world *off* the chessboard. What if it is similar with the analytical approach? We can manage to explain well and analyze chess squares in black and white, but the most

---

[35] See also Caldwell, *Beyond Positivism*, 112.
[36] Wittgenstein, *Tractatus Logico-Philosophicus*, paragraph 7.
[37] So time can flow in both directions, so to speak.

important things occur on the largest chess square, the 65th square. After all, that's where the players are.

The things that we cannot (scientifically or analytically) talk of, and should pass in silence, cry out, as they "are the things that matter the most and are the things that we want to talk about."[38] There are areas of life (probably the most important) that *must be passed over in silence by* analytical science (if the analysis is taken honestly and purely scientifically). Most of our life's interests as human beings, and perhaps even as scientists, lie on that 65th square. Giving unequivocal (scientific) answers to real questions is harder than it looks.

So there is double-trouble for economists; we live in an unusual state of schizophrenia. A theoretical economist must forget about the real world (he must dream, just like Descartes), otherwise he will not get far in his models. His reward tends to be conclusions that are just as abstract and inapplicable to the real world as the model itself. But when an economist has to talk about practical economics—for example, about economic policy he must often forget the exact models, throw out unnecessary sophisticated theoretical apparatus, and speak from experience.[39]

And there is the final implication for economists: Economists should be humble—we must be aware that we did not think up the economy, nor did we build it. As I have tried to show, the economy itself existed far before the teachings about it. It is something as archetypal as humanity itself. We are not the architects of the economy; we are only (more- or less-traveled) tourists who observe with great awe a magnificent and ancient city. We are in the same situation as if we were to observe a clock face and try to reveal the principle of the clock's mechanism hidden inside. Over time we would be able to predict where the hands would be at an arbitrary time in the day. If an extraterrestrial were to see such a clock, or a person who did not know how it worked, they could create an arbitrary number of theories to explain the movement of the hands. From this, on the basis of given methods and academic disputes, they would choose the best, whether this was according to the criteria of mathematical elegance, simplicity, political expedience, on the basis of inborn conceptions of how such a machine *should* work, and so on. (At the same time, it could be doubted that the theory which would have proposed an explanation through a complicated relationship between springs and many varied circles would win in such a contest.)

The truth would be shown only at the moment when the clock would break down and have to be fixed—only then do we find out whether we *really understand how the clock works*. Not only do economists not know

---

[38] "But what many in the Circle misunderstood was that Wittgenstein did not believe that the unsayable should be condemned as nonsense. On the contrary, the things we could not talk about were those that really mattered." Edmonds and Eidinow, *Wittgenstein's Poker*, 163.
[39] See Mini, *Philosophy and Economics*, 16.

how to fix the mechanism that stops working according to their vision, but they cannot even agree on what brings it back to proper functioning.

But how can this hidden principle be recognized if we are not able to view it directly? We will eternally fumble about humbly before a living mechanism that we did not construct—like uncomprehending students who stand in amazement before this colossal miracle called market economy and hope that it does not stop, because just as in the legend of Prague's astronomical clock, nobody other than Master Hanuš—who created it—knows how to fix it. Economists only know how to comment on the economy and fine-tune it, as long as everything is functioning generally well.

BEAUTIFUL ECONOMICS

So, in times when the economy is dazzling and growing, there seems to be no reason to doubt the abilities of economic science. But is it to the doctor's credit that the child grows? He can certainly contribute with better or worse advice, but if the child is essentially healthy, you cannot tell the difference between a good and bad doctor. A good doctor, or economist, can be much better identified in the times of sickness, crisis.

From time to time it is argued (usually by economists) that economics is the queen of the social sciences. We were so fascinated with the growth of the global economy in recent years that we completely forgot how clueless economics is in times of crisis. The models stop working. They seem to work well when they work and not when they don't . . . So what now?[40]

It would appear in times of crisis, when changes are too sharp and too frequent, that standard mathematical models cannot be used. In their construction we must rely on sufficiently long time order; in the meantime, however, we must also turn to history and intuition for inspiration. How often has a person heard this sentence from analysts: "The model tells us this, but we think. . . ." The model must be complemented with intuition.[41] And this must be admitted.

Although thinking like an economist is a practical mental exercise, it is similar to playing chess. Now, chess is quite useful—it helps us to think strategically, but it would be preposterous to argue that the world is a chessboard and that moves on it correspond to the real movements of armies, that *real* horses move in the L-shaped motion. In addition, if a person gets into his or her role as an economist too much, he or she stops considering

---

[40] Joseph Schumpeter advises to get free of it and draw from historical experience. The entire German historical school refuses abstract timeless models and returns to history as its only teacher.

[41] Let's leave behind the question whether such models can even be built without using intuition.

whether life can be played on different strings than the selfish-economic ones. Schumpeter also had something similar in mind: "General history (social, political, and cultural), economic history, and more particularly industrial history are not only indispensable but really the most important contributors to the understanding of our problem. All other materials and methods, statistical and theoretical, are only subservient to them and worse than useless without them."[42]

There are pieces of knowledge that an economist can learn from abstract models (just as in the case of chess), and there are situations when abstraction is the only thing we have. What's more, at the moment when you have learned a given method of consideration, it is hard to get rid of the mental image in your head. Whenever you are confronted with the given problem, the image automatically comes back to mind. The model is sometimes useful but sometimes misleading; in both cases we must be aware that it does not describe reality but only its rational abstraction. It is therefore a fiction; hopefully a useful one, but still only a fiction. *An economist must be aware of these fictions.* Let the economist use his models, but he must, as Wittgenstein said, climb above them. He must look around, must not completely believe them (they are parables!), and must not *completely* devote himself to them. He must know where they are and are not useful. Otherwise he may cause more harm than good.

THE QUESTION THAT DRIVES US

This book can be perceived as a postmodern criticism of mechanistic and imperial mainstream economics. Instead of this imperialism, methodological dadaism—as Feyerabend refers to it—might be more of use. Let us use economic schools according to how they fit given matters and not according to which axiomatic system is closer to our worldview. Let us give up efforts to find one school that is "right" or is "closer to the truth," and rather let us order them according to their usefulness for a particular reality.

Inspiration comes involuntarily; there is neither a scientific nor rigorous method for it. Revel in it. Our education teaches us to apply rigorousness, but at the same time we neglect the other side of knowledge, which is cognition itself, discovering mysteries, fleeting inspiration, openness to the muses, the fineness and sensitivity of the spirit. All these are the characteristics that are at least as important as the rigorous scientific method itself. Without inspiration, burning questions, and enthusiasm for the issue, there is no discovery. For "it's the question that drives us,"[43] as Trinity puts it in the film *The Matrix*.

---

[42] Schumpeter, *Business Cycles: A Theoretical, Historical and Statistical Analysis of the Capitalist Process*, 20.
[43] Wachovski and Wachovski, *The Matrix*, 1999.

Conclusion

Hic sunt leones[1]

> *In the middle of the forest there's an unexpected clearing*
> *that can only be found by those who have gotten lost.*
> *The clearing is surrounded by a forest that is choking itself.*
> Tomas Tranströmer[2]

Throughout this book we have sought and inquired about the spirit of economics. Does such a thing exist? I have tried to show that it does. And just what is the spirit of economics? Is it in its place or dislocated? What is the meaning of economics, and what is its role in the context of the whole? This was something I have tried to discover and describe on the previous pages.

The real question therefore isn't whether the market economy works or not. The real question is (and we ask it really), whether it works in the way we want it to work. The question of whether something works is itself nonsensical unless it is related to the meaning and the purpose of the given phenomenon. Only according to this can we judge whether something (doesn't) work. The question of the functioning of the market or the invisible hand is, in reality, an inherently normative question: How do we want it to work?

BODY WITHOUT SOUL: ZOMBIE ECONOMICS

… but this is even more complicated, because even a tool can "come alive" and gain its own meaning, unfortunately different than what we wanted

---

[1] A legend found on old maps: Unexplored blank spaces where the explorer did not get to were fittingly marked Here there are lions.

[2] Swedish poet, winner of the Nobel Prize for Literature in 2001. This is the beginning of one of his best-known poems. We can only speculate as to whether Tranströmer's hope of the lost exactly expresses the hope of the time. That answers only come after questions—never the other way around—and that only the lost can find it. When we search for something (meaning), in the same breath we admit that we have lost it. We have the feeling that we should have it, but do not. A child does not search for the meaning of its life—isn't this precisely because it has it, that it lives—and therefore doesn't search for it?

to give it. It becomes its own meaning. Many stories, old as well as new, tell of how the tool becomes the master. Something that should serve us somehow comes alive, gains its own logic and starts to work against us... Have we thus dislocated the spirit of economics? After many years of artificially peeling away meaning, ethics, and normativity from economics, we must not be surprised that economics sometimes even behaves like this: Without meaning and unfairly, living its own life. At least it can be heard as a rebuke of contemporary protests against the current form of "growth capitalism."

What happens when the body is separated from the soul and the soul from the body? The horror genre offers us a lesson: If something that should be together and work together is divided (body and soul), on one side what we get is a body without a soul, a zombie. A zombie is a human, or rather the body of a human, who has lost its human dimensions, compassion, humanity, gentleness—and is only after one thing: To feed and to reproduce (through biting, so even this reproduction is pretty effective because it is a byproduct of eating). The ghastliness of the entire situation is usually then exacerbated because someone who was close to us (a friend, family member, child, wife, or husband) and who was with us suddenly turns against us.

But there are other stories which warn against the tool becoming the master. The modern myth of *The Matrix* tells of how something that was supposed to serve us becomes our master: In the end it is not tools and technology which serve people, but people who serve machines (they are shackled slaves from birth) and (the machines' own) technology. The *R.U.R* robots from Čapek's play, the genie from Aladdin's lamp or the Golem from the beautiful Prague Jewish legend all similarly go out of control. From newer stories we can recall films such as *A.I. (Artificial Intelligence)* or *I, Robot*, where robots suddenly discover their own (different) life, meaning. It is even a frequent theme of Kundera's stories: A play that has been begun gains a life of its own and enslaves its actors, who initially felt like directors. The puppetmaster becomes the puppet, the faithful servant becomes the master, and an innocent play, from a joke, becomes a straitjacket.

In other words, it appears impossible to separate questions of good and evil from economics, or to separate meaning from tools, ethics from economics, even though the last generation has tried so bitterly. If we continue this way, we won't ever completely pound the soul out of economics, but maybe economics will gain its own *telos* (or meaning) and begin to work *for itself*, and not as we wish. In other words, a moral vacuum does not exist. Other morals, possibly not human, are created.

But there is another dimension to the analogy of economics as body and soul. Let's go back for a moment to the horror genre. When the body is separated from the soul, we not only get the zombie (a body without a soul), but also a ghost (a soul without a body). Ghosts are just as scary, but for different reasons than zombies: Ghosts don't attack us. What is horrifying about them is their silent gaze; vacant, reproachful, accusatory. They want *something* from us; something evil, unjust, violent happened to them and they haunt us. So to use this picture: The soul torn away from the body is in itself the same source of fear, a kind of constantly accusing superego, which often makes absurdly large demands. Even this can happen with ethics—the soul of economics—if it is dislocated: It becomes unrealistic, too demanding. It will expect this of economics and require too much, more than economics itself can handle.

Economics must simply stand on both legs—to have a body and a soul. It is no accident that economics as a field was originally a subset of moral philosophy. And it is this image that nicely supplements Adam Smith's forgotten second book, which discusses morals and sentiments and even has them in its title. Here, then, is that missing, neglected leg which causes economics and economies to limp.

VALUES WITHOUT PRICES

How could it not limp when we try to do accounting with values where only some have prices? It seems to me that this is the primary difficulty of economics: Many things have value, but only certain values have prices. A train, an advertisement or a nail file certainly have their value and also have their price (because there is a market for these values); other values (friendship, the smile of a child, clean air, etc.) are unquestionable values, but have no price (there is no market for them, they are not freely exchangeable). This is why economics is limping and sometimes has devastating impacts; often values with prices are set against values without prices.

From time immemorial, the hard murders the soft. The "blacksmith" Cain kills the "breeze" Abel; Agent Smith (a blacksmith) constantly wants to destroy Neo (Neo escapes, he defends himself, but he does not want to destroy). The soft must be protected from the hard. Economics is similar in this. So a large billboard has its value and its price, while the beautiful view (which that billboard can block) has only a value and not a price. What do we do with this? How do we find a balance? There are three ways to bridge this problem: The first is to try to find or express the price of the value of the view—in this regard there are even attempts to go in the direction of economic consideration (the "price" of clean air approximates CO_2 permits, etc.). The second possibility is simply not to allow the market here; ban billboards from beautiful places in the same way that factories cannot be built in city parks. And the third possibility is to soften hard numbers, to take the price of the advertisement as *fuzzy*.

THE DARK ROOM AND THE SIMULATION OF CERTAINTY

If we find ourselves in a situation of fundamental uncertainty, is it useful to simulate certainty? In other words: Can an accurate prediction of the future be dangerous? Let's imagine we're in a room where light fails and the room is so dark that you can't see a step in front of you and no one knows which direction the door is in. Now someone's voice is heard, someone with great authority, who announces: "I know where the door is. Hurry after me, follow my voice." If people in a situation of fundamental uncertainty believe this prediction and run at full speed toward the voice, they could all run into a wall, or even worse, fall out a window. What would happen if no one made such a prediction? People would fall on all fours, on hands and knees, and slowly they would grope their way around the room until they found the door. Yes, this is not a rapid strategy, but definitely one where no one would smash their nose or break an arm.

I think it is this groping, this uncertainty, that we lack. The simulation of certainty is a very dangerous thing. We have run too far in darkness. We have had the feeling that we have eliminated risk and have insured ourselves against everything unexpected. We have exchanged stability (expressible, for example, in low public debt) for speed (GDP growth on steroids).

NANO- AND MEGA-UNITS AND THE ECONOMICS OF THE MIDDLE

At the same time, in life there are spheres where we work without money, even though we are handling great value there—and this is in the nanosphere of family, friends, lovers, and so on. In this area we exchange value, but in doing so we use neither money nor precision. We even behave ineffectively and intentionally unselfishly in this sphere. When we behave selfishly, we at least try to make it look like it's not about self-interest, that we are doing things *for someone else*, not for ourselves. In other words, the rules that govern economics do not work here; respectively, we do not want them to work. This "nanoeconomy" is explored, for example, by behavioral economics.

But what happens when other rules apply not only in nanoeconomies, but also in hyper-units? As far as the bankruptcy of major units such as states or important companies goes, it appears that we also behave differently here; we forgive, we help, and we don't adhere to precise agreements, because adhering to them could mean the collapse of the system. The classical rules of economics may work well in the medium space— but in the extremes (large or small) they collapse. In this regard no "general theory" exists, because even Keynes in his book *General Theory* speaks of this middle measure. Just as in theoretical physics, it's useful to think differently on the small quantum level than in normal measures (here Newton "suffices," even though we know that this is just an approximation of reality) and again differently on large measures, where the general theory is "valid." At the same time, we all suspect that there must be a unifying theory of everything, but thus far we haven't come up with anything better.

Perhaps there is a similar situation in economics. Economics can work in common dimensions, similar to Newton's classical deterministic and mechanistic physics.[3] In other words, economics can work in unimportant areas. In questions of health, love, death, and state bankruptcy there must be other, more general rules at work.

GILGAMESH AND WALL STREET—FROM WALL TO WALL

As these words are being written, protests on Wall Street are at their peak. And once again they're striking against a *wall*. The end of this book returns to its beginning. Gilgamesh, who for his wall tried to turn people into maximally effective robots without humanity, deserved the first documented protest in history: People complained to the gods. Today we complain to politicians and institutions. But the complaint seems similar: We do not want to build this wall so gruelingly, we do not want to become something different; in the vehement construction of this wall, which isn't perceived as our own, we do not want to lose (our) human souls.

And while we're on this symbolism: Right next to Wall Street stands a symbol of the market—a raging bull, slightly larger than life, cast from bronze, which slightly brings gold to mind. A bull in an attack position, one whose horns provoke fear. Why did we choose this as the symbol of the market? We first notice that it primarily is about an animal, an irrational animal, one which neither excels in its ingenuity nor is known for its friendship to man. It can't be saddled. And why is the only way to ride (for a short while) on a bull called a rodeo? Why haven't we chosen as a symbol a calmer animal, one more friendly to man, a domesticated animal like a horse or a dog? It seems this symbol is completely appropriate. And the most important question: Why are we surprised when the markets act the way they do?

During the protests, the bull found itself behind a wall, but this time behind a protective wall, protected by a police cordon. The question we must ask is this: Who was that wall protecting? Was it protecting the people from the bull, or the bull from the people? If you are a member of Occupy Wall Street, you will think it's necessary to protect people from the madness of the market, against its cruel and unjust impacts. If you are a member of the Tea Party movement, you will probably instead request

---

3 Following the example of mechanistic physics we today have an idea—it is a kind of universally accepted and living myth that economics is a tool, an area, where rules are valid similar to the cold, mechanical, independent-of-humans, inexorable, and exact rules of physics of the last century. It appears to me that this is a mistaken idea. After all, contemporary physics already knows the borders of exactness (Planck's uncertainty, the uncertainty of the position of small particles before the collapse of wavelength) and knows that it is impossible to be completely precise. Quantum physics is not mechanical but probabilistic, just as we know that particles do not behave independent of their observer (Schrödinger's cat and the experiment with light particles).

that the markets be protected from the irrational prohibitions of politicians, regulators, etc.

Nevertheless, even here we meet with the theme of (in)humanity, the wall. Isn't the main objection of the occupiers of Wall Street the fear that economics is a body without a soul, a zombie that will destroy us? Even here the symbolism of the wall appears, the animal, the protection from nature (the animal symbolizing the market) or the protection of nature (naturalness?) from people. The raging bull in the city is ultimately a similar symbol to the wild Enkidu in the city of Uruk, a wild natural force in the middle of civilization.

OUR (UN)NATURALNESS

Almost all archetypal myths speak of a certain decision, a *trade-off*, between growth through knowledge and harmony (with nature or one's own naturalness). Enkidu, who changes from animal into man, "acquired reason, but animals ran from him," Eve and Adam lose their Edenic harmony with each other and their surroundings in exchange for a taste of the Tree of the Knowledge of Good and Evil. In Greek myths, humankind is cursed because Prometheus stole (technical) knowledge from the gods, and harmonic labor, which was once pleasant, became unpleasant.

That harmony with nature, that naturalness, was lost. And we've been searching for it ever since. Man is naturally unnatural and unnaturally natural. We're more natural when we aren't natural. This is true psychologically and religiously, but especially economically.

An example: Man's first possession after the fall in the story of the Garden of Eden was clothing. Not because of cold, but to cover up their private parts (in this regard the first property was "unnecessary," a-biotic, morally-ideologically). They weren't cold; they started to own because they were embarrassed. The first possessions did not come from physical need, but from psychological-moral shame and a feeling of "nakedness." So they started to be ashamed of their naturalness, literally of their nature. The sheepskin, which they were later covered with so they would not be ashamed, was symbolic: We feel better in another's skin. Our own is too intimate. And ever since, man has felt more himself if he's wearing a Hugo Boss suit. On the other hand, if we were to sit here naked, naturally, as we were at birth, we would feel very unnatural.

This natural unnaturalness, this a-harmony, is the core of economics to this day. This "surface tension," the existential disquiet between the interior and exterior—the externalization of my own feelings of inner insufficiency, that a compensation should be there—is the beginning of all economics.

One of the ways to read the crisis is that the economy is calling for a forced sabbath. We are not listening to this voice and are constantly trying to whip (ourselves) toward greater performance. It would be enough for the economy to turn around just a bit, so that in the event of a downturn in demand (instead of laying off 20 percent of employees) we worked 20 percent less. In other words, to go home on Thursday night or to decrease peoples' pay.

The economy is exhausted, as is nature, our machines, and even ourselves.

THE CRISIS OF GROWTH CAPITALISM AND THE PROBLEM OF THE THIRD BEER

What we're now going through isn't as much a crisis of capitalism as it is a crisis of "growth capitalism." After all, capitalism (how else should we name the current state of economics after thousands of years of western civilization's development?) was the same before the crisis as it is now. Why did the protests against unfair capitalism only come now? Why only now does it bother us that the economy does not divide wealth fairly?

Imagine there are three people sitting at a table, but on the table there are only two pints of beer dancing on the table. How do we fairly distribute them? Should the poorest, the richest, or the lady go without beer? Should the alcoholic get it preferentially, or the person who has never tasted beer in his life? Should the one who brewed it get it, or the one who owns the pub? These are complicated economic-philosophical questions which necessarily touch on philosophy (what are rights and what is property?), ethics (what is fair?), sociology (which rights emerge from social standing?) or even psychology (whether and how to act) and other fields. Regardless, the question is one of redistribution: How to distribute wealth, and who "de-serves" the beer and why, under which makeup do rights emerge in society.

We have solved this complicated problem by having a third beer magically appear on the table. At once the problem is solved; everybody takes one and that's that. Let's notice that all of a sudden the question of justice disappears as if it is rounded (everybody gets one, and it's all the same who and how they deserve it), and the topic of fair distribution of wealth somehow instantly vanishes. Giving everyone one beer seems to us to be roughly (the word roughly is important) fair, and on the contrary the demands of one of the revelers for two beers (for whatever reason) seem strange, if all are thirsty for a beer.

This magic third beer in this dilemma symbolizes economic growth. And our current problem: The third beer hasn't suddenly appeared. The economy is simply not growing. So we must logically return to the philosophical questions we "resolved" with economic growth. The pleasant, comfortable and elegant solution is growth. It solves, it seems, all problems. This is precisely why we have the anxious panic of it "not growing." But what if we've grown all that we will? Constantly and possibly erroneously we live in the notion that now we are talking about a sort of temporary cooldown, that it is normal to grow, and constantly. So growth will soon return and everything will be once again like old times. Growth simply solves everything.

Fair enough, but what about when it doesn't grow? How do we divide the beers then? We need to prepare for longer periods of non-growth, which could last for decades, because as soon as the real, non-steroidal growth returns, it will (I hope!) be an imperative to decrease the existing public debt as soon as possible, sooner than we are hit by another crisis. In other words, to quickly collect wood before the next winter hits. European and American public debt is unbearably large; it is on the verge of bursting—and must be decreased quickly. Paying down debt means having public finance surpluses. So firstly growth cannot be returned with debt, as we have been accustomed to in the past (this "source" has been exhausted), and secondly, surplus public finance (the only way to quickly decrease the debt) means a slowdown in economic growth. Those who want to power their economies through debt must be prepared to slow it down through surplus, which will pay down the debt.

We have let ourselves be bribed by growth (the third beer) and have neglected (or "resolved") philosophical-economic questions of the just distribution of wealth. In other words, it is true that when we get rich in general, it's almost all the same to us how we get rich; we don't ask too much for justice. But when all of a sudden there's no growth, or even when we get poor—we're much more sensitive to justice. This asymmetry may be because we are who we are. The economy was roughly as (un)just a generation ago as it is today, but we're only dealing with the theme of injustice now. This is why it's about the crisis in growth capitalism. Capitalism and democracy can certainly exist without growth (otherwise we'd be talking about a very strange, weak system which holds on due to the bribe of growth), even if everything goes better with the third beer.

SUMMARY

We have studied the development of the economic soul from the very bedrock of written human memory on this planet. All of this left traces, even in today's times. We all have in ourselves the stories we live and the ones our ancestors passed on to us. We have also inherited others, often unknowingly. There is a piece of the wild Enkidu in every one of us, a bit of the tyrannical and heroic Gilgamesh, a large piece of Plato's influence, mechanical dreams shared with Descartes, and others. There are the words and deeds of Jesus and the prophets that resonate in our heads from millennia past. They help us make our own life stories and give reason or meaning to our own deeds. And these often unknown parts of our life stories (and the story of our civilization) shine forth and reveal themselves, especially in times of crisis.

We have tried to show the history of want from the very beginnings of Creation in the Old Testament. "Original sin" could also be interpreted in terms of excessive consumption. The ancient Greeks devoted much of their philosophy to economic issues. So did Christianity. Their keywords and principles in the Gospels are of economic or social origin. Thomas Aquinas and others have also contributed greatly to principles that were later attributed to Adam Smith, who elucidated on them at the right time in history. We have tried to study the heritage of the Cartesian scientific approach and have shown highlights of the economics of good and evil in the writings of Bernard Mandeville and Smith.

In the second part of the book, I have tried to show that the riddle of consumption has always been with us, that humans are naturally unnatural, and that we will always strive for more, no matter how much plenty there is around us. That hideous want has been with us since Pandora and Eve, and it is connected to the toils of labor. Even the most ancient civilizations knew what we are—at great pains—(re)discovering today. I have also shown how we have chosen the Hedonists' program (increasing the supply of goods) over the Stoic (decreasing our demand for goods). The quest for self-control is up to us. It is not for nothing that the Old Testament writes that "He who is slow to anger is better than the mighty, and he who rules his spirit, than he who captures a city."[4] Or, as Milton puts it, "He who reigns within himself and rules his passions, desires, and fears is more than a king."[5]

Living on the Edge

It appears that contemporary economics (and also some economic policy based on it) should leave some new ideas behind and—on the other hand—return to many of the old ideas. It should abandon the persistent dissatisfaction, artificially created social-economic shortcomings, while it should rediscover the role of sufficiency, resting, and gratitude for what we have. And, by the way, we really do have a lot; from a material-economic standpoint the most in the history of Western Greek-Jewish-Christian civilization ... or any civilization known to ever walk this planet. We should therefore leave behind this material daintiness and the excessive emphasis on the happiness material prosperity can provide. The reason for this rethinking is that economic policy following material goals inherently leads to debt. Any economic crisis will become much worse if we are to constantly shoulder the burden of this debt. This burden should be repaid fast—before the next major economic crisis hits our system and finds us unprepared: Having not learned our lesson, and being pampered.

---

4   Proverbs 16:32.
5   Milton, The Poetical Works of Milton, 106.

Those who constantly live on the edge should not be surprised when that edge cuts. Those who cut the (competitive) edge should not complain when that edge cuts them. Those who fly too high and too close to the sun, like the fabled Icarus, cannot be surprised when their wings sometimes melt; the higher he flew, the farther he fell. And we have skated too long on an edge that is very sharp. Skating and flying moderately were not enough for us; perhaps the time has come to return to safer and more pleasant altitudes.

There's a song that says that rules and laws are created by lawyers and poets. Poets (in the wider meaning of the term) give rules meaning and spirit; lawyers give them form and letter. Similarly, we may say that a great economist can be either an outstanding mathematician or an excellent philosopher. It seems to me that we have given lawyers and mathematicians too large a role at the expense of poets and philosophers. We have exchanged too much wisdom for exactness, too much humanity for mathematization. It brings to mind an extremely detailed ivory tower, but one that has its foundations built on sand. It goes without saying that one parable speaks of how a wise builder pays more attention to his foundations than to the baroque decorations on the tip-tops of his building's towers. When the rain comes, the cathedral will not fall like a house made of sugar.

we're on the topic of towers, isn't the confusion of scientific language—the inability for understanding between individual scientific fields—also a result of each of the fields climbing up to the highest heights, where it tends to be empty and lonely, leaving the common lowlands empty? Isn't the confused scientific language similar to what happened long ago during the construction of the Tower of Babel? True, staying low to the ground does not offer such a view to a distance, but, on the other hand, this is the place where people live. And isn't it better—as is often said—to be roughly right than precisely wrong?

If we let up on our sophistication and speak clearly and understandably, albeit more simply, we may understand each other more. And we would be more aware of how much these isolated disciplines mutually need each other so that the building would hold together fast.

If I've written about what we should abandon, the question of what to return to should come more easily. The answer appears as follows: Step down from Babylon's ivory tower before the confusion of languages (no one understanding anyone or anything) is completed.

I do not reproach the progress that science has made until now, but as economists, we must constantly repeat what we know and what we do not know—and what we believe. We know much, but there is no doubt that there is ever more of what we still do not know and probably never will. Too happily have we run away from these moral principles, principles on which economics should stand. Economic policy has been set loose, and a deficit psychosis in the form of gigantic debt is the result. Before setting out in search of new horizons, however, it is time for economic retro. Ultimately, if a mathematician reveals an error in a calculation, he does not continue with it. He neither covers up the mistake nor resolves it. He must return to the point where the error occurred, correct it, and then calculate further.

Learning from the crisis appears to be our only hope. Good times are not an appropriate time for scrutiny and reflection, let alone for a substantive change of direction in the original spirit of the word repentance. The truth appears in crisis—frequently in its unpleasant nakedness (the emperor wears no clothes!), but in all its vehemence.

The debt crisis is not just an economic or consumer crisis. It is much deeper and wider. Our era lacks moderation. I am not calling here for a return to nature or to the natural state of things, nor am I urging the denial or rejection of material things. Material things have their role, and are one of many sources of happiness (but not the only one, as we have been acting in recent years). I am calling for us to become aware of our own satiation; I am calling on us to become aware that we must be grateful for what we have. And we really have a lot.

We are so wealthy and strong that we do not have external limits. We have overcome nearly everything, and have long been able to do as we please. The fact that we did not do very much good in recent years with this freedom is a sad realization.

Life Is Elsewhere, in Us

Sometimes it seems to me that our human history can be summarized in the following way: We have to be more and more advanced to enjoy and come to terms with the simple things of life. Our fathers and mothers played with wooden toys—in fact, all generations from time immemorial did—and they were as happy doing so as our children are with their electronics. But wooden toys will not do the trick for our kids anymore—as they did two generations ago. We have to have more and more sophisticated toys, theories, and books to realize and enjoy the simple things and facets of life. Our abstract and technical knowledge seems to be more and more advanced; our understanding of the real life in and around us seems to stay constant.

We all live in stories, be they stories for children or stories for adults. Indeed, life seems to be made of not much else than stories. That's why we like to talk so much: Scientists tell their own stories to each other, and as Roy Weintraub notes, "all theory is autobiography."[6] In stories, we all know, as a child does, that our stories are not a true representation of the world around us, but they have some relevance to it, a connection we can sometimes hardly pinpoint.

Overall this book is an attempt to show that there is a much broader and fascinating story of economics than its mathematical perception. In one way, perhaps this book represents an ineloquent attempt to point out

---

[6] Weintraub, How Economics Became a Mathematical Science, 6.

the soul of the economy and economics, their animal spirits. And, like every soul, this one needs to be attended to, cared for, and nurtured. The economy has a soul, one we should not lose—and one that we should know about and appreciate it before we go on to make our claims about the external world.

This book has also tried to be an antithesis to the prevailing wanna-be value-free, zero-moral, positivistic, and descriptive-looking economics. There are many more normative elements in economics than we are ready to admit and to work with.

This book has attempted to offer a counterbalance to the reductionist, analytical, and mathematical model–based approach to economics. It also makes a limited attempt to offer a deeper connection and more points of communication with other fields—philosophy, theology, anthropology, history, culture, psychology, sociology, and others. In fact, I have attempted to show that there is much more of all of the above than mathematics and analytics behind our models, that mathematics is just the visible tip of the iceberg of economics and that the rest of the problem is much softer, more mystical, and does not offer itself easily to deterministic model-building. In fact, I am in no way against mathematics, but I wanted to show that it is not as important as we have made it out to be. What economics needs is not more mathematics but more of everything else. I believe that to make economics more relevant, we need more meta-economics. It was often said that ethics and soft skills[7] are the icing on the cake of mathematical analysis. In this book I have tried to show that it's exactly the other way around: Mathematical analysis is the icing on the cake of a much deeper and wider economic development. And while we should not ignore what the numbers tell us (so, even numbers talk!), we equally cannot ignore all that cannot be modeled. And in most decision making, these seem to be crucial decisions.

Those reading carefully have noticed that this is not a book of answers—but it has tried to offer areas where certain answers might be. This is more of a deconstruction of economics through a historical reconstruction. So in some ways this book has tried to take a step forward with alternative schools of economics and a step backward from the mainstream perception of the economy and economic anthropology. For economists, the question "what do we think a human being is?" has to be rethought. Perhaps we also teach economics in a strange way. Although we are the strongest believers in human freedom of choice, we do not allow students to choose their own school of economic thought; we teach them the mainstream only. After they are safely indoctrinated for a couple of years, only then may they learn of alternative, "heretical" approaches—and a history of their own field. Even the history of economics is often thought of

---

[7] A term used in sociology, marks unique characteristics such as empathy, communicativeness, self-criticism or leadership abilities, etc.

as a display of "trials and errors" of the (stupid and primitive) history before us—before we finally hit the mainstream truth, which the past was so clumsily grasping for. This book tries to take the exactly opposite tack, to take our present state of the art with a grain of salt and take the ideas of our forefathers a bit more seriously.

Let us hope that we will be treated as kindly by our sons and daughters. Wild things are not in the past, in heroic stories and movies, or in distant jungles. They are within us.

Bibliography

Adams, Douglas. *The Hitchhiker's Guide to the Galaxy*. London: Picador, 2002.

Aeschylus. *Prometheus*. Translated by Herbert Weir Smyth. Cambridge, MA: Harvard University Press, 1926.

Akerlof, George A., and Robert J. Shiller. *Animal Spirits: How Human Psychology Drives the Economy, and Why It Matters for Global Capitalism*. Princeton, NJ: Princeton University Press, 2009.

Anzenbaucher, Arno. *Úvod do filozofie* [Introduction to Philosophy]. Prague: Státní pedagogické nakladatelství, 1990.

Aquinas, Thomas. *Contra Gentiles: On the Truth of the Catholic Faith*. Vol. 3, *Providence*. New York: Hanover House, 1955–57.

Aquinas, Thomas. *De Regno: On Kingship, to the King of Cyprus*. Translated by Gerald B. Phelan. Toronto: The Pontifical Institute of Mediaeval Studies, 1949.

Aquinas, Thomas. *The Summa Theologica of St. Thomas Aquinas, Second and Revised Edition*. 2008. http://www.newadvent.org/summa/.

Archibald, Katherine G. "The Concept of Social Hierarchy in the Writings of St. Thomas Aquinas." *Historian* 12, no. 50 (1949–50): 28–54.

Arendt, Hannah. *The Human Condition*. Chicago: University of Chicago Press, 1998.

Argyle, Michael. *The Psychology of Happiness*. London, New York: Methuen, 1987.

Aristophanes. *Ecclesiazusae*. London: Harvard University Press, 1947.

Aristotle. *The Complete Works of Aristotle: The Revised Oxford Translation*. Edited by Jonathan Barnes. Princeton, NJ: Princeton University Press, 1995.

Aristotle. *Nicomachean Ethics*. Translated by T. Irwin. Indianapolis, IN: Hackett Publishing, 1985.

Aristotle. *Nicomachean Ethics*. Translated by W. D. Ross. Oxford: Clarendon Press, 1933.

Augustine. *City of God*. Edinburgh: Eerdmans, 2002. http://etext.lib.virginia.edu/ebooks/.

Augustine. *Confessions*. Translated by Henry Chadwick. New York: Oxford University Press, 1991.

Augustine. *Enchiridion on Faith, Hope, and Love*. Washington, DC: Regnery, 1996.

Balabán, Milan, and Veronika Tydlitátová. *Gilgameš: Mytické drama o hledání věčného života* [Gilgamesh: A Mythic Drama on the Search for Immortality]. Prague: Vyšehrad, 2002.

Bassham, Gregory, and Eric Bronson. *The Lord of the Rings and Philosophy: One Book to Rule Them All*. Chicago: Open Court, 2003.

Bauman, Zygmunt. *Modernity and the Holocaust*. Ithaca, NY: Cornell University, 2000.

Becchio, Giandomenica. *Unexplored Dimensions: Carl Menger on Economics and Philosophy (1923–1938)*. Advances in Austrian Economics, 12. Bradford: Emerald Group Publishing, 2009.

Becker, Gary S. *The Economic Approach to Human Behavior*. Chicago: University of Chicago Press, 1976.

Becker, Gary S. "Milton Friedman." In *Remembering the University of Chicago: Teachers, Scientists and Scholars*, edited by Edward Shils. Chicago: University of Chicago Press, 1991.

Beckett, Samuel. *Waiting for Godot: Tragicomedy in Two Acts*. New York: Grove, 1982.

Bell, Daniel. "The Cultural Contradictions of Capitalism." *Journal of Aesthetic Education* 6, no. 1 (January–April 1972): 11–38.

Berkeley, George. *A Treatise Concerning the Principles of Human Knowledge*. Oxford: Oxford University Press, 1998.

Bhagwati, Jagdish N. *In Defense of Globalization*. Oxford: Oxford University Press, 2007.

Bimson, John J. *The Compact Handbook of Old Testament Life*. Minnapolis, MN: Bethany House, 1998.

Bishop, Matthew. *Economics: An A–Z Guide*. London: Economist, 2009.

Blaug, Mark. *The Methodology of Economics; or, How Economists Explain*. Cambridge: Cambridge University Press, 1980.

Blecha, Ivan. *Filosofická čítanka* [Philosophical Reader]. Olomouc: Nakladatelství Olomouc, 2000.

Boli, John. "The Economic Absorption of the Sacred." In *Rethinking Materialism: Perspectives on the Spiritual Dimension of Economic Behavior*, edited by Robert Wuthnow, 93–117. Grand Rapids, MI: Eerdmans, 1995.

Bonhoeffer, Ditrich. *Ethics*. New York: Touchstone, 1995.

Bourdieu, Pierre. *Outline of a Theory of Practice*. Cambridge, New York: Cambridge University Press, 1977.

Brandon, Samuel G. F. "The Epic of Gilgamesh: A Mesopotamian Philosophy." *History Today* 11, no. 1 (January 1961): 18–27.

Brickman, Philip, Dan Coates, and Ronnie Janoff-Bulman. "Lottery Winners and Accident Victims: Is Happiness Relative?" *Journal of Personality and Social Psychology* 36 (1978): 917–927.

Brookes, Bert B. "Schumacher: Meta-Economics versus the 'Idolatry of Giantism.'" *The School of Cooperative Individualism*. http://www.cooperativeindividualism. org/brookes_on-e-f-schumacher.html (accessed 2010).

Bruni, L. *Civil Happiness: Economics and Human Flourishing in Historical Perspective*. London and New York: Routledge, 2006.

Buber, Martin. *I and Thou*. Translated by Ronald Gregor Smith. Hesperides Press, 2008.

Buchanan, James M. *Economics and the Ethics of Constitutional Order*. Ann Arbor: University of Michigan Press, 1991.

Buckle, Henry Thomas. *History of Civilization in England*. London: Parker and Son, 1857–1861.

Bunt, Lucas N. H., Phillip S. Jones, and Jack D. Bedient. *The Historical Roots of Elementary Mathematics*. New York: Dover, 1988.

Bury, J. B. *The Idea of Progress*. London: Macmillan, 1920.

Caldwell, Bruce J. *Beyond Positivism*. London: Routledge, 1994.

Campbell, Joseph. *The Hero with a Thousand Faces*. 2nd ed. Princeton, NJ: Princeton University Press, 1968.

Campbell, Joseph. *Myths to Live By*. New York: Viking, 1972.

Campbell, Thomas Douglas. *Adam Smith's Science of Morals*. London: Allen & Unwin, 1971.

Čapek, Karel. *R.U.R.: Rossum's Universal Robots*. National Theatre, Prague, Czech Republic, January 25, 1921.

Čapek, Karel. *R.U.R.: Rossum's Universal Robots*. Prague: Aventinum, 1920.

Cheal, David J. *The Gift Economy*. New York: Routledge, 1988.

Chesterton, G. K. *St. Thomas Aquinas*. Middlesex: The Echo Library, 2007.

Chesterton, G. K. *Orthodoxy*. Redford, VA: Wilder Publications, 2008.

Class, Heinrich. *Wenn ich der Kaiser wär: Politische Wahrheifen und Notwendigkeiten*. Leipzig: Weicher, 1912.

Colins, Chuck, and Mary Wright. *The Moral Measure of the Economy*. New York: Orbis Books, 2007.

Comte, Auguste. *Cours de philosophie positive* [Course of Positive Philosophy]. Paris: Bachelier, 1835.

Cox, Steven L., Kendell H. Easley, A. T. Robertson, and John Albert Broadus. *Harmony of the Gospels*. Nashville, TN: Holman Bible, 2007.

Davies, Norman. *Europe: A History*. London: Pimlico, 1997.

Davis, Philip J., and Reuben Hersh: *Descartes' dream: the world according to mathematics*. Boston: Harcourt, Brace, Jovanovich, 1986.

Defoe, Daniel. *The Political History of the Devil (1726)*. Edited by John Mullan and William Robert Owens. London: Pickering and Chatto, 2005.

Descartes, René. *Discourse on the Method; and, Meditations on First Philosophy*. 4th ed. Edited by David Weismann. New Haven, CT: Yale University Press, 1996.

Descartes, René. *Discourse on the Method of Rightly Conducting One's Reason and of Seeking the Truth in the Sciences*. City: Wildside Press, 2008.

Descartes, René. *Meditations on First Philosophy*. Sioux Falls: NuVision, 2007.

Descartes, René. *Principles of Philosophy*. Translated by V. R. Miller and R. P. Miller. Dordrecht: Kluwer Academic, 1984.

Descartes, René. "Treatise on Man." In *The Philosophical Writings of Descartes*, edited by Dugald Murdoch, John Cottingham, and Robert Stoothoff. Cambridge: University of Cambridge, 1985.

Detienne, Marcel. *The Masters of Truth in Archaic Greece*. New York: Zone Books, 1999.

Diamond, Jared. *Why Is Sex Fun? The Evolution of Human Sexuality*. New York: Basic Books, 2006.

Diderot, Denis. *Diderot's Selected Writings*. Edited by Lester G. Crocker. Translated by Derek Coltman. New York: Macmillan, 1966.

Diener, E., J. Horowitz, and R. A. Emmons. "Happiness of the Very Wealthy." *Social Indicators Research* 16 (April 1985): 263–274.

Dixit, Avinash K., and Barry Nalebuff. *Thinking Strategically: The Competitive Edge in Business, Politics, and Everyday Life*. New York: Norton, 1991.

Durkheim, Emile. *The Division of Labor in Society*. Translated by George Simpson. New York: Free Press, 1947.

Eagletton, Terry. *On Evil*. Yale University Press, 2010.

Eckstein, Walther. *Theorie der ethischen Gefühle*. Leipzig: Meiner, 1926.

Edmonds, Dave, and John Eidinow. *Wittgenstein's Poker*. New York: Ecco, 2001.

Eliade, Mircea. *Cosmos and History: The Myth of the Eternal Return*. New York: Harper Torchbooks, 1959.

Eliade, Mircea. *The Myth of the Eternal Return*. London: Routledge & Kegan Paul, 1955.

Eliade, Mircea. *The Sacred and the Profane: The Nature of Religion*. New York: Harcourt Brace, 1959.

Elster, Jon. *Nuts and Bolts for the Social Sciences*. Cambridge: Cambridge University Press, 1989.

Emmer, Michele. *Mathematics and Culture*. Berlin, Heidelberg, New York: Springer-Verlag, 2004.

Epicuros. *Principal Doctrines. Epicurus & Epicurean Philosophy*, 1996. http://www.epicurus.net/en/principal.html.

Epicurus. *Principal Doctrines*. Translated by Robert Drew Hicks. The Internet Classics Archive, 1925. http://classics.mit.edu/Epicurus/princdoc.html.

Estes, Clarissa Pinkola. *Women Who Run with the Wolves*. New York: Ballantine Books, 2003.

Etzioni, *Amitai. Moral Dimension: Toward a New Economics*. New York: Free Press, 1988.

Fajkus, Břetislav. *Současná filosofie a metodologie* [Philosophy and the Methodology of Science]. Prague: Filosofický ústav AV ČR, 1997.

Falckenberg, Richard, and Charles F. Drake. *History of Modern Philosophy: From Nicolas of Cusa to the Present Time*. Translated by A. C. Armstrong. New York: Kessinger, 1893.

Ferguson, Niall. *The Ascent of Money: A Financial History of the World*. New York: Penguin Press, 2008.

Ferguson, Niall. *The War of the World: Twentieth-Century Conflict and the Descent of the West*. New York: Penguin, 2006.

Feyerabend, Paul K. *Against Method*. 3rd ed. London, New York: Verso, 1993.

Fisher, Irving. "Fisher Sees Stocks Permanently High." *New York Times*, October 16, 1929, 2.

Fitzgerald, Allan, John C. Cavadini, Marianne Djuth, James J. O'Donnell, and Frederick Van Fleteren, eds. *Augustine through the Ages: An Encyclopedia*. Grand Rapids, MI: Eerdmans, 1999.

Force, Pierre. *Self-Interest before Adam Smith: A Genealogy of Economic Science*. Cambridge: Cambridge University Press, 2003.

Fox, Justin. *The Myth of Rational Markets*. New York: Harper Business, 2009.

Frank, Robert. Conference on "Understanding Quality of Life: Scientific Perspectives on Enjoyment and Suffering," Princeton, NJ, November 1–3, 1996.

Frankel, Viktor E. *Man's Search for Meaning*. London: Hodder and Stoughton, 1964.

Frazer, James George. *The Golden Bough: A Study in Magic and Religion*. New York: Oxford University Press, 1994.

Friedman, Milton. *Essays in Positive Economics*. Chicago, London: University of Chicago Press, 1970.

Fromm, Erich. *To Have or to Be*. New York, London: Continuum, 2007.

Fukuyama, Francis. *The Trust: The Social Virtues and the Creation of Prosperity*. New York: Free Press, 1996.

Gadamer, Hans-Georg. *The Idea of the Good in Platonic-Aristotelian Philosophy*. New Haven, CT. Yale University Press, 1988.

Gaede, Erwin A. *Politics and Ethics: Machiavelli to Niebuhr*. Lanham, MD: University Press of America, 1983.

Gaiman, Neil, and Terry Pratchett. *Good Omens: The Nice and Accurate Prophecies of Agnes Nutter, Witch*. London: Viktor Gollancz, 1990.

Galbraith, John Kenneth. *The Affluent Society*. Boston: Houghton Mifflin, 1958.
Galbraith, John Kenneth. *The Affluent Society*. Boston: Houghton Mifflin, 1998.
Galileo, Galilei. *Dialogues concerning the Two Great Systems of the World*. Translated by Stilman Drake. Ann Arbor: University of Michigan Press, 1970.
George, Andrew R. *The Babylonian Gilgamesh Epic: Introduction, Critical Edition and Cuneiform Texts*. Oxford: Oxford University Press, 2003.
Goethe, Johann W. *Goethe's Faust*. Translated by Walter Kauffman. New York: Anchor Books, 1961.
Graeber, David. *Toward an Anthropological Theory of Value*. New York: Palgrave, 2001.
Green, David. "Adam Smith a sociologie ctnosti a svobody [Adam Smith and the Sociology of Virtue and Freedom]." *Prostor* 7, no. 28 (1994): 41–48.
Groenewegen, John. *Transaction Cost Economics and Beyond*. Recent Economic Thought. Boston: Kluwer, 1995.
Groenewegen, Peter. *A Soaring Eagle: Alfred Marshall, 1842–1924*. Aldershot, UK: Edward Elgar, 1995.
Halík, Tomáš. *Stromu zbývá naděje. Krize jako šance* [There is Hope. Crisis as an Opportunity]. Praha: Nakladatelství Lidové noviny, 2009.
Hall, Joseph. *Heaven upon Earth and Characters of Virtues and Vice*. Edited by Rudolf Kirk. New Brunswick, NJ: Rutgers University Press, 1948.
Halteman, Richard J. "Is Adam Smith's Moral Philosophy an Adequate Foundation for the Market Economy?" *Journal of Markets and Morality* 6 (2003): 453–478.
Haney, Lewis Henry. *History of Economic Thought: A Critical Account of the Origin and Development of the Economic Theories of the Leading Thinkers in the Leading Nations*. New York: Macmillan, 1920.
Hare, M. R., J. Barnes, and H. Chadwick. *Zakladatelé myšlení: Platón, Aristoteles, Augustinus* [Founders of Thought: Plato, Aristotle, Augustine]. Prague: Svoboda, 1994.
Harris, H. S. *The Reign of the Whirlwind*. York Space, 1999. http://hdl.handle.net/10315/918.
Harth, Phillip. Introduction to "The Fable of the Bees; or, Private Vices, Public Benefits," by Bernard Mandeville.
Hasbach, Wilhelm. *Untersuchungen über Adam Smith und die Entwicklung der Politischen Ökonomie*. Leipzig: Duncker und Humblot, 1891.
Hayek, Friedrich A. *Law, Legislation, and Liberty*. London: Routledge and Kegan Paul, 1973.
Hayek, Friedrich A. *New Studies in Philosophy, Politics, Economics, and the History of Ideas*. London: Routledge and Kegan Paul, 1978.
Hayek, Friedrich A. *The Trend of Economic Thinking: Essays on Political Economists and Economic Thinking*. Vol. 3. Edited by W. W. Bartley and Stephen Kresge. London: Routledge, 1991.
Hayter, David, and Alex Tse. *Watchmen*. Directed by Zack Synder. Produced by Warner Bros. Pictures. 2009.
Heffernanová, Jana. *Gilgameš: Tragický model západní civilizace* [Gilgamesh: A Tragic Model of Western Civilization]. Prague: Společnost pro Světovou literaturu, 1996.
Heffernanová, Jana. *Tajemství dvou partnerů: Teorie a metodika práce se sny* [The Secret of Two Partners]. Prague: Argo, 2008.
Heidegger, Martin. *Philosophical and Political Writings*. Edited by Manfred Stassen. New York: Continuum, 2003.

Heidel, Alexander. *The Gilgamesh Epic and Old Testament Parallels.* Chicago: University of Chicago Press, 1949.

Heilbroner, Robert L. *The Wordly Philosophers: The Lives, Times, and Ideas of Great Economic Thinkers.* New York: Simon and Schuster, 1953.

Hejdánek, Ladislav. "Básník a Slovo [Poet and the Word]." In *České studie: Literatura, Jazyk, Kultura* [Czech Studies: Literature, Language, Culture], edited by Mojmír Grygar, 57–81. Amsterdam, Atlanta: Rodopi, 1990.

Heller, Jan. *Jak orat s čertem: kázání* [How to Plow with the Devil]. Prague: Kalich, 2006.

Hendry, David F. "Econometrics: Alchemy or Science?" *Economica* 47 (1980): 387–406.

Hengel, Martin. *Judentum und Hellenismus.* Tubingen: Mohr, 1969.

Henry, Matthew. *Matthew Henry's Commentary on the Whole Bible.* http://www.apostolic-churches.net/bible/mhc/.

Hesiod. *Works and Days. In Hesiod: Theogony, Works and Days, Testimonia,* edited by Glenn W. Most. Cambridge, MA: Harvard University Press, 2006.

Hesiod. *Theogony.* In *Hesiod: Theogony, Works and Days, Testimonia,* edited by Glenn W. Most. Cambridge, MA: Harvard University Press, 2006.

Hildebrand, Bruno. *Die Nationalökonomie der Gegenwart und Zukunft.* Frankfurt am Main: Erster Band, 1848.

Hill, Roger B. *Historical Context of the Work Ethic.* Athens: University of Georgia, 1996.

Hirsch, Fred. *Social Limits to Growth.* 1st ed. Cambridge, MA: Harvard University Press, 1976.

Hirschman, Albert O. *The Passion and the Interests: Political Arguments for Capitalism before Its Triumph.* Princeton, NJ: Princeton University Press, 1997.

Hobbes, Thomas. *Leviathan.* Oxford: Oxford University Press, 1996.

Horsley, Richard A. *Covenant Economics.* Louisville: Westminster John Knox, 2009.

Hume, David. *Selections.* Edited by Charles William Hendel. New York, Chicago: C. Scribner's Sons, 1927.

Hume, David. *A Treatise on Human Nature.* NuVision Publications, 2008. http://www.nuvisionpublications.com.

Hume, David. *Enquiries Concerning the Human Understanding and Concerning the Principles of Morals.* Oxford: Clarendon Press, 1902.

Hurtado-Prieto, Jimena. *Adam Smith and the Mandevillean Heritage: The Mercantilist Foundations of "Dr. Mandeville's Licentious System."* Preliminary version. February 2004. Available at http://phare.univ-paris1.fr/hurtado/Adam%20Smith.pdf

Husserl, Edmund. *Cartesian Meditations.* London: Nijhoff, 1977.

Huxley, Aldous. *Brave New World.* New York: Harper, 1958.

Inglehart, Ronald. *Culture Shift: In Advanced Industrial Society.* Princeton, NJ: Princeton University Press, 1990.

Inglehart, Ronald. *World Values Survey.* 2009. http://www.worldvaluessurvey.org/ (accessed 2010).

Irwin, William, ed. *The Matrix and Philosophy: Welcome to the Desert of the Real.* Illinois: Carus Publishing Company, 2002.

Johnston, Louis D., and Samuel H. Williamson. *What Was the U.S. GDP Then?* 2008. http://www.measuringworth.org/usgdp/ (accessed 2010).

Jung, Carl G. "The Archetypes and the Collective Unconscious." In *The Archetypes and the Collective Unconscious: The Collected Works*, edited by R. F. C. Hull. Princeton, NJ: Princeton University Press, 1990.

Jung, Carl G. *Psychology and Religion*. New Haven, CT: Yale University Press, 1962.

Jung, Carl G. *Výbor z díla VIII – Hrdina a archetyp matky* [Collected works vol. 8 – Hero and the Archetype of a Mother]. Prague: Nakladatelství Tomáše Janečka – Emitos, 2009.

Kahn, Charles H. *Plato and the Socratic Dialogue*. Cambridge: Cambridge University Press, 1996.

Kalenská, Renata. "Někdy se mě zmocňuje pocit . . ." *Lidové Noviny*, November 15, 2008. http://www.lidovky.cz/nekdy-se-me-zmocnuje-pocit-dca-/ln_noviny. asp?c=A081115_000040_ln_noviny_sko&klic=228612&mes=081115_0.

Kant, Immanuel. *Critique of Judgment*. Indianapolis: Hackett, 1987.

Kant, Immanuel. *Introduction to the Metaphysics of Morals*. Whitefish, MT: Kessinger, 2004.

Kant, Immanuel. *Religion within the Limits of Reason Alone*. New York: Harper & Brothers, 1960.

Kant, Immanuel. *The Metaphysical Elements of Ethics*. Rockville: Arc Manor, 2008.

Kaye, B. Introduction to *The Fable of the Bees*, by Bernard Mandeville. Oxford: Clarendon Press, 1924.

Kerényi, Karl. *Gods of the Greeks*. London: Thames & Hudson, 1980.

Kerkhof, Bert. "A Fatal Attraction? Smith's 'Theory of Moral Sentiments' and Mandeville's 'fable.'" *History of Moral Thought* 16, no. 2 (1995): 219–233.

Keynes, John Maynard. *Collected Writings of John Maynard Keynes*. Edited by Austin Robinson and Donald Moggridge. London: Macmillan for the Royal Economic Society, 1971–89.

Keynes, John Maynard. "Economic Possibilities for Our Grandchildren." In *Essays in Persuasion*, edited by John Maynard Keynes, 358–373. New York: W. W. Norton, 1930.

Keynes, John Maynard. *Essays in Persuasion*. New York: W. W. Norton, 1963.

Keynes, John Maynard. *First Annual Report of the Arts Council (1945–1946)*. http:// www.economicshelp.org/blog/economics/quotes-by-john-maynard-keynes/

Keynes, John Maynard. *General Theory of Employment, Interest, and Money*. London: Macmillan, 1936.

Kierkegaard, Sören. *Concluding Unscientific Postscript to Philosophical Fragments*. Edited by Charles Moore. Rifton, NY: Plough, 1999.

Kirk, G. S., J. E. Raven, and M. Schofield. *The Presocratic Philosophers*. Cambridge: Cambridge University Press, 1983.

Kirk, Rudolf, ed. *Heaven upon Earth and Characters of Virtues and Vices*, by Joseph Hall. New Brunswick, NJ: Rutgers University Press, 1948.

Kline, Morris. *Mathematical Thought from Ancient to Modern Times*. New York: Oxford University Press, 1972.

Kmenta, Jan. Review of *A Guide to Econometrics*, by Peter Kennedy. *Business Economics* 39, no. 2, April 2004.

Knies, Carl G. A. *Die Politische Oekonomie vom Standpunkte der geschichtlichen Methode*. Braunschweig: C. A. Schwetsche und Sohn, 1853.

Knight, Frank Hyneman. "Liberalism and Christianity." In *The Economic Order and Religion*, edited by Frank Hyneman Knight and Thornton Ward Merrian. New York, London: Harper & Brothers, 1945.

Knight, Frank Hyneman. *Freedom and Reform: Essays in Economics and Social Philosophy*. New York: Harper & Brothers, 1947.

Kolman, Vojtěch. *Filozofie čísla* [The Philosophy of Numbers]. Prague: Nakladatelství Filosofického ústavu AV ČR, 2008.

Komárek, Stanislav. *Obraz člověka a přírody v zrcadle biologie* [Image of Man and Nature in the Mirror of Biology]. Prague: Academia, 2008.

Kratochvíl, Zdeněk. *Filosofie mezi mýtem a vědou od Homéra po Descarta* [Philosophy between Myth and Science from Homer to Descartes]. Prague: Academia, 2009.

Kratochvíl, Zdeněk. *Mýtus, filosofie, věda I. a II. (Filosofie mezi Homérem a Descartem)* [Myth, Philosophy, and Science]. Prague: Michal Jůza & Eva Jůzová, 1996.

Kugel, James L. *The Bible as It Was*. 5th ed. Cambridge, MA: Belknap Press, 2001.

Kuhn, Thomas S. *The Structure of Scientific Revolutions*. Chicago: University of Chicago Press, 1969.

Kundera, Milan. *Immortality*. New York: Perennial Classics, 1999.

Kundera, Milan. *Laughable Loves*. London: Faber, 1999.

Lacan, Jacques. *The Four Fundamental Concepts of Psycho-Analysis*. London: W.W. Norton, 1998.

Lacan, Jacques. "The Signification of the Phallus." In *EcritÉcrits: A Selection*, translated by Alan Sheridan, 311–323. London: Tavistock/Routledge, 1977.

Lalouette, Claire. *Ramessova říše—Vláda jedné dynastie*, Prague: Levné knihy, 2009 [in original *L'empire de Ramsès*. Paris: Fayard, 1985].

Lanman, Scott, and Steve Matthews. "Greenspan Concedes to 'Flaw' in His Market Ideology." *Bloomberg*, October 23, 2008. http://www.bloomberg.com/apps/ne ws?pid=newsarchive&sid=ah5qh9Up4rIg.

Leacock, Stephen. *Hellements of Hickonomics, in Hiccoughs of Verse Done in Our Social Planning Mill*. New York: Dodd, Mead, 1936.

Leontief, W. "Theoretical Assumptions and Nonobserved Facts." *American Economic Review* 61 (1971): 1–7.

Levin, Samuel M. "Malthus and the Idea of Progress." *Journal of the History of Ideas* 27, no. 1 (January–March 1966): 92–108.

Lévi-Strauss, Claude. *Myth and Meaning: Cracking the Code of Culture*. London: Schocken, 1995.

Lévi-Strauss, Claude. *The Elementary Structures of Kingship*. Edited by R. Needham, J. Harle Bell, and J. R. von Sturmer. Boston: Beacon, 1969.

Lewis, Clive Staples. "Evolutionary Hymn." In *Poems*, 55–56. San Diego: Harcourt, 1964.

Lewis, Clive Staples. *The Four Loves*. New York: Harcourt Brace Jovanovich, 1960.

Lewis, Clive Staples. *Letters of C. S. Lewis*. Edited by W. H. Lewis. New York: Harcourt, Brace & World, 1966.

Lewis, Clive Staples. *A Preface to Paradise Lost*. New Delhi: Atlantic Publishers and Distributors, 2005.

Lewis, Clive Staples. *The Weight of Glory and Other Addresses*. 2nd ed. New York: Macmillan, 1980.

Lewis, Thomas J. "Persuasion, Domination, and Exchange: Adam Smith on Political Consequences of Markets." *Canadian Journal of Political Science* 33, no. 2 (June 2000): 273–289.

Liddell, H. G., and R. Scott. *Greek-English Lexicon*. 9th ed. Oxford: Clarendon, 1996.

Limentani, Ludovico. *La morale della simpatia: Saggio sopra l'etica di Adamo Smith nella storia del pensiero inglese*. Genova: A. F. Formíggini, 1914.

Locke, John. *Two Treatises of Government*. Cambridge: Cambridge University Press, 2003.

Lowry, S. Todd. "Ancient and Medieval Economics." In *A Companion to the History of Economic Thought*, edited by Warren J. Samuels, Jeff Biddle, and John Bryan Davis, 11–27. Oxford: Blackwell Publishing, 2003.

Lowry, S. Todd. *The Archaeology of Economic Ideas: The Classical Greek Tradition*. Durham, NC: Duke University Press, 1988.

Lowry, S. Todd. "The Economic and Jurisprudential Ideas of the Ancient Greeks: Our Heritage from Hellenic Thought." In *Ancient and Medieval Economic Ideas and Concepts of Social Justice*, edited by S. Todd Lowry, and Barry Gordon. New York: Brill, 1998.

Lowry, S. Todd, and Barry Gordon, eds. *Ancient and Medieval Economic Ideas and Concepts of Social Justice*. New York: Brill, 1998.

Luther, Martin. "Martin Luther's Last Sermon in Wittenberg, Second Sunday in Epiphany, 17 January 1546." In *Dr. Martin Luthers Werke: Kritische Gesamtausgabe*, 51–126. Weimar: Herman Boehlaus Nachfolger, 1914.

Macfie, Alec L. "The Invisible Hand of Jupiter." *Journal of the History of Ideas* 32 (October–December 1971): 595–599.

Macfie, Alec L. *The Individual in Society*. London: Allen & Unwin, 1967.

MacIntyre, Alasdair. *After Virtue*. 3rd ed. Notre Dame, IN: University of Notre Dame Press, 2008.

MacIntyre, Alasdair. *A Short History of Ethics: A History of Moral Philosophy from the Homeric Age to the Twentieth Century*. London: Routledge & Kegan Paul, 1998.

Mahan, Asa. *A Critical History of Philosophy*. New York: Phillips & Hunt, 2002.

Malthus, Thomas. *An Essay on the Principle of Population*. Oxford: Oxford University Press, 2008.

Mandeville, Bernard. *A Letter to Dion*. The Project Gutenberg. http://www.gutenberg.org/files/29478/29478-h/29478-h.htm.

Mandeville, Bernard. "An Essay on Charity, and Charity-Schools." In Mandeville, *The Fable of the Bees*. Middlesex: Penguin, 1970.

Mandeville, Bernard. *The Fable of the Bees; or, Private Vices, Public Benefits*. Edited by Phillip Harth. Oxford: Clarendon Press, 1924; and later version Middlesex: Penguin, 1970.

Mankiw, Gregory N. *Principles of Economics*. Mason, GA: South-Western Cengage Learning, 2009.

Marshall, Alfred. *Principles of Economics*. London: Macmillan for the Royal Economic Society, 1961.

Martindale, Wayne, and Jerry Root, eds. *The Quotable Lewis: An Encyclopedic Selection of Quotes from the Complete Published Works*. Wheaton, IL: Tyndale, 1989.

Marx, Karl. *Capital*. Vol. 1. Edited by Ben Fowkes. London: Penguin, 1990.

Marx, Karl. *On the Jewish Question*. Edited by Helen Lederer. Cincinnati: Hebrew Union College–Jewish Institute of Religion, 1958.

Marx, Karl, and Friedrich Engels. *Manifesto of the Communist Party*. New York: Cosimo, 2009.

Mauss, Marcel. *The Gift: Forms and Functions of Exchange in Archaic Societies*. London: Cohen & West, 1966.

McCloskey, Deirdre N. *The Bourgeois Virtues: Ethics for an Age of Commerce.* Chicago: University of Chicago Press, 2006.

McCloskey, Deirdre N. "The Rhetoric of Economics." *Journal of Economic Literature* 21 (June 1983): 481–517.

McCloskey, Deirdre N. *The Secret Sins of Economics.* Chicago: Prickly Paradigm Press, 2002.

Merton, Robert K. *Social Theory and Social Structure.* New York: Free Press, 1968.

Mill, John Stuart. *Autobiography.* The Harvard Classics, 25. Edited by C. E. Norton. New York: Collier & Son, 1909.

Mill, John Stuart. *Collected Works of John Stuart Mill. Vol. 10, Essays on Ethics, Religion, and Society.* Edited by John M. Robson. London: Routledge and Kegan Paul, 1979.

Mill, John Stuart. *Essays on Some Unsettled Questions of Political Economy.* London: Parker, 1844.

Mill, John Stuart. *Utilitarianism.* Forgotten books, 2008. www.forgottenbooks.org.

Mill, John Stuart. *Principles of Political Economy: With Some of Their Applications to Social Philosophy.* Edited, with an Introduction, by Stephen Nathanson. Indianapolis, IN: Hackett, 2004.

Mini, Piero V. *Philosophy and Economics: The Origins and Development of Economic Theory.* Gainesville: University Presses of Florida, 1974.

Mirowsky, Philip. *Machine Dreams: Economics Becomes a Cyborg Science.* Cambridge: Cambridge University Press, 2002.

Mirowsky, Philip. *More Heat Than Light: Economics as a Social Physics, Physics as Nature's Economics.* Cambridge: Cambridge University Press, 1989.

Mises, Ludwig van. *Human Action: A Treatise on Economics.* 4th ed. Edited by Bettina Bien Graves. Irvington-on-Hudson, NY: Foundation for Economic Education, 1996.

Mlčoch, Lubomír. *Ekonomie důvěry a společného dobra* [Economic Trust and the Common Good]. Prague: Karolinum, 2006.

Montesquieu, Charles de Secondat. *Spirit of Laws.* Edited by Anne M. Cohler, Basia Carolyn Miller, and Harold Samuel Stone. Cambridge: Cambridge University Press, 1989.

Morrow, Glenn R. "Adam Smith: Moralist and Philosopher." *Journal of Political Economy* 35 (June 1927): 321–342.

Muchembled, Robert. *A History of the Devil: From the Middle Ages to the Present.* Cambridge, UK: Polity, 2003.

Mumford, Lewis. *The City in History: Its Origins, Its Transformations, and Its Prospects.* San Diego, New York, London: Harcourt, 1961.

Myers, David G. "Does Economic Growth Improve Human Morale?" *New American Dream.* http://www.newdream.org/newsletter/growth.php (accessed 2010).

Nelson, Robert H. *Economics as Religion: From Samuelson to Chicago and Beyond.* University Park: Pennsylvania University Press, 2001.

Nelson, Robert H. *Reaching for Heaven on Earth: The Theological Meaning of Economics.* Savage, MD: Rowman & Littlefield, 1991.

Nelson, Robert H. *The New Holy Wars: Economic Religion vs. Environmental Religion in Contemporary America.* Pennsylvania: Pennsylvania State University Press, 2010.

Neubauer, Zdeněk. *O čem je věda? (De possest: O duchovním bytí Božím)* [What Is Science About?]. 1st ed. Prague: Malvern, 2009.

Neubauer, Zdeněk. *Přímluvce postmoderny* [Advocate of Postmodernity]. Prague: Michal Jůza & Eva Jůzová, 1994.

Neubauer, Zdeněk. *Respondeo dicendum: autosborník k desátému výročí padesátých narozenin [Respondeo dicendum: In Honor of Tenth Anniversary of Fiftieth Birthday]*, 2 ed. Edited by Jiří Fiala. Prague: O. P. S., 2002.

New International Version of the Holy Bible. Grandville, MI: Zondervan, 2001.

Nin, Anais. *The Diary of Anais Nin, 1939–1944*. New York: Harcourt, Brace & World, 1969.

Nisbet, Robert A. *The History of the Idea of Progress*. New Brunswick, NJ: Transaction, 1998.

Nisbet, Robert A. "The Idea of Progress." In *Literature of Liberty: A Review of Contemporary Liberal Thought* 2 (1979): 7–37. Available at http://oll.libertyfund.org.

Novak, Michael. *The Catholic Ethic and the Spirit of Capitalism*. New York: Free Press, 1993.

Novak, Michael. *Duch demokratického kapitalismu* [The Spirit of Democratic Capitalism]. Prague: Občanský Institut, 2002.

Novotný, Adolf. *Biblický slovník* [Biblical Dictionary]. Prague: Kalich, 1992.

Novotný, František. *The Posthumous Life of Plato*. Prague: Academia, 1977.

Nussbaum, Martha C. *The Fragility of Goodness: Luck and Ethics in Greek Tragedy and Philosophy*. New York: Zone Books, 1999.

Oates, Whitney J., and Eugene O'Neill. *The Complete Greek Drama*. New York: Random House, 1938.

O'Connor, Eugene Michael. The Essential Epicurus: Letters, Principal Doctrines, Vatican Sayings, and Fragments. Buffalo, NY: Prometheus, 1993.

Oncken, August. "The Consistency of Adam Smith." *The Economic Journal* 7 (September 1897): 443–450.

Orwell, George. *1984*. New York: Signet, 1981.

Palahniuk, Chuck. *Fight Club*. Directed by David Fincher. Produced by 20th Century Fox. 1999.

Palahniuk, Chuck. *Fight Club*. New York: Henry Holt, 1996.

Pascal, Blaise. *Pensées*. New York: Penguin Classics, 1995.

Pass, Christopher, Bryan Lowes, and Leslie Davies. *Collins Dictionary of Economics, Second Edition*. Glasgow: HarperCollins, 1993.

Pasquinelli, Matteo. *Animal Spirits: A Bestiary of the Commons*. Rotterdam: NAi Publishers, 2008.

Patinkin, Don. *Essays on and in the Chicago Tradition*. Durham, NC: Duke University Press, 1981.

Patočka, Jan. *Kacířské eseje o filosofii dějin* [Heretical Essays in the Philosophy of History]. Prague: OIKOYMENH, 2007.

Patterson, Stephen, and Marvin Meyer. *The "Scholars' Translation" of the Gospel of Thomas*. http://home.epix.net/~miser17/Thomas.html.

Pava, Moses L. "The Substance of Jewish Business Ethics." *Journal of Business Ethics* 17, no. 6 (April 1998): 603–617.

Payne, Jan. *Odkud zlo?* [Whence Evil?]. Prague: Triton, 2005.

Penguin Classics. *The Epic of Gilgamesh*. Translated by N. K. Sandars. London, New York: Penguin Group, 1972.

Pieper, Thomas J. *Guide to Thomas Aquinas*. Notre Dame, IN: University of Notre Dame Press, 1987.

Pirsig, Robert M. *Zen and the Art of Motorcycle Maintenance*. Toronto, New York, London: Bantam Books, 1976.

Plato. *Complete Works*. Edited by J. M. Cooper and D. S. Hutchinson. Cambridge: Hackett, 1997.

Polanyi, Karl. "Aristotle Discovers the Economy." In *Primitive, Archaic, and Modern Economies: Essays of Karl Polanyi*, edited by Karl Polanyi and George Dalton, 78–115. Boston: Beacon Press, 1971.

Polanyi, Michael. *Personal Knowledge: Towards a Post-Critical Philosophy*. London: Routledge & Kegan Paul, 1962.

Pope, Alexander. "The Riddle of the World." In *Selected Poetry and Prose*, edited by Robin Sowerby, 153–154. London: Routledge, 1988.

Popper, Karl. *The Open Society and Its Enemies*. New York: Routledge, 2003.

Popper, Karl. *The Poverty of Historicism*. London, New York: Routledge & Kegan Paul, 1957.

Punt, Jeremy. "The Prodigal Son and *Blade Runner*: Fathers and Sons, and Animosity." *Journal of Theology for Southern Africa* 119 (July 2007): 86–103.

Radin, Paul. *The Trickster: A Study in American Indian Mythology*. London: Routledge & Kegan Paul, 1956.

Rádl, Emanuel. *Dějiny Filosofie: Starověk a středověk* [History of Philosophy: Ancient and Medieval]. Prague: Votobia, 1998.

Raphael, David D. *The Impartial Spectator: Adam Smith's Moral Philosophy*. Oxford: Oxford University Press, 2007.

Rawls, John. *Lectures on the History of Moral Philosophy*. Cambridge: Harvard University Press, 2000.

Redman, Deborah A. *Economics and the Philosophy of Science*. Oxford: Oxford University Press, 1993.

Rich, Arthur. *Business and Economic Ethics: The Ethics of Economic Systems*. 4th ed. Leuven, Belgium: Peeters, 2006.

Rich, Arthur. *Wirtschaftsethik*. Gütersloh: Mohn, 1984–1990.

Roll, Erich. *A History of Economic Thought*. 3rd ed. Englewood Cliffs, NJ: Prentice Hall, 1964.

Rothbard, Murray N. *Economic Thought before Adam Smith: Austrian Perspectives on the History of Economic Thought*. Vol. 1. Cheltenham, UK: Edward Elgar, 1995.

Rousseau, Jean-Jacques. *Discourse on the Origin of Inequality*. Oxford: Oxford University Press, 1994.

Rushdie, Salman. *Fury: A Novel*. Toronto: Vintage Canada, 2002.

Russell, Bertrand. *Mysticism and Logic and Other Essays*. London, New York: Longmans, Green, 1918.

Sallust. *On the Gods and the World*. Translated by Thomas Taylor. Whitefish, MT: Kessinger, 2003 [1793].

Schor, Juliet B. *The Overworked American: The Unexpected Decline of Leisure*. New York: Basic Books, 1993.

Schumacher, Fritz Ernst. *Small Is Beautiful: Economics as if People Mattered*. London: Vintage Books, 1993.

Schumpeter, Joseph A. *Business Cycles: A Theoretical, Historical, and Statistical Analysis of the Capitalist Process*. New York, Toronto, London: McGraw-Hill, 1939.

Schumpeter, Joseph A. "The Common Sense of Econometrics." *Econometrica* 1, no.1 (1933): 5–12.

Schumpeter, Joseph A. *History of Economic Analysis*. London: Routledge, 2006.

Scitovsky, Tibor. *The Joyless Economy: The Psychology of Human Satisfaction*. New York: Oxford University Press, 1992.

Sedláček, Tomáš. "Spontaneous Rule Creation." In *Cultivation of Financial Markets in the Czech Republic*, edited by Michal Mejstřík, 317–339. Prague: Karolinum, 2004.

Sen, Amartya Kumar. *On Ethics and Economics*. Oxford: Blackwell, 1987.

Shakespeare, William. *The Merchant of Venice*. First Folio. 1623.

Shaw, George B. *Man and Superman*. Rockvill: Wildside Press, 2008.

Shils, Edward. *Remembering the University of Chicago: Teachers, Scientists, and Scholars*. Chicago: University of Chicago Press, 1991.

Shionoya, Yuichi. *Schumpeter and the Idea of Social Science: A Metatheoretical Study*. Cambridge: Cambridge University Press, 2007.

Sigmund, Paul E., ed. *St. Thomas Aquinas on Politics and Ethics*. New York: W. W. Norton, 1987.

Simmel, Georg. *Peníze v moderní kultuře a jiné eseeje* [Money in Modern Culture]. 2nd ed. Edited by Otakar Vochoč. Prague: Sociologické nakladatelství, 2006.

Simmel, Georg. *The Philosophy of Money*. London: Routledge and Kegan Paul, 1978.

Simmel, Georg. *Simmel on Culture: Selected Writings*. Edited by David Frisby, and Mike Featherstone. Thousand Oaks, CA: Sage, 1997.

Simon, Herbert A. *An Empirically-Based Microeconomics*. Cambridge: Cambridge University Press, 1997.

Sims, Christopher A., Stephen M. Goldfeld, and Jeffrey D. Sachs. "Policy Analysis with Econometric Models." *Brookings Papers on Economic Activity* 1982, no. 1 (1982): 107–164.

Sipe, Dera. "Struggling with Flesh: Soul/Body Dualism in Porphyry and Augustine." *An Interdisciplinory Journal of Graduate Students*. http://www.publications.villanova.edu/Concept/index.html.

Šmajs, Jozef. *Filozofie: Obrat k Zemi* [Philosophy: Back to Earth]. Prague: Academia, 2008.

Smith, Adam. *Adam Smith's Moral and Political Philosophy*. Edited with an introduction by Herbert Wallace Schneider. New York: Hafner, 1948.

Smith, Adam. "Essays on Philosophical Subjects." In *The Glasgow of the Works and Correspondence of Adam Smith, III*, edited by D. D. Raphael and A. S. Skinner. Oxford: Oxford University Press, 1980.

Smith, Adam. *An Inquiry into the Nature and Causes of the Wealth of Nations*. Library of Economics and Liberty, 1904. http://www.econlib.org/library/Smith/smWN13.html.

Smith, Adam. *An Inquiry into the Nature and Causes of the Wealth of Nations*. Oxford: The Clarendon Press, 1869.

Smith, Adam. *Lectures on Jurisprudence*. Oxford: Oxford University Press, 1978.

Smith, Adam. *The Theory of Moral Sentiments*. London: H. G. Bonn, 1853.

Smith, Adam. *The Theory of Moral Sentiments*. In *The Glasgow Edition of the Works and Correspondence of Adam Smith, I*, edited by D. D. Raphael and A. L. Macfie. Indianapolis: Liberty Funds, 1982.

Smith, David Warner. *Helvetius: A Study in Persecution*. Oxford: Clarendon Press, 1965.

Sojka, M. *John Maynard Keynes and Contemporary Economics*. Prague: Grada, 1999.

Sokol, Jan. *Člověk a svět očima Bible* [Man and the World in the Eyes of the Bible]. Prague: Ježek, 1993.

Sokol, Jan. "Město a jeho hradby [The City and Its Walls]." *Vesmír* 5, no. 2 (May 5, 2002): 288–291.

Sombart, Werner. *The Jews and Modern Capitalism*. New Brunswick, NJ: Transaction, 1997.

Sousedík, Stanislav. *Texty k studiu dějin středověké filosofie* [Texts on the Study of the Medieval History of Philosophy]. Prague: Karolinum, 1994.

Spiegel, Henry William. *The Growth of Economic Thought*. 3rd ed. Durham, NC: Duke University Press, 1991.

St. John of the Cross. *Dark Night of the Soul*. New York: Dover, 2003.

Steven L. Cox, and Kendell H. Easley. *Harmony of the Gospels*. Nashville, TN: B&H Publishing, 2007.

Stevenson, Betsey, and Justin Wolfers. *Economic Growth and Subjective Well-Being: Reassessing the Easterlin Paradox*. Cambridge, MA: Centre for Economic Research NBER, 2008.

Stigler, George J. "Economics, The Imperial Science?" *Scandinavian Journal of Economics*, vol. 86, no. 3 (1984), 301–14.

Stigler, George J. *The Essence of Stigler*. Edited by Kurt R. Leube and Thomas Gale Moore. Stanford: Hoover Institution Press, 1986.

Stigler, George J. "Frank Hyneman Knight." In *The New Palgrave: A Dictionary of Economics*, edited by John Eatwell, vol. 3, 55–59. New York: Stockton Press, 1987.

Stiglitz, Joseph E. *Globalization and Its Discontents*. 1st ed. New York: W. W. Norton, 2002.

Suppe, Frederick. *The Structure of Scientific Theories*. Urbana: University of Illinois Press, 1977.

Taleb, Nassim. *The Black Swan: The Impact of the Highly Improbable*. New York: Random House, 2007.

Tamari, Meir. "The Challenge of Wealth: Jewish Business Ethics." *Business Ethics Quarterly* 7 (March 1997): 45–56.

Tarantino, Quentin. *Reservoir Dogs*. Directed by Quentin Tarantino. Produced by Miramax Films. 1992.

Tassone, Giuseppe. *A Study on the Idea of Progress in Nietzsche, Heidegger, and Critical Theory*. Lewiston, NY: Mellen Press, 2002.

The Economist. *Economics A–Z: Animal Spirits*. The Economist Newspaper Limited. 2010. http://www.economist.com/research/economics/alphabetic.cfm?letter=A (accessed 2010).

The International Standard Bible Encyclopedia. 1939. http://www.international standardbible.com/(accessed 2010).

The Pervert's Guide to Cinema. Directed by Sophie Fiennes. Presented by Slavoj Žižek. 2006.

Thoreau, Henry David. *Civil Disobedience and Other Essays (The Collected Essays of Henry David Thoreau)*. Stilwell, KS: Digireads.com Publishing, 2005.

Tocqueville, Alexis de. *Democracy in America*, trans. and eds., Harvey C. Mansfield and Delba Winthrop. Chicago: University of Chicago Press, 2000.

Tolkien, John Ronald Reuel. *The Lord of the Rings*. Boston: Houghton Mifflin, 2004.

Turner, Jonathan. *Herbert Spencer: A Renewed Appreciation*. Beverly Hills, CA: Sage, 1985.

Vanek, Jaroslav. *The Participatory Economy: An Evolutionary Hypothesis and a Strategy for Development*. Ithaca: Cornell University Press, 1974.

Veblen, Thorstein. *Essays in Our Changing Order*. Edited by Leon Ardzrooni. New Brunswick, NJ: Transaction, 1997.

Veblen, Thorstein. "The Intellectual Pre-Eminence of Jews in Modern Europe." *Political Science Quarterly* 34 (March 1919): 33–42.

Volf, Miroslav. "In the Cage of Vanities: Christian Faith and the Dynamics of Economic Progress." In *Rethinking Materialism: Perspectives on the Spiritual Dimension of Economic Behavior*, edited by Robert Wuthnow, 169–191. Grand Rapids, MI: Eerdmans, 1995.

Voltaire. *The Philosophical Dictionary for the Pocket (Dictionnaire Philosophique)*. London: Thomas Brown, 1765.

Von Skarżyński, Witold. *Adam Smith als Moralphilosoph und Schoepfer der Nationaloekonomie*. Berlin: Grieben, 1878.

Wachovski, Andrew, and Lawrence Wachovski. *The Matrix*. Directed by Andrew Wachovski, and Lawrence Wachovski. Produced by Warner Bros. Pictures. 1999.

Wachtel, Paul L. *The Poverty of Affluence: A Psychological Portrait of the American Way of Life*. New York: Free Press, 1983.

Walther, Eckstein. Introduction to *The Theory of Moral Sentiments*, by Adam Smith. Leipzig: Felix Meiner, 1926.

Weber, Max. *Ancient Judaism*. New York, London: Free Press, 1967.

Weber, Max. *Economy and Society*. Edited by Guenther Roth and Claus Wittich. Berkeley, Los Angeles, London: University of California Press, 1978.

Weber, Max. *The Protestant Ethic and the Spirit of Capitalism*. New York, London: Routledge, 1992.

Weber, Max. *The Sociology of Religion*. Boston: Beacon, 1963.

Weber, Max. *Wirtschaft und Gesellschaft*. Grundrisse der verstehenden Soziologie, Tubingen 1972, pages 369–370.

Weber, Max, and Jan Škoda. *Autorita, Etika a Společnost* [Authority, Ethics, and Society]. Prague: Mladá fronta, 1997.

Weintraub, Roy E. *How Economics Became a Mathematical Science*. Durham, NC: Duke University Press, 2002.

Werhane, Patricia H. "Business Ethics and the Origins of Contemporary Capitalism: Economics and Ethics in the Work of Adam Smith and Herbert Spencer." *Journal of Business Ethics* 24, no. 3 (April 2000): 19–20.

Wesley, John. *Wesley's Notes on the Bible*. Grand Rapids, MI: Christian Classics Ethereal Library. http://www.ccel.org/ccel/wesley/notes.html.

Whitehead, Alfred North. *Adventures of Ideas*. New York: Free Press, 1985.

Whitehead, Alfred North. *Process and Reality: An Essay in Cosmology*. New York: Free Press, 1978.

Whitehead, Alfred North. *Science and the Modern World*. Cambridge: Cambridge University Press, 1926.

Willis, Jim. *God's Politics: Why the Right Gets It Wrong and the Left Doesn't Get It*. San Francisco: HarperSanFrancisco, 2005.

Wimmer, Kurt. *Equilibrium*. Directed by Kurt Wimmer. Produced by Dimension Films. 2002.

Wittgenstein, Ludwig. *Tractatus Logico-Philosophicus*. New York, London: Routledge & Kegan Paul, 1974.

Wolf, Julius, ed. "Das Adam Smith–Problem." *Zeitschrift für Socialwissenschaft* 1, Berlin: 1898.

Wuthnow, R., ed. *Rethinking Materialism: Perspectives on the Spiritual Dimension of Economic Behavior*. Grand Rapids, MI: Eerdmans, 1995.

Xenophon. *The Education of Cyrus*. Edited by H. G. Dakyns. London: Dent, 1914.

Xenophon. *Hiero*. Edited by H. G. Dakyns. Whitefish, MT: Kessinger, 2004.

Xenophon. *Xenophon: Memorabilia, Oeconomicus, Symposium, Apology*. Edited by E. C. Marchant and O. J. Todd. Cambridge, MA, and London: Harvard University Press, 1977.

Yates, Frances A. *Giordano Bruno and the Hermetic Tradition*. London: Routledge & Kegan Paul, 1964.

Yates, Frances A. *The Rosicrucian Enlightenment*. London, New York: Routledge & Kegan Paul, 2003.

Yoder, John Howard. *The Politics of Jesus*. Grand Rapids, MI: Eerdmans, 1972.

Zeyss, Richard. *Adam Smith und der Eigennutz*. Tübingen: Verlag der H. Laupp'schen Buchhandlung, 1889.

Žižek, Slavoj. *The Parallax View*. Cambridge, MA, and London: MIT Press, 2009.

Žižek, Slavoj. *The Plague of Fantasies*. New York, London: Verso, 1997.

Index